The Changing Languages of Europe

Dedicated to Wim Blockmans
and the wonderful people of NIAS

The Changing Languages of Europe

BERND HEINE & TANIA KUTEVA

OXFORD
UNIVERSITY PRESS

OXFORD
UNIVERSITY PRESS

Great Clarendon Street, Oxford OX2 6DP

Oxford University Press is a department of the University of Oxford.
It furthers the University's objective of excellence in research, scholarship, and education by publishing worldwide in

Oxford New York

Auckland Cape Town Dar es Salaam Hong Kong Karachi
Kuala Lumpur Madrid Melbourne Mexico City Nairobi
New Delhi Shanghai Taipei Toronto

With offices in

Argentina Austria Brazil Chile Czech Republic France Greece
Guatemala Hungary Italy Japan Poland Portugal Singapore
South Korea Switzerland Thailand Turkey Ukraine Vietnam

Published in the United States
by Oxford University Press Inc., New York

First published 2006

British Library Cataloguing in Publication Data

Data available

Library of Congress Cataloguing in Publication Data

Data available

Typeset by SPI Publisher Services, Pondicherry, India
Printed in Great Britain
on acid-free paper by Biddles Ltd., King's Lynn

ISBN 0-19-929733-9 978-0-19-929733-7
0–19–929734–7 978–0–19–929734–4

Foreword

A number of students of language have pointed out that the way grammatical meanings are expressed in a given language is strikingly similar to what is found in some neighbouring language or languages, even though the forms used in these expressions are entirely different, and in spite of the fact that the languages concerned may be genetically only remotely related or even unrelated. The main goal of this book is, first, to show that such observations are far from being coincidental; rather, that such cross-linguistic similarities are more common than is widely believed. Second, we will argue that there is a principled way to account for such similarities and, third, that these similarities are the result of processes of conceptualization that are the same across cultures.

The present book focuses on grammatical change in Europe. It has benefited greatly from discussions with and comments and data from many colleagues, in particular the following: Sasha Aikhenvald, Walter Bisang, Peter Blumenthal, Natalia Bugay, Irma Canovic, Michela Chennamo, Hilary Chappell, Ulrike Claudi, Bernard Comrie, Eva Csató, Östen Dahl, Andrii Danylenko, Ulrich Detges, Bob Dixon, Bridget Drinka, Carola Emkow, Zygmunt Frajzyngier, Victor Friedman, Jost Gippert, John Haiman, Martin Haspelmath, Daniel Jacob, Lars Johanson, Christa Kilian-Hatz, Christa König, Yaron Matras, Luca Melchior, Maj-Britt Mosgaard-Hansen, Salikoko Mufwene, Ulrich Obst, Lukas Pietsch, Karl-Heinz Röntgen, Suzanne Romaine, Peter Siemund, Thomas Stolz, Elvira Veselinović, Nigel Vincent, Julija Vuckovski, Andreas Wesch, Debra Ziegeler, as well as many others. Special thanks are also due to Monika Feinen, for her invaluable technical assistance. Finally, we express our deep gratitude to Meike Pfaff, Barbara Sevenich, and Stefanie Lorkowski for having assisted us in ways that go far beyond technical details, and for all the work they did on an earlier version of this volume.

We are also deeply indebted to the Center for Advanced Study in the Behavioral Sciences, Stanford, and the Institute for Advanced Study, LaTrobe University, and in particular the Research Centre for Linguistic Typology in Melbourne and its directors Bob Dixon and Sasha Aikhenvald, who offered the first-named author hospitality to work on this book; the second-named author thanks the Max Planck Gesellschaft for providing financial support and in particular to Bernard Comrie, the director of the Linguistics

Department of the Max Planck Institute for Evolutionary Anthropology, Leipzig, for offering a most stimulating atmosphere for the finalizing stage of the book. We are grateful to these institutions for their generosity and understanding. Our gratitude also extends to our colleagues Lenore Grenoble and Lindsay Whaley, Dartmouth College who offered the first-named author academic hospitality and the means to work on this book when he was invited as a visiting professor from March to June 2002. Our final thanks are due to the Netherlands Institute for Advanced Study (NIAS) and its rector Wim Blockmans for the outstanding hospitality we were able to enjoy in 2005–6 at the finalizing stage of the book.

Contents

List of Tables

List of Maps

List of Figures

Abbreviations

A	subject of transitive clauses
a.n.	authors' note
ABL	ablative
ABSOL	absolutive
ACC	accusative
ADE	adessive
AL	allocutive
ALL	allative
ANIM	animate
AOR	aorist
AP	adverbial particle
ART	article
BEN	benefactive
CAU	causative verb
COM	comitative
COMP	comparative
COMPC	complementary conjunction
COND	conditional
CONJ	conjugational verb, conjunction
CONT	continuous
COP	copula
D	determiner
DAT	dative
DEF	definite
DEM	demonstrative
DET	determiner
DIM	diminutive
DIR	directive
DO	direct object
DUR	durative
ELA	elative
ENZ	enunciative
ERG	ergative
F	feminine
FACT	factitive
FREQ	frequentative
GEN	genitive
IDEO	ideophone

IM	interrogative marker
IMP	imperative
INDF	indefinite
INDIC	indicative
INE	inessive
INF	infinitive
INFR	inferred
INSTR	instrumental
INTER	interrogative
INTR	intransitivizer
IRR	irrealis
LOC	locative
LOG	logophoric marker
M	masculine
MOD	modal
N	noun, neuter
NEG	negation
NF	non-wnal
NFIN	non-wnite
NMZ	nominalization
NOM	nominative
NOMIN	nominalizer
NON	non-
O	object
OBL	oblique
OM	object marker
OPT	optative
Q	question
PART	partitive
PAST	past
PERF	perfect
PFV	perfective
PL	plural
PM	predicate marker
POSS	possessive
POT	potential
PPA	active perfect participle
PPLE	participle
PPP	past passive participle
PRES	present
PRET	preterit
PROG	progressive
PRS	present

PRT	preterite
PTC	particle
PTCP	participle
PWOc	Proto Western Oceanic
Q	question marker
REL	relative clause marker
REM.P	remote past
REP	reported
S	subject of intransitive clauses; subject
SAE	Standard Average European
SB	subjunctive
SE	demonstrative determiner *se* in finnish
SG	singular
SOV	subject–object–verb word order
SR	subordinator
SVO	subject–verb–object word order
TAM	tense, aspect, and modality
TOP	topic
TRN	transnumeral
TRS	transitive suyx
TZ	transitivizer
V	verb
VIS	visual
VSO	verb–subject–object word order
1, 2, 3	wrst, second, third person

1

Europe as a Linguistic Area

Europe is moving towards political unity, and dramatic progress has been made in this process over the last fifty years. In this book we wish to demonstrate that there is a much older process leading towards unity in Europe, namely a linguistic one: as a result of cultural, social, economic, and political exchange across national and regional boundaries, the languages and dialects of Europe have become increasingly alike.

All scholars who have worked on Europe as a linguistic area agree that genetic relationship is not an appropriate parameter to describe the structural affinities characterizing European languages, pointing out that the areal distribution of language structures frequently cuts across genetic boundaries. Processes such as 'balancing' (*Ausgleich*) or 'superposition' have been invoked to account for the linguistic uniformity of European languages, but it remains largely unclear how exactly such processes are to be defined.

In the present chapter we will summarize previous work that has been done on this issue, present the main findings that have been made and discuss problems associated with this research. Subsequently, we will describe the methodology that will be used in the chapters to follow.

1.1 Europe's linguistic diversity

How many languages are spoken natively in Europe? This is a seemingly easy question, but it is not really easy to answer: the exact number of languages spoken in Europe varies depending on how one defines Europe, and there is no universal agreement on how Europe should be delineated (see Stolz 2006 for detailed discussion). Should one take it as a geographical, a political, a historical, or a cultural entity? Should one trace a borderline north or south of the Caucasus? Since there are some forty languages spoken in the Caucasus, this is not a trivial issue.

But it is not only problems of a geographical, socio-political, or other nature that make it hard to come up with an uncontroversial delimitation of Europe and its linguistic diversity. The problem starts with how to define a language. Should one rely on linguistic, sociolinguistic, or any other criteria? In an influential monograph, Décsy (1973: 2) proposed a figure of sixty-two European languages—in doing so, he ignored languages such as Catalan or Sardinian since they are claimed to have a social status that disqualifies them from being recognized as full languages. There are also other linguists who, although for different reasons, maintain that the number of languages in Europe does not exceed fifty or sixty (e.g. Nelde, Ureland & Clarkson 1986: 1). On the other hand, there are also scholars who maintain that the number of languages is much larger; van der Auwera (1998*b*: 6), for example, proposes a list of 140 languages to be found within the geographical confines of Europe.

On the basis of the genetic relationship patterns recognizable in European languages, Europe cannot be defined as a linguistic unit. Table 1.1 provides an overview of the main genetic stocks represented in Europe and of the languages that will figure in the present work. To be sure, the continent is dominated by languages belonging to the Indo-European family. This is most obvious when one looks at the numbers of speakers: hardly more than 5 per cent of Europeans speak non-Indo-European languages as their mother tongues. Furthermore, the western part of Europe consists only of Indo-European languages, the one exception being Basque. However, there is also much genetic and structural diversity in Europe, mostly in its extreme east; in van der Auwera's catalogue of 140 European languages, only slightly more than half (74) belong to the Indo-European family.

1.2 Major themes of research

More recently, a number of studies have been devoted to the typological diversity of European languages. What surfaces from this research is that genetic relationship is not an appropriate parameter to describe or account for the structural affinities characterizing European languages—rather, that there are many linguistic properties cutting across genetic boundaries. There are a number of questions that arise when one wishes to determine whether Europe forms a linguistically defined unit. A survey of the history of areal work on European languages suggests that it is most of all the following questions that have occupied scholars:

(i) Is there something like a European area that can be defined linguistically and, if so, how can it be delimited?
(ii) Is there anything that could be defined as the areal centre of European languages?
(iii) Are there any linguistic properties setting European languages off from languages in other parts of the world?

TABLE 1.1. Language families and main languages represented in Europe

Family	Sub-family	Branch	Main languages
Indo-European	Romance	Western	Portuguese, Spanish, Catalan, French, Occitan, Romansch
		Eastern	Italian, Rumanian
			Sardinian
	Germanic	Western	German, Dutch, Frisian, English
		Northern	Swedish, Danish, Norwegian, Icelandic, Faroese
	Celtic	Goidelic	Irish, Scots Gaelic
		Brittanic	Welsh, Breton
	Baltic		Latvian, Lithuanian
	Slavic	Western	Polish, Sorbian, Czech, Slovak
		Eastern	Russian, Ukrainian, Belorussian
		Southern	Slovenian, Serbian, Croatian, Macedonian, Bulgarian
	Greek		Modern Greek
	Albanian		Albanian
	Indo-Aryan		Romani
Finno-Ugric	Finnic		Finnish, Karelian, Estonian, Livonian, Votic, Ingrian, Vesp; Sa(a)mi; Mordvin
	Ugric		Hungarian
	Samoyed		Nenets
Altaic	Turkic		Turkish, Tatar, Bashkir, Karaim, Chuvash
'Caucasian'			Georgian, Abkhaz, Chechen, Lezgian, etc.
Afroasiatic	Semitic	Maghreb	Maltese
Basque			Basque

(iv) If Europe really is a linguistic area, what are the motivating forces underlying areal relationship?

(v) Is it possible to divide the languages of Europe into significant, smaller units independent of genetic relationship?

Each of these questions has been addressed in some detail in the relevant research, and in the following paragraphs we will review the main findings that have been made in the course of this research. Before doing so, a few words on the terminology used in this chapter seem in order (for terms to be used in subsequent chapters, see Section 2.1).

A notion to be discussed in detail in this chapter is that of *linguistic area*. This term was defined by Murray Emeneau as standing for 'an area which includes languages belonging to more than one family but showing traits in common which are found not to belong to the other members of (at least) one of the families' (Emeneau 1956: 16, fn. 28). Since then, a number of alternative definitions have been proposed,[1] and various kinds of linguistic groupings have been identified which, supposedly as a result of language contact 'show traits in common'; we will refer to all these groupings summarily as linguistic areas. The term *sprachbund* (from German *Sprachbund* = 'language union'), introduced by Nikolai Trubetzkoy in 1923, will be reserved for linguistic areas that are defined by a distinct set of linguistic properties whose presence cannot be explained with reference to genetic relationship, parallel development (drift), universal constraints on language structure, or to chance. Furthermore, there are linguistic areas consisting of languages that are characterized by a high degree of mutual intertranslatability; following Ross (1996, 2001, forthc.) we will reserve the label *metatypy* for such groupings.[2] And finally there are areas that are the result of one and the same historical process, more specifically of the same process of grammaticalization;[3] such groupings will be called *grammaticalization areas* (Heine & Kuteva 2005).

1.2.1 *Delimiting Europe as a linguistic area*

Areal relationship among the languages of Europe is a topic that has a long history. Relying on nineteenth-century typological notions, Lewy summarized what many authors before and after him expressed in some way or other (see also Becker 1948; Wagner 1959, 1964):

> Die europäischen Sprachen sind wohl alle zu den flektierenden zu rechnen,—die ja durchaus nicht die Regel bilden. [The European languages presumably all belong to the inflectional ones—which certainly do not form the rule (among the world's languages)] (Lewy 1942: 26).

A number of authors in the past have suggested that this property pointed out by Lewy, as well as other properties claimed to be common to European

[1] While language contact is not mentioned in Emeneau's classic definition, other authors have proposed contact as a defining property of linguistic areas, as in the following widely-used definition by Sherzer: 'A *linguistic* area is defined... as an area in which *several* linguistic traits are shared by languages of the area and furthermore, there is evidence (linguistic and non-linguistic) that contact between speakers of the languages contributed to the spread and/or retention of these traits and thereby to a certain degree of linguistic uniformity within the area' (Sherzer 1973: 760).

[2] Metatypy can be defined as the wholesale restructuring of a language's semantic and syntactic structures as a result of language contact, leading to a new typological profile in the replica language on the one hand, and to a large degree of direct intertranslatability between the model and the replica language on the other (see e.g. Ross 1996: 182).

[3] The term grammaticalization will be discussed in more detail in Section 1.5.

languages cannot be accounted for with reference to genetic relationship but require an account in terms of areal diffusion, and that there is something like a European sprachbund. In Lewy's (1942: 21) view, the history of Europe is 'the history of the Indo-Europeanization of Europe'. Others again maintain that this history can be seen in a more general development from a synthetic-inflectional towards an analytic-isolating language structure (e.g. Hinrichs 2004). Becker (1948) proposes to treat the languages of Europe as a distinct unit mainly on the basis of similarities in their idiomatic structures. For Thomas (1975: 47), calquing (or loan translation) played a crucial role in the rise of such a unit, in that it 'produced a convergence of the lexical and semantic systems of the languages of Europe, helping to create the European *Sprachbund*'. It remains unclear, however, how exactly this sprachbund should be defined.

Since the 1990s, considerable headway has been made in defining patterns of areal relationship in Europe within the project 'Typology of Languages in Europe' (usually referred to as the EUROTYP project; see König & Haspelmath 1999). What surfaces from this research is that there is in fact some justification in considering Europe to be an areal unit of some kind (see especially Bechert *et al.* 1990; Bernini & Ramat 1996; Dahl 1990, 2000*b*; Kuteva 1998; Haspelmath 1998, 2001; van der Auwera 1998*b*; König & Haspelmath 1999; Stolz 2006). The following discussion is far from being a full account of this work; rather, we will be confined to a few salient hypotheses that have been proposed within this paradigm.

Some of these works, in particular that by van der Auwera (1998*c*), focus on a nuclear European area (see Section 1.2.2). Others, again aim to establish a more extended unit within Europe. Kortmann (1998*a*, 1998*b*: 507ff.) proposes distinguishing between a core and a peripheral area, using mainly syntactic criteria (see Section 1.2.3). His core area includes the Romance languages, West Germanic, mainland Scandinavian Germanic, Slavic, Hungarian, Albanian, and Greek. Languages of his peripheral area include insular Scandinavian North Germanic, Basque, Celtic, Baltic, Armenian, Altaic, Uralic (except Hungarian), Caucasian languages, Indo-Iranian, and Semitic languages, and he adds that, compared to the core area, the languages of the periphery are highly heterogeneous with reference to the properties compared.

Kortmann (1998*a*: 214–15) goes on to propose a west–east divide within Europe's core area. Establishing that the five most important sources from which adverbial subordinators are constructed in European languages are adverbs, adpositions, complementizers, interrogatives, and relativizers, he then observes that in the classical languages Latin and Greek, (case-marked) interrogatives and relativizers were by far the most important sources for adverbial subordinators. But these two languages differ in their proportions of temporal subordinators as opposed to causal, conditional, and concessive subordinators, and Kortmann finds corresponding proportions in modern European languages, where the languages in the western part of the core area reflect the sphere of influence of Latin while the languages of the eastern part reflect that of Classical Greek (Kortmann 1998*a*: 221)—even if Latin turns out overall to have provided the major model. He concludes (see also Section 1.2.4, (iv)):

Thus it has been observed before (Solta 1980: 73) that Church Latin and Classical Latin as the language of the learned played a much more important role in creating the relative unity of the West Romance languages than Vulgar Latin. Likewise it is well known that the Greek church language, directly and indirectly (via Old Church Slavonic), has been of great importance on the Balkan Peninsula (Kortmann 1998*b*: 535).

Based on their work on equative and similative constructions, Haspelmath and Buchholz (1998: 326–7) propose a different classification of their 'Standard Average European' (henceforth: SAE) area. The core area, where all four criteria they distinguish are fulfilled, consists of Romance, West Germanic including Yiddish, most Slavic languages, Lithuanian, the Indo-Aryan language Romani, and Greek. Not included in the core are the North Germanic languages, the Slavic languages Serbian/Croatian and Macedonian, Albanian, and the Finno-Ugric languages Finnish, Estonian, and Hungarian. Basque, Maltese, Turkish, and the languages of the extreme east of Europe, with the exception of Georgian and Armenian, do not meet any of their four criteria.

What surfaces from this kind of work is that there is a widespread belief that it is possible to regard European languages as forming a linguistic area—one that consists almost entirely of Indo-European languages, with the possible exception of Hungarian. When it comes to details, however, there is not much agreement. In particular, there is general disagreement on which languages exactly should belong to Europe as a linguistic area, or core area, which languages are central within this area and which are more peripheral, and which ones should be excluded from the area (see van der Auwera 1998*c*: 816 for a survey).

However, there is also more substantial disagreement, as suggested by the following examples. Hock (1986: 508–9) treats Insular Germanic as core and Mainland Germanic as transitional, and while some authors would exclude Slavic languages from the core (e.g. Haarmann 1976*b*: 123–7), others (e.g. Hock 1986: 508–9; Lazard 1990: 250; Haspelmath 2001) maintain that Slavic languages belong to the core; for Décsy (1973), Russian is a 'Standard Average European' language like French, German, and Italian. Notoriously controversial is the taxonomic status of Celtic languages such as Irish, Breton, and Welsh, which are sometimes included (Ramat & Bernini 1990), sometimes excluded from core European (Hock 1986: 508–9; Haspelmath 1998: 273, 2001: 1505).

If there is general agreement among the various scholars on how to delimit Europe as a linguistic area, then it concerns on the one hand Basque and Maltese, which occupy a marginal position in all classifications, and on the other hand the languages of Europe's extreme east, in particular the languages of the Caucasus and Turkish: none of the various classifications associates languages such Lezgian, Mari, Udmurt, Tatar, or Turkish with Europe as a linguistic area. But even here there are problems of delimitation: two of languages of the east, Georgian and Armenian, are not generally excluded from the area, and in van der Auwera's (1998*c*: 823) classification based on adverbial domains these two languages even belong to the same areal grouping as Greek, Albanian, and Spanish, that is, languages that are generally classified as core European languages by other authors.

In some of the works reviewed above there is a more global perspective, suggesting, for example, that there may be some more fluid areal macro-groupings that also contribute to a better understanding of the relationship patterns obtaining among European languages. In this vein, Koptjevskaja-Tamm (2002: 215) draws attention to a distinction, surfacing in the Circum-Baltic region, between languages behaving in accordance with an Indo-European-dominated SAE area on the one hand and a Central Eurasian type on the other, the latter being represented by language families such as Turkic, Mongolic, Dravidian, Uralic, and others.

Since the end of the last century, searching for Europe's linguistic unity has become an issue attracting attention beyond the confines of linguistic analysis; note that the EUROTYP project, which resulted in an unprecedented amount of typological information on the languages of Europe, was sponsored by the European Science Foundation, and terms such as 'Eurolinguistics' (or *Europäistik*) have been proposed to deal with the study and promotion of linguistic unity in Europe (Reiter 1999; Ureland 2004). Van Pottelberge (2005) therefore raises the question of whether such socio-political goals, or implicit ideological orientation, might not have had some bearing on the linguistic results obtained, such as the ones summarized in this section.

1.2.2 *Searching for Europe's centre*

That Europe as a linguistic area has internal structure in terms of a centre and a periphery is an old assumption. It was Décsy (1973: 29–30) who first proposed a central European sprachbund; following Whorf (1941, 1956: 138), he called it the *SAE-Bund* (the Standard Average European area). The languages included are French, German, English, Italian and, somewhat surprisingly, Russian. Décsy's classification is not entirely coherent, drawing on an array of different kinds of criteria. In the case of this postulated sprachbund, he gives precedence to sociolinguistic over linguistic properties: observing that languages such as Spanish, Portuguese, or Dutch should be assigned to the *SAE-Bund* on the basis of their linguistic structure, he nevertheless excludes them from this areal unit since they are spoken by less than fifty million people; in accordance with this taxonomic preference, Russian is allocated to his *SAE-Bund*.

In the recent work of the EUROTYP framework, more rigid taxonomic principles have been applied in a search for Europe's linguistic centre. In fact, this topic has become a popular one, leading scholars to look for languages that are most centrally 'European'. Based on an enormous amount of data on adverbial constructions, van der Auwera (1998*c*: 823–5) proposes a 'Charlemagne *Sprachbund*', a minimal area consisting of French, Dutch, and German, with Italian and Polish being close to this centre area—named after the first ruler of an area where nowadays French, German, Italian, and Dutch are spoken. Thieroff (2001: 228) finds van der Auwera's classification largely confirmed by his analysis of fourteen features of tense, aspect, and mood in twenty European languages, in that French, German, and Italian, although not Dutch, exhibit the highest number of his features.[4] In spirit, this unit is in accordance with what has been written more recently on Europe as a linguistic area; however, it is not exactly the same as the central units proposed by other authors. Haspelmath (1998: 273) also adopts van der Auwera's notion of a Charlemagne *Sprachbund*, but his nucleus is not the same as that of van der Auwera: instead of Italian as a whole, Haspelmath limits it to northern Italian dialects, while (Standard) Italian and Polish are excluded, being in the same areal grouping as Slavic languages such as Czech, Slovenian, Serbian/Croatian, and Bulgarian.

A different notion emerges in Haspelmath's (2001: 1505) later classification: based on a comparison of thirty-nine European languages and nine morphosyntactic features, he concludes that the nucleus is made up of two languages only, French and German, since they have all nine features considered, while Dutch and Italian have one feature less, being in the same group as languages such as Sardinian and Albanian, with Polish occupying a fairly marginal position.

[4] Mention should be made, however, that Thieroff's (2001) comparisons are biased in favour of German, which is the focus of his analysis.

Both Haspelmath's French-German nucleus and van der Auwera's Charlemagne *Sprachbund* are attractive hypotheses. But there are also problems:[5] first, unlike Haspelmath's nucleus, van der Auwera's grouping rests essentially on only one set of properties relating to the structure of adverbial constructions. Second, it is not based on unambiguous quantitative evidence: as the data provided by van der Auwera (1998*c*, Map 6) suggest, the languages having the maximal score of five properties for the five adverbial domains analysed are French, Dutch, and German, while Italian and Polish have a lower score of four properties. On the basis of this situation, one would expect that, if Italian is a member of the 'Charlemagne *Sprachbund*', then Polish should be one, too.[6] Third, van der Auwera's analysis of tense–aspect properties of European languages on the basis of Thieroff (2000) shows that French and German stand out among other European languages in having all eight tense and aspect properties included in the analysis, while Italian has seven, Dutch five, and Polish is fairly marginal with only three of the properties.

But Haspelmath's nucleus hypothesis is not entirely convincing either, for one simple reason: there is a difference of merely one feature separating the nucleus from languages such as Dutch and Italian, that is, languages that have been named by various other authors as displaying a high concentration of European properties.

To conclude, while there is a widespread feeling that something like an areal nucleus does exist in Europe, it is largely unclear which languages exactly belong to it. However, there is agreement to the effect that if there are European languages that occupy a central position on account of their linguistic properties then they are located mostly or exclusively in the western half of the continent. There is also agreement that, if there is a nucleus consisting of a small number of languages characterized by an exceptional density of areal relationship, that nucleus includes German and French,[7] possibly also Dutch and Italian, less centrally in addition other Romance languages, but not English.

Nevertheless, there remains a question relating to the criteria used in areal taxonomy: to what extent do the criteria selected by the authors referred to

[5] Van Pottelberge (2005) observes that the languages figuring time and again in these notions of a European nucleus are exactly those spoken in the European Economic Community (the predecessor of the European Union), which consisted of Germany, France, Italy, The Netherlands, Belgium, and Luxembourg. He goes on to speculate that this fact might not be coincidental but could be an implicit result of the research orientation of the authors concerned.

[6] Van der Auwera (1998*c*: 824) acknowledges this fact, observing that French, Dutch, and German are 'at the very center', while Italian and Polish are 'very close to the center'.

[7] Note, however, that even here there is no total agreement: According to Lewy (1942), French belongs to the Atlantic and German to his Central Area.

above determine how an areal grouping will look like? For example, Stolz (2006) observes that depending on which mix of properties one decides to draw on, it may be Russian rather than French, Dutch, and German that turns out to be the centre of Europe's languages.

1.2.3 *The search for 'Euroversals'*

Looking for linguistic characteristics that may define Europe's languages was one of the main typological goals since the beginnings of European areal typology. For earlier scholars, important parameters of comparison were provided on the one hand by nineteenth-century morphological typology. For example, we noted in Section 1.2.1 that Lewy (1942: 17) classified all European languages as inflectional. This view was adopted by Haarmann (1976*a*: 110) in a restricted form, who also maintained that all European languages have an inflectional component. On the other hand, there was an attempt to integrate linguistic and extra-linguistic observations—with the effect that many of the resulting classifications, for example, that of Décsy (1973), are based on a mixture of linguistic, historical, cultural, and other criteria. Finally, a search for Europe's linguistic unity was also associated with philological models, where the borrowing of lexical and grammatical forms, such as derivational elements from the classical languages Greek and Latin, was viewed as a significant factor in uniting the languages of Europe (e.g. Blatt 1957; Pagliari & Belardi 1963).

At the same time, that search was also about finding key properties that would allow one to single out Europe as a typological unit. The term 'Europeme' was proposed to identify linguistic properties found in Europe and nowhere else (Décsy 1973: 196). Haarmann (1976*b*: 108–12) proposed a catalogue of sixteen Europemes, that is, structural properties to be found in all sixty-five European languages of his sample (which excludes the Caucasus). The criteria used to formulate these Europemes were highly general—to the extent that they apply not only to European languages but also to many other languages in the world,[8] even if they exclude a number of non-European languages.

Other lists of European properties were proposed by Hock (1986: 505–9) and Thomason and Kaufman (1988: 315–25). Summarizing the typological work of the last three decades, van der Auwera (1998*c*: 815–16) provides the

[8] For example, according to Haarmann's (1976*a*: 108) first two Europemes, the number of simple segmental phonemes is between 10 and 110, and the number of consonant phonemes exceeds that of vowel phonemes in all European languages, but such generalizations also apply to most other languages of the world.

following list of twelve linguistic features that were mentioned in the course of previous work:

(i) analytic expression formats;
(ii) simplified case paradigms;
(iii) presence of definite and indefinite articles;
(iv) use of 'have' and 'be' as auxiliaries;
(v) non-Pro-Drop character;
(vi) relatively fixed verb-second (SVO) sentence level word order;
(vii) phrasal word order: prepositions and postposed genitives;
(viii) accusativity;
(ix) agreement of the finite verb with the subject;
(x) passive allows the agent;
(xi) agent and subject are not identical;
(xii) lexical and phraseological similarities.

While pointing out properties widely found in European languages, the list is not entirely satisfactory in that it contains features that are fairly general. For example, features such as (vi), (viii), (ix), or (x), as well as others, can be found in many languages of the world. Even if taken in conjunction, the features do not seem entirely appropriate to distinguish European from non-European languages.[9]

Compared to this large range of features, Kortmann (1998*a*, 1998*b*: 507ff) relies on a highly restricted set of features in order to define a linguistic core area of Europe. This core, which includes the Romance languages, West Germanic, North Germanic (mainland Scandinavian), Slavic, Hungarian, Albanian, and Greek, is characterized by the following properties: (a) having SVO order (except for Hungarian, which has SOV), (b) using mainly prepositions (Hungarian again being an exception), (c) employing predominantly finite subordinate clauses, and having a large, semantically highly differentiated inventory of free adverbial subordinators placed clause-initially. Note that Kortmann's work is centrally concerned with adverbial subordination.

Kortmann maintains that defining Europe as a linguistic area and searching for Euroversals are different goals and should therefore be treated separately: in the case of the former goal, he is concerned with searching for a European core area, which he defines on the basis of the three properties listed above. With regard to the latter goal, he presents a list of twenty-five Euroversals (plus a

[9] For example, an African language such as Swahili exhibits nine of the twelve features, which would make it a candidate for status as a European language in line with some languages spoken within Europe. Note that even feature (xii) applies to Swahili, which—as a result of a century of language contact with English—has acquired lexical and some phraseological patterns from English.

number of sub-Euroversals) which bear no relationship to his core area but are derived from generalizations on adverbial subordinators in all European languages, including Caucasian, Altaic, and Semitic languages spoken on the European continent. Accordingly, rather than being Europe-specific implications, some of these Euroversals look like universal predications, that is, generalizations on languages across the world. Consider the following cases:

(1.1) Selected Euroversals of Kortmann (1998*b*: 545)

Euroversal 19.2: If a European language predominantly employs clause-final subordinators, then, if it has any adpositions, it is predominantly postpositional.

Euroversal 20.2: If a European language employs adverbial subordinators in clause-final position, it is SOV.

Now, what defines Kortmann's European core area in particular is the presence of SVO order, prepositions, and adverbial subordinators in clause-initial position. Accordingly, neither of these Euroversals is really relevant to his area, which is characterized by the non-applicability of the properties addressed in these two Euroversals.

Overall it turns out that the fewer criteria a given author chooses for typological comparisons, the more likely it is that s/he came up with classifications of European languages that disagree with those of other authors. A case in point is the stimulating work by Ramat and Bernini (1990) on negation. Observing that a number of European languages can be singled out as marking sentence negation by either discontinuous forms, for example, French *Je ne sais pas* (I NEG know NEG) 'I don't know', or postverbal forms, for example, Frisian *Jan is der net* (Jan is here NEG) 'Jan is not here', they propose calling languages having either of these expressions as Europe's core languages. The result is, for example, that the Celtic languages Breton and Welsh belong to the core whereas no Balkanic, Slavic, or Finno-Ugric language does. Whilst these authors draw attention to a strategy for encoding negation that is highly relevant for understanding Europe's areal history, this criterion on its own is not sufficient for an areal classification of Europe as a whole.

To some extent, recent work is a direct continuation of that of earlier scholars. A new term, 'Euroversal' has been coined, used alongside or as a replacment for the older Europeme (van der Auwera 1998*b*: 11–12, 1998*c*: 813; Kortmann 1998*b*: 536ff). Kortmann introduces the term Euroversal as a quantitative notion, used to identify morphosemantic properties of adverbial subordinators shared by more than 80 per cent of the modern European languages.

Not all scholars working on Europe as a linguistic area, however, use the terms Europeme or Euroversal. For example, rather than mentioning either of these terms, Haspelmath (1998, 2001) simply talks about 'features' characterizing 'Standard Average European' (see Section 1.3).

The terms Euroversal and Europeme can receive, and have in fact received, two different definitions. On the one hand, they are understood as linguistic properties found in most or all European languages but which may also be found in non-European languages. On the other hand, they are defined as linguistic properties that distinguish European languages from languages in other parts of the world, that is, that are specific to Europe. The former is the definition used by most scholars, where it remains unclear how to delimit Euroversals from language universals—in other words, the generalizations apply to most or all languages in the world. In fact, these scholars are aware of this situation but are not overly concerned about it since, for most of the phenomena studied by them, there is no adequate information on their worldwide distribution anyway, as van der Auwera acknowledges in a summarizing appraisal:[10]

> Euroversals, whether authors in the preceding chapters explicitly called them that or not, are claims that are to hold for all or most of the languages of Europe. In this modest and very tentative way, some of the Euroversals are possible Universals. It seems reasonable to assume that the more the Euroversals depend on semantic and/or functional factors, the higher the chance that the Euroversals are Universals. Still there is no way to predict which Euroversals, if any, could qualify as Universals and the only way to find out is to study a sample of the world's languages. This cannot be done here (van der Auwera 1998*c*: 813–14).

The second kind of definition has not been used in a rigid format by any of the typologists concerned—for the reasons mentioned above: research on Europe as a linguistic area has focused on information on European languages; looking for corresponding information on a worldwide scale was clearly beyond its scope. However, there are a few researchers who use a worldwide perspective, most notably Haspelmath (1998, 2001; see Section 1.2.7 below). Whilst not exactly in accordance with the second definition, Haspelmath's procedure of looking for features that are widespread in Europe but

[10] Summarizing his seminal work on adverbial subordinators in Europe, Kortmann comes to essentially the same conclusion as van der Auwera: 'The status of these Euroversals still needs to be determined on the basis of studies on adverbial subordinators working with the same methodology as this study on more European languages and, above all, on a representative sample of non-European languages. Only then will it be possible to decide which of the generalizations made here are truly distinctive of the languages of Europe and which ones instantiate universals in the domain of adverbial subordinators (Kortmann 1998*b*: 551).

uncommon elsewhere in the world corresponds to the definition, at least in spirit. Interestingly, as we observed above, Haspelmath is among those who do not use terms such as Euroversal or Europeme.

Haspelmath is not the only one to relate structures of European languages to those found in other parts of the world. In her crosslinguistic study of tense, aspect and modality, Kuteva (1998) finds that there is a noteworthy typological distinction manifested in grammaticalization behavior. She concludes that, while auxiliation in European languages involves almost exclusively general event schemas of auxiliation, i.e., general verbal notions such as 'be', 'have', 'go', or 'come', auxiliation in other parts of the world may well concern both general and specific instantiations of event schemas, the latter including lexically more specific verbs such as 'walk', 'think', 'taste', or 'bury'.

1.2.4 *The motivating forces of areal relationship*

Another theme concerns the linguistic and extra-linguistic factors that can be held responsible for areal relationship in Europe. What surfaces from the work that has been done on this issue is that the only factor that clearly—and trivially—can be held responsible is language contact. However, in spite of all this work, we still know very little on the sociolinguistic history of Europe and about the patterns of crosslinguistic interaction characterizing Europe's linguistic history.

According to Haspelmath (1998: 272) there are, in particular, five main historical factors that need to be considered if one wants to reconstruct what 'created the surprisingly similar patterns that are found in SAE (Standard Average European) languages', which are:

(i) retention of Proto-Indo-European structures and processes of assimilation of non-Indo-European to Indo-European languages;
(ii) influence from a common substratum of a pre-Indo-European population in Europe;
(iii) contacts during the great transformations at the transition from late antiquity to the early Middle Ages in Europe;
(iv) Latin and the common European culture of the Middle Ages;
(v) the common European culture from the Renaissance to the Enlightenment.

We will now look at each of these factors in turn.

(i) Haspelmath rejects the possibility that retention of Proto-Indo-European structures was responsible for the presence of pan-European morphosyntactic features, on the following grounds:

> Thus, Indo-European SAE languages must have developed their special characteristics long after the breakup of the Proto-Indo-European proto-language, at a time when they were already spoken in Europe (Haspelmath 1998: 284).

It would seem, however, that things are slightly more complex. Among the twelve features that he draws on to define Europe as a linguistic area, there is one technically known as the 'dative external possessor'.[11] It is not found in English; the following German example illustrates this feature, where the inalienable possessor 'child' is encoded as a participant in the dative (DAT) case:

(1.2) German

Die	Mutter	wäscht	dem	Kind	die	Haare.
the	mother	washes	the.DAT	child	the	hair

'Mother is washing the child's hair.'

Haspelmath (1998: 284) observes that this feature 'seems to have an impeccable Proto-Indo-European ancestry', to be found in virtually all ancient Indo-European languages, such as Old Indic, Old Iranian, Homeric Greek, Latin, Gothic, and Old Church Slavonic. In light of this observation, one is well advised to take the conclusion he reaches in the above quotation with care, even if he adds that the dative external possessor is the only feature exhibiting such an Indo-European connection.

(ii) That the modern European languages have been shaped by influence from languages of a pre-Indo-European population in Europe is an old, and a controversial hypothesis. Whilst recent research has adduced new evidence in support of such a hypothesis (e.g. Vennemann 1994; Nichols 1995), we side with Haspelmath in maintaining that so far this evidence is not really strong enough to demonstrate that a substratum ante-dating the presence of Indo-European languages in Europe has contributed significantly to Europe as a linguistic area. The substratum hypothesis fails in particular to account for the many properties that demonstrably have arisen in European languages in the course of the last millennium, as we hope to show in the following chapters.

(iii) Haspelmath (1998: 285) hypothesizes that it was the time of the great transformations at the transition from late antiquity to the Middle Ages that can be held responsible for most of the features characterizing the structural unity of Europe. In fact, the time between 400 and 1200 AD saw a number of dramatic transformations in Europe, such as the decline of the Western

[11] For a critical appraisal of this feature, see Van Pottelberge (2005).

Roman Empire, and the Germanic, Romance, and Slavic migrations, leading to the emergence of the modern insular Celtic, Germanic, Romance, and Slavic languages.

This hypothesis is a strong one, but it cannot account for all the features, as in fact Haspelmath admits. As we will see in the following chapters, quite a number of processes of linguistic transfer across European languages clearly occurred in later periods. For example, the contact-induced growth of a polysemy between comitative and instrumental case marking, which will be our concern in Chapter 5, took place in a number of European languages much later than in the Middle Ages (Stolz 2001; Stolz, Stroh and Urdze 2003: 71), and a number of the typological properties characterizing Irish English (Hiberno-English) appear to be the result of language contact in Ireland roughly between 1700 and 1900 (see, e.g., Siemund 2004*a*, 2004*b*; Pietsch 2004*a*, 2004*b*, 2004*c*).

(iv) One factor frequently invoked to account for the diffusion of linguistic properties across Europe has been seen in the classical languages, most of all in Latin, to a lesser extent also in Greek (see Section 1.2.1). The Christian church, culture and writing, Roman law, and scholarship were all important vehicles disseminating Latin in the emerging European languages and nations, mostly as written media. Accordingly, Kortmann (1998*b*: 523) draws attention to the fact that the great majority of languages belonging to his European core area have a rich and long literary tradition of more than 300 years, and he adds:

> Moreover, the languages with a long literary tradition are also those with the most elaborate, semantically most differentiated inventories of adverbial subordinators, while those largely lacking a literary tradition . . . have considerably smaller sets of subordinators for the specification of interclausal relations (Kortmann 1998*b*: 523).

That the two classical languages had an impact on the structure of modern European languages is a salient theme especially in earlier works; note, for example, that Blatt (1957: 473) hypothesized that the modern European syntax bears 'the stamp of the Latin genius'. As mentioned above (see Section 1.2.1), an interesting correlation is suggested by Kortmann (1998*a*: 214–15): Based on evidence on the structure of adverbial subordinators he concludes that Europe's core area can be divided into a western and an eastern half, where the former reflects the structural influence of Latin and the latter that of Greek, even if overall Latin's contribution was more substantial than that of Greek.

Beyond any reasonable doubt, Latin and Classical Greek have had a deep impact on the lexicon of modern European languages; the overall contribution of these two languages to structural changes in the other European languages, however, is still largely unclear. What is clear, however, as has also been pointed out by some of the authors dealing with this subject, is that there are quite a number of general developments in the European languages that cannot be explained with reference to Latin and Classical Greek. For example, Kortmann (1998*b*: 476–8) found that the structure of adverbial clauses has changed considerably in the course of the last two millennia. The structure of adverbial subordinators became more complex: while in the classical languages, subordinators consisting of more than one word accounted for 23.3 per cent of all items, their number increased to 45.2 per cent in the modern languages. At the same time, adverbial subordinators lost syntactic and semantic polyfunctionality.

There are many, and even more obvious examples to suggest that the structural influence of Latin and Greek had its limits, and that some linguistic structures in European languages are the result of innovation. For example, Latin had no articles whatsoever, and the same applies to Proto-Germanic, while the presence of both definite and indefinite articles in modern Romance and Germanic languages is considered by many to be a paradigm argument in favour of Europe as a linguistic area; accordingly, the presence of articles cannot possibly be due to inheritance (see Chapter 3).

Unfortunately, not all properties characterizing modern European languages are demonstrably unambiguous[12] innovations independent of Latin influence. One example may suffice to illustrate the problem involved. As we will see in more detail in Chapter 6, the polysemy of words such as English *who, what, where, which,* etc. between an interrogative and a clause-subordinating function, which is another strong case of a pan-European property, can be traced back—at least to some extent—to Latin, where such words exhibited roughly the same range of functions as they do in the modern languages. The presence of this polysemy in the Romance languages is, presumably, at least to some extent due to genetic inheritance, but Latin also appears to have influenced the diffusion of this polysemy to some non-Romance languages via its role since the Middle Ages. Haspelmath (1998) points out that this might not apply to all the properties to be widely found in modern European languages. He admits, however, that the rise of two of these properties, verbal negation with a negative indefinite and postnominal relative clauses with inflected resumptive relative pronouns, may well have been

[12] As an anonymous reviewer of an earlier version of this book rightly observes, '[C]hanges can obliterate older structures. These changes may be internal (a plausible example is the typological shift English and so many other European languages underwent from OV to VO), and others contact-induced. A synchronic language state is always the result of change, and little is ever of "unambiguous" origin.'

influenced by Latin, even if 'Latin probably only helped reinforce these structures in those languages where they existed already independently as variants' (Haspelmath 1998: 275).

Such observations suggest that, once again, we are left with a situation where no meaningful generalizations seem possible.

(v) Haspelmath (1998: 272) argues that the rise of the pan-European features discussed by him cannot be due to factors relating to the common European culture from the Renaissance to the Enlightenment since a time-span of 300–500 years is not sufficient to account for the presence of these features. Even if this point is well taken, we will see in the following chapters that, nevertheless, the last five centuries of European history have seen some dramatic developments towards the rise of new functional categories as a result of language contact, and some of these developments in fact concern pan-European properties discussed by Haspelmath. Accordingly, we are reluctant to accept that this phase of European history 'can be discarded from the outset', as he puts it.

In addition to (v), and the other factors discussed above, there must have been another factor that Betz (1944) refers to as *europäischer Sprachausgleich*, a continuous levelling process whereby neighbouring languages constantly adjust to one another—with the effect that over a period of more than 1,000 years the languages concerned accumulate larger amounts of structures of other languages spoken in the same area. Such levelling processes are particularly strong in regions and situations characterized by intense language contact, and Europe's history offers a wide range of such situations. They are more likely to occur in situations of sociolinguistic asymmetry, where there is, for example, a linguistic minority exposed to a dominant language—but again, levelling does not require unusual sociolinguistic settings (see Chapter 7).

The findings made above suggest that the distinction between what is genetically inherited (that is, due to common descent) and what is due to contact-induced innovation is a thorny issue and one in need of much more scholarly attention than it has received so far.

1.2.5 *Areal groupings within Europe*

Since its beginnings, work on areal relationship has focused on European languages, and one major goal of earlier scholars was to demonstrate that there are a number of distinct areal groupings within Europe.[13]

[13] Scholars working in this tradition are portrayed by Stolz (forthc.) as using a segregating approach, according to which not all European languages resemble each other to the same extent.

In fact, the only widely accepted linguistic area in Europe are the Balkans, claimed to be the paradigm case of a sprachbund,[14] even if there are scholars who have problems with the relevance of such a linguistic unit (see Hinrichs 1999 for references). Fairly uncontroversial members of this area are Albanian, Modern Greek, Rumanian, Bulgarian, Macedonian, perhaps also Balkan Romani and the southernmost varieties of Serbian/Croatian—all Indo-European languages. Not all authors use the same catalogue of properties or the same number of properties to define the sprachbund (see Sandfeld 1930; Schaller 1975; Solta 1980; Joseph 1992; van der Auwera 1998*a*; Hinrichs 1999), but the following are distinguished by most authors: (a) a stressed mid-to-high central vowel; (b) a vowel inventory without phonological contrasts of quantity, openness, or nasalization; (c) the merger of genitive and dative cases; (d) periphrastic futures based on verbs for 'want'; (e) postposed definite articles; (f) 'pleonastic' use of weak object pronominal forms in combination with full noun phrases; (g) a superessive marker ('on') for numerals between '11' and '19'; (h) infinitive loss and its replacement with finite clauses; (i) the replacement of synthetic adjectival comparative forms with analytic ones; and (j) the presence of evidential or admirative verb forms. The Balkan sprachbund developed over a period of 1,500 years (Hinrichs 1999: 454), but the main period was between 800 and 1700 AD.

There have also been a number of attempts to identify other areal groupings within Europe, starting with Lewy (1942), the first major attempt to arrive at an areal sub-classification of Europe (see Stolz 2006). Based on a combination of morphosyntactic criteria, Lewy divided the eighteen languages he studied in some detail into five areal groupings, summarized in Table 1.2.

With the exception of the Balkans, which had already been defined earlier by Sandfeld (1930), none of the groupings proposed in Table 1.2 has been confirmed as a significant linguistic area by subsequent researchers. However, some of his groupings, especially his Atlantic grouping, had an impact on subsequent generations of students of language contact and linguistic prehistory in Europe (especially Wagner 1959, 1970; Ureland 1978a). And much the same applies to the other attempts at areal language classification in Europe that followed Lewy (1942), such as Décsy (1973), Haarmann (1976*a*, 1976*b*), Ureland (1985*b*), Sarhimaa (1991), and Wintschalek (1993). Décsy (1973), for example, classified the sixty-two European languages he analysed into ten areas, where SAE is one of them, consisting of French, German, Italian, and Russian (see Section 1.2.2 on this issue), but the evidence supporting his

[14] For convenient summaries see e.g. Joseph (1992) or Feuillet (2001); see also Bahner (1986).

TABLE 1.2. Lewy's (1942) classification of eighteen European languages based on typological and areal characteristics

	Structural characteristic	Areal group	Languages
I	Isolation of inflection	Atlantic	Basque, Spanish, Italian, French, Irish, English, Swedish
II	Word inflection	Central	German, Hungarian
III	Demonstrative	The Balkans	Rumanian, Albanian, Greek
IV	Stem inflection and subordination	Eastern	Latvian, Russian, Finnish, Mordvin, Cheremis
V	Fully subordinating	Arctic	Yurak (Samoyed)

groupings is in many cases of doubtful value; like that of Becker (1948) and Wagner (1959, 1964), Décsy's work is characterized appropriately by Stolz (2006) as being based on a 'somewhat speculative and impressionistic approach with strong affinities to *Völkerpsychologie*'.

In more recent work on areal relationship in Europe, a number of groupings within Europe have been proposed. Groupings that have received some scholarly attention are in particular the Circum-Baltic region, the Middle Volga region (or the Volga-Kama *Sprachbund*), and the Circum-Mediterranean area. Whilst none has so far received general recognition as a sprachbund, this work is of a different nature than that of the period prior to 1990: based on systematic comparisons and on contemporary notions of typological linguistics, it has brought about a wealth of new findings on the areal relationship patterns in specific regions of Europe.

The Circum-Baltic area, or 'superposition zone' is said to include, but is not necessarily confined to Baltic (Lithuanian, Latvian), Slavic (North Kashubian), Germanic (Swedish), and Finnic (Livonian, Estonian, Finnish) languages (Stolz 1991; Nau 1996; Dahl & Koptjevskaja-Tamm 2001*b*; Koptjevskaja-Tamm & Wälchli 2001; Koptjevskaja-Tamm 2002; see also Décsy 1973: 68; Haarmann 1976*b*: 106). Dahl and Koptjevskaja-Tamm (2001*b*: xviii–xix) list more than thirty languages and dialects as potentially belonging to the area, adding that 'the notion Sprachbund is not satisfactory for characterizing the linguistic situation' of this area. That the status of this area as a distinct sprachbund is in fact controversial is suggested by the fact that there exist a number of contrasting notions of it, and that there is no single typologically distinctive property shared by all languages of the area (Koptjevskaja-Tamm 2002: 212); Nau (1996) concludes that this is a linguistically highly complex area characterized by many layers of micro- and macro-contacts and various kinds of mutual influences stretching over a long period of time (see also Koptjevskaja-Tamm and Wälchli 2001: 627; Koptjevskaja-Tamm 2002).

The Middle Volga region combines the Finno-Ugric languages Mari, Udmurt, and Mordva and the Turkic languages Tatar, Bashkir, and Chuvash. The former are autochthonous, while Turkic-speaking peoples entered the region in and around the eighth century. Russian added to shaping language contact and linguistic transfer after Russia annexed the Volga-Kama region in 1552. According to Johanson (2000*c*), the paramount linguistic property of this area consists of a set of reduced (lax) vowels, even if there are various other properties as well, transferred both from Turkic to Finno-Ugric languages and from Finno-Ugric to Turkic languages. Note further that Wintschalek (1993) has proposed a Volga-Kama *Sprachbund* that contains all the languages mentioned by Johanson (2000*c*) but is not confined to them.

A number of attempts have been made to demonstrate that there is a Circum-Mediterranean linguistic area (see especially Cristofaro & Putzu 2000; Cristofaro 2000; Grandi 2002; Ramat & Stolz 2002; Stolz 2002*a*, 2002*b*), exposing many—to some extent unexpected—typological similarities among the languages of the Mediterranean world. Such similarities include: (a) word iteration; (b) animacy-based differential object marking; (c) invariable relativizers; (d) possessive clitics or pronominal affixes; and (e) augmentative suffixes (Stolz 2003–4). However, whilst being intuitively plausible as a historically defined linguistic unit, and in spite of the fact that there are a number of grammatical isoglosses cutting across genetic boundaries, evidence for an overall Circum-Mediterranean sprachbund is so far not entirely convincing.

Finally, van der Auwera (1998*c*: 828–9) tentatively proposes three linguistic areas or *Sprachbünde* that may be distinguished in Europe: the Balkan sprachbund as a relatively uncontroversial linguistic area, and two others that have so far not been recognized as such. The first consists of Dutch, French, German, Italian, and Polish (corresponding largely to his 'Charlemagne *Sprachbund*'), and the second includes English, Danish, Norwegian, and Faroese. The criteria used by van der Auwera all concern property clusterings in adverbial domains.

To conclude, none of the areal groupings within Europe that have been proposed, not even the Balkans, are linguistically entirely satisfactory—to the extent that it is possible to define them in terms of a set of linguistic properties that are found exclusively within that grouping but nowhere else, at least not in neighbouring languages (see Campbell *et al.* 1986: 561 for a critical appraisal).

1.2.6 *On mapping*

The recent typological work on European languages within the EUROTYP framework has yielded an enormous range of information on structural diversity. The main goal of this work was to study areal relations among European languages by defining the geographical distribution of both individual properties and bundles of properties. Accordingly, two main taxonomic parameters were employed: typology and geography. Typology was employed to determine whether property P_x of language L1 is the same as or different from property P_y of language L2—in other words, typology was based on discrete categorization and cross-linguistic taxonomy, even if in a number of cases discrete categorization was supplemented by graded categorization of the form 'language L1 has more of property P_x than language L2'. The geography parameter was employed to demonstrate that the distribution of typological sameness or difference somehow makes sense, that is, that there is a systematic correlation between typological and geographical patternings. This research activity resulted in an extensive range of maps showing the areal distribution of linguistic properties.

Maps in this paradigm are of two kinds: They involve either isogloss mapping or isopleth mapping. Isogloss mapping is a technique whereby, within a given region, languages exhibiting the same property are marked as being areally the same—that is, as sharing the same isogloss (cf. van der Auwera's (1998*b*: 15) notion of 'name map'). Isogloss mapping has dominated much of the areal-typological work of the EUROTYP era, resulting in a plethora of maps (see especially the contributions in van der Auwera 1998*b*; Haspelmath 2001). There are some variations in the use of this technique, depending, for example, on whether priority is given to the linguistic or the geographical component of classification (see van der Auwera 1998*b*: 19–20).

Isopleth mapping (or quantified isogloss mapping) has been applied implicitly in many of the works mentioned (see also Haspelmath and Buchholz 1998: 327). Explicitly, it has been employed in sprachbunds whose status is held to be fairly uncontroversial, such as South Asia (Masica 1976), the Balkans (van der Auwera 1998*a*), and Meso-America (van der Auwera 1998*a*). Isopleth maps are designed on the basis of the relative number of properties that languages of a linguistic area share: languages having the same number of properties, irrespective of which properties these are, are assigned to the same isotope or areal unit and, depending on how many properties there are in a given language, the relative position of that language *vis-à-vis* other languages of that linguistic area can be determined.[15]

[15] 'In these maps the demarcation lines, called isopleths, mark off areas with languages displaying the same number or *plethora* of features, but not necessarily the same features' (van der Auwera 1998*a*: 260).

What isopleth maps achieve is that they show the geographical distribution of the relative number of features making up a sprachbund. For example, on the basis of ten features that are said to be characteristic of the Balkan languages, van der Auwera (1998*a*: 261–3) finds that Bulgarian is the most central Balkanic language, being 'included in all isoglosses', that is showing all ten Balkanic features employed by him. Isopleth mapping is a convenient way of establishing structural characteristics of sprachbunds, such as their boundary and their core structures. It is not of much help, however, when it comes to determining how the relationship among individual languages of a sprachbund is to be described, other than establishing that language L1 has more of the properties defining the sprachbund than L2.

1.2.7 *Haspelmath (2001)*

Haspelmath's study of 2001 marked a new era in work on Europe as a sprachbund. What distinguishes it from previous studies are, in particular, the following points. First, it is based on a wide range of different features, extending from nominal to verbal, from morphological to syntactic issues, and from clause-internal structure to clause combining. Second, more than that of other authors, the catalogue of features used by him is maximally diagnostic of properties characterizing European languages. Third, Haspelmath's study relies on a vast amount of data relating to worldwide distribution; accordingly, unlike most other authors who have written on this general issue, he is in a position to relate the structures of European languages to what is found elsewhere in the world. And fourth, he offers comprehensive data for thirty-nine European languages on nine of the features proposed by him, with the result that the reader is in a position to verify or falsify his hypotheses.

Haspelmath concludes that Europe can be defined as a sprachbund, which he calls Standard Average European (SAE), a term first proposed by Whorf (1941; see especially Whorf 1956: 138), and also used by other scholars (e.g. Garvin 1949; Décsy 1973: 29; van der Auwera 1998*c*).[16] He proposes the following parameters, or SAE features as he calls them (Haspelmath 2001: 1494–501):

(i) definite and indefinite articles;
(ii) postnominal relative clauses with inflected, resumptive relative pronouns;

[16] Note that Whorf did not use 'Standard Average European' as a term of linguistic typology, nor did he define it by means of linguistic properties (see Van Pottelberge 2005 for a critical discussion).

(iii) a possessive perfect ('have'-perfect) formed with 'have' plus a passive participle;[17]
(iv) a preponderance of generalizing predicates to encode experiencers;
(v) a passive construction formed with a passive participle plus an intransitive copula-like verb;
(vi) a prominence of anticausatives in inchoative–causative pairs;
(vii) dative external possessors;
(viii) verbal negation with a negative indefinite;
(ix) particle comparatives in comparisons of inequality;
(x) equative constructions based on adverbial-relative clause structures;
(xi) subject person affixes as strict agreement markers; and
(xii) differentiation between intensifiers ('emphatic reflexives') and reflexive pronouns.

Whilst these are the features he uses for areal-typological generalizations, he adds a number of further features most of which strike us as being equally diagnostic of Europe as a linguistic area, such as verb fronting in polar interrogatives, comparative marking on adjectives (see below), markers used for conjoining noun phrases ('A and-B' conjunction), comitative–instrumental syncretism (see Chapter 5), and suppletive forms for second person ordinal numerals.

The list of twelve features presented above is not identical with the one in Haspelmath (1998), an earlier version containing eleven features of which nine are also present in the 2001-version, while the remaining two ('A and-B' conjunction, and verb fronting in polar interrogatives) are excluded from the main list in Haspelmath (2001) as they are less well-documented. In the 1998-version of SAE, Haspelmath had distinguished the following kinds of language groupings:

(a) The nucleus, comprising Dutch, German, French, and northern Italian dialects; hence, it includes van der Auwera's (1998*b*: 824) 'Charlemagne *Sprachbund*',[18] but it is not coextensive with it (see Section 1.2.2).
(b) The core, which in addition includes the other Romance (Spanish, Portuguese, Italian, Rumanian) and Germanic languages (English, Icelandic, Norwegian, Swedish, Faroese), West Slavic (Czech, Slovenian)

[17] As we will see in Chapter 4, our definition of possessive perfects differs from that of Haspelmath in not restricting them to the requirement that there be a transitive 'have'-verb. Accordingly, our definition covers a larger set of constructions than that of Haspelmath.

[18] Note that in van der Auwera's (1998*c*) 'Charlemagne *Sprachbund*', Italian is treated as a whole, that is, northern Italian dialects are not mentioned.

and South Slavic (Bulgarian), and Balkan languages (Albanian, Modern Greek).
(c) The periphery, consisting of East Slavic (Russian, Ukrainian, Belorussian), Baltic (Latvian, Lithuanian), Finnic and Hungarian, Basque, Maltese, Armenian, and Georgian.
(d) The Celtic languages (Irish, Welsh, Breton), which are not part of SAE (Haspelmath 1998: 273).

This classification is somewhat modified in his later study (Haspelmath 2001: 1505), where he arrives at the following classification: on the basis of nine of the twelve features selected, the resulting groupings are: the nucleus of SAE consists of French and German only, where all nine features are found, followed by a second group having eight of the features, which consists of Dutch plus all the Romance languages of the sample except Rumanian and Albanian, a third group with seven features, which consists of English, Rumanian, and Greek, a fourth group with six features containing Icelandic, Norwegian, Swedish, and Czech, and finally a fifth group with five features consisting of all Slavic and Baltic languages. All the remaining fifteen languages are clearly marginal, having at best two features (see Map 1.1).

A convention. As we saw above, there are as many different notions of what an SAE language is as there are scholars who have worked on this issue (see especially van der Auwera 1998*c*: 816). But only Haspelmath's (2001: 1505) systematic analysis just summarized offers a way of defining SAE languages based on fairly unambiguous quantitative evidence: there is clearly a twofold classification of the languages of Europe. On the one hand there are languages having five or more of the nine features analysed by Haspelmath, on the other hand there are languages having at best two features. In the remainder of this book we will adopt this classification, calling the former group, but not the latter group, SAE languages. On the basis of this convention, the following will be referred to as SAE languages:

(i) all Romance languages;
(ii) all Germanic languages;
(iii) all Slavic languages;
(iv) the Baltic languages Latvian and Lithuanian;
(v) Albanian;
(vi) Greek;
(vii) Hungarian.

Accordingly, languages of the second group, such as Finnish, Estonian, Maltese, Basque, Turkish, the Celtic languages, Georgian, Armenian, etc.,

MAP 1.1. Number of morphosyntactic features found in European languages (according to Haspelmath 2001)

will not be called SAE languages. But we will no longer be concerned with what a nuclear area of Europe should look like, mainly for the reasons given in Section 1.2.2.

Haspelmath's (1998, 2001) notion of an SAE sprachbund compares well with the one that exists on the Balkan sprachbund—both in terms of the evidence presented, the results obtained, and also in terms of historical plausibility. On the basis of Haspelmath's (2001: 1505) quantitative evidence, it is possible to hypothesize that a given language that has five or more of the nine features studied by him is very likely to be one spoken in Europe, while a language spoken anywhere else in the world can be expected to have hardly more than two of the features.

However, we will use this notion exclusively for convenient reference; as we will see in Section 1.3, even this notion raises a number of questions. Note further that Haspelmath's proposal is heavily biased in favour of Indo-European languages since, with the exception of Hungarian, all SAE languages belong to this family. Furthermore, it is also biased in favour of the languages of Europe's western half; consequently, a number of authors have suggested that SAE should more appropriately be called 'Standard Average Western European' (see van der Auwera 1998*c*: 817 for details), and there would be reasons to follow this suggestion. Still, as Haspelmath (2001: 1505) rightly points out, the latter term would also be misleading in view of the fact that his SAE group includes languages such as Greek, Albanian, Latvian, and Russian, which would not really qualify as western European languages.

With the above remarks we do not wish to aim at an evaluation of the different hypotheses that have been voiced on areal taxonomy in Europe—not only because such an endeavour would be premature at the present stage of research but also because areal taxonomy is not a central issue of this book. Accordingly, the terminological convention proposed in this section has no bearing on the content of the following chapters, which will not be concerned with how European languages differ from one another but rather with how they are, or are becoming, alike.

1.3 Discussion

In the preceding section we saw that there are many answers to the questions we posed in the introduction to that section. These answers raise a number of further questions, such as the following:

(a) On the basis of all the evidence that has been produced, is it really possible to argue that there is a European sprachbund or linguistic area with clearly defined boundaries?

(b) Suppose we took any randomly chosen geographical region in the world: would we find there less linguistic homogeneity across genetic boundaries than we find in Europe?

(c) To what extent are the areal relationship patterns to be found in Europe the product of what is a commonplace in areal linguistics, namely that neighbouring languages are likely to be more alike than languages that are geographically separated?

(d) To what extent are these patterns the product of the criteria used to identify them? For example, if one were to choose a set of criteria based on worldwide cross-linguistic parameters, how likely is it that Europe stands out as a typological unit *sui generis*?
(e) With the possible exception of the Balkan sprachbund, are there really any areally defined linguistic groupings within Europe?

Problems that we encountered in the preceding paragraphs include the following: apart from French, no single European language is agreed upon by all authors to belong to Europe's core—not even Dutch or German. Languages that are treated as being peripheral European languages by some authors, such as Russian, are classified as core European by others. And, ignoring some rather trivial universal linguistic properties, there is not a single property that sets European languages off from other languages, that is to say, that is found in Europe but nowhere else in the world, and there is also no property that is found everywhere else in the world but not in Europe.

There are a number of possible reasons for this situation. One concerns the choice and evaluation of criteria presumed to be diagnostic of areal relationship. Different scholars have taken different stances on what should be a criterion for areal taxonomy. This problem is addressed by van der Auwera in the following way:

> The fact that the assignment differs from one linguist to the next is not negative. They make their assessment relative to different structural features. Thus, Dahl (1990: 3) hesitates about Italian, probably because he is about to discuss the non-Pro-Drop character of some European languages, a feature lacking in Italian; Lazard (1990: 246) does not give a top ranking to English, because the conjugation of the finite verb is nearly insensitive for person (van der Auwera 1998*c*: 817).

These observations suggest, first, that areal relationship is a complex notion, second, that it exhibits different manifestations in different domains of language structure, and third, that it is in many cases unclear whether a certain isogloss or bundle of isoglosses is due to historical relationship of any kind, or to coincidence. But there are also questions of a more general nature, relating to what the notion sprachbund can contribute to a better understanding of language structure, linguistic relationship, and/or of historical reconstruction.

One question concerns the magnitude of linguistic evidence. None of the more widely accepted sprachbunds that have been proposed so far is based on a larger amount of linguistic evidence; usually there are at best a dozen linguistic criteria that have been recruited in defining such areas. Considering that any given language consists of thousands of different structural properties, one may wonder what such a small number of structural similarities can contribute to an understanding of a linguistic relationship among the languages concerned.[19]

Another question concerns the contribution that a study of sprachbunds can make to understanding the history of the languages concerned and the way and the extent to which this history was shaped by language contact. Since linguistic areas are hypothesized to be the result of historical events, they might be expected to provide a tool for historical reconstruction. It would seem, however, that none of the sprachbunds that are generally accepted lives up to this expectation. Neither work on the Balkans or Meso-America nor on any other established linguistic area has contributed substantially to reconstructing the history of contact processes of the languages concerned.

With reference to Europe, these observations raise the following questions: What is the eventual benefit of defining Europe as a sprachbund? What can be achieved in this way that has not been achieved in the case of well-established sprachbunds such as the Balkans or Meso-America?

But there are also questions relating to grammatical taxonomy. The analyses that we reviewed in the preceding sections were based on discrete categorization of grammatical forms and structures. The kind of problems associated with these analyses can be illustrated with a few examples from Basque. For good reasons, this language is classified in all the areal typologies that we discussed as being fairly marginal. But there is an alternative view on this issue. This may be demonstrated with reference to some of the features proposed by Haspelmath (2001) as being diagnostic of SAE.[20]

The first feature that Haspelmath lists is (i) the presence of definite and indefinite articles (2001: 1494). He observes that Basque has a definite but no indefinite article. This observation is problematic in several ways. One problem, relating to definite articles, will be discussed later; the second problem concerns indefinite articles: Basque *does* have an indefinite article, *bat*, which is used for all canonical functions associated with such articles, such as presentative, specific, and non-specific indefinite reference, and which can be inflected. The following is a typical example containing two instances of the indefinite article (see Sections 3.3.3, 7.2.1):

[19] We are grateful to an anonymous reviewer for having drawn our attention to this fact.

[20] Note that, unlike Haspelmath's (2001) account, which is based essentially on a comparison of written and/or standard languages, the following discussion also draws on non-standard data, that is, on dialectal variation.

(1.3) Basque (Haase 1992: 60)

Fraide seindu çahar **bat**- ec ikuss- i cie- la Ainguru **bat**....
brother holy old a- ERG see- PTCP PRT- SR angle a
'[One reads] that an old holy Brother saw an angle....'

What might have induced Haspelmath to decide that Basque has no indefinite article is the fact that this article does not appear to be entirely obligatory, to be used in all contexts where indefinite reference is involved, or where an indefinite article would be used in languages like Spanish, French, or German.

The second SAE feature that Basque is said to lack is (ii) the presence of a postnominal relative clause with inflecting relative pronouns introducing the relative clause, where the pronoun signals the head's role within the relative clause (Haspelmath 2001: 1494–5). However, there is such a construction in Basque; consider the following example, taken from the written language:

(1.4) Basque (Haase 1992: 152)

Hiri bat ba- zen, **zoin**- tan ez bait- zen eliza- rik.
town one ENZ- PRT.3.SG which- TRN.INE NEG SR- PRT.3.SG church- PART
'There was a town where there was no church.'

A third SAE feature that is said to be absent in Basque is (iii) a possessive perfect ('have'-perfect) formed with 'have' plus a passive participle (Haspelmath 2001: 1495). That Basque, nevertheless, has a construction of this kind is suggested by examples such as the following, where the verb *ukan* 'have' plus the transitive participle are used to form a recent perfect with transitive verbs:

(1.5) Basque (Haase 1992: 92)

ikus- i dut.
see- PTCP PRES.3.SG<1.SG
'I have seen.' (Lit. 'I have it seen')

This construction appears to have been created only during the twentieth century on the model of Romance languages (Haase 1992: 92–3). That Haspelmath (2001) did not take it into account in his classification may be due to its young age of grammaticalization; but once again, one could take a different stance on this issue.

A fourth feature characterizing SAE languages concerns (v) participial passives plus an intransitive copula-like verb (Haspelmath 2001: 1496–7). Once again, Basque has such a construction, even though it was replicated only in the course of the twentieth century from Romance languages. As in canonical SAE languages, the Basque passive also uses the main verb in a participial form and an intransitive copula verb, *izan* 'be', and as in SAE languages there may be an agent, encoded by the ablative-partitive case suffix -*(r)ik*:

(1.6) BASQUE (Haase 1992: 132)

A(b)antxü	xakür	bat-	eta-	(r)ik	ausiki	izan	tzün.
almost	dog	one-	TRN-	ABL/PART	bite.PTCP	be.PTCP	PRT.3.SG.2.AL

'He was almost bitten by a dog.'

Note that the structural properties mentioned are of fairly recent origin, they presumably arose in the course of the last four or five centuries as a response to the interaction of Basque speakers with their Romance-speaking neighbours (Haase 1992: 158; see also Section 7.2.1). However, these observations suggest that there are a number of problems with the standard approach that we surveyed in the preceding sections, such as the following:

(a) This approach relies heavily or exclusively on standard and/or written languages, which do not always really reflect what is going on in a language.
(b) It tends to rely on what appears to be the most salient construction, ignoring alternative constructions that are also used to express the grammatical function at stake. Accordingly, certain kinds of relevant typological information are likely to be ignored within this approach.
(c) Another problem relates to the requirement inherent in this approach that categorization must be discrete, that is, that language L has either property P_1 or P_2—other possibilities being discarded. One effect this requirement has is that to some extent arbitrary decisions have to be made in cases where both P_1 and P_2 exist as more or less equivalent options in one and the same language.
(d) A problem related to (c) concerns cross-linguistic structural equivalence: whether property P_1 in language L_1 is really structurally equivalent to property P_1 rather than to P_2 in language L_2 is in some cases not easy to decide, but this issue can influence the results obtained. We may illustrate this with another example from Basque. In Haspelmath's (2001: 1494) classification of SAE features, Basque is treated as a language that has a definite but no indefinite article. As we saw above, this taxonomy can be questioned since there is a fairly productive indefinite article. But perhaps a more serious problem

exists with the definite article: Haase (1992: 53–4) observes that the primary function of the 'definite article' *-a* is to individualize referents, and these referents can be, and not uncommonly are, indefinite or even non-specific, as in the following examples:

(1.7) BASQUE (Haase 1992: 53)

Gizon-	a	hiz.	diela	urti-	a
man-	ART	PRS.2.SG	before	year-	ART

'You are a man.' 'a year ago'

To be sure, Haspelmath's decision that Basque has a definite article can be justified on the grounds that *-a* is more likely to mark definite than indefinite reference. However, one may argue that *-a* is not really structurally equivalent to definite articles in SAE languages. In this case, a taxonomic conclusion that one could draw from the observations made is that, rather than having a definite but no indefinite article, Basque has an indefinite but no definite article—hence, quite the opposite of what a discrete-categorization approach of the kind employed by the typologists cited suggests.

Furthermore, there are two more general problems associated with this kind of approach:

(e) The work that has been done recently on Europe as a linguistic area—as well as on other areas prominent in sprachbund linguistics such as Meso-America, South Asia, or Ethiopia—aims at studying linguistic relationship across genetic boundaries. One may wonder, however, whether the approach adopted in that work is really optimal for studying areal relationships. All Romance languages, for example, have been shown to share at least seven out of the nine features used by Haspelmath (2001). The approach used does not allow analysts to determine which of these features are due to genetic inheritance and which are due to language contact. Thus, the possessive perfects of the Romance languages can presumably be traced back to some extent to Late Latin—hence, there is reason to assume that the modern Romance languages have this property, at least to some extent, on account of either genetic inheritance or parallel development (i.e. drift; Sapir 1921; LaPolla 1994) rather than of areal relationship. And much the same applies to the polysemy between interrogative and relative clause markers (e.g. French *qui* 'who'), which is another feature widely accepted as a feature specific to SAE: this polysemy was already fully grammaticalized in Latin (see Chapter 6). Once again, the fact that it is found in all modern Romance languages is therefore likely to be due largely to its genetic history within the Romance language family, and is therefore of limited value for determining areal, that is, contact-induced relationship.

This suggests that, if indeed the goal is to study areal relationship, then the question arises whether the various features really should all be given the same weight in areal classification. For example, if we observe that Romance languages have a possessive perfect then this information is obviously less relevant to areal classification than the fact that Macedonian has one, since we know that in the case of Macedonian genetic relationship can be ruled out as a motivating factor (see Chapter 4).

(f) A final problem, and one that is of central concern to the present book, is that this approach does not fully account for the dynamics underlying grammatical categorization in European languages. This dynamics can be reflected in dialect variation, in contextual variation, or in the coexistence of different use patterns employed for the expression of a given grammatical function, and especially in language change.

We may illustrate this last point with the following example. Among the features mentioned by Haspelmath (2001: 1501–2) in support of a European sprachbund, in addition to the twelve listed in Section 1.2.7, there is the presence of special comparative markers on adjectives, such as inflectional (e.g. *big* vs. *bigg-er*) or suppletive forms (*good* vs. *better*). It would seem that this feature involves two separate properties: one concerns the presence vs. the absence of degree markers such as *-er* or *more* in English. Indeed, compared to other parts of the world, Europe stands out as an area where degree markers are especially common, whereas most languages elsewhere in the world do without a degree marker, in that the comparative of inequality is simply expressed by a standard marker, that is, forms corresponding to English *than* (see Stassen 1985). The second property concerns the use of synthetic vs. analytic degree markers. Inflectional and suppletive forms such as the ones we mentioned for English are synthetic ones, while the English particle *more* is an instance of an analytic degree marker. Once again, European languages are typologically unusual in exhibiting a concentration of synthetic degree markers that is clearly higher than in other parts of the world. To conclude, Haspelmath's hypothesis is well-founded with reference to both properties.

But there is also another perspective to this situation. Although synthetic degree markers are not only found in Indo-European languages but also in Basque and Finno-Ugric languages (Haspelmath 2001: 1502), their presence appears to be largely genetically rather than areally determined, and it would seem that the history of European languages of the last two millennia is characterized more by a decline of synthetic markings than by anything else. The Romance languages are a paradigm case, where synthetic markers survive at best as relics (such as French *bon* 'good' vs. *meilleur* 'better', Italian *buono* 'good' vs. *migliore* 'better'), in other languages, such as English or Greek, synthetic markers have lost in productivity. A particularly interesting case is provided by the Balkan languages, where the decline of synthetic degree markers is considered to be one of the main criteria for defining that sprachbund, to be observed in Bulgarian, Macedonian, Albanian, Rumanian, as well as in Modern Greek (see Section 1.2.5). Even more important from an areal perspective, however, is the fact that a number of European languages tend to give up their synthetic degree markers in situations of language contact; we will substantiate this point in the next chapter (Section 2.6).

To conclude, as a first approximation, Haspelmath (2001: 1501–2) is correct in arguing that, compared to other regions in the world, SAE is characterized by a remarkable density of synthetic markings. With regard to the areal dynamics of European languages, however, his decision to draw on this property as a parameter of areal relationship is not really helpful: there appears to be a drift away from this kind of marking rather than anything else. Since our interest in this book is not with genetically determined structures but rather with understanding areal phenomena as the result of processes induced in some way or other by language contact, we will have little to say on typological generalizations of the former kind. Accordingly, within the framework to be used here, the gradual process of decline of synthetic degree markers is of greater interest as a potential 'Euroversal' or 'Europeme' than the fact that this property is present in many European languages.

What we argue in the following chapters is that, if one relies on data such as the ones we presented on Basque or on the evolution of synthetic degree markers, it is likely that a different areal map of Europe will emerge—one where Basque, as a result of more recent processes, would presumably not occupy an entirely peripheral position, as it does in previous classifications; we will return to this issue in Chapter 7.

Typological work of the past decades was to a large extent preoccupied with a rigid, discrete categorization of linguistic structures, where the central question was whether or not a given language has category C for function F, rather than, for example, what the nature of the category used to express F is. A typical example can be seen in Dahl's (2000a) notion of a 'futureless area' in Europe, which is based on the classification of Europe's languages into those that have a future category used obligatorily in sentences having future time reference, and those that have no such category. Accordingly, the German *werden*-future is not a future since its use is not obligatory in sentences with future reference, for example *Ich fliege morgen nach Berlin* (I fly tomorrow to Berlin) 'I am going to fly to Berlin tomorrow'—consequently, German is treated as belonging to Europe's futureless area. Now, as Thieroff (2000: 288–9) shows, all languages that are classified as 'futureless' by Dahl do have special devices to mark future time reference and these devices can be used optionally in future contexts, and he treats these as languages with a weakly grammaticalized future. We will return to this issue in Section 2.2.

Conclusions. With these observations we do not mean to question the significance of the work just summarized: this work is empirically sound, typologically relevant, and highly useful for studying areal phenomena. What we wanted to achieve mainly with the above remarks is to prepare the reader for the fact that the approach used in the present book is different, in that it attempts to highlight language contact and its products as a dynamic phenomenon, by studying language use and language variation across space and time.

In spite of all the problems discussed in this section, one should be aware that the typological work of the last two decades has provided sufficient evidence to suggest that the linguistic map of Europe has been shaped significantly by language contact of various kinds and in various periods within the course of the last two millennia. What this work has revealed in particular are generalizations such as the following:

(i) There are clusterings of linguistic properties in Europe that are unlikely to occur in other parts of the world.
(ii) At least some of these clusterings are unlikely to be due to genetic relationship or coincidence.
(iii) These clusterings are particularly pronounced in the languages of western and central Europe, even if this may be due to some extent to the fact that we know much more about these languages than the languages of eastern Europe.

On the basis of such observations, in what follows, we will take the following assumptions as cornerstones for analysing the network of areal relationships in Europe: the typological similarity characterizing European languages is to some extent due to language contact processes that took place in the course of the last two millennia. These processes were complex but exhibit an overarching pattern: on the one hand, there are the earlier classical languages, Greek and Latin, that provided relevant models of transfer (see e.g. Kortmann

1998*a*, 1998*b*). On the other hand, there are also a number of modern European languages, most of all Romance and Germanic languages, that served as models. Third, there are also regional areal groupings, including but not being confined to the Balkans, the Baltic region, and the Mediterranean region, that have created a complex areal network in Europe which appears to be elusive to straightforward taxonomic order. And finally, there was a wide range of social networks across speech communities at all times of European history that contributed to linguistic assimilation of one kind or other.

1.4 A case study: from perfect to past time reference

As may have become clear from the preceding sections, areal linguistics within the EUROTYP tradition has been the subject of a wide range of studies, and it has produced a wealth of typological information on the languages of Europe. What this rich research activity has revealed is that there are multiple networks of typological similarities both uniting and dividing the languages of Europe. At the same time, the approach adopted in most of these studies presents a specific perspective of areal relationship—one based on a discrete typology of grammatical categorization without due reference to the factor of time. There are a number of exceptions in this work, however, where information on language-internal diversity, variation characterizing the nature of grammatical categories, and variation across time is taken into account in order to study areal relationship, and we will now have a look at one of these exceptions with a view to proposing an alternative perspective on studying an areal relationship. The case that we are concerned with is Thieroff's (2000) typological analysis of tense–aspect categories in Europe (see also Breu 1994: 56–8; Abraham & Conradie 2001; Drinka 2003*a*, 2003*b*).

1.4.1 *The areal dimension*

Using a compositional analysis to describe and compare the structure of tense–aspect marking in the languages of Europe, Thieroff proposes a set of categories, such as perfect (= anterior, i.e. event time before point of reference), aorist (= perfective past, result/end-state in the past), future, imperfect,[21] preterite, and progressive, and he defines tense–aspect forms in terms of whether they are marked or unmarked for these categories. For example,

[21] No definition is given by the author; he observes that this category covers the semantic fields of imperfective past and counterfactuality (Thieroff 2000: 277).

the English form *sang* is said to be marked for preterite but unmarked for anterior, future, or progressive, and English verb forms marked for preterite include *sang, was singing, had sung, would sing*, etc. What this means is, first, that Thieroff (2000) aims at reconciling grammatical functions and expression forms, in that he proposes that all these forms have the preterite marker, and, second, that there is no one-to-one correlation between conventional notions such as deictic time and his categories; for example, he uses the term 'past' as a cover term for both the categories preterite and imperfect.

However one may wish to view the categories proposed by Thieroff, they enable him to describe some major traits in the development of the tense–aspect domain of European languages. In particular, he argues that there is a general development to be observed in European languages leading from perfects expressing current relevance (= present anteriors) to past tense markers, and that this development can be described in terms of a four-stage model[22] of the following kind (see also Chapter 4):

(i) *Stage 0*: This stage is characterized by the presence of a perfect, more precisely a present anterior form expressing current relevance but having no aorist/preterite function.

(ii) *Stage 1*: The perfect spreads into the domain of the past, assuming functions of an aorist/preterite, and it competes with the already existing markers expressing past time reference. One innovation characterizing this stage is that the perfect marker can now combine with itself to form a pluperfect (= event time before reference time, and reference time before speech time). At a more advanced stage, however, the existing aorist/preterite is marginalized.

(iii) *Stage 2*: Aorist/preterite is completely lost, there is now only one form for the semantic fields of current relevance, perfective past, and imperfective past. The erstwhile perfect can no longer be combined with past time markers to form pluperfects.

(iv) *Stage 3*: The erstwhile perfect marker starts to take over other typical features of past time markers. It can no longer be combined with future markers to form future perfects, and it acquires modal uses.

22 Thieroff actually distinguishes five stages; however, there is reason to reduce his stages 1 and 2 to one stage, as he himself does as well in the graphic presentation of the stages (Thieroff 2000: 285). Note further that our rendering of his findings is confined to a few points that are of interest to our subject matter. We are ignoring, e.g., the differences between Germanic languages, marking a distinction −preterite vs. +preterite, and Romance languages, marking a distinction non-past vs. imperfect vs. aorist.

What is important for our discussion is, first, that we are dealing with a well-documented process of grammaticalization leading from perfect (or anterior) to past time markers (see Bybee *et al.* 1994 for details). This means that the development in all cases concerned is unidirectional, leading from present anterior to past tense markers—that is, we will not expect any language to undergo a development from past time to perfect marker. And in the same way as perfect markers gradually assume the functions of past time markers, the older past time markers tend to decline, and they may eventually disappear altogether.

Second, the various stages distinguished by Thieroff exhibit a clear areal patterning (see Map 1.2). Stage 0 is the situation found in northern, western, and southeastern Europe, it includes all Germanic languages except German, as well as Finnish, Estonian, Lithuanian, Basque, the Romance languages Portuguese, Spanish, and Catalan, as well as Bulgarian and Greek. Within the centre of the stage-0 area there is the stage-1 area, surrounded by stage-0 languages. It includes Standard German (or Northern German), Upper Sorbian (which is spoken in Eastern Germany), French, Standard Italian (but not Northern Italian), Serbian/Croatian, Rumanian, and Albanian. The stage-2 area is geographically a centre within the stage-1 centre, surrounded by stage-1 languages; it consists of Southern German, Northern Italian, and Hungarian. The final stage-3 area is located east of the stage-2 area, it comprises the Slavic languages Slovenian, Lower Sorbian, Polish, Czech, Belorussian, Ukrainian, and Russian.

On the basis of this distribution, the following more general development can be sketched: the earliest stage of evolution (stage 0) is retained in the peripheral regions of Europe, that is, in northern, western, and southeastern Europe. The more central part of Europe experienced an innovation, in that the stage-0 marker was grammaticalized to a stage-1 marker, and this grammaticalization proceeded further to stage 2 in the most central area. Finally, in the Slavic languages, spoken to the east of the stage-2 area, the last stage 3 has been reached, where the grammaticalization process from perfect to past time marker is nearing completion.

The following case may further illustrate the nature of the process discussed here, as well as of many other processes to be discussed in the next chapters. Among the Slavic languages there is a general process whereby the two synthetic aspect–tense forms imperfect and aorist were given up; but whereas the imperfect was lost early, the aorist was retained much longer. Breu (1994: 58) observes that in Italian it is the other way round: while the imperfect is retained, the aorist (i.e. the *passato remoto*) is disappearing, being replaced

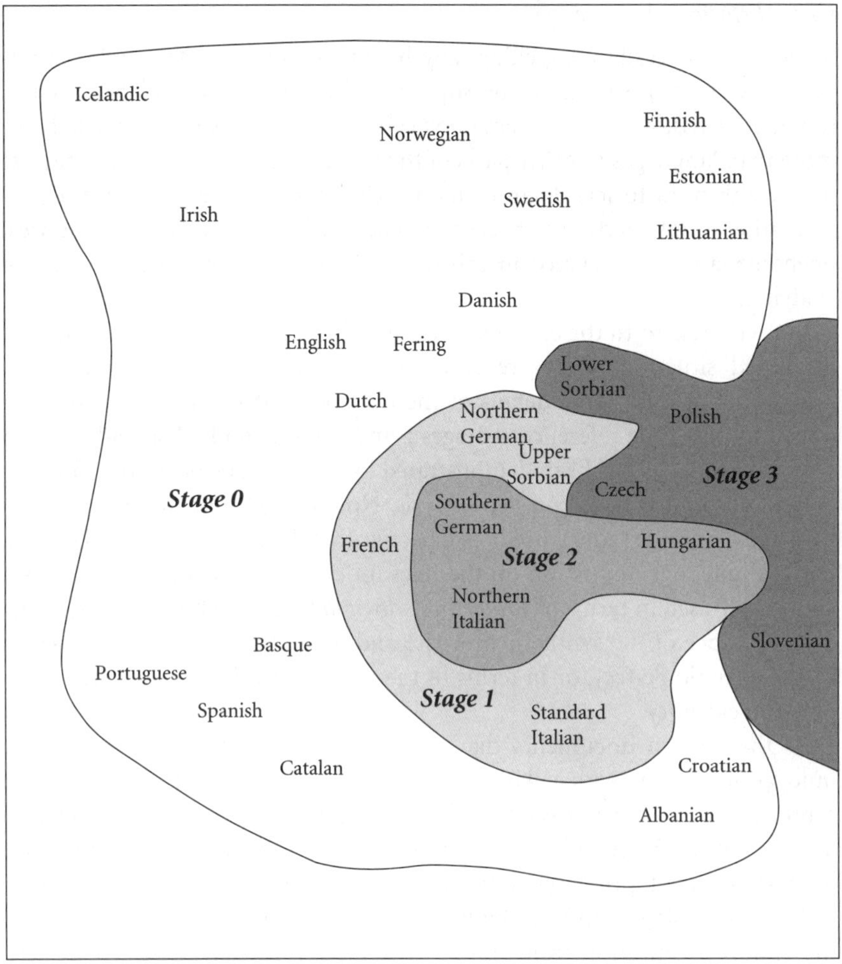

MAP 1.2. Areal patterning of the grammaticalization from perfect to past time markers in the languages of Europe (based on Thieroff 2000: 285)

with the analytic perfect (*passato prossimo*). Now, there is a Slavic-speaking minority living in Molise, southern Italy, speaking a dialect of Croatian. Having been in close contact with Italian for nearly five centuries, these Croatian speakers—unlike Croatian speakers in Croatia—abandoned the Slavic mode of aspect–tense marking and adopted the Italian one instead. Accordingly, they have retained their Slavic imperfect but gave up the aorist; Breu concludes that in this way Molise Croatian has acquired *einen romanischen Typ im slawischen Gewande* (a Romance type in a Slavic dress).

1.4.2 *Historical evidence*

In order to be really compelling, any hypothesis on a contact-induced linguistic relationship needs to be supported by diachronic evidence. In this respect, discussion in the present book can rely on a nearly optimal data basis: more than languages in other parts of the world, European languages dispose of a wealth of historical documentation. Unfortunately, however, this documentation is not nearly as rich as one would like it to be: for many of the areal phenomena to be discussed in this book, there is no appropriate historical evidence.

But with regard to the case discussed in this section, we are in a somewhat privileged situation: there are early written documents that allow us to reconstruct at least some details of the development from perfect aspect at stage 1 to past time reference at stages 2 and 3 and a gradual spread through central Europe, as has been demonstrated by Drinka (2003*a*, 2003*b*), and the present account is based on her analysis. Note that Drinka, following Abraham and Conradie (2001), uses a perspective that differs from that of Thieroff. For example, her discussion on the relevant change from stage 1 to stages 2 and 3 is phrased in terms of *Präteritumschwund* (preterite loss), that is, of the disappearance of the synthetic preterite and its replacement in this function by the analytic perfect, or in terms of the reinterpretation of the perfect as a preterite category.

As the written documents that are available suggest, the centre of this innovation was the vernacular Parisian French of the twelfth and thirteenth centuries, where the perfect first came to be used for past time reference. Speakers in southern and western France, or in Normandy and Brittany, have been slow in adopting the innovation. Documents dating from 1263–97, collected in Cologne and nearby locations, show that a first major spread of the grammaticalization from stage 1 to stage 2 must have affected western dialects of German bordering French by the thirteenth century: in these documents, analytic perfects predominate over synthetic preterites in contexts where past time reference is intended.

Subsequently, this grammaticalization appears to have spread to south-eastern dialects of German: fifteenth-century documents from the Bavarian towns of Nürnberg and Augsburg show a rapid increase in replacement of the preterite by the perfect; by 1536, the old preterite system had ceased to operate productively, and the perfect had come to predominate. Another direction of spread affected northern Italian dialects, where the French-like pattern was adopted by the end of the sixteenth century.

We have no historical information on how and when this grammaticalization spread to the neighbouring Slavic languages Czech, Slovak, Slovenian, and northern Croatian and Serbian, where the analytic perfects (with active resultative *l*-participle + BE) were used to mark the preterite. But the geographical distribution of this grammaticalization attests to its areal spread:

It should be noted that the closer that each of these three languages lie to the center of the nuclear area, the more features of PS [*Präteritumschwund*; a.n.] they possess, with more southerly Serbian in the process of developing PS, Croatian further along in the process, and Slovenian, as the westernmost South Slavic language, having given up all trace of anteriority (Drinka 2004: 224).

Drinka's (2003*a*, 2004) analysis also allows for reconstructing at least some of the motivating forces that can be held responsible for the areal spread of the grammaticalization process discussed in this section. In the critical period between the twelfth and the fourteenth centuries when the analytic perfect began to be extended to contexts where it could be understood to express temporal rather than aspectual contours of an event, Paris was a cultural and intellectual centre in Europe. Gothic art and architecture, courtly manners and ideals, scholasticism, and other cultural values spread into adjacent parts of Germany and across Europe. French played an important role as the language of administration along the French–Germanic border, and a large number of official documents in the western parts of the German-speaking area were written in French. It therefore comes as no surprise that grammatical conventions such as the use of the analytic perfect for past time reference gradually encroached upon the languages and dialects most strongly exposed to the impact of Parisian culture.

The spread of this innovation to southern dialects of German or to northern Italian dialects is less easy to account for, even if there are some extra-linguistic factors that might have contributed to this process. That it did not extend to Middle Low German in northern Germany is related to the fact that, whereas the western and southern dialects of German were adopting many French innovations, French influence on Low German dialects was much less pronounced; rather, cultural exchange was mediated more prominently via Middle Dutch.

What surfaces from these observations is, first, that there are good reasons to assume that the grammaticalization of the analytic perfect in some German dialects from stage 1 to stage 2 can be linked to more general processes of cultural diffusion in Europe and, second, that northern French is likely to have played a crucial role in linguistic diffusion; we will deal with a similar example in Section 2.7.

1.4.3 *Discussion*

The example considered in the present section was meant to draw attention to an alternative perspective of studying areal relationship—one that will be adopted in the chapters to follow. This perspective is based on the following observations: first, the development of grammatical categories tends to be determined by areal factors; second, it cuts across language and dialect boundaries. As we saw above, the areal distribution of stages unites different languages and at the same time separates dialects of one and the same language (for more examples, see Breu 1994: 57–8). Accordingly, an analysis that ignores language-internal variation is likely to miss relevant information on the areal patterning of linguistic structures.

Third, this development is gradual: rather than leading straight from one category to another, it involves a number of intermediate stages. Fourth, with the gradual replacement of one category with another, the former does not necessarily disappear entirely but tends to survive in some contexts, at least for quite some time. In the end, however, replacement may be complete. For example, the old past tense has survived in northern and Standard German, which are stage 1: *ich machte es* (I make.PAST it) 'I made it', while in southern German dialects, which are stage 2, it is essentially lost, having been replaced with the erstwhile perfect, for example, *ich habe es gemacht* (I have it made) 'I made it' (Breu 1994: 57).

Fifth, the development is in accordance with principles of grammaticalization, proceeding gradually from less grammaticalized to more strongly grammaticalized functional markers. What is important for our purposes is that grammaticalization processes in the languages of Europe tend to pattern areally, that is, they are likely to be propelled and/or accelerated by language contact.

And finally, developments such as the grammaticalization of perfect (or anterior) categories to markers of past time reference are diachronic processes and hence can be accounted for by means of historical evidence—in other words, hypotheses on these developments can be verified or falsified.

1.5 Theoretical background

Our investigation is carried out within the framework of grammaticalization theory. Grammaticalization is defined as the development from lexical to grammatical forms, and from grammatical to even more grammatical forms.

Since the development of grammatical forms is not independent of the constructions to which they belong, the study of grammaticalization is also concerned with constructions, and with even larger discourse segments. In accordance with this definition, grammaticalization theory is concerned with the genesis and development of grammatical forms. Its primary goal is to describe how grammatical forms and constructions arise and develop through space and time, and to explain why they are structured the way they are.

The main motivation underlying grammaticalization is to communicate successfully. To this end, one salient human strategy consists in using linguistic forms for meanings that are concrete, easily accessible, and/or clearly delineated to also express less concrete, less easily accessible and less clearly delineated meaning contents. To this end, lexical or less grammaticalized linguistic expressions are pressed into service for the expression of more grammaticalized functions. Accordingly, grammaticalization is a process whereby expressions for concrete (= source) meanings are used in specific contexts for encoding grammatical (= target) meanings.

There is a wide range of parameters that have been proposed (see e.g. Heine *et al.* 1991; Hopper & Traugott [1993] 2003; Bybee *et al.* 1994; Lehmann [1982] 1995); in our model it is the four parameters listed in example (1. 8) (see Heine & Kuteva 2002); alternative parameters that have been proposed, such as syntacticization, morphologization, obligatorification,[23] subjectification, etc., can be accounted for as being derivative of these parameters.

(1.8) PARAMETERS OF GRAMMATICALIZATION
- (a) extension (or context generalization): use in new contexts suggests new meanings,
- (b) desemanticization (or 'semantic bleaching'), i.e. loss in meaning content,[24]

[23] Some students of this paradigm of linguistics argue that obligatorification, whereby the use of linguistic structures becomes increasingly more obligatory in the process of grammaticalization, should be taken as a definitional property of this process. As important as obligatorification is (see Lehrmann [1982] 1995), it is not a *sine qua non* for grammaticalization to take place, and it is also not restricted to this process, occurring also in other kinds of linguistic change, such as lexicalization. Within the present theoretical framework, obligatorification is a predictable by-product of decategorialization.

[24] Some students of grammaticalization do not distinguish desemanticization as a distinct parameter and rather prefer to describe semantic development in terms of notions such as invited inferences, subjectification, or pragmatic strengthening (e.g. Hopper & Traugott [1993] 2003). It would seem, however, that the parameter desemanticization allows for more generalizations than either invited inferences, subjectification, or pragmatic strengthening do: there are many grammaticalization processes that involve desemanticization but no inferencing, subjectification, or strengthening. For example, the process from case–gender–number suffixes in Latin to plural suffixes in Romance languages such as Italian (*-i*) or Spanish (*-s*) involved the desemanticization of case and gender but, as far as we are aware, neither invited inferencing nor subjectification or pragmatic strengthening.

(c) decategorialization, i.e. loss in morphosyntactic properties characteristic of lexical or other less grammaticalized forms, and
(d) erosion (or 'phonetic reduction'), i.e. loss in phonetic substance.

While three of these parameters involve a loss in properties, there are also gains: in the same way as linguistic items undergoing grammaticalization lose in semantic, morphosyntactic, and phonetic substance, they also gain in properties characteristic of their uses in new contexts. Grammaticalization requires specific contexts to take place and it can be, and has been, described as a product of context-induced reinterpretation. Accordingly, context is a crucial factor in shaping the structure of grammatical forms—to the extent that these forms may express meanings that cannot immediately be derived from their respective source forms.

1.6 Conclusions

As the preceding discussion suggests, the goal of this volume is not to look for another taxonomy of the languages of Europe: We are not aiming to propose another European linguistic area or sprachbund. Rather than viewing areal relationship as a product, we will describe it as a process induced by language contact, and rather than describing Europe as a linguistic area, we will be concerned with the forces that led, and are leading to areal relationship in Europe.

What we observed in Sections 1.4 and 1.5 was meant to illustrate the kind of phenomena that we will be concerned with in this book, and the way we will approach the study of areal relationship in Europe. The examples that we will consider in the present volume are meant to demonstrate that European languages are becoming increasingly alike. Note that the processes looked at here do not involve borrowing, that is, a transfer of phonetic substance or form-meaning units (see Section 2.1); rather, what happens is that speakers in contact with another language may gradually change their modes of expression and of structuring linguistic discourse in the direction of what they regularly observe in the other language. Most of these changes involve minor use patterns—they are minute to the extent that neither the speakers nor trained linguists are usually aware of them. But in some cases they may accumulate and give rise to new grammatical structures and, hence, to new patterns of areal relationship in Europe. Based on findings made within the framework of grammaticalization theory, we will attempt to reconstruct how new grammatical structures evolve in situations of language contact, and how this affects the linguistic landscape of Europe.

Chapter 2 is concerned with the way we will approach the study of contact-induced language change. It deals on the one hand with the pragmatics underlying the process, described in terms of use patterns, and on the other hand with regularities in the emergence of new grammatical categories. The subsequent Chapters, 3 through 6, are each devoted to one particular functional domain. In Chapter 3 this domain is reference marking, it concerns more specifically the system of articles found in European languages. Obligatory markers for definite and indefinite reference are cross-linguistically not very common; in the languages of (western) Europe, however, they are a salient structural characteristic. This has not always been the case: two millennia ago there were essentially no real articles in the languages of Europe. In this chapter we show how articles are spreading throughout Europe.

Like articles, constructions commonly termed 'have'-perfects, or possessive perfects as we will refer to them, were largely unknown in the early history of European languages. In Chapter 4 we are concerned with the rise and spread of possessive perfects across Europe.

A functional pattern found in all SAE languages concerns case polysemy, or case syncretism, between a comitative ('together with') and an instrumental ('by means of') meaning. Elsewhere in the world this is not really a common structure: only roughly one out of four languages of the world has this case polysemy. In Chapter 5 it will be argued that there is an ongoing process in Europe whereby languages distinguishing comitative and instrumental case markings are gradually adopting this polysemy pattern as a result of language contact.

In most languages of Europe there is another polysemy pattern to the effect that one and the same marker (e.g. English *who*) is used to introduce both questions and subordinate clauses. This situation is cross-linguistically unusual, and in Chapter 6 we attempt to account for why such a polysemy pattern exists and why it is to a large extent confined to the languages of Europe or to languages that have been in contact with Indo-European languages.

Chapter 7 is concerned with the question of how contact between SAE languages and other languages affects the typological profile of the languages concerned. With the spread of European languages to other parts of the world, these languages have been exposed to interaction with a wide range of languages spoken on other continents, and in this chapter we will therefore not be confined to the European continent; rather, our discussion will also include contact situations in Central America, West Africa, and South East Asia. Two kinds of situation will be discussed: on the one hand, we will deal with situations where European languages acted as models (Section 7.2), on the other hand there will also be examples where other languages provided the models for shaping European languages (Section 7.3).

Contact-induced language change has been described as being highly variable and unpredictable. In the concluding Chapter 8 we will argue, based on findings made in the previous chapters, that there are both regularities and constraints in the way grammatical forms and constructions behave in situations of language contact.

The present book may be viewed as furnishing further evidence in support of the sprachbund hypothesis. However, discussion is restricted in a number of ways. First, our goal is not with conventional areal typology, hence we will not be concerned with many issues that have been central to typological studies carried out in the course of the past decades, such as finding representative samples of languages, devising questionnaires, etc. Second, for reasons of space, we will be confined to only a very small number of typological properties. Third, in accordance with the general theme of this book, we will be confined to one specific issue, namely grammatical replication. And fourth, we will have little to say about what has been called the nucleus of European languages (but see Section 2.7); rather, we will focus on the fringe ends of (western) Europe, in particular on Slavic, Finno-Ugric, Baltic, Celtic languages, and Basque—the reason for this limitation being that we want to study how languages that contrast typologically with 'prototypical' European languages are affected by language contact.

There are two kinds of ideal sociolinguistic settings that we will be confronted with. On the one hand, we will deal with L2>L1 transfers, where a dominant language, L2, typically an SAE language, was spoken as a second language and provided the model for replication for speakers of L1, the first language. On the other hand, there are also L1>L2 transfers, where speakers use their L1 as a model in replicating grammatical structures in their L2. A number of previous studies suggest that these two kinds of settings have different effects on language change. For example, it has been argued that 'interference' is more dramatic in L1>L2 transfers than in L2>L1 transfers (Breu 1996: 22). The data that are available to us do not necessarily support such claims. Furthermore, it is widely assumed that L1>L2 transfer leads to or is indicative of replacement of L1 by L2. While this is frequently so, it is not necessarily the case; as we will see in Chapter 7, Basque (L1) contacts with Romance languages (L2) involved not only L2>L1 transfers but also L1>L2 transfers; still, Basque does not appear to be in danger of being replaced by these Romance languages.

On the whole, the distinction between the two settings is of minor importance for the kinds of transfers that we will be concerned with. To be sure, grammatical change in European languages on the basis of L2>L1 transfer is much better documented and, accordingly, our data will overwhelmingly be taken from this kind of transfer. However, we did not find any significant differences in the nature and the linguistic structure between the two kinds of settings.

Our interest is with the languages of Europe; still, we will also need to look at languages in other parts of the world, for the following reasons. First, because we are using a model that is claimed to apply to languages anywhere in the world; hence, we will rely on generalizations derived from findings made on many languages worldwide. Second, we will do so for contrastive purposes: in order to establish what is specifically European, it is important to know what is not. And third, we wish to know how European languages behave in situations of language contact. While the European continent offers a rich laboratory to approach this issue, European languages have also been massively exposed to contact with languages in other parts of the world. In Chapter 7 we will therefore also deal with the role and the fate of European languages in sociolinguistic situations that have hardly any parallels within Europe.

In order to avoid any possible misunderstandings, the following convention should be taken into account. Our concern is with how people in Europe used and are using their languages in interaction with other people and languages. Nevertheless, we will sometimes draw on shorthand phrasings that are literally incorrect or misleading, or both. For example, when we say that a given language has developed a new functional category, then it goes without saying that languages cannot do such things—rather, what we mean is that it is the speakers using these languages who do.

2

Grammatical Replication

That languages can undergo structural change as a result of contact is by now widely accepted. Many different views have been expressed on how this change can be described and how it is constrained and, to this end, hierarchies of borrowability have been proposed (e.g. Whitney 1881; Weinreich [1953] 1964; Moravcsik 1978; Matras 1998*a*; Myers-Scotton 2002). But many of the generalizations that were proposed have turned out to be of doubtful value, in that they can be shown to be contradicted by a larger body of evidence (see especially Harris & Campbell 1995: 121–50). Generalizations that have been proven to be wrong include overall hypotheses, for example the claim, made quite frequently in some way or another, that borrowing is only possible when the languages concerned are structurally compatible, similar, or 'harmonious', and also more specific hypotheses, such as Weinreich's ([1953] 1964: 41) well-known claim that free grammatical forms are more easily borrowed than bound ones.

The extensive work that has been carried out more recently suggests, in a nutshell, that 'virtually anything can (ultimately) be borrowed' (Harris & Campbell 1995: 149; see also Thomason & Kaufman 1988: 14). Somewhat pessimistically, Curnow (2001: 434) therefore concludes that we may never be able to develop universal constraints on borrowability on the basis of the data available and that attempts to develop a universal hierarchy of borrowing should perhaps be abandoned. Still, there are a few generalizations proposed by Moravcsik (1978) and others that appear to be robust, that is, to hold at least as strong tendencies. For example, that nouns are more easily borrowed than verbs and other word class items, and that grammatical words tend to be borrowed together with the linear arrangement properties characterizing their use in the donor language appear to be fairly uncontroversial generalizations. But on the whole, present-day contact linguistics does not seem to provide much encouragement to look for universals of language change in this field.

Nevertheless, in the present book we argue that there are constraints on contact-induced language change. But rather than dealing with language contact in all its linguistic and sociolinguistic manifestations, we will be confined to one aspect of it, namely to grammatical replication. To this end, we will rely on the framework of grammaticalization theory. Much of the literature on language contact is concerned with linguistic categories and the relations holding among them. In Section 2.2 we will see that there are phenomena below the level of categories, and we will deal with such phenomena in terms of use patterns, a notion that is elusive to linguistic taxonomy, relating to pragmatic parameters such as context and frequency of use. Grammaticalization theory as a tool of analysis has been introduced in Section 1.5; its relevance for the study of language contact is discussed in Section 2.3, and its limits in Section 2.4. Some factors constraining grammatical replication are pointed out in Section 2.5. In the subsequent Section 2.6 we are concerned with a question that was raised in the preceding chapter (Section 1.5.1), namely how our framework relates to the distinction between internal and external language change, and in Section 2.7 we present an example concerning the development of verbs meaning 'to threaten' in European languages to illustrate the kind of analysis used in this work.

The main goal of this chapter is to provide a basis for understanding the processes to be discussed in subsequent chapters, that is processes that appear to be going on in European languages, leading to an increased structural equivalence among these languages.

2.1 Introduction

Grammatical replication is a process whereby a language, called the replica language (R), creates a new grammatical structure (Rx) on the model of some structure (Mx) of another language, called the model language (M).[1] It concerns meanings and the structures associated with them, but not forms, that is, phonetic substance is not involved. Grammatical replication contrasts with lexical replication, that is, with the replication of lexical structures (usually referred to as calquing or loanshift), and both contrast with borrowing, which—in our terminology—concerns phonetic substance, that is, either sounds or form–meaning units such as morphemes, words, or larger entities.

This means that we will be working with a number of restrictions. First, we will use the term borrowing in a narrower sense than many other authors do, using the term contact-induced linguistic transfer as a cover term for both replication and borrowing.[2] Second, we will be concerned neither with lexical

[1] We are using the phrase 'a language' as a shorthand for 'speakers of a language'; it goes without saying that languages cannot do such things.

[2] For a justification of these conventions, see Heine & Kuteva 2003, 2005.

replication nor with borrowing. Third, contact-induced word order change phenomena—as long as they do not concern grammaticalization—are beyond the scope of our investigation (for an insightful account of word order typology as a natural result of contact phenomena, see Stilo 1985, 2005).

2.2 Grammatical use patterns

For good reasons, students of language contact take grammatical (or functional) categories to be the basic unit for describing and understanding grammatical change. As our work suggests, however, there is yet another notion that appears to be equally relevant to understanding the process leading to new grammatical structures, especially in the initial phases of the process. With this notion we mean grammatical use patterns (in short: use patterns), which have the properties listed in (2.1).

(2.1) PROPERTIES OF USE PATTERNS

(a) They are associated with some specific grammatical meaning.

(b) They are recurrent pieces of linguistic discourse. Such pieces may consist of a clause, a phrase, or even a single form used in some specific context.

(c) Their use is optional, that is, they may, but need not, be employed for the expression of that grammatical meaning.

(d) They are the primary units figuring in the initial stage of grammatical replication.

Unlike fully grammaticalized categories, use patterns are optional structures marking the beginning of grammaticalization; they tend to be variants restricted in their occurrence to particular contexts, and/or to specific social layers of speakers, registers, or regions.

Use patterns are in a number of ways similar to a number of alternative theoretical notions that have been proposed, in particular to speech formulas (Pawley 1992: 22, 1994: 14, 16), or what is described in usage-based models of functional linguistics as constructions, or in the sociolinguistic literature as variable rules. All these notions have in common that they are based on the assumption that there are structures that can be reduced neither to general rules of syntax or grammatical categorization nor to forms of unstructured linguistic or sociolinguistic variation. Nevertheless, use patterns must be distinguished from all these notions in that their defining properties, especially (2.1d), are shared by none of these notions.

We may illustrate use patterns with the following example from Swedish, involving present tense uses of the verb *bli* 'become' (Dahl 2000*c*). Example

(2.2a) shows its general change-of-state meaning in a past tense sentence. This may also be the meaning intended in (2.2b), but (2.2b) can also be understood as having future reference, hence it can be translated in English by either (2.2bi) or (2.2bii). In (2.2c), however, illustrating the context of a weather forecast, there is a use pattern where the verb *bli* can only be understood as expressing a specific meaning, namely future time reference: it does not imply a change of state since it can be used, for example, when it is already cold at the time it is uttered.

(2.2) SWEDISH (Dahl 2000*c*: 351–3)

(a) Festen blev trevlig.
party.DEF become.PAST pleasant
'The party became pleasant.'

(b) Du blir snart en stor pojke.
you.SG become.PRES soon a big boy
(i) 'You'll soon become a big boy.'
(ii) 'You'll soon be a big boy.'

(c) Det blir kallt imorgon.
it become.PRES cold tomorrow
'It will be cold tomorrow.'

Example (2.c) is suggestive of a discourse unit that would not normally be described as a grammatical category; but it can be described as a use pattern consisting of the verb phrase, being associated with a specific grammatical meaning in certain contexts, namely future tense, and being optional for the expression of that meaning: It may, but need not, be employed when events in the future are to be expressed.[3] It must be emphasized, however, that *bli* is never used with an infinitive in the way German *werden* 'become' can be, and syntactically, *bli* does not really differ from English *become* (Dahl, p.c.).

2.2.1 *From minor to major use pattern*

One salient mechanism characterizing the processes that may take place in particular contexts in a situation of intense language contact involves use patterns that may give rise to entirely new use patterns. More commonly, however, there is already something that we will call a minor use pattern, which is activated because there is a model provided by another language, and it develops into a major use pattern in the direction of that model. We will

[3] Dahl (2000*c*: 353) says that 'what we are here dealing with is, in principle, a special use of verbs of becoming rather than a future tense marker. But there is still a clear link to future time reference.' The exact contexts in which this special use occurs are not entirely clear.

refer to this process as the replication of use patterns, where replication has the following effects in particular:

(2.3) THE RISE OF MAJOR USE PATTERNS
- (a) An existing use pattern is used more frequently.
- (b) It is used in new contexts.
- (c) It may become associated with a new grammatical function.

Major use patterns are thus defined with reference to minor use patterns, differing from the latter in the properties listed in (2.3). Furthermore, speakers are usually not aware that there is a minor use pattern, whilst they are more likely to recognize a major use pattern, and in grammatical descriptions, minor use patterns tend to be ignored, whilst major use patterns are more likely to be pointed out by grammarians.

Compared to Swedish *bli* 'become', the corresponding German item *werden* 'become' can be described in terms of a major use pattern: there is no more ambiguity, which cannot be said of the Swedish verb, that is, whenever it used with infinitival (main) verbs as complements, the change-of-state meaning of *werden* is lost, the only meaning being future reference.

Note that German *werden* 'become' meets all the criteria pointed out in (2.3) above as characteristics of a major use pattern:

- (i) While there are no data on the frequency of occurrence of the two items, it is reasonable to assume that German *werden* is more common as a future marker than its Swedish counterpart *bli.*
- (ii) German *werden* occurs in more, and in a larger set of contexts—including contexts where it can co-occur with its change-of-state counterpart, cf. (2.4a).
- (iii) While Swedish *bli* exhibits relics of the semantics characterizing the change-of-state verb (see Dahl 2000*a*: 352–3), German *werden* (when used with infinitival verbs as complements) has been desemanticized to the effect that it has lost its association with its lexical source, the change-of-state verb: it is a future tense marker[4] comparable with such markers in many other languages of the world.

Still, unlike future tense markers in other languages, the German *werden*-future is a use pattern rather than a fully-fledged grammatical category: first, its use is optional when future reference is to be expressed. Accordingly, sentence (2.4b), which has the future marker, is largely equivalent to (2.4c),

[4] In some traditions of German linguistics, *werden* is portrayed as a marker having primarily modal rather than tense functions. But much the same claim could be made with reference to future markers in many other languages.

where there is no future marker. And second, it also exhibits constraints in the sociolinguistic contexts in which it occurs. For example, the future-marked sentence (2.4b) is more constrained than (2.4c), being less likely to occur in spoken than in written discourse, or in informal than in formal contexts.

(2.4) GERMAN

(a) Der Sommer wird schön werden.
the summer FUT.3.SG beautiful become.INF
'The summer will be beautiful.'

(b) Der Vortrag wird am Freitag stattfinden.
the lecture FUT.3.SG on Friday take.place
'The lecture will take place on Friday.'

(c) Der Vortrag findet am Freitag statt.
the lecture takes on Friday place
'The lecture will take place on Friday.'

These are not the only differences separating Swedish *bli* from German *werden* as future markers; there are others[5] that we ignore here as we are concerned exclusively with illustrating the difference between minor and major use patterns. But there are also similarities between the two languages, and it is those to which we now turn.

In his survey of future markers in Europe, Dahl (2000*b*: 325–7) points out that there is what he calls the northern European 'futureless area', where present tenses tend to be employed for prediction-based future time reference. This area largely coincides with that of future use patterns based on verbs for 'become'. In fact, such future use patterns are not restricted to Swedish and German; they cover most of the Germanic and Finnic languages in Europe[6] (English being an exception; Dahl 2000*c*: 357, 359).

That this distribution is suggestive of areal relationship—hence of language contact of some kind—is suggested by the following observations. First, a development from verbs meaning 'become' to markers of future reference appears to be cross-linguistically rare (see Bybee *et al.* 1994); that it occurs across languages in a compact area of Europe is therefore unlikely to be due to coincidence. And second, the area cuts across genetic boundaries, that is, it includes languages of two different language families; it is therefore also unlikely that the area of the 'become'-to-future use pattern is the result of genetic relationship. The only reasonable hypothesis, therefore, is one in terms of language contact.

[5] A more fundamental difference can be seen in the fact that Swedish *bli* never combines with an infinitive.

[6] Dahl does not provide information on the structure of these use patterns in the other languages of the area.

TABLE 2.1. A pathway of grammaticalization of 'become'-futures in some languages of northern Europe

Stage	0	I	II	III
Structure		Minor use pattern	Major use pattern	Functional category
Main characteristics	Lexical use	Grammatical function appearing in specific contexts	Use in more contexts; regular association with grammatical function	Obligatory marker of the grammatical function

But there is yet another perspective to this situation, which Dahl summarizes in the following way:

It is thus possible that even if the Germanic and Baltic-Finnic verbs of becoming cannot be regarded as future copulas, the extensions of their use that we can observe represent the first step in such a grammaticalization path (Dahl 2000*c*: 360).

Whilst the information on both the synchronic and the diachronic situation of the 'beome'-futures in this area is scanty, it nevertheless suggests the following scenario of grammaticalization: at stage I there evolved a minor use pattern in the languages of northern Europe, where the 'become'-verb acquired grammatical uses as a marker of future time reference in specific contexts. In at least one language, German, the minor use pattern developed further into a major use pattern: it was extended to new contexts and became a marker consistently associated with marking future reference, even if its use remains optional. Whilst the Swedish 'become'-future represents stage I and its German counterpart stage II, none of the languages concerned has reached stage III, where the use pattern would give rise to a grammatical category used obligatorily as a future tense marker. Thus, we can reconstruct the evolution as in Table 2.1.

As we saw above, the northern European 'become'-future covers only stages I and II of the scenario proposed in Table 2.1, while other European languages have not proceeded beyond stage 0. There is no information on how the pattern arose and spread across northern Europe.[7] The fact that the German use pattern is the most strongly grammaticalized would seem to suggest that it provided the model for diffusion; relative degree of grammaticalization offers an important parameter in the diffusion of grammatical structures; we will

[7] Dahl (2000*c*: 357–8) suggests that there may already have been such a use pattern in Gothic.

return to this issue in Section 2.5. Still, in want of further evidence, we will leave this issue with respect to the north European 'become'-future unresolved.

2.2.2 *The role of use patterns in language contact*

The example just examined illustrates a problem inherent in the analysis of contact-induced grammatical change: in many cases, the evidence to establish that language contact was a contributing factor is scarce. In such cases, the study of use patterns provides a convenient tool for identifying possible sources of change, as the following examples may illustrate.

Nominal compounding is a mechanism that is important in Germanic languages, but not in French and other Romance languages. Now, speakers of Germanic languages exposed to intense contact with French tend to decrease the amount of compounding and to increase the use of attribute patterns on the model of French. The result is that in situations where speakers of languages such as German or Dutch are regularly exposed to French as a dominant language,[8] they tend to shift from compounding to attributive use patterns. For example, Taeldeman (1978: 52) reports that in Dutch varieties spoken in Flanders, there is a pattern [adjective–noun] on the model of French instead of the inherited compounding pattern, for example *Culturele Raad* (French: *Conseil Culturel*) instead of *Cultuurraad* 'Cultural Council', or *academisch jaar* instead of *academiejaar* 'academic year', or *administratieve kosten* instead of *administratiekosten* 'administrative costs'.

Similar observations have been made in the contact situation of eastern Belgium between French and German (Riehl 2001: 257). German speakers in this part of Belgium may use the German compound *Herbstzeit* (lit.: 'autumn time') 'autumn', but they also use an attributive/possessive pattern instead, saying *Zeit des Herbstes* ('time of the autumn') on the model of French *le temps d' automne* ('the time of autumn'). In much the same way, Riehl found that in South Tyrol, northern Italy, where the official language is Italian, German speakers tend to develop the possessive pattern into a major use pattern, whereas in Standard German compounding would be preferred. Accordingly, in an attempt to replicate the possessive construction of Italian, German speakers say, for example *das Bündel von Trauben* 'the bunch of grapes' instead of *das Traubenbündel* ('the grape bunch') on the model of Italian *il grappolo d'uva.*

Note that none of these processes has affected the structure of grammatical categorization. The Dutch or German speakers concerned did not develop new constructions or categories for marking attributive possession, nor did

[8] Concerning the term 'dominant language', see Johanson (1992).

they give up compounding; nevertheless, there clearly is grammatical change among these speakers in that there appears to be a gradual transition from one use pattern to another on the model of French and Italian, respectively.

One effect that the change from minor to major use pattern may have is that it leads from what is usually described as a marked structure to an unmarked structure. Turkish is commonly portrayed as a verb-final language, but there are pragmatically marked structures where the verb precedes its complement. For example, Friedman (2003: 66) notes that a sentence such as *Erol' **dur** iyi öğrenci*, where the verb occurs in non-final position, would have a pragmatically marked meaning like 'It is Erol who is the good student' in Standard Turkish. But Turkish varieties spoken on the Balkans have been strongly influenced by Balkan languages, and in West Rumelian Turkish dialects spoken in Macedonia, the above sentence would be an unmarked sentence equivalent to the English 'Erol is a good student'—corresponding to the unmarked Macedonian sentence *Erol e dobar učenik* 'Erol is a good student'. This suggests that under the influence of Macedonian and perhaps other Balkanic verb-medial (= SVO) languages, speakers of West Rumelian Turkish dialects have developed one of their pragmatically marked minor use patterns into an unmarked pattern—thereby establishing syntactic equivalence with the language or languages of their Balkanic neighbours. Consequently, in these Turkish dialects of Macedonia the verb occurs far more frequently in a non-final position than it does in Standard Turkish.

To conclude, what we wanted to show in the present section is that use patterns play an important role in situations of language contact, in that a given language may acquire a minor use pattern or develop an existing minor use pattern into a major one when another language offers an appropriate model. Accordingly, use patterns provide a relevant parameter for studying areal relationship. The evidence available suggests in fact that much of what happens in terms of linguistic transfer among languages in contact concerns use patterns, and it is only in very few cases that transfer proceeds further to the level of fully-fledged grammatical categories.

2.2.3 *Use patterns and code-switching*

Code-switching, that is, the alternation of morphemes from two (or more) different languages within the same discourse, sentence, or constituent, has been shown to be an important force in contact-induced grammatical change (see especially Myers-Scotton 1993, 2002). However, since it concerns the manipulation of lexical and grammatical forms—hence relates to borrowing rather than replication—it is not within the scope of the present work (see Section 2.1 above). However, it can also be instrumental in inducing the rise of new use patterns. The following example from the contact situation between Spanish and the Aztecan language Nahuatl shows how this may happen.

Nahuatl verbs take a pronominal object proclitic when a nominal object follows, compare Example (2.5a). Such a clitic is not allowed in the local variety of Spanish—that is, it is possible to say (2.5b) but not (2.5c). However, when, in this code-switching situation, the object is a Nahuatl noun, the use of the pronominal object proclitic is obligatory, as in (2.5d). We seem to be dealing with a new use pattern, triggered by the grammaticalization parameter of extension (see Section 2.3, Example (2.6)), where the object pronoun has acquired a new context, and this context is determined by code-switching.[9]

(2.5) NAHUATL–SPANISH CODE-SWITCHING (MacSwan 1999: 170–2; McConvell 2004: 3–4; **bold** = Spanish, *italics* = Nahuatl)

(a)	**Mi**	**hermana**	*ki-*	*tlasojtla*	*in*	*Juan.*
	My	sister	3.O.SG-	love	D	Juan
	'My sister loves Juan.'					
(b)	**Veo**	**(a)**	**la**	**muchacha.**		
	see.1.S.SG	*a*	the	girl		
	'I see the girl.'					
(c)	***La**	**veo**	**(a)**	**la**	**muchacha.**	
	3.O.SG	see.1.S.SG	*a*	the	girl	
(d)	**La**	**veo**	**(a)**	*in*	*ichpochtle.*	
	3.O.SG	see.1.S.SG	*a*	D	girl	
	'I see the girl.'					

Code-switching may, but need not, play a role in the rise of new contact-induced use patterns. In the data that we were able to access it is rarely mentioned as a contributing factor; we therefore have little to say about it in this work.

2.3 Grammaticalization and grammatical replication

As we observed in Section 1.5, contact-induced grammatical change in general and grammatical replication in particular are constrained in a significant way, in that they follow general principles of grammaticalization, that is, it is essentially unidirectional,[10] leading from concrete meaning contents to less

[9] Note that this interpretation differs from that proposed by both MacSwan (1999) and McConvell (2004). For a similar example from the Spanish–Basque contact situation, see Section 7.3.1.

[10] As more recent research has shown, there are examples contradicting the unidirectionality hypothesis (see especially Campbell & Janda 2001; Newmeyer 1998: 260 ff.); however, as acknowledged by these scholars, such examples are few, accounting for less than one-tenth of all cases of grammatical change (Newmeyer 1998: 275–6, 278; Haspelmath 1999; Heine 2003*b*).

concrete ones, more specifically from lexical to grammatical, and from grammatical to even more grammatical meanings (see also Heine and Kuteva 2003, 2005). In the present book we wish to demonstrate that this also applies to language contact in Europe. To this end, we will describe grammatical replication in terms of the set of parameters (or criteria) of grammaticalization presented in Section 1.5.1 (1.8), repeated here for convenience.

(2.6) PARAMETERS OF GRAMMATICALIZATION
- (a) extension (or context generalization): use in new contexts suggests new meanings,
- (b) desemanticization (or 'semantic bleaching'), i.e. loss in meaning content,
- (c) decategorialization, i.e. loss in morphosyntactic properties characteristic of lexical or other less grammaticalized forms, and
- (d) erosion (or 'phonetic reduction'), i.e. loss in phonetic substance.

We will now illustrate these parameters by using examples from cases of language contact in Europe.

2.3.1 *Extension*

One of the parameters that is central both to the rise of new use patterns and to the transition from minor to major use patterns concerns (context) extension, that is, the use of an existing linguistic structure is used more frequently and in new contexts which tend to suggest a new meaning. This is exactly the parameter that characterizes grammaticalization processes in their early stages (see (2.3) above). Once used with a new range of contexts, the category concerned is likely to receive a new semantic interpretation arising in these contexts—that is, extension is a prerequisite for desemanticization to take place. Still, extension does not necessarily lead to desemanticization and category change: as the following examples show, there is extension but apparently no dramatic change in the meaning of the grammatical category concerned.

Maltese, historically, is a western Arabic dialect which has been influenced by a number of different languages, in particular by Italian and more recently by English. One effect of the Italian influence was that the Maltese preposition *ta'*, expressing the periphrastic genitive, was extended to new contexts on the model of the use patterns characterizing the Italian preposition *da*. For example, like Italian *da*, it can be used without a possessee noun phrase before proper names, for example *Ta' Kolina* 'At Kolina's (restaurant)', or with verbal nouns (where Italian speakers would use an infinitive), for example *tal-biza'* ('of-fright') 'frightfully' (for more examples, see Drewes 1994: 101). In this way, the Maltese genitive marker has developed into a grammatical category with a new structure and a considerably extended range of functions.

Essentially, the same kind of influence was exerted by English, the second major model language for Maltese. For example, the Maltese preposition *fuq* 'on top of, upon' has been extended to new contexts where it appears to acquire additional functions by replicating uses of the English preposition *on* in phrasal constructions, for example *fuq it-tv* 'on television', *fuq btala* 'on holiday', *fuq parir ta'* 'on the advice of', *fuq talba ta'* 'on the request of' (Drewes 1994: 101). Once again, the outcome is that an existing grammatical category of Maltese is changed through contact-induced extension on the model of another language.

Like the preceding example, the following one consists simply in the extension of an existing grammatical category to contexts where it could not previously be used. Language contact between Slovenian and German speakers in Trieste had *inter alia* the effect that the Slovenian pattern of reflexive marking was replicated to some extent by German speakers (Morfill [1885] 1971: 269). Replication had the effect, first, that the German reflexive pronoun *sich* came to be used in new contexts on the model of the Slavonic reflexive marker *se*, for example with verbs such as *lernen* 'learn', which do not take a reflexive pronoun in Standard German, and, second, that the German pronoun, which is restricted to third person referents, was extended to second and first persons, for example *wir waschen sich* (we wash REFL) 'we wash ourselves', that is, its use spread across all three categories of personal deixis.

In Yiddish, another Germanic language which descended from Middle High German, the reflexive *zix*, a cognate of High German *sich*, was also extended from third person to all person/number categories. It is possible that this process was also induced by contact with the Slavic languages of the region where Yiddish was spoken, but we are not aware of any reliable evidence to strengthen this hypothesis. However, it would seem that contact-induced extension has also affected this language, as the following observation by Kemmer suggests:

> Yiddish appears to use *zix* in all of the middle contexts in which it occurs in German, but also in some additional ones that closely parallel the use of *-sja* in Russian, with which it has been in more recent contact (Kemmer 1993: 262).

In other words, the examples we are concerned with here do not involve structural change (e.g. development of a polysemy that formerly did not exist); rather, what is involved is type extension (extension to new 'hosts'), which is an issue related to productivity.[11]

[11] With thanks to an anonymous reviewer for having this pointed out to us.

2.3.2 *Desemanticization*

This parameter of grammaticalization concerns the rise of new grammatical meanings, in that an existing structure when used in new contexts is desemanticized, that is loses parts of its meaning and is reinterpreted in these contexts as expressing a new, grammatical meaning. The English verb *make*, for example, is a lexical item which has lost its lexical meaning in certain contexts where it is reinterpreted essentially as a grammatical marker expressing causativity, as in *The dust made me sneeze.*

Such a process can be observed quite commonly in situations of, and being induced by, language contact. The verb *(la)schar* of the Rhaeto-Romance language Surselvian has the lexical meaning 'leave' similar to its cognates *laisser* in French or *lasciare* in Italian and, in the same way as its cognates, it is also used as a permissive auxiliary ('allow someone to do'). Surselvian speakers are in close contact with German, where the corresponding verb *lassen* 'let' can also be used as a permissive auxiliary ('permit'). But the German verb has an additional grammatical meaning: it is used as a causative auxiliary ('cause to do'). Now, under German influence, Surselvian speakers tend to generalize their verb *(la)schar* so that it is also used as a causative auxiliary (Stimm 1984). What this suggests is that *(la)schar* is undergoing a grammaticalization process on the model of German *lassen*, whereby the Surselvian verb is desemanticized and reinterpreted as a causative auxiliary.

A process alternative to 'let' developing into a causative auxiliary appears to be ongoing in some Flemish varieties in Flanders, Belgium, which have been strongly influenced by French (Taeldeman 1978): the French causative construction based on *faire* 'make, do', illustrated in (2.7a), has provided the model for Flemish speakers, who tend to replace their causative construction based on the auxiliary *laten* 'let' (2.7c) by a use pattern based on *doen* 'do' on the model of French *faire*, cf. (2.7b), where the verb *doen* loses its lexical meaning and is desemanticized to a causative auxiliary as a result of language contact.

(2.7) FRENCH AND DUTCH VARIETIES IN BELGIUM (Taeldeman 1978: 60)

(a)	On	m'	a	**fait**	examiner	si	[. . .].
	(one	me	has	made	examine	whether)	
(b)	Men	heeft	me	**doen**	onderzoeken	of	[. . .].
(c)	Men	heeft	me	**laten**	onderzoeken	of	[. . .].

'They made me inquire whether [. . .].'

Desemanticization does not mean that there is only loss in semantic substance; rather, there may be new meaning components evoked by the new contexts. The result can be that a grammatical category arises that is semantically quite dissimilar from its source. In Irish, there is a spatial or temporal use pattern of the kind [X is after Y] which has been grammaticalized into verbal aspect category called the 'hot-news' perfect; what this category expresses is an event that is located at a point that is separated from but temporally close to the moment of speaking, for example *John has just arrived* (see Harris 1991: 201ff.), cf. (2.8).

(2.8) Irish (Harris 1991: 205)

Tá	sí	tréis	an	bád	a dhíol.
be:NON-PAST	she	after	the	boat	selling

'She has just sold the boat.'

Around the late seventeenth century, the same grammaticalization appears to have taken place in Irish English (Sullivan 1980: 205; Filppula 1986; Boretzky 1986: 25; Harris 1991: 201 ff; Siemund 2004*a*, 2004*b*), giving rise to a corresponding category in this variety of English, cf. (2.9), and there can be hardly any doubt that this was a replication on the model of Irish, for the following reasons. First, the development of a prepositional structure with 'after' taking a non-finite verb as a complement to a marker of verbal aspect is a very rare process in the languages of the world. Second, that such a structure gives rise to a 'hot-news' perfect is, again, cross-linguistically fairly uncommon; that the same process occurred in neighbouring languages can therefore hardly be accounted for either with reference to universally available options of grammaticalization or to coincidence. And finally, that contact between Irish and Irish English has led to substantial replication in the latter on the model of the former is well documented (see e.g. van Hamel 1912; Siemund 2004*b*; Heine & Kuteva 2005).

(2.9) Irish English (Siemund 2004*a*)
Tell mother we are just after receiving Her letter.
'Tell mother we have just received her letter.'

The verbal aspect category that arose in Irish English is, on the one hand, the result of the desemanticization of a fairly concrete conceptual schema, on the other hand its specific function cannot be reduced entirely to meaning loss.

2.3.3 *Decategorialization*

One common process leading to decategorialization concerns major-category items such as nouns and verbs that are used in specific contexts where they develop into minor categories such as adpositions, tense–aspect markers, or derivational elements, thereby losing the cardinal properties characteristic of free forms, becoming clitics or affixes of other major-category items. The following Finnish example, volunteered by Nau (1995: 86–7), may illustrate the process concerned. Presumably on the model of English *top* (and Swedish *topp*), speakers of Finnish have extended the use of their noun *huippu* 'top, peak' to act as a modifier of nouns in compounds, thereby assuming a schematic meaning, which is 'an outstanding, very important X', for example *huippuhenkilö* 'an outstanding personality ', *huippuurheilija* 'a top sportsman', or *huipputekniikka* 'top technology'. This use pattern is found especially in journalese, but it is not the only one of its kind. Nau describes a second one, involving the Finnish noun *avain* 'key', which has also given rise to a compounding pattern on the model of English 'the key X', for example *avainasema* 'key position', *avainhahmo* 'key figure', or *avainkysmys* 'key question'. In such contexts, the nouns *huippu* and *avain* have lost categorial properties of nouns, such as being pluralized, case-marked, being free in their occurrence, and they behave to some extent like grammatical markers.[12]

2.3.4 *Erosion*

Erosion, or loss in phonetic substance, is usually the last process to occur when a grammaticalization process takes place, and in the following chapters we will have little to say about it, for the following reason: most of the cases discussed here concern periods of contact that were simply too short to have had a distinct effect on the phonetic substance of the structures undergoing grammaticalization.

However, there are a few cases where contact-induced grammatical change also involved erosion; the following example is one of them. Spoken in Germany and having been affected by nearly a millennium of contact with German, Lower and Upper Sorbian have acquired optional definite and indefinite articles on the model of German by grammaticalizing, respectively, one of their demonstratives and the numeral for 'one' (Boretzky 1986: 17; Lötzsch 1996: 52–3). In the course of this process, the two items underwent erosion, in that the Upper Sorbian demonstrative *tón* (masculine nominative singular) loses its stress when expressing the function of a definite article, and the Upper Sorbian numeral *jedyn* 'one' (masculine singular) is usually shortened to a monosyllabic form *jen* in its article uses but not in its numeral uses. As this example shows, erosion involves segmental and suprasegmental elements: the change from *jedyn* to *jen* led to loss of phonetic segments,

[12] However, Dahl (p.c.) draws our attention to the fact this holds true more generally for nouns used as the first elements of compounds. For instance, in the word *avainnippu* 'bunch of keys', *avain* behaves structurally like the above examples, but it is not part of this use pattern because it lacks the schematic meaning characterizing this pattern.

while the loss of distinctive stress is a paradigm example of suprasegmental erosion.

2.3.5 *Replica vs. ordinary grammaticalization*

In creating new functional categories in situations of language contact, speakers have two choices in replicating what they find in the model language: they may either replicate the process that they assume to have taken place in the model language, or they may draw on universal strategies of grammaticalization in forming a new use pattern or category. This distinction is referred to in Heine and Kuteva (2003, 2005), respectively, as replica and ordinary grammaticalization. Replica grammaticalization can be illustrated with the example from Irish English that was just presented: in Irish, a use pattern of the kind [X is after Y] has been grammaticalized to a 'hot-news' perfect, and speakers of Irish English appear to have chosen exactly the same grammaticalization process to develop an equivalent category. Ordinary grammaticalization means that speakers create a use pattern or category they find in another language without being concerned with how this structure may have arisen in that language; in other words, the conceptualization pattern underlying the category in the replica language differs from the one in the model language.

2.3.6 *Conclusions*

In the preceding paragraphs we have discussed the four parameters of grammaticalization independently of one another. More commonly, however, several parameters are simultaneously involved, as the following example may show. Kostov (1973: 110–13) reports that the Lovāri variety of Romani spoken in Hungary has been drifting typologically towards Hungarian in that Lovāri speakers, using Hungarian as a second mother tongue, grammaticalized their own locative adverbs to derivational[13] verbal prefixes in an attempt to replicate Hungarian verbal prefixes, thereby introducing structural equivalence and a new morphosyntactic pattern. That this is a fairly productive pattern is suggested by the fact that the use of the new prefixes is not confined to their own verbs; rather, Lovāri speakers also apply them to verbs borrowed from Hungarian. Kostov (1973: 113) mentions that verbal composition of this kind was not unknown to Lovāri speakers; what Lovāri speakers have done under Hungarian influence is to increase the frequency of use of a rare type of expression, and expand and elaborate it—that is, they appear to have developed a minor use pattern into a major one.

[13] Kostov (1973: 110–11) refers to the process as verbal compounding rather than derivation.

Contact-induced grammatical change in this case involved at least two of the parameters of grammaticalization: extension, whereby the use of locative adverbs was extended to new contexts, and decategorialization, in that these adverbs gradually lost their independent word status and were decategorialized to appendages of other words, that is to verbal prefixes.

That higher frequency of use is a salient characteristic of contact-induced grammatical change has also been pointed out by a number of authors working on language contact (e.g. Stolz 2003–4). In many cases, frequency and extension to a larger range of contexts jointly contribute to the rise of new use patterns. In contacts between Macedonian, Albanian, and other Indo-European Balkan languages on the one hand and dialects of West Rumelian Turkish dialects in Macedonia on the other, the former acted as models for the latter; we have seen one example of this in Section 2.2. Friedman furthermore notes:

> The use of the optative-subjunctive to express indirect imperatives and clauses of goal also occurs in other Turkic languages and dialects [. . .], but the far greater frequency and wider range of such uses in Balkan Turkish indicate the influence of non-Turkish Balkan languages (Friedman 2003: 62).

Most of the cases to be discussed below are of this kind: they involve an interaction of different parameters leading to increased frequency, contextual expansion and, in some cases, to the gradual emergence of new grammatical constructions and categories.

In this section we have reviewed a number of what can be assumed to be cases of contact-induced language change, and all are in accordance with universally attested processes of grammaticalization. What they suggest is that grammatical change is unidirectional irrespective of whether it is language-internally or language-externally motivated (see Section 2.6). There are a few exceptions, or possible exceptions, and we will point them out in the course of this book; on the whole, however, they are rare.

2.4 Restructuring vs. contact-induced grammaticalization

While most cases of grammatical replication concern grammaticalization, some do not, and we will refer to the latter as cases of restructuring (Heine & Kuteva 2005: 3.4.3). As a rule, contact-induced grammatical change of the type examined here involves an activity whereby speakers create new use patterns or categories on the model of some other language by using principles of grammaticalization. But in some kinds of change there is no new creation; what happens is simply that, as a result of language contact, an existing structure is rearranged or replaced with some other structure, or, as we will say here, it is restructured. Thus, we consider contact-induced grammaticalization and restructuring to be two different manifestations of grammatical replication.

'Restructuring' is a ubiquitous term, it has been used in a number of linguistic traditions, especially in contact linguistics (e.g. Aikhenvald 2002), and most of all in pidgin/creole studies (see, e.g., the contributions in Neumann-Holzschuh & Schneider 2000); we will use the term here strictly in the sense defined above. Restructuring is included in what Harris and Campbell call (syntactic) borrowing (or at least one of the ways in which they use the term borrowing):

> We use the term **borrowing** to mean a change in which a foreign syntactic pattern (either a duplication of the foreign pattern or at least a formally quite similar construction) is incorporated into the borrowing language through the influence of a donor pattern found in a contact language (Harris & Campbell 1995: 122).

As we will see below (especially in Section 7.2.3), however, these authors also treat cases as borrowing that are fairly clear instances of contact-induced grammaticalization.

There are two main kinds of processes that qualify as cases of restructuring: loss and rearrangement of existing structures. Loss refers to changes whereby a language, as a result of contact, loses categorial distinctions, that is, it becomes structurally impoverished in some way *vis-à-vis* the situation of this language prior to contact. The following examples illustrate two different kinds of loss.

The first case concerns two Germanic languages, English and German, but the contact situation is not in Europe but in the USA. German has an elaborate paradigm of discourse markers, including *ja*, *denn*, *doch*, *mal*, *schon*, etc., commonly called modal particles (more recently also referred to as focus particles). English does not have any clear equivalents for these particles, and Salmons (1990: 461ff) observes that German–English bilinguals in the USA (e.g. in Texas and Indiana), have almost entirely given up the use of these particles, thereby replicating the situation characterizing their model language English. Replication in this case involved restructuring, leading to the loss of a conceptual domain that arguably constitutes a central component of the discourse structure of German as spoken in Europe.

The second example is more complex, it concerns Molise Croatian or Molisean, a Slavic variety spoken in Molise, southern Italy, which offers a rich laboratory for the analysis of language contact (Breu 1994, 1996). Like other Slavic languages, Croatian is a three-gender language distinguishing masculine, feminine, and neuter, while Italian has only two genders, lacking a neuter category. Molisean has been heavily influenced by Italian, and one of the results of this contact was that Molisean lost the neuter gender of nouns, in that the former neuter nouns were assigned as a rule to the masculine gender—thereby achieving structural equivalence with Italian. Now, similar cases of loss are not uncommon in Indo-European languages, such as the Romance languages, and one might therefore wonder whether the Molisean loss of the neuter gender was necessarily due to Italian influence. As Breu convincingly shows, however, contact must have been involved in this particular case. For example, while Italian has lost its neuter gender, the variety of Italian spoken in the Molise area has retained relics of the neuter gender in specific contexts, and Molisean has also retained its neuter gender in the corresponding contexts, namely with adjectives and pronouns in impersonal utterances. Loss in this case led to a reorganization of gender assignment in the replica language. We will return to this example below.

Rearrangement of existing structures involves changes in the ordering and/or the syntactic relations of constituents. For example, when the Indo-Aryan language Romani (Romanes) came into contact with languages of the Balkans, it is said to have replaced the verb-final (SOV) order inherited from its Indo-Aryan past by SVO (and VSO), which is characteristic of the Balkan languages (Matras 1996: 64); see Section 2.2. Contact-induced word-order change is perhaps the most commonly observed manifestation of restructuring, and a number of examples can be found in dialects of West Rumelian Turkish spoken in Macedonia (Friedman 2003: 50ff). For example, on the model of Indo-European Balkanic languages such as Macedonian and Albanian, speakers of these Turkish dialects have reversed the genitive and its head in possessive constructions; for example *babasi Alinin* 'the father of Ali' instead of Standard Turkish *Ali'nin babası* (Friedman 2003: 61).

Molise Croatian also provides an example to illustrate reordering: nominal attributes in this Slavic variety have changed from preposed to postposed position, thereby matching the structure of the Italian model language. That we are dealing with a contact-induced change is suggested, for example, by the fact that Italian may use word order to express a functional distinction between a differentiating (postposing) and descriptive (preposing) use of attributes. Exactly this distinction has been replicated by Molisean speakers, see (2.10).

(2.10) Molise Croatian (Breu 1996: 31)

(a) jena hiža mala
one house big
'a big house (not a small one)'

(b)	jena	mala	hiža
	one	big	house
	'a big house'		

Rearrangement of a more complex type involves the replacement of one type of syntactic organization with another type as a result of language contact. There is a wealth of examples in the relevant literature (see especially Thomason & Kaufman 1988); we may illustrate the process with one example of contact between two European languages, even if the arena of contact was not on the European continent. Harris and Campbell (1995: 124–5) observe that Finnish as spoken in the USA has replicated (or borrowed in their terminology) a number of constructions from English. For example, Finnish does not permit infinitival complements of nouns or adjectives with subject raising, while English does. Finnish speakers in the USA have replicated the English construction, leading to sentences such as the following that are unacceptable in Standard Finnish:

(2.11) AMERICAN FINNISH (Harris & Campbell 1995: 125)

oli	aivan	liian	kauan	häne-	n	odottaa.
was	really	too	long	he-	GEN	to.wait

'It was entirely too long for him to wait.'

This example suggests that in a situation of language contact, the available syntactic structure used for marking complex complements was replaced with a new structure replicated from the model language, with no grammaticalization process involved.

As we observed above, we will treat contact-induced grammaticalization and restructuring as distinct manifestations of grammatical replication. Observations on a larger body of instances of grammatical replication suggest, first, that the former is much more common than the latter (see Heine & Kuteva 2005). And second, they also suggest that many cases that have been attributed to the latter can equally well be analyzed in terms of the former. This also applies to the cases discussed above. Take, for example, the case of gender loss in Molise Croatian that we mentioned above. In the same way as loss of the neuter gender can be described as restructuring, it can also be interpreted as an instance of grammaticalization. One of the main parameters of grammaticalization concerns extension (see Section 2.3), whereby existing grammatical categories are extended to new contexts. Accordingly, the change characterizing Molisean can also be viewed as an extension process whereby the use of the masculine gender category was extended to contexts previously reserved for neuter nouns, with the ultimate effect that the neuter category was eliminated, and that the semantic content of the masculine category was redefined.

A more detailed analysis of presumed cases of restructuring, also treated under labels such as 'reanalysis' and 'resyntacticization', in fact reveals that many of these cases can more profitably be interpreted as being suggestive of grammaticalization. A paradigm case is provided by what Nadkarni (1975) calls the Dravidianization of an Indo-Aryan language in India, whereby speakers of the Saraswat Brahmins dialect of the Indo-Aryan language Konkani replicated a grammaticalization process that had taken place earlier in the Dravidian language Kannada—with the result that a complex interrogative construction consisting of both a word question and a polar (yes–no) question turned into a relative clause construction. While Appel and Muysken (1987: 159) refer to this case as resyntacticization, it is in accordance with principles of grammaticalization as we will see in Chapter 6, where we will deal with similar instances of this process.

The linguistic data discussed in this book concern basically contact-induced grammaticalization. Accordingly, whenever there is a case of restructuring, we will draw the reader's attention to this fact.

2.5 On the nature of replication

The observations made in the preceding sections suggest that grammatical replication is severely constrained. One of the most salient constraints is the unidirectionality of grammatical replication. For example, we will expect that in a situation of language contact, speakers may replicate a grammaticalization process from a demonstrative attribute to a definite article, or from numeral 'one' to an indefinite article (see Section 2.3), while we will not expect a process in the opposite direction, that is, where language contact leads to a development from definite article to demonstrative or from indefinite article to numeral. In the present section we will point out two further characteristics of grammatical replication.

One of these characteristics concerns the structure of the linguistic material transferred from one language to another. Grammatical replication may affect virtually any domain of language structure; first and foremost, however, it is a semantic-conceptual process, leading to the rise of new meaningful structures on the model of another language. The following example clearly illustrates that grammatical replication involves—primarily—the transfer of semantic-conceptual, and not morphosyntactic, structure.

The Indo-Aryan language Romani offers a perhaps extreme case of how speakers can adapt their modes of grammatical categorization to those of their neighbours. In the Balkans, adaptation had the effect that Romani speakers developed a de-volitive future, that is, a future tense historically derived from a verb for 'want' (cf. the English *will*-future); elsewhere in Europe they found other models and, accordingly, developed other kinds of future categories. In the dialect of Wales they developed a de-allative future using a verb for 'go' presumably on the model of English *be going to* (Boretzky 1989: 368), cf. (2.12).

(2.12) ROMANI OF WALES (Boretzky 1989: 369)
brišindo džala te del.
(rain goes to give)
'It is going to rain.'

In Russian Romani dialects there is a future tense using the verb *l-av* 'take' as an auxiliary (e.g. *l-av te xav* 'I am going to eat')—a grammaticalization that is cross-linguistically quite unusual. Now, Ukrainian has two future tenses, and one of them also uses the verb 'take' as a future auxiliary. Boretzky (1989: 369) suggests that Vlach Romani speakers acquired their 'take'-future when they crossed Ukrainian territory.

Quite a different situation is found in the Sinti variety that was influenced by German: there is no formal future expression in this variety; rather, the present tense is used to refer to events in the future. This is exactly the situation found in colloquial German,[14] where the present tense is also used in appropriate contexts for future events; conceivably, what this suggests is that absence of a salient model prevented grammaticalization to take place.[15]

That de-volitive futures generally found in Balkan languages are due to language contact is suggested, for example, by the fact that the Romani varieties spoken on the Balkans have developed a future category marked with *ka*(*m*)-, which is derived from the verb *kam-av* 'want, love' (Boretzky 1989: 368). Still, in view of the cross-linguistically widespread distribution of de-volitive futures, a development based exclusively on universal principles of grammaticalization, unaffected by language contact, can never be entirely ruled out. There is, however, additional evidence to suggest that this grammaticalization was contact-induced: whilst the various Romani varieties developed a number of different future tenses, it is only the varieties spoken on the Balkans that acquired a de-volitive future (Boretzky & Igla 1999: 729); note that the presence of a de-volitive future is widely held to be a salient

[14] German has a conventionalized future category, the *werden*-future, but it is rarely used in spoken discourse; see Section 2.2.

[15] Note that an alternative interpretation of the same situation is that, on the model of colloquial German, the Sinti extended the use of their present tense also to contexts denoting futurity.

property of the Balkan sprachbund (see Sandfeld 1930; Schaller 1975; Solta 1980; Joseph 1992).

But the Balkan varieties of Romani provide further evidence that the rise of new future tenses has been shaped primarily by contact. We observed above that there is a less common source for future tense markers based on the grammaticalization of obligation markers typically involving a possession schema, that is a possessive verb 'have' plus a non-finite main verb—French and other Romance languages providing paradigm examples of this pathway of evolution. The Geg dialect of Albanian and varieties of Macedonian and Bulgarian have drawn on this pathway to develop future tenses, and Romani speakers in contact with these Balkan languages appear to have replicated this pathway. Now, the Romani equivalent of a 'have'-verb is a construction literally meaning 'is me' (*si man*) to designate 'I have'; accordingly, these Romani speakers replicated the possession schema to create a future tense, as illustrated in (2.13).

(2.13) Romani, Prizren dialect (Boretzky & Igla 1999: 719)
Hi ma te džav lesa.
is me that go.1.SG he.INSTR
'I will go with him.'

Another example showing that it is conceptual-semantic rather than morphosyntactic structures that are the primary target of grammatical replication is suggested by the following case concerning the possessive perfect in Irish (see also Chapter 4). Whilst there are no indications that there was a possessive perfect in Middle Irish (eleventh to seventeenth century), Modern Irish has a possessive construction based on the Location Schema [Y is on X], using the preposition *ag* 'at' to present the possessor, (2.14a). In the languages of western and central Europe, possessive constructions of the kind 'I have a cat' have given rise to possessive perfects ('I have seen a cat'), and the same process has occurred in Irish, (2.14b), even if it has not gone beyond the initial stage of development in Irish, being restricted to transitive verbs and human subjects, and expressing resultative meanings.[16] Given the areal and historical situation of Irish, in addition to the fact that the development from possessive construction to perfect aspect category is cross-linguistically rare, the most plausible hypothesis is that Irish acquired this construction as a result of contact with European languages that had undergone this development earlier, most likely with English.

[16] Cf. Harris (1984), who observes that the Irish possessive perfect, referred to by him as 'PII', 'is realized as a possessive construction which incorporates a verbal adjective as object complement (possession in Irish is expressed prepositionally as "object-of-possession is at possessor")' (Harris 1984: 319).

(2.14) Modern Irish (Elvira Veselinović, p.c.)

(a) Tá teach agam.
is house on.1.SG
'I have a house.'

(b) Tá an litir scríofa agam.
be.PRES ART letter to.write.PPP on.1.SG
'I have written the letter.' (Lit. 'The letter is a written one on me.')

If this assumption is correct, this would mean that Irish replicated the conceptual strategy of using a possessive schema for developing the aspectual notion of a perfect, but not the morphosyntax used for the expression of possession and the perfect: whereas English, like other Germanic and Romance languages, encodes both the possessor and the agent of the perfect as the clausal subject, Irish treats the possessor and the perfect agent like an adjunct by means of a locative phrase. In other words, Irish must have replicated a grammaticalization process from possessive to perfect concept but not the syntax associated with these concepts.

Another characteristic of grammatical replication is that the replica structure is usually less grammaticalized than the corresponding model structure. This can be illustrated with the following example from Estonian (Stolz 1991: 70–3). The fellow Finnic language Finnish expresses verbal negation periphrastically by means of a separate verb inflected for person using the present tense personal affixes, (2.15a). In the Baltic languages Latvian and Lithuanian, verbal negation is expressed by means of the affix *ne-*, prefixed to the finite verb, (2.15c). Estonian has a long history of contact with Baltic languages in general and with Latvian in particular and has been strongly influenced by Latvian (Stolz 1991). It would seem that Estonian has adapted its earlier Finnic structure of negation to that of the Baltic languages: it has grammaticalized the third person singular form of the Finnic negation verb to an invariable negation marker *ei* which may not be separated from the following main verb by any other element, thus having acquired nearly prefixal status, (2.15b). However, it has not gained all the properties of a prefix (Stolz 1991: 71).

(2.15) The structure of negation in Finnic and Baltic languages (Stolz 1991: 70–2)

(a) Finnish
e- n lue.
NEG- 1.SG read
'I don't read.'

(b) Estonian

mina	ei	loe.
(I.NOM	NEG	read)

'I don't read.'

(c) Latvian

es	ne-	gribu.
(I.NOM	NEG-	want.1.SG)

'I don't want.'

Thus, Estonian has developed a structure of verbal negation that contrasts sharply with that of the fellow Finnic language Finnish and is nearly identical with that of the genetically unrelated Baltic languages. Nevertheless, it differs from its Baltic models in the fact that it is less grammaticalized: first, it has not quite reached the prefixal status characterizing the situation in the latter and, second, in its southern dialects the Estonian negator has retained the verbal property of still being inflected for tense.[17]

This example illustrates that replica categories and structures are not the same as their corresponding model categories and structures; rather, they differ in a principled way from their corresponding model structures in that they tend to be less grammaticalized, being used less frequently, being associated with a smaller range of contexts, and/or exhibiting a lower degree of morphosyntactic obligatoriness, etc. (see Heine & Kuteva 2005 for discussion). However, this generalization is in need of qualification: it applies generally to cases of replication in their younger stages of evolution; the longer the contact situation continues, the more the replica categories approach the structure of their models, and in cases of an extended period of contact, the two may become structurally nearly identical.

Grammatical replication concerns linguistic meanings and structures, but not forms. Accordingly, in this book we will have little to say about the transfer of forms, that is, borrowing. Still, borrowing and replication are not always independent of one another. A few cases of contact-induced transfer have been reported that jointly involve replication and borrowing, Aikhenvald (2002: 239) calls this process grammatical accommodation (see Heine & Kuteva 2005, section 6.3.1 for examples). But it may also happen that borrowing provides a basis for replication, as the following example illustrates (Rot 1991: 58). Hungarian borrowed a number of verbs containing the derivational prefix *aus-* ('out') from German. Being aware that there is an element in these verbs associated with the meaning 'out', Hungarian speakers acti-

[17] We are grateful to Dahl (p.c.) for having drawn our attention to the latter fact. However, Dahl considers this not to be a compelling case of replication since it may be argued that Estonian can be said to be reverting to what is the most common type of negation in the languages of the world.

vated their own prefix (or preverb) *ki-* as an equivalent of German *aus-* and extended its use to verbal roots of Hungarian (Finno-Ugric) origin, such as the following:

(2.16) HUNGARIAN (Rot 1991: 58)

ad	'give'	ki-ad	'give out'
fő	'boil'	ki-fő	'boil out'
lök	'push'	ki-lök	'push out'

As the description by Rot suggests, borrowing was a prerequisite for grammatical replication: on the model of German *aus*, Hungarian *ki-*was extended to new verbs as part of a grammaticalization process.

2.6 Internal vs. external change

A problem that confronts the approach used here is that in most cases it is hard to prove that grammatical replication has in fact taken place and this approach therefore has to rely on circumstantial evidence; for example, particulars of the socio-historical circumstances characterizing the language-contact situation may provide clues for or against a replication hypothesis. But there is an even more important problem, one that we discussed in Section 1.5.1, namely the question of whether the processes described in this book are really externally induced, that is, due to language contact, or, alternatively, to internal development. As has been established elsewhere (Heine & Kuteva 2003), there is reason to assume that contact-induced grammaticalization simultaneously implies both. We will now substantiate this assumption.

One salient line of grammaticalization concerns an evolution as sketched in (2.17), according to which free linguistic forms may, in appropriate contexts, turn into clitics of other words, which again may develop into derivational and/or inflectional affixes. At a more advanced stage, affixes again can be lost, and they may be replaced with new free forms, thereby giving rise to a new cycle of grammaticalization (cf. Givón's (1971) well-known scale of grammaticalization; see also Heine & Reh 1984).

(2.17) A COMMON EVOLUTION OF GRAMMATICAL FORMS
free form > clitic > affix > renewal.

Accordingly, it is always possible that affixes undergo what is technically known as *renewal*. This is especially likely when affixes have lost most of their meaning, categorial distinctiveness, and/or phonetic substance, no longer being able, for example, to carry stress—the evolution of case inflections in Romance languages or English being a case in point. Note, however, that renewal is not necessarily contingent on the particular state of a given form; given, for example, sufficient external motivation it may also affect a clitic, or even a free form.[18]

While grammaticalization theory accounts for renewal in a principled way, there is another factor that has been held responsible for it, namely language contact; however, many of the cases where this factor has been invoked turn out to be controversial. But, language contact can also be a contributing factor, as the following examples may show.

One characteristic of many Indo-European languages, not commonly found in other language families, can be seen in the presence of suffixal inflections (degree markers) on adjectives to express degrees of comparison, that is, to form comparative and superlative categories (English *small*, *small-er*, *small-est*) or, alternatively, by suppletive forms (*good*, *better*, *best*), both of which tend to be referred to as synthetic forms or constructions. These forms have turned out to be vulnerable to loss and replacement, and in a number of Indo-European languages, such as the Romance languages, they have been replaced with free forms—that is, they have given rise to a new grammaticalization cycle. An alternative hypothesis that has been proposed is language contact, and in fact, there is some evidence to suggest that renewal is particularly common in situations of language contact (e.g. Danchev 1989; Heine & Kuteva 2005). The general question that arises, therefore, is which of the two hypotheses, internal grammaticalization or externally motivated (i.e. contact-induced) change, accounts for renewal.

There have been some discussions on this issue with regard to the development from a synthetic (affixal or suppletive) to an analytic (free form) comparative construction in English, and it would seem that ultimately the issue has remained unsolved. For example, the fact that the analytic construction became particularly common in Late Middle English may be suggestive of a replication on the French model, while the fact that the English superlative (*most*) is not an exact structural replica of the corresponding French superlative (*le plus*) has been taken as posing a problem to this hypothesis.

Nevertheless, there are pieces of evidence that seem to be supportive of the external-motivation hypothesis, such as the following. In the fifteenth century, the analytic forms were still rare in Northern English, while in Southern English, which was presumably more strongly exposed to French influence, these forms had become current at least a century earlier (Danchev 1989: 169). That this is not an isolated piece of evidence is suggested by the following

[18] We are grateful to Östen Dahl for having drawn our attention to this observation.

examples. In German, the synthetic comparative construction is well established, for example *schön* 'beautiful', *schön-er* ('beautiful-COMP') 'more beautiful'. But in the dialect of Luxembourg, which has a history of centuries of intense contact with French, instances of an analytic comparative can be found, for example *mehr schön* ('more beautiful'), presumably on the model of French *plus beau* ('more beautiful') (Alanne 1972; Danchev 1989: 170).

The Dutch varieties spoken in Flanders, including Algemeen Nederlands, have been massively influenced by French, leading to a number of new grammatical use patterns or to the extension of already existing patterns (Taeldeman 1978), an example of which was seen in Section 2.2. One of these processes involved the French comparative of inequality, illustrated in (2.18a), which gave rise to an analytic use pattern with the particle *meer* 'more' being used on the model of French *plus*, (2.18b), this pattern coexisting side by side with the inherited synthetic construction using the comparative suffix *-er*, (2.18c).

(2.18) FLEMISH AND FRENCH (Taeldeman 1978: 58)

(a) Dans ce restaurant les plats du jour sont **plus** variés.
(in this restaurant the dishes of day are more varied)

(b) In dat restaurant zijn de dagschotels **meer** gevarieerd.

(c) In dat restaurant zijn de dagschotels gevarieerd- **er.**
'In this restaurant, the dishes of the day are more diverse.'

More examples of this kind are not hard to find. The Slavic Croatian minority living in Molise, southern Italy, has a 500-year history of intense contact with the host language Italian, resulting in massive transfers from Italian to Molisean, the Croatian variety spoken by this minority; we have already seen some examples in the preceding sections. These transfers involved, once more, the marking of the comparative of inequality (Breu 1996: 26): speakers of Molisean have given up the conventional Slavic synthetic construction by replicating the analytic Italian construction, using *veče* on the model of Italian *più* 'more' as degree marker. Thus, while Standard Croatian uses the synthetic form *lyepši* 'more beautiful', Molisean has *veče lip* ('more beautiful') instead.

Once again, one might argue that this renewal would have happened anyway without necessarily requiring a language contact hypothesis. But there is one piece of evidence which supports the latter hypothesis. While Italian, like all other Romance languages, has given up the use of synthetic degree markers, there are a few synthetic forms left in Italian, and in exactly these cases the synthetic forms have survived in Molisean at least as optional variants. Thus, where Italian has *migliore* or *più buono* 'better', Molisean as well has this variation: *bolji* or *veče dobar* 'better', and in these cases there is also a third form, consisting of the old comparative form with the new degree marker: *veče bolji* ('more better'). This coexistence seems to suggest that there was a four-stage evolution of the kind sketched in (2.19), which is in accordance with what one commonly finds in cases of grammaticalization.

(2.19) A SCENARIO OF EVOLUTION FROM SYNTHETIC TO ANALYTIC COMPARATIVE CONSTRUCTION

Stage 1: There is a synthetic form (e.g. Molisean *bolji* 'better').
Stage 2: An analytic degree marker is added (*veče bolji*).
Stage 3: Redundancy is eliminated in that after the degree marker the positive (basic) form is used (*veče dobar*).
Stage 4: The old synthetic form disappears (this stage has not been reached in our example).

But perhaps the best-known example of a contact-induced evolution from synthetic to analytic comparative marking comes from the Balkans, where it is widely held to provide one of the defining properties of this sprachbund. In the languages of the sprachbund there was a gradual transition from synthetic suppletive adjectival forms to analytic constructions by means of preposed markers, such as Bulgarian *pó-*, Albanian *më-*, Rumanian *mai-*, and Modern Greek *πιό-*, although Greek has retained many of the earlier synthetic comparative structures (Schaller 1975: 149; Solta 1980: 229). One suggestion that this renewal is an instance of contact-induced replication is demonstrated by the fact that it affected languages of the Balkan sprachbund but not, or much less so, genetically related languages not belonging to the sprachbund (Solta 1980: 229).

An example that can presumably be linked to the Balkan situation, even though it involves borrowing rather than grammaticalization, concerns a Polish dialect spoken in Rumania (Bukovina). The Polish speakers of this dialect have borrowed the Rumanian degree marker *mai* as *maj* 'more' and have replicated the analytic construction of Rumanian. Thus, instead of the traditional Polish comparative *nowszy* 'newer' they use *maj novyj* ('more new'). Replication on the model of Rumanian has also affected the superlative, where Rumanian places the adjectival article before the degree marker *mai*: in this Polish dialect there is one way of forming superlatives by placing the demonstrative attribute (e.g. *ten*) before the degree marker; note that Polish has no articles but, as we will see in Chapter 3, the most common way of developing new definite articles is via the grammaticalization of demonstrative attributes. Accordingly, the Polish construction *ten maj vjel'ki* 'the biggest' is an exact replica of Romanian *cel mai mare* 'the biggest' (Breu 1996: 34).

A similar development appears to have occurred in a Slavic language in contact with a fellow Slavic language, where the latter, but not the former, belongs to the Balkan sprachbund: there is a Russian minority living in two villages in Bulgaria, and the language of this minority has been influenced by contact with the dominant language Bulgarian. One effect of this influence, once again, is that the Russian spoken by this minority is losing its synthetic comparative in favour of an analytic construction modelled on the pattern of the Bulgarian *pó*-construction mentioned above (see Breu 1996: 34 for details).

To conclude, there is evidence to the effect that the transition from a synthetic to an analytic mode of marking the comparative of inequality was, at least in part, induced by language contact: once languages having synthetic comparatives were exposed to intense contact with languages having analytic ones, such as the Romance languages, there was a gradual transition towards the analytic construction.

Essentially the same kind of observations can be made with reference to case marking, where renewal means that old case suffixes are replaced with adpositions. When this happens, the existing case suffixes are first strengthened by adpositions (which take their own case suffixes) before they are lost (consider the scenario in (2.19)). Such a situation is reported once again from the Croatian minority in Molise, southern Italy. Slavic languages express case distinctions by means of case suffixes while Italian uses prepositions instead. Now, in the contact situation of southern Italy, speakers of Molise Croatian tend to add prepositions having functional equivalents in corresponding Italian prepositions to nouns marked by case suffixes. In this way, the instrumental case suffix is strengthened by the comitative preposition *z* 'with' to present instrumental participants on the model of Italian *con*, and in attributive possession, a new construction [possessee *do* possessor.GEN] was created on the model of Italian [possessee *di* possessor], where the Croatian allative preposition *do* 'to, toward' (governing the genitive case) was selected as an equivalent of the Italian possessive marker *di* (Breu 1990*b*: 54, 1996: 26–7). This evidence suggests that we are dealing with the first step towards renewal, where the Croatian case suffixes have not been lost but—under the influence of Italian—appear to be giving way to prepositions as the primary means of marking case distinctions.

That case renewal can be contact-induced is somehow a commonplace in Balkan linguistics. For example, the fact that the two Slavic languages spoken on the Balkans, Bulgarian and Macedonian, gave up their case inflections in favour of prepositions is attributed to the contact situation within this sprachbund (Breu 1994: 45).[19] In a similar fashion, contact with the Balkan languages is said to have been responsible for speakers of the Indo-Aryan Romani (Romanes) to increasingly replace their agglutinating case suffixes with newly-created prepositions (Matras 1996: 65). This change is reflected in language-internal variation, where conservative dialects still rely on case suffixes while in other varieties, prepositions can be used for nearly all case functions with the exception of the genitive.

More generally, in the examples considered above, there is evidence to the effect that a process from synthetic to analytic modes of expression tends to be propelled or accelerated by situations of language contact. A number of examples are provided by Friedman (2003) on contact in Macedonia between Macedonian and Albanian on the one hand and dialects of West Rumelian Turkish (WRT) on the other, where the former provide a model for the latter. This author concludes:

> Morphosyntactic contact phenomena in the verb-phrase reflect tendencies to eliminate non-finite forms and move in a direction from agglutination toward analyticity—both of which tendencies are also characteristic of the Indo-European Balkan languages from which the WRT constructions are evidently calqued. These tendencies are realized by substituting the optative-subjunctive or conditional for the infinitive, by substituting lexical items of phrases for affixes of interrogation and negativity, and by replacing participial constructions with connectors plus finite verb forms (Friedman 2003: 62).

To conclude, there is evidence in favour of language contact as a factor contributing to the evolution (renewal) from affixal or suppletive (= synthetic) to free-form (= analytic) expressions. At the same time, there is also robust evidence to support the grammaticalization scale in (2.17): such a renewal may occur without necessarily being propelled—or enhanced, for that matter—by language contact. The loss of a phonologically eroded affix followed by the emergence of a new, more expressive analytic structure with the same function, which runs the same *free form>clitic>affix* grammaticalization path is commonly attested as part of language-internal grammatical change (Heine *et al.* 1991).

Crucially, whilst synthetic comparatives or case inflections—whether under conditions of language contact or not—may be replaced with analytic ones, replacement in the opposite direction, that is where analytic comparatives or

[19] According to Breu (1994: 45), it was Romance influence that was responsible for the loss of case inflections in Bulgarian and Macedonian, but his hypothesis is not backed by appropriate evidence.

case markers are replaced with synthetic ones, is not impossible but is fairly unlikely to happen. A plausible explanation why in contact situations—just as in non-contact-related situations—it is analytic constructions that replace synthetic ones, and not the other way round, may be the fact that contact-induced grammatical change involves, typically, grammaticalization processes, which, typically, exemplify analytic structures in their incipient and intermediate stages (as opposed to the static end results of such processes, that is, suffixes); see Heine and Kuteva (2005: 258–9).

What this suggests is, first, that the two kinds of account—internal vs. external change—neither contradict one another nor are they mutually exclusive; rather, they tend to complement one another in producing grammatical change (see Danchev 1984, 1988, 1989 for similar observations). It would seem that, not infrequently, language contact either triggers grammatical change that might easily have happened without language contact, or else it strengthens or accelerates an ongoing grammatical change. Second, and consequently, these findings suggest that the frequently raised question of whether a given change is internally or externally motivated is in quite a number of cases simply redundant.

Third, and for our purposes most importantly, contact-induced grammatical change is in accordance with principles of grammaticalization: languages such as English, Luxembourgian German, Algemeen Nederlands, Molise Croatian, etc. tend to replace their synthetic comparatives with analytic ones, while it is less likely that a language in a situation of contact replaces its analytic comparatives or adpositional cases with synthetic constructions or inflections.[20] This suggests that contact-induced grammatical change is constrained and—to a limited extent also—predictable (but see Section 2.4).

2.7 A case study

Work on Europe as a linguistic area, which we discussed in Chapter 1, aimed to search for linguistic properties that are common in Europe but uncommon or absent elsewhere in the world. In the present section we will discuss a case that appears to qualify as such a property, and it is one that illustrates the methodology used in this book. However, unlike the cases examined in

[20] Our interest here is exclusively with renewal. It may, and in fact frequently does, happen that analytic constructions are gradually grammaticalized to synthetic constructions, both with and without language contact—in accordance with the scenario of evolution sketched in (2.17). But this relates to another part of the grammaticalization cycle; we will look at such cases in the following chapters.

subsequent chapters, this property primarily concerns Standard Average European (SAE) languages.

2.7.1 *'Threaten' constructions*

This property relates to the 'polysemy' of verbs meaning 'threaten'. We will now look at a number of European languages to examine whether we are really dealing with a phenomenon that is both typologically and areally significant.

German. The German verb *drohen* 'threaten' is associated with four main constructions, which are illustrated in (2.20); for reasons that will become clear later, we will refer to them as the stage 1, 2, 3, and stage 4 constructions.[21]

(2.20) GERMAN

(a) Karl **droht** seinem Chef, ihn zu verklagen. — Stage 1
Karl threatens to.his boss him to sue
'Karl threatens his boss to take him to court.'

(b) Uns **droht** nun eine Katastrophe. — Stage 2
to.us threatens now a disaster
'We are now threatened by a disaster.'

(c) Das Hochwasser **droht** die Altstadt zu über-schwemmen. — Stage 3
the flood threatens the old.town to flood
'The flood risks flooding the old town.'

(d) Mein Mann **droht** krank zu werden. — Stage 4
my husband threatens sick to become
'My husband risks falling ill/threatens to fall ill.'

Stage 1 *drohen* takes human agents as subject referents,[22] experiencers (encoded in the dative case), and a range of other participants, including infinitival complements, as in (2.20a), complement clauses introduced by *dass* 'that', and direct and indirect speech clauses. Compared to stage 1, stages 2, 3, and 4 have a limited syntactic potential: stage 2 takes only inanimate

[21] The following discussion relies to a large extent on findings made within an ongoing research project carried out by Hiroyuki Miyashita. We wish to express our gratitude to him for allowing us to use these findings. In grammars of German, stages 2 and 4 are not normally distinguished. Stage 1 *drohen* is treated as a lexical verb while stage 3 *drohen* tends to be classified as modal (*Modalitätsverb*) or semi-modal (*Halbmodalverb* or *Halbmodal*), and while some grammarians treat stage 3 *drohen* as an auxiliary, others reject such an analysis, and still others say that *drohen* is not an auxiliary but is closely related to auxiliaries. Finally, there are also some authors who maintain that there is no distinction in category status between stages 1 and 3 (see Heine & Miyashita 2005 for more details).

[22] In addition to human referents, non-human animate ones are to some extent also allowed.

subjects and experiencer arguments, the latter encoded in the dative case, while stages 3 and 4 have no arguments other than subjects and infinitival complements; what distinguishes the latter two is that stage 3 takes inanimate and stage 4 human subjects. Since stage 1 also has human subjects, the stage 4 construction is frequently ambiguous, depending on whether the subject referent can be understood to act intentionally and/or to control the event described by the infinitival verb (= stage 1), or else whether s/he is conceived of as being unable to control the event (= stage 4). For example, (2.20d) is normally interpreted with reference to stage 4; but given appropriate contextual information, as in (2.21), it may also be interpreted as an instance of stage 1, in that the subject referent can be understood to act intentionally and to control the event:

(2.21) GERMAN

Mein	Mann	**droht**	krank	zu	werden,
my	husband	threatens	sick	to	become
falls	ihm	der	Urlaub	verweigert	wird.'
if	to.him	the	leave	refused	is

'My husband threatens to fall ill in case he doesn't get leave.'

Another distinction concerns the meaning of *drohen*: whereas stage 1 *drohen* is a lexical verb having a meaning paraphrasable as in (2.22a), *drohen* of stages 2, 3, and 4 has a reduced, schematic meaning, as paraphrased in (2.22b), we will call it functional[23] *drohen*. Functional *drohen* expresses the epistemic modality of probability, but there are the following meaning components in addition: (i) the concept 'something undesirable happens', (ii) aspectuality, in that almost invariably its use involves a change of state, and (iii) deictic time, in that the event expressed by the infinitival verb is conceived of as taking place soon—that is, a concept that in a number of languages is expressed by a distinct functional category, usually referred to as a near or immediate future tense. The distinguishing properties of the four constructions are summarized in Table 2.2.

(2.22) A PARAPHRASE OF THE MEANING OF GERMAN LEXICAL (2.22a) VS. FUNCTIONAL *drohen* (2.22b)

(a) 'Someone points out that s/he intends to do something that is undesirable to someone else.'

(b) 'Something undesirable is likely to happen soon.'

Our reason to refer to the four constructions as 'stages' is that their presence in Modern High German is the result of a historical process leading from stage

[23] Functional *drohen* is also referred to as modal, epistemic, evidential *drohen*.

TABLE 2.2. Distinguishing properties of the four *drohen* constructions of German

Stage	Subject	Verbal meaning	Complements
1	Animate	Lexical	Infinitival verb, experiencer, prepositional (*mit* + NP), clausal (*dass* + S), direct and indirect speech
2	Inanimate	Functional	Experiencer
3	Inanimate	Functional	Infinitival verb
4	Animate	Functional	Infinitival verb

1 via stages 2 and 3 to stage 4. Neither in Old High German nor in Middle High German is there any significant trace of functional *drohen* while there is abundant evidence of lexical stage 1 *drohen*, exemplified in (2.23).

(2.23) MIDDLE HIGH GERMAN (Hartmann von Aue, *ca.* 1170–1210)
hêrre waz wil der leu? uns dunket daz er uns **dreu**.
man what wants the lion to.us seems that he to.us threaten
'Sir, what does the lion want? It seems to us that he is threatening us.'
Stage 1

Stage 2 arose in Early New High German in the first half of the sixteenth century, when the construction began to be extended productively from human to inanimate subject referents; an example is provided in (2.24).

(2.24) SIXTEENTH-CENTURY GERMAN (Hans Sachs, 1494–1576)
dergleichen auch ohn-zahlbar sorgen,
such also countless sorrows
troen im abendt und den morgen.
threaten him evening and the morning
'Countless sorrows of this kind were threatening him evening and morning.'
Stage 2

It is only roughly two centuries later that stage 3 evolved, that is, when *drohen* turned into what is frequently described as a modal auxiliary. Early attestations of it are found in the first half of the eighteenth century; (2.25) illustrates the construction.

(2.25) EIGHTEENTH-CENTURY GERMAN (Gottsched, 1738)
[...] wasser in ein meer zu giessen,
water in a sea to pour

welches ohnedem überzulaufen **drohet.**
which anyway to.run.over threatens
'[...] to pour water into a sea that risks running over anyway.' Stage 3

The final stage 4 construction emerged in the late eighteenth century, when the functional *drohen* construction of stage 3 was generalized to allow human subject referents unable to control the event described by the infinitival verb, as exemplified in (2.26).

(2.26) EIGHTEENTH-/NINETEENTH-CENTURY GERMAN (Goethe, 1749–1832, *Hermann und Dorothea* [40, 320])
es knackte der fuss, sie **drohte** zu fallen, [...].
it cracked the foot she threatened to fall
'Her foot cracked, she was about to fall down [...].' Stage 4

By the first half of the nineteenth century, all four *drohen* constructions had established themselves and have remained largely unchanged for two centuries, up to present-day German—that is, a grammaticalization process that started in the sixteenth century came to a standstill around the early nineteenth century. Thus, the presence of the four constructions distinguished in (2.20) is due to historical processes that took place within a timespan of hardly more than two and a half centuries.

This process is a canonical case of auxiliation, whereby a construction involving a lexical verb gradually develops into an auxiliary construction (see e.g. Heine 1993; Bybee *et al.* 1994; Kuteva 2001), and it is in accordance with the parameters proposed in Section 2.3: extension had the effect that the use of *drohen* at stage 1 was extended to contexts where it could occur with inanimate subjects, giving rise to stages 2 and 3, and at stage 4 it was further extended to contexts involving human subjects. Via desemanticization, *drohen* lost its lexical semantics, paraphrased in (2.22a), and was reduced to expressing a grammatical function at stages 3 and 4—even if some its lexical properties survived, as (2.22b) shows. Decategorialization had the effect that *drohen* lost most of its valency properties, such as selecting a range of nominal and clausal complements (see Table 2.2): At stages 3 and 4, the infinitival verb is the only complement allowed, and it is now the infinitival verb that determines the valency of the construction.

Spanish. But German *drohen* is not an isolated case, as we will now show with examples from Spanish.[24] The Spanish verb *amenazar* 'to threaten' is associated with a range of constructions which have striking equivalents to the

[24] The following discussion is based largely on pioneering work by Bert Cornillie (2004*a*, 2004*b*, 2005*a*, 2005*b*); the reader is referred to this work for a more detailed treatment.

German *drohen* constructions distinguished in (2.20), as (2.27) show.[25] Example (2.27a) illustrates stage 1, where there is a human subject and lexical *amenazar*, and the construction is associated with a range of complements comparable to German stage 1 *drohen*. Example (2.27b) is suggestive of stage 2, where there is an inanimate subject, while (2.27c) exhibits the auxiliary-like stage 3 construction with inanimate subjects, and (2.27d) roughly the same construction with a human subject, that is, stage 4. And in the same way as German *drohen*, Spanish *amenazar* has a lexical function at stage 1 but a grammatical function with the remaining constructions—roughly as paraphrased in (2.22) above.

(2.27) SPANISH (Cornillie 2004*b*, 2005*b*)

(a) El MBL vuelve a **amenazar** con dejar la coalición. Stage 1
(the MBL turn at threaten with to.leave the coalition)[26]
'The MBL [Movimiento Bolivia Libre] once again threatens to leave the coalition.'

(b) [...] y la tormenta **amenazaba** un día desastroso, [...]. Stage 2
(and the thunderstorm threatened a day disastrous)
'[...] and the thunderstorm threatened a disastrous day [...].'

(c) El sol **amenazaba** con quemar la cara de Juan. Stage 3
(the sun threatened with to.burn the face of Juan)
'The sun threatened to burn John's face.'

(d) [...] un grupo de niños indisiplinados que Stage 4
(a group of boys unruly that
amenazan convertirse en delincuentes juveniles.
threaten turn.REFL in delinquents juveniles)
'[...] a group of undisciplined youths who "threaten" to turn into juvenile delinquents.'

In a similar way as in German, the variety of different constructions characterizing present-day Spanish is the result of a grammaticalization process leading from stage 1 to stage 4. Up to the fifteenth century, stage 1 was essentially the only construction available to speakers of Spanish, as in (2.28).[27]

[25] It goes without saying that there are also differences. One concerns the fact that Spanish *amenazar* frequently, although not always, requires the preposition *con* 'with' to introduce the infinitival verb (see Cornillie 2004*b*).

[26] The glosses are ours; the author does not provide glosses.

[27] Note that lexical *amenazar* occurs with an infinitive introduced by the preposition *de*, while in Present-Day Spanish *con* is more popular than *de*.

(2.28) Thirteenth-century Spanish (Alfonso X., *General estoria*, 1272–1284; Cornillie 2004*b*: 358)
[...] dios mesura el de ty & esto te **amenaza** de fazer.
(God plans it of you and this you promises of to.do)
'[...] God plans the same for you, he threatens to do this to you.'
Stage 1

The first attested cases of functional *amenazar* date back to the end of the fifteenth century, where there are cases of both stage 2, (2.29), and stage 3, (2.30). The earliest stage 2 attestation with nominal object dates from a dictionary entry in 1492.

(2.29) Fifteenth-century Spanish (Antonio de Nebrija, 1492. *Dictionarium latino–hispanicum*. Salamanca; Cornillie 2005*b*)
milagro que **amenaza** mal
(miracle that threatens evil)
'miracle that portends evil' Stage 2

(2.30) Fifteenth-century Spanish (Bartholomaeus Anglicus, 1494; Cornillie 2005*b*)
Refirma el diente que se anda & **amenaza** de se caer.
(Repair the tooth that itself move and threatens of itself to.fall)
'Repair the tooth that moves and threatens to fall.' Stage 3

There is remarkable variety in marking the infinitival complement: it may be either of the prepositions *de* or *con*, or there may be no preposition. All early examples involve complements expressing a change of state (Cornillie 2004*b*: 362).

It is only in the course of the nineteenth century that stage 4 *amenazar* arose (Cornillie, p.c.), but we are not aware of any early attestation of it. In that century there is also a gradual extension in the infinitival verbs from change of state to copular verbs (Cornillie 2005*b*).

French. A comparable structure is found in French, where the verb *menacer* 'to threaten' is associated with a similar range of constructions: the examples in (2.31) illustrate stage 1 (2.31a), stage 2 (2.31b), and stage 3 (2.31c). Whereas Spanish *amenazar* usually takes the preposition *con*, French *menacer* takes the preposition *de*.

(2.31) French
(a) Les délégués ont **menacé** de quitter la salle.
(the delegates have threatened *de* to.leave the hall)
'The delegates threatened to leave the hall.' Stage 1

(b) Les pluies **menacent** nos récoltes.
(The rains threaten our harvests)
'The rains threaten our harvest.' (Kissine 2004: 227) Stage 2

(c) Le village **menaçait** d' être définitivement aplati
(the village threatened *de* to.be definitely flattened
contre la falaise.
against the cliff)
'The village threatened to be definitely flattened out against the cliff.'
(Zola, *Joie de vivre*, 1884, p. 896; *Trésor de la langue française*)
Stage 3

In Old French, *menacer* (or *menacier, manecier*) was a stage 1 lexical verb, but stage 2, taking a complement introduced by *de* is attested around 1200, meaning 'something constitutes a threat to someone', and a stage 3 construction was established before 1300, first attested in 1200 (Tobler-Lommatzsch, *Altfranzösisches Wörterbuch* V, p. 1389), for example *menacer de tomber* 'threaten to fall (down)'. There is no information on the rise of *menacer* of stage 4.

English. A similar situation is found in English: the examples in (2.32) illustrate the stage 1 and stage 3 constructions; as in German, there is no linking preposition between 'threaten' and the infinitival verb.

(2.32) English (Traugott 1993, 1997)
(a) [...] a handful of Tory MPs who are **threatening** to abstain or vote against repatriation of Vietnamese boat people.
(b) Should such developments **threaten** to materialise, the pressure for an easier monetary policy [...] could be steep.

Like German *drohen* and Spanish *amenazar*, the English verb *threaten* has also gone through all four stages (see Traugott 1993, 1997). It is only the lexical stage 1 use of this verb that can be traced back to Old English, (2.33), where it occurred with a range of arguments: an intransitive use, used with nominal object complements, with non-finite *to*-complements, and with finite *that*-complements (Traugott 1993: 349).

(2.33) Old English (850–950, Paris Psalter, p. 15; Traugott 1993: 349)
ðu ðreast and bregst Þa ðeoda Þe us **ðreatigað**
you harass and terrify the nations that us threaten
'You harass and terrify the nations that threaten us.' Stage 1

In the seventeenth century, *threaten* occurs with nominal object complements, with an epistemic meaning 'portend, presage', where the subject is construed as the source of the threat, being an argument of the predicate (Traugott 1993: 350). There are now non-human subjects and meanings of the type: 'there is something about the subject that leads to an expectation of the proposition coming into being' (Traugott 1997: 188), and the object is frequently indefinite. The following is the first attestation of this stage 2 construction:

(2.34) SEVENTEENTH-CENTURY ENGLISH (before 1627 AD; Traugott 1993: 350)
This fire was the more terrible, by reasone it was in a conspicuous place, and **threatned** danger unto many, and was altogether unapproacheable for remedy. Stage 2

It took more than a century before the stage 3 construction emerged: in the eighteenth century, a non-intentional epistemic use arose with infinitival complements, with a shift from control to raising verb status, where 'the speaker views the proposition as likely, and evaluates it negatively' (Traugott 1993: 350), see example (2.35).

(2.35) EIGHTEENTH-CENTURY ENGLISH (*c.* 1780 AD; *Mirror* No. 81; Traugott 1997: 189)
I am sometimes frightened with the dangers that **threaten** to diminish it [my estate]. Stage 3

There is no information on when exactly stage 4 arose. The following example is from present-day English, where the subject referent can be understood as being unable to control the event described by the infinitival verb:

(2.36) PRESENT-DAY ENGLISH (1992, *Independent*; Traugott 1993: 351)
[...] the hapless, aggrieved house-husband **threatens** to become as rigid and unexamined a comic invention as the grotesquely intrusive mother-in-law once was. Stage 4

Dutch. Much of what we observed in German, Spanish, and English can be found in Dutch: the verb Dutch *dreigen* 'to threaten' exhibits a similar distinction between lexical and functional constructions: (2.37a) illustrates stage 1, (2.37b) stage 2, and (2.37c) stage 3.

(2.37) DUTCH (Verhagen 2000)

(a) De rector **dreigde** het onderwijs voor onbepaalde tijd
the headmaster threatened the teaching for indefinite time

te zullen staken.
to shall suspend
'The headmaster threatened to suspend teaching indefinitely.' Stage 1

(b) Oorlog **dreigt**. (Bert Cornillie, p.c.)
'War looms.' Stage 2

(c) Het debat **dreigde** uit de hand te lopen.
the debate threatened out the hand to run
'The debate threatened to get out of hand.' Stage 3

And the little historical information that is available suggests that the development of *dreigen* was similar to that of the other languages just examined: while lexical *dreigen* has a long history, functional *dreigen* of stage 3 is documented only from the sixteenth century on, see (2.38).

(2.38) Sixteenth-century Dutch (1566; Verhagen 2000: 203)
Het schip, twelck **dreycht** te sincken [...].
the ship which threatens to sink
'The ship, which threatens to sink [...].' Stage 3

Other SAE languages. Further examples from western European languages are not hard to come by. Italian *minacciare* 'to threaten' offers another case, as can be seen in the following examples.

(2.39) Italian (Luca Melchior, p.c.)
(a) **Minaccia** di denunciarmi.
threatens *di* sue.me
'He threatens to sue me.' Stage 1
(c) La casa **minaccia** di cadere.
the house threatens *di* collapse
'The house "threatens" to collapse.' Stage 3

The following examples are from the Rhaeto-Romance language Friulian of northern Italy. As in Italian, the infinitival verb *menaçâ* 'to threaten' is introduced by the preposition *di*. We have found no indications that Friulian has a stage 4 construction. While it is possible to make an utterance such as *Peter al menace di inmalâsi* (Peter 3.M.SG threatens *di* get.sick) 'Peter is about to get sick', it is not considered to be fully grammatical.

(2.40) Friulian (Luca Melchior)
(a) Al **menace** di denunçâmi.
3.M.SG threaten *di* sue.me
'He threatens to sue me.' Stage 1

(b) 'E **menace** ploe.
3.F.SG threaten rain.F
'There "threatens" to be rain.' Stage 2

(c) La cjase 'e **menace** di colâ.
the house 3.F.SG threaten *di* collapse
'The house "threatens" to collapse.' Stage 3

Finally, there is a range of similar constructions in Scandinavian languages; the following examples are from Danish, where—as in Spanish—the 'threaten' verb and the infinitival verb are linked by a comitative preposition ('with'):

(2.41) DANISH (Maj-Britt Mosegaard-Hansen, p.c.)
(a) Han **truede** med at fyre hende.
he threatened with to fire.INF her
'He threatened to fire her.' Stage 1

(b) Et tordenvejr **truer.**
a thunderstorm threatens
'There is war/a thunderstorm "threatening".' Stage 2

(c) Bolden ramte vasen, som vaklede og **truede**
ball hit vase which tottered and threatened

med at falde ned.
with to fall.INF down
'The ball hit the vase, which tottered and threatened to fall down.
'Stage 3

(d) Torben **truede** med at blive kriminel.
Torben threatened with to become.INF criminal
'Torben "threatened" to turn into a criminal.' Stage 1/4

The fact that some Danish speakers definitively do not accept the use of the 'threaten' verb with an animate subject and an epistemic meaning—as in the example below—is indicative that the grammaticalization of this verb does not appear to have progressed much further than stage 3 in Danish:

(2.42) DANISH (Jan Lindschow, p.c.)
*Peter **truer** med at blive syg.
Peter threatens with to become ill
'Peter is about to fall ill/risks falling ill.'

On the whole, it seems to be the case that the more we move towards the geographical periphery of Europe, the lower the degree of the 'threaten' auxiliation process. Thus we have no indicaions that this process has taken place in Sardinian, in the southernmost part of Europe, for instance. If we look at eastern Europe, here, again, there seems to exist areal gradience of decreasing degree of 'threaten' auxiliation the further we are from western European languages. For instance, Serbian has reached stage 3 of the process. In other words, it is possible to use the 'threaten' verb with inanimate subjects such as 'the tree', 'the bridge', 'the wall', etc. with the epistemic meaning of (2.22b), that is, 'something (undesirable) is likely to happen soon':

(2.43) SERBIAN (Ana Drobnjakovic, p.c.)

Drvo	**preti**	da	padne.
tree	threatens	to	fall

'The tree risks falling down/is about to fall down.'

Note, however, that the 'threaten' verb construction is only one—and definitely not the first choice—of a variety of ways to express the meaning 'something (undesirable) is likely to happen soon'; some of them involve auxiliary use of the volitional verb 'want', others employ specific adverbial expressions:

(2.44) SERBIAN (Ana Drobnjakovic, p.c.)

Drvo	hoće	da	se	sruši.
tree	wants	COMP	REFL	collapse

'The tree is about to collapse/risks collapsing.'

(2.45) SERBIAN (Ana Drobnjakovic, p.c.)

Drvo	samo	što	se	ne	sruši.
tree	only	that	REFL	not	collapse

'The tree is about to collapse/risks collapsing.'

A stage 4 use of the 'threaten' verb in Serbian is judged to be impossible:

(2.46) SERBIAN (Ana Drobnjakovic, p.c.)

*Petar	**preti**	da	se	razboli.
Peter	threatens	COMP	REFL	fall.ill

'Peter risks falling ill/is about to fall ill.'

Moving eastward in Europe, Bulgarian shows only a stage 2 auxiliation of the verb 'threaten':

(2.47) BULGARIAN

(a)

Ivan	me	**zaplašva**,	če	šte	me	dade	pod	sud.
Ivan	me	threatens	that	will	me	give	under	court

'Ivan threatens me to take me to court.' Stage 1

(b) **Zaplašva** ni katastrofa.
threatens us disaster
'We are threatened by a disaster.' Stage 2

(c) *Dŭrvoto **zaplašva** da padne.
tree.DEF threatens COMP fall
'The tree threatens to fall.' *Stage 3

(d) *Mŭžŭt mi **zaplašva** **da** se razbolee.
husband my threatens COMP REFL fall.ill
'My husband risks falling ill/threatens to fall ill.' *Stage 4

As for the easternmost Slavic languages such as Ukranian and Russian, for instance, no epistemic use of the 'threaten' verb is acceptable there, either. The following example illustrates the situation in Russian:

(2.48) RUSSIAN
(a) Ivan **ugrožaet** **mne** podat' na menja v sud.
Ivan threatens me give on me.ACC in court
'Ivan threatens me to take me to court.' Stage 1

(b) Nam **grozit** katastrofa.
us threatens disaster
'We are threatened by a disaster.' Stage 2

(c) *Derevo **grozit** upast'.
tree threatens fall
'The tree threatens to fall.' *Stage 3

(d) *Moj mužščina **grozit** zabolet'.
my husband threatens fall.ill
'My husband risks falling ill/threatens to fall ill.' *Stage 4

In sum, we would say that the auxiliation of the 'threaten' verb seems to be a grammaticalization process specific to SAE: we are not aware of any language outside Europe having the same profile, namely a verb meaning 'threaten' which simultaneously exhibits a distinction between lexical and functional readings and is associated with the range of constructions that we have distinguished in this section. Note, however, that there are considerable differences in the extent of productivity exhibited by the functional 'threaten' constructions in the various European languages. There are languages, such as German, where all four constructions are fully productive, but there are also languages, such as English, where productivity is severely limited, and in other languages, especially those of Europe's eastern hemisphere, functional 'threaten' constructions constitute no more than what one might wish to describe as 'idiomatic' use patterns. More research on this issue is required.

2.7.2 *Discussion*

The data presented in the preceding section lead to the conclusion that the structural profile that 'threaten' verbs in SAE languages exhibit may qualify as a property characterizing SAE languages: This profile is widespread in Europe but hard to find in other parts of the world. However, there are other traits that distinguish this case from the ones summarized in Chapter 1, and that are used by the authors concerned to establish Europe as a linguistic area. First, the presence of this structural profile is the result of a grammaticalization process leading from main verb 'threaten' of stages 1 and 2, to an auxiliary-like item at stages 3 and 4, and from a lexical meaning at stage 1 to modal meaning at stages 2, 3, and 4.

As the available historical data suggest, this process started out in the various languages with the stage 1 construction, where the 'threaten' verb had the semantics and the syntactic potential of a canonical lexical verb, being a speech-act verb taking a range of different arguments, which as a rule included a human agent, an inanimate undergoer or a clausal complement, or a direct or indirect speech clause, an experiencer, and/or a means complement introduced by comitative or ablative markers. At stage 2, the construction was extended to inanimate subject referents, with the effect that the meaning of the 'threaten' verb underwent desemanticization: rather than expressing the semantics of a lexical verb as in (2.22a), the verb was reduced to the schematic meaning of (2.22b), mainly expressing epistemic modality; however, it remained the main verb of the clause. Stage 3 represents the next stage of grammaticalization, where an infinitival verb originally being a complement of the 'threaten' verb assumes the role of the new main verb—with the effect that the 'threaten' verb, that is, the erstwhile main verb, underwent decategorialization towards an auxiliary. Stage 4 can be viewed as a further instance of desemanticization, in that the subject is no longer restricted to inanimates but is generalized, now occurring with human referents.

This process is a fairly recent one. As Table 2.3 suggests, it set in between the fifteenth and seventeenth centuries and was concluded in the nineteenth century—with one notable exception, which is French.

To conclude, we are faced with the following situation: somewhere between the fifteenth and nineteenth centuries, a number of SAE languages experienced a series of developments, all proceeding in the same direction from 'threaten' as a lexical verb to a functional marker, and from the 'threaten' of

TABLE 2.3. A chronological overview of first attestations of stages in the grammaticalization of 'threaten' constructions in SAE languages

Stage	French	Spanish	German	Dutch	English
1	Before 1100	Before 1500	Before 1500	Before 1500	Before 1500
2	1200	1495	1560		1627
3	1200	1494	1738	1566	1780
4		Nineteenth century	*c.* 1800		

stage 1 to stage 4. And the result of these developments is the same in the modern SAE languages: the verb for 'threaten' shows both lexical and functional uses and is associated with a range of different constructions.

Note that this is not an isolated case. Approximately the same development from lexical verb to modal auxiliary, involving the same four stages of evolution and taking place in the same period between the fifteenth and the nineteenth centuries, affected verbs for 'to promise' in exactly the same languages, namely *versprechen* in German, *prometer* in Spanish, *promettre* in French, *beloven* in Dutch, *promise* in English,[28] etc. (see Traugott 1993, 1997; Cornillie 2004*b*; Verhagen 2000). And once again, French is an exception: lexical *promettre* is attested as from 980, while stage 2 uses of *promettre* appear around 1160[29] and stage 3 uses around 1200 (*Trésor de la langue française*).

The question is how this situation is to be accounted for. Genetic inheritance does not appear to be an explanatory parameter: the process cannot be traced back to the ancestors of the modern European languages, such as Proto-Romance or Proto-Germanic. Whilst it may have been a contributing factor in the development of some Romance languages, it is demonstrably irrelevant in the case of 'threaten' verbs in Germanic languages, where this situation has a history of less than five centuries.

Rather than genetic inheritance, one might argue that it was drift, that is parallel development, that accounts for the situation: the languages concerned are in a number of ways structurally alike. Accordingly, they dispose of similar

[28] The following sentence, which is the title of Traugott (1993), illustrates the structurally related uses of the stage 3 situation of both *promise* and *threaten* in present-day English: *The conflict promises/threatens to escalate into war.*

[29] The following is the first attestation of French *promettre* as a stage 2 construction:

et le ciel et mer li **promet** mort
and the sky and sea him promises death
'and the sky and the sea promise him death'
(*Enéas*, ed. J.-J. Salverda de Grave, 262, *c.* 1160; *Trésor de la langue française*)

means for developing new structures, and it would therefore not be surprising if this would have led to a situation where each of these languages underwent the same grammaticalization process independent of one another, that is without there being any historical connection to be held responsible for parallel development. But such a possibility does not seem to be plausible either since it does not account for the fact that this development took place around the same time in the history of European languages.

And grammaticalization on its own does not provide a comprehensive explanation either. On the one hand we are dealing with a universally attested case of a grammaticalization process leading from lexical main verb to modal auxiliary (Heine 1993; Bybee *et al.* 1994; Kuteva 2001). On the other hand, the particular development of 'threaten' verbs in SAE languages cannot be explained exhaustively in terms of grammaticalization theory. To be sure, this theory is able to take care of facts such as the temporal sequence of development stages and the relative degree of evolution of the various constructions, but it does not provide a satisfactory answer to the following questions: (a) Why did this process happen within one particular phase of the history of European languages? (b) Why did it happen within a geographically contiguous area of western Europe but not elsewhere in Europe? (c) And why are there no examples of this particular grammaticalization process in languages in other parts of the world?

The only reasonable explanation that offers itself is one in terms of language contact. Accordingly, we argue that the emergence of distinct 'threaten' constructions in the western half of Europe is the result of diffusion across languages. This raises the further question of where the ultimate source of the process is to be sought. On the basis of the diachronic data provided above (see Table 2.3) it would seem that there is an answer: the process appears to have started in French roughly 300 years earlier than in other European languages; there is therefore reason to hypothesize that French provided the model for the spread. As our discussion in Section 1.4 suggests, the case discussed here is in no way exceptional. We observed there that northern France in general and Paris in particular were in a culturally and intellectually privileged situation between the twelfth and the fourteenth centuries, being a centre of cultural diffusion across much of Europe. We therefore hypothesize that the process started in French and later spread to other European languages.

The observations made in this section are relevant to subsequent discussions, for the following reasons. First, they show that there is no 'proof' that language contact was responsible for grammatical change; nevertheless, there is evidence to hypothesize that contact-induced replication played at least a contributing role in the process concerned. Second, grammatical replication is a complex process, consisting simultaneously of both internal development and of effects that one language has on another. Third, this development from less to more strongly grammatical structure has all the properties characterizing grammaticalization, including the fact that it involves a number of different stages of evolution—in our example four stages. And finally, these observations also suggest that traditional accounts in terms of calquing or loan translation, whereby a grammatical concept or structure of one language is simply copied in another language, is not really helpful for understanding the nature of grammatical replication.

2.8 Conclusions

The question that we were centrally concerned with in this chapter was how language contact affects, or may affect, the grammatical structure of a given language. Being confined to grammatical replication, we were dealing with one specific spectrum of phenomena characterizing contact-induced language change. Thus we described grammatical replication as part of a network of a number of types of linguistic transfer, which can summarily be represented as in Figure 2.1.

We outlined a model of what we call grammatical replication, the central components of which are use patterns on the one hand and grammaticalization on the other. We observed that a minor use pattern—in many cases a pattern already existing in the language—develops into a major use pattern associated with a particular grammatical meaning, which in turn may develop into an incipient category, and eventually into a fully-fledged grammatical category; it is the influence of the model language that determines which of all

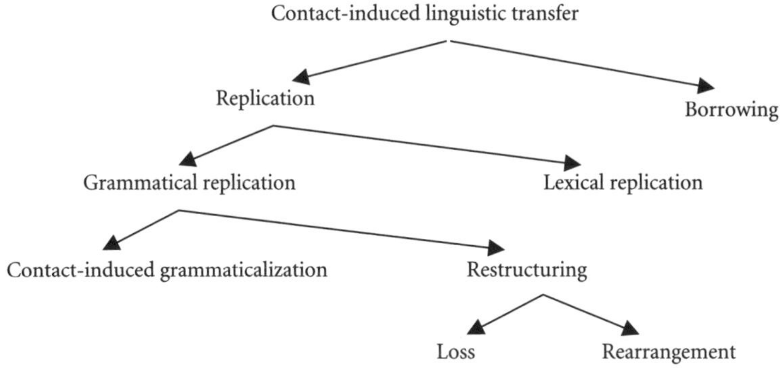

FIGURE 2.1. The main types of contact-induced linguistic transfer

the existing minor use patterns will evolve into a major pattern associated with a particular grammatical meaning. There is a high level of optionality built into this model, especially at the initial stages of the process. What is optional is the choice of a minor use pattern which corresponds to a pattern of the model language (compare the notion of 'formula of equivalence') rather than other minor use patterns existing in the replica language.

Grammaticalization was found to be the main driving force shaping the emergence and development of new grammatical structures in situations of language contact. There are processes, discussed under the label restructuring in Section 2.4, that do not conform to the unidirectionality principle, but as a rule do not contradict this principle either. What this means is that grammatical change is constrained to quite some extent, and therefore to predictable limits. Our discussion in the following chapters will be based on this observation, where we will attempt to reconstruct a number of processes leading to an increase in structural equivalence among the languages of Europe.

3

The Rise of Articles

In this chapter we will argue that language contact must have played an important role in the development of articles in European languages. We will base our argument on two areal-typological accounts encompassing the languages of Europe. The first account involves definite articles, the second indefinite ones. For the former account we were able to find geographical linguistic studies which point in the direction of the same geographical pattern as the one we outline here (e.g. Schroeder to appear). When it comes to indefinite articles, we are not aware of any comprehensive areal-typological study dealing with the languages of Europe. Our account of indefinite articles in Europe is therefore based on publications on individual languages and—in isolated cases—on elicited data from informants.

3.1 Introduction

Articles are only one of a variety of means that encode definiteness and indefiniteness in the languages of Europe, other means being in particular word order, sentence stress, case oppositions, verbal agreement suffixes, or adjectival suffixes.

The use of articles is anchored in general human conceptualization capacities such as foregrounding (or individuating) of an entity against the background of a developing 'textual' world or a shared situational world: both the definite and the indefinite articles individuate an entity out of a group of entities. The function of the definite article is to individuate qualitatively. Even though both definite and indefinite articles mark grammatical categories involving the same conceptualization area, there is no systematic connection between the occurrence of definite and indefinite articles. A language may have both a definite and an indefinite article (e.g. English), or it may have none (e.g. Ukrainian), or it may mark only definiteness (e.g. Icelandic, Welsh, Irish, Scots-Gaelic) or only indefiniteness (e.g. Turkish or Kirmanji) by means of one article, or more than one article, and provide other means to mark the other.

Our working definition of definite articles applies to a morphological device (free morpheme, clitic, or affix) which has as its primary function the marking of the identifiability of a referent of a noun phrase for both speaker and hearer. Identifiability in this sense is a pragmatic category (and not a category of objective truth) based on the 'mental object' that emerges in the universe of discourse, for example:

(3.1) ENGLISH
She was fanatic about spartan life: she wanted to have a single room, with just a small table and a chair. **The** chair should be comfortable and **the** table stable enough for her to write; that was all she wanted.

Here the referents of the noun phrases *table* and *chair* in the second sentence—marked by the definite article *the*—are no particular objects existing in the objective world and yet they are identifiable as mental objects for both speaker and hearer since they have been introduced in the previous sentence.

As a working definition of indefinite articles we will accept nominal determiners whose functions include that of marking specific indefinite reference.[1] Specific indefinite reference typically involves a speech act where the referent of a noun phrase is identifiable for the speaker (it may be thought of as familiar/known to the speaker); importantly, this referent is presented by the speaker in such a way that it is left unidentified for the hearer, see (3.2a). This is the reason why such markers are very appropriate means of presenting the first mentioning of participants in discourse, see (3.2b).

(3.2) ENGLISH
(a) I knocked again and **a** little girl opened the door.
(b) Once upon a time there lived **an** old man [...].

The majority of the world's languages do not have definite and/or indefinite articles. According to a survey carried out by Dryer (1989*a*: 85), about two-thirds of the languages of the world do not employ articles, and less than 8 per cent of the languages of his sample of roughly 400 languages have both definite and indefinite articles. These results are largely compatible with the results of our investigation of 100 languages representative of the languages of the world. On the basis of the latter, we can say that there exist well-recognized definite articles deriving from a demonstrative in 5 per cent of our sample languages; another 7 per cent of all languages present an incipient stage of development of the definite article derived from a demonstrative, and

[1] Note that outside Europe such a definition might be problematic, due to the fact that for two Polynesian languages (Tongan, Maori) it has been proposed that the definite article has extended its use to specific indefinite reference (Hawkins 2004: ch. 4, p. 20).

yet another group of languages—constituting 3 per cent of our sample—have definite articles deriving from a source other than a demonstrative (e.g. third-person pronouns). For the remaining 85 per cent of our sample languages we either had no conclusive data or they were languages that do not employ definite articles. The results for the languages with indefinite articles were: 6 per cent with well-established indefinite articles deriving from the numeral 'one', another 10 per cent with incipient-stage indefinite articles deriving from 'one', and 2 per cent with indefinite articles deriving from sources other than 'one'. In the remaining 82 per cent again, either no conclusive information was available or it was explicitly stated that the languages made no use of indefinite articles.

Compared to this quantitative distribution, the situation found in Europe is typologically unusual: both definite and indefinite articles are found in all Romance languages and almost all Germanic languages plus Balkan languages such as Modern Greek, Albanian, Bulgarian,[2] and Macedonian (Haspelmath 1998: 274). Compared to Dryer's worldwide figure of 8 per cent, over 39 per cent of European languages (15) have both definite and indefinite articles on the basis of Haspelmath's sample, and an additional 15 per cent (6) have definite but no indefinite articles.

3.2 Evolution

While articles are widespread in Standard Average European (SAE) languages, this was not always so: the Old European languages had essentially no articles. Articles are clearly not a genetic feature of Indo-European; Indo-Iranian languages have generally lacked articles throughout their history (Haspelmath 1998: 274). The only exception seems to have been Old Greek. Mycenean Greek (attested for the period between the fourteenth and the twelfth centuries BC) had no article; however, the article starts to appear in Homeric Greek and is established as a normal feature in older prose (Putzu & Ramat 2001: 127).

The growth of articles in European languages is the result of developments that occurred roughly in the course of the last two millennia. Neither ancient Celtic languages, such as Celtiberian, Gaulish, Lepontic, or Galatian, nor Italic languages or Classical Latin had articles (Nocentini 1996; Putzu & Ramat 2001: 122), nor can articles be reconstructed back to Proto-Germanic. It is only in Vulgar Latin that a definite article arose, documented as *le* in Old French. It was not used regularly for definite reference; rather it served to present

[2] In Haspelmath (2001: 1494), Bulgarian is treated as a language that has a definite but no indefinite article. See Section 3.2.3 below.

participants that were either identifiable from the context or co-text or else were prominent in discourse (Epstein 1993: 131–44). Articles are said to have arisen in European languages during the time of the great migrations at the transition between antiquity and the Middle Ages; they appear to be 'well in place once the vernacular languages appear in the written record toward the end of the first millennium AD' (Haspelmath 1998: 285).

In Old High German, the demonstrative attribute had already intruded the domain of definite-reference expression. However, the demonstrative-derived article was still weakly grammaticalized: it tended to be omitted when the referent was uniquely identifiable. For example, there are articles in (3.3a), while in (3.3b) there are none since *árma joh hénti* 'arms and hands' are identifiable via the following participial construction. Note that (3.3a) shows both the article and the demonstrative uses of the plural demonstrative *thie* 'these'.

(3.3) Old High German (Demske 2001: 115)

(a)

thie	árma	joh	**thie**	hénti	thie	zeigont	wóroltenti.
the	arms	and	the	hands	these	show	world.end

'the arms and the hands, they stand for the end of the world.'

(Otfrid, V.1.20)

(b)

Sálig	thiu	nan	wérita,	than	imo	fróst	derita;
blessed	this.F	him	protected	before	him	frost	harmed

árma	joh	hénti	inan	hélsenti!
arms	and	hands	him	caressing

'Blessed be she who protected him before the frost harmed him; [blessed be] the arms and hands that caressed him!'

(Otfrid, I.11.45)

In this section we will first consider language-internal grammaticalization of articles (Section 3.2), and will then focus our attention on language contact in the development of both the definite and the indefinite article in the languages of Europe (Section 3.3).

3.2.1 *Definite articles*

It is a well-established fact that the most common historical source of definite articles is a demonstrative attribute (see, e.g., Greenberg 1978*b*; Diessel 1999). However, it is not just any kind of demonstrative that tends to evolve into a definite article. We will first take a look at the different kinds of demonstrative, and will then summarize the main results of the research on the evolution of definite articles.

It is possible to distinguish between two major groups, exophoric and endophoric demonstratives. Exophoric demonstratives refer to entities in the situation surrounding the speaker and the hearer:

(3.4) ENGLISH (Levinson 1983: 66)
(a) **This** finger hurts.
(b) **This** city stinks.

Endophoric demonstratives serve language-internal, that is discourse-organization purposes. They can be further subdivided into anaphoric (3.5a), discourse-deictic (3.5b), and recognitional demonstratives (3.6) (Diessel 1999: 93). Anaphoric demonstratives refer to noun phrases introduced in discourse at a prior time; they keep track of discourse participants, while discourse-deictic demonstratives refer to whole propositions.

(3.5) ENGLISH
(a) I met a very nice dentist last month. Since I need a couple of new fillings, I decided to go to **that** dentist.
(b) Could you say **that** again?

Finally, recognitional demonstratives are used to indicate that the hearer is able to identify the referent, based on specific shared knowledge, whereby they do not have a referent in the preceding discourse or in the surrounding situation (that is, recognitional demonstratives are 'discourse new, and hearer old'), see (3.6).

(3.6) ENGLISH (Gundel *et al.* 1993: 278, cited in Diessel 1999: 106)
I couldn't sleep last night. **That** dog (next door) kept me awake.

Whereas exophoric, anaphoric, and discourse-deictic demonstratives can be used both adnominally and pronominally, the recognitional demonstrative can only be used adnominally.

Out of the four types of demonstrative pronouns, it is the anaphoric, adnominal, demonstrative that has been traditionally held to give rise to definite articles (see Diessel 1999: 128, and all the references therein).

There exist, in fact, numerous examples where the anaphoric demonstrative has developed into a definite article, and the reason seems to be that its inherent deictic semantics makes it a very appropriate source for definite articles. Since the adnominal anaphoric demonstrative serves a discourse-internal function—to refer to the same referent as its antecedent and thus track participants of the preceding discourse—it serves as a common strategy to establish major participants in the universe of discourse. Its use involves non-topical antecedents that tend to be somewhat unexpected, contrastive, or emphatic. At a next stage of development, the adnominal anaphoric demonstrative becomes a definite article, whereby its use is gradually extended from non-topical antecedents to all kinds of referents in the preceding discourse. Thus Diessel (1999: 109–29), summarizing the relevant research, proposes the following sequence of stages for the development of definite articles:

(3.7) (Adapted from Diessel 1999: 113, 128–9)
Exophoric demonstrative > anaphoric demonstrative > definite article

This is, no doubt, a gross oversimplification whereby numerous language-specific developments are levelled up for the sake of theoretical generalizations, which is what the following example from Latin and Romance languages shows. In a recent study of the determiner-system in Romance, Vincent (1997) convincingly argues that in the development of the article system in Romance languages there was at least one more salient stage. It is a stage between anaphoric demonstrative and definite article, where there existed two 'proto-articles', *ille* and *ipse.* In Classical Latin, *ille* is a marker of distal deixis, that is, it indicates distance from both speaker and addressee, and *ipse* is a marker of emphasis or contrast. Whereas—in Classical Latin—*ille* has both a distal and an anaphoric role, *ipse* has a contrastive-identitive function instead (Vincent 1997: 154–5). And yet, at the 'proto-article' stage, that is in Late Latin, both *ille* and *ipse* mark definiteness in the nominal phrase. More precisely, the two items had distinct although overlapping functions. *Ille* had specialized as a definiteness marker in a cataphoric function, that is to say, it was used as a definite first mention followed by a restrictive relative clause:

(3.8) LATE FOURTH-CENTURY AD LATIN (Vincent 1997: 156)
[...] ubi se tamen MONTES **illi**, inter quos ibamus, aperiebant et faciebant vallem infinitam ingens [...].
'[...] where in the meantime the mountains, between which we were going, opened out and formed an endless valley [...].'

Ipse, on the other hand, had become specialized in an anaphoric function:

(3.9) LATE FOURTH-CENTURY AD LATIN (Vincent 1997: 156)
[...] ubi se tamen montes **illi**, inter quos ibamus, aperiebant et faciebant vallem infinitam ingens... Vallis autem **ipsa** ingens est valde, iacens subter latus montis Dei [...].
'[...] where in the meantime the mountains, between which we were going, opened out and formed an endless valley... The valley is indeed truly huge, lying under the side of the mountain of God' [...].

Later, at the final, definite-article stage—in what Vincent (1997: 168) refers to as Proto-Romance—*ille* and *ipse*[3] become generalized as fully-fledged articles independent of syntactic structure (i.e. having cataphoric vs. endophoric function).

A rather fine-grained—and yet, cross-linguistically valid—description of the development *demonstrative pronoun>definite article* is offered by Hawkins (2004, ch. 4) who proposes a comprehensive account of the gradual semantic/pragmatic progression in the evolution of definite articles. Hawkins identifies the following major stages. First, the deictic restriction is abandoned (that is, no contrast between entities near the speaker/hearer or far from the speaker/hearer). As a result, at this initial stage, the definite article can identify the referent relative to some whole pragmatic set, which can be either the whole (visible) situation or the whole previous text (within memory). This stage is limited to anaphoric references to the previous text and/or to objects existing in the immediate situation of utterance (e.g. the 'anaphoric' articles of early Germanic such as Gothic *sa*).

Second, the definite article can be used in a broader range of contexts at this stage because the pragmatic sets now expand from visible (*mind the step*) to non-visible and larger situations (*the king has abdicated*), and from anaphoric references based on previous mention (*a house*: *the house*) to inferences based on general knowledge as well as to stereotypic 'frames' such as *a house*: *the door* (e.g. the Hausa definite suffix -*n*).

Third, the definite article can now be used universally or generically, with little or no pragmatic delimitation (*The lion is a mammal*), for example the definite articles of the middle and modern periods of the Germanic languages. Fourth, the definite article is extended to encode specific indefinite reference in addition to definiteness. At this stage, the definite article can simply assert existence. As a result, the range of possible uses is now very large (including pragmatically identifiable references, generic references, purely existential claims; for example Tongan *e*, Maori *te*). Finally, there are even further extensions as the definite/indefinite article is recruited for purely syntactic purposes, agreement and noun class marker, etc. so that, in the end, all connections to definiteness/indefiniteness are lost (e.g. in Bantu languages).[4]

[3] Note that an *ipse*-derived article survives today in Balearic Catalan (Vincent 1997: 154).

[4] Hawkins (2004: ch. 4, p. 21) explicitly points out that '[E]ach stage maintains the usage possibilities of the previous one and introduces more ambiguity and polysemy, but expands the grammatical environments and the frequency of usage of the definite article. . . . In order to understand these extensions, we will need to examine more formal and syntactic aspects of definiteness, and their processing'. We will not go into further details here; instead we would like to refer the reader to Hawkins (2004) for an insightful application of a processing approach to the grammaticalization of the demonstrative into the definite article.

Relating Hawkins' (2004) sequence of stages in the development of the definite article to the group of languages we are concerned with here, that is European languages, we are not aware of any language in Europe that has reached the fourth stage. A possible exception here could be Swedish as spoken in north-eastern Scandinavia in the so-called peripheral Swedish dialect area (Dahl 2004). In this area, the article can even be used in contexts involving non-specific indefinite reference (see Dahl's 2004: 174 discussion of 'low referentiality uses'):

(3.10) NEDERKALIX, NORRBOTTEN (Dahl 2004: 174)

Jä skå tåla åom fördä,
I shall speak.INF about for.you.DAT

måmme, åt jä ållti veillt hå **i** kjaatt
mother that I always want.SUP have a cat

män hä gja jo ät håå kjatta
but it go.PRES as.you.know not have.INF cat.DEF

når man båo ini **i** höreshöus.
when one live.PRS in a rent-house

'I want to tell you, Mother, that I have always wanted to have a cat—but it isn't possible to have a cat (lit. the cat) when you live in an apartment house.'

3.2.2 *Indefinite articles*

The starting point of the grammaticalization from 'one' to indefinite article involves, in the vast majority of attested cases, the numeral 'one'. On the basis of data from both geographically and genetically related and unrelated languages, Heine (1997*b*: 70ff) proposes a five-stage grammaticalization development for indefinite articles. At the initial stage (the numeral stage), the item for 'one' functions as a numeral (that is, the language lacks an indefinite article):

(3.11) FINNISH (Laury 1997: 37)

Siitä katos aena yöllä **yks** omena.
SE-ELA disappear always night-ADE one apple

'Every night one apple disappeared from it.'

At stage 2 (the presentative marker stage), the article introduces a new participant presumed to be unknown to the hearer and this participant is then taken up as definite in subsequent discourse:

(3.12) RUSSIAN

Žyl	da	byl	**odin**	starik [. . .].
lived	PTC	was	one	old.man

'Once upon a time there was an old man [. . .].'

Stage 3 (the specific indefinite marker stage) is characterized by an extension in use whereby the item for 'one' can also be used to mark a discourse participant known to the speaker but presumed to be unknown to the hearer, irrespective of whether or not the participant is expected to come up as a major discourse participant. Nevertheless, the use of the article is still associated with subsequent mentions, even though it does not have to be a major discourse participant as in a stage 2 situation:

(3.13) STREET HEBREW (Givón 1981: 36)

ba	hena	ish-	**xad**	etmol	ve-	hitxil	le-	daber	ve- hu[. . .].
came	here	man-	one	yesterday	and	started	to-	talk.and-	he

'A man came in yesterday and started talking and he [. . .].'

The following stage 4 (the non-specific indefinite marker stage) allows for the article to be used when a participant is introduced whose referential identity is known to neither the hearer nor the speaker:

(3.14) ENGLISH

Draw **a** dog!

At the final stage 5 (the generalized article stage), the article can be expected to occur on all types of nouns, with the exception of a few contexts involving, for instance, definiteness marking, proper nouns, nationality-denoting nouns, predicative clauses, etc. In some varieties of western European languages, proper nouns can be used with the definite article; in informal varieties of German it is acceptable to use it with personal names, for example *Ich bin der Peter* (I am the Peter) 'I am Peter'. Spanish is said to be an example of a stage 5 language, where the article is generalized to the extent that it can even be used in contexts involving plural nouns:

(3.15) SPANISH (Heine 1997*b*: 73)

un	día	ven-	ían	**un-**	o-	s	hombres [. . .].
one	day	come-	3PL.PRET.IMPERF	one-	M-	PL	men

'One day there came some men [. . .].'

3.3 Contact-induced grammaticalization of articles

The discussion in the preceding section was meant to show that the evolution of articles is on the one hand a straightforward, unidirectional process; on the other hand, it is also a complex one, being shaped by the particular discourse-pragmatic forces at work in a given language. In the present section we will try to determine what this means with reference to the languages of Europe, especially to Europe's peripheral languages, and how evolution in these languages has been affected by language contact. Unfortunately, our treatment will remain a sketchy first approximation of the subject matter since, for many of these languages, information on the evolution of articles is scarce.

3.3.1 *Introduction*

Cross-linguistic typological observations suggest that areal diffusion must have played a role in the rise and development of articles in European languages but its exact contribution is for the most part unclear. While western Europe presents a history leading from a situation without articles to one where articles have been fully conventionalized, there is no such history in the eastern part of Europe. Based on the standard varieties of European languages, the conclusion drawn in areal typological research is that '[in a] large part of eastern Europe there are no articles at all (East Slavic, West Slavic, Finno-Ugrian other than Hungarian, Turkic, Nakh-Dagestanian, Kartvelian)' (Haspelmath 1998: 274). More precisely, no articles are said to exist in Slavic languages other than Bulgarian, Macedonian, and North Russian, or in Finno-Ugric languages other than Hungarian. And in those languages where they are found, their presence has been related to language contact. This is fairly uncontroversial in the case of Bulgarian and Macedonian: while the ultimate historical source of articles in these two Slavic languages is essentially opaque,[5] it is widely believed that it was areal pressure within the Balkan sprachbund that contributed to their rise. The situation is less clear in the case of North Russian, which—unlike Standard Russian—has a suffixed definite article (Breu 1994: 53–4).[6]

[5] As in most other cases of Balkanisms, there are several conflicting hypotheses. One of them holds substrate influence from Romance languages responsible, another one claims Greek influence, and a third invokes some pre-Romance 'Urbevölkerung auf dem Balkan' which first influenced Balkan Romance and later Slavic languages (Breu 1994: 53).

[6] Again, no reliable information exists on how the article originated. On the one hand, it is claimed to be due to an Old Nordic substrate (note that there is a postposed definite article in Swedish and other northern Germanic languages); others consider the possibility of a Finnic substrate—perhaps surprisingly since Finnic languages generally lack articles.

In other words, there are reasons why eastern Europe tends to be portrayed as an area lacking articles, and this is why we will focus on the situation in this part of Europe in what follows.

What one usually finds in the grammatical descriptions of the languages of this area is that the notions of definiteness and indefiniteness are encoded by (a) syntactic means, (b) morphological means, and (c) lexical means—none of which are classified as articles. The grammar of Croatian and Serbian, for instance, states:

> Das Kroatische bzw. Serbische als eine artikellose Sprache hat eine vergleichbare morphologische Kategorie nicht [Croatian/Serbian as a language without articles has no morphological category comparable (to definite and indefinite articles).] (Kunzmann-Müller 1994: 91).

According to Kunzmann-Müller (1994: 91), definiteness and indefiniteness in Croatian and Serbian can be expressed syntactically by means of word order and intonation.[7] Another way to encode definiteness and indefiniteness in Croatian and Serbian involves the opposition between the accusative and the genitive ('partitive genitive'), which is restricted to the position of the direct object on the one hand, and to a limited number of nouns (denoting material, plural nominals, etc.) on the other. Finally, Kunzmann-Müller (1994: 92) points out that the demonstrative pronoun (along with a number of other pronouns) as well as the numeral 'one' are used as lexical means to express definiteness and indefiniteness, respectively:

(3.16) CROATIAN and SERBIAN (Kunzmann-Müller 1994: 92)

O	**tom**	malom	čovjeku	ne	zna	se
about	*that*	little	man	not	know	REFL
ništa	zato što	on	nije	imao	sredstava	da
nothing	because	he	not	had	means	to

ostavi	kakvo	svjedočanstvo	o	sebi	i	svom	osobnom
leave	what	document	about	self	and	his	particular

načinu	života.
way	of.life

'On *the* little man one knows nothing because he had no means to leave behind any testimony of himself and his personal way of life.'

[7] 'Das Merkmal Determiniertheit erhält ein kroatisches bzw. serbisches Substantiv, wenn es sich in thematischer Position befindet; zur Kennzeichnung von Indeterminiertheit wird es hingegen in die rhematische Position gebracht, d.h. stärker zum Satzende hin platziert' (Kunzmann-Müller 1994: 91).

(3.17) CROATIAN and SERBIAN (Kunzmann-Müller 1994: 92)

U	M.	su	prespavali	kod	**jedne**	obitelji
In	M.	are	slept	at	one	family
koju	je	očuto	poznavao	netko	iz	grupe.
which	is	apparently	knew	someone	of	group

'In M. they spent a night with *a* family whom someone from the group knew.'

The last two examples—with the demonstrative pronoun and the numeral 'one' encoding definiteness and indefiniteness, respectively—are reminiscent of what in western European languages like German, for instance, are traditionally classified as the definite and the indefinite article. The reasons why it is not acceptable to speak of articles in languages such as Croatian and Serbian are—we believe—threefold. First, the demonstrative and the numeral 'one' in most eastern European languages are not obligatorily used to mark definiteness and indefiniteness, respectively, in the nominal phrase; in contradistinction to this, western European languages such as German, or English, or French have to obligatorily mark the nominal phrase for definiteness/indefiniteness.

Second, what is usually examined for the presence/absence of articles are the standard varieties of particular languages; by looking at dialects, however, as well as at the colloquial varieties of languages, a clearer—and frequently—different picture emerges. Therefore, in the present chapter, we are interested in both the standard and the non-standard varieties of the languages discussed as well as in both their written and colloquial varieties.

Third, it is a matter of methodology whether a structure is considered a grammatical category or not. In what follows we will be using the methodology applied in grammaticalization studies and the notion of use pattern (see Section 2.2). The traditional methodology makes it difficult to identify a particular form as an article unless that form has acquired the status of a fully-fledged, highly-grammaticalized category. What we traditionally consider to be the definite and the indefinite articles are, however, the result of a grammaticalization process that takes place over long periods of time—sometimes many centuries—and not the static, ready-made products of something that has always been there, thriving in the system. Hence, our methodology capitalizes on the dynamics of the process leading from the demonstrative and the numeral 'one' to the definite and the indefinite article, and the fluid discourse structures giving rise to new use patterns.

Such a methodology allows us—we argue—to recognize articles at various stages of their development, which otherwise would remain unnoticed. Each of these stages has its semantic, morphosyntactic, and—in the case of more advanced stages—phonological characteristics, too.

At the core of our method there is a mechanism—technically termed context-induced reinterpretation (Heine *et al.* 1991)—which combines cognitive-semantic and discourse-pragmatic factors. This mechanism allows for the replacement of meanings in particular contexts—on the basis of inferences which can be invited through such contexts—by stronger grammatical meanings. The following example from Bulgarian can be used as an illustration:

(3.18) BULGARIAN

(a)

Az	imam	**edno**	dete.
I	have.1SG.PRES	one	child

'I have one child.'

(b)

Vidjax	**edno**	dete.
see.1SG.AOR	one	child

'I saw one child.'/'I saw a child.'

(c)

Edni	deca	dojdoxa	da	mi	pomognat
one.PL	children	come.PL.AOR	to	me	help
tazi	sutrin.				
this	morning				

'Some/certain children came to help me this morning.'

The example in (3.18a) illustrates the initial meaning of the morpheme *edno* as the numeral 'one' in Bulgarian. In specific contexts, in which the quantity aspect of the nominal phrase is not of importance, as in (3.18b), a particular process takes place in the minds of Bulgarian speakers whereby the initial concept of the numeral 'one' gets reinterpreted in the sense of 'selecting for mental viewing' an entity and placing it into the world of discourse. Note, however, that the initial, numeral-'one' sense of the item *edno* is suppressed but not eliminated. Now, there also exist other contexts, where this initial, numeral-'one' sense can be entirely ruled out, especially contexts where the noun is in the plural, as in (3.18c). In such contexts then, there is a use pattern where only the grammatical meaning of the indefinite article is present.

The methodology we employ here enables us to reveal a picture of the distribution of the articles in Europe, which is more diversified than the traditionally assumed east–west demarcation line of absence vs. presence of articles. In the course of our description we will show that in a fine-grained analysis of the empirical data—where we will be taking advantage of the diagnostic properties which grammaticalization theory offers, especially in the early stages of the process—language contact turns out to be a relevant factor in the evolution of articles in Europe.

As pointed out above, cross-linguistically there are fairly common pathways in which articles arise: definite articles are highly likely to develop out of demonstrative attributes, and indefinite articles out of numeral attributes for 'one' (see, e.g., Greenberg 1978*a*; Givón 1981; Diessel 1999; Heine & Kuteva 2002). At the earliest stage of their evolution, these markers tend to exhibit the characteristics of what we have described elsewhere (Heine & Kuteva 2005) as minor use patterns, where their use as definite or indefinite reference markers is rare, restricted to specific contexts and/or specific groups of speakers. Gradually, minor patterns may turn into major use patterns, where the new function occurs more frequently and in more contexts, resulting in the emergence of incipient categories.

There is some evidence to suggest that a number of languages of eastern Europe are on the way to acquiring articles in this way. It has been recognized in the literature already that this happens on the model of neighbouring Germanic or Romance languages. That it is language contact which is a crucial factor in propelling (or accelerating) this process has been pointed out by a number of scholars working on these languages; compare Putzu's (2002: 250) observation, echoed by a number of other authors, that only those Slavic languages 'which have been subject to strong areal interference developed the definite article'.

What has not been spelled out clearly so far is the particular geographical pattern of influence of the articles in western and partially central Europe on eastern European languages. As we will show in the course of our description below, this west-to-east influence seems to be strongest in the southern part of the demarcation line (with languages like Albanian and Bulgarian having clearly identifiable articles) and weakest in the northern part of that line.

With respect to definite articles in European languages, Schroeder (to appear) has shown that there exists a geographical continuum between western European languages (with separate forms for the demonstrative and the definite article, e.g. English) via central European languages (where the definite article has the same form as the demonstrative pronoun, e.g. German) to eastern European languages (with demonstratives but no definite articles, e.g. Russian). What our study adds to Schroeder's results is that it pays more attention to dialectal and colloquial varieties and to the contexts of use of the demonstrative as definite article in some of the European languages.

3.3.2 *Definite articles*

With the exception of North Russian (see above), the easternmost Slavic languages of Europe, Ukranian, Russian, and Belorussian, have no definite articles.

Ukranian. The definite article in an English sentence is never rendered by means of a specialized grammatical form in Ukrainian. The following is an example of an endophoric context, where what corresponds to the English definite article is the unmarked form of the noun *drug* 'friend' in Ukrainian:

(3.19) UKRAINIAN

Ja	xoču	mati	druga.	Drug	povinen	maty	dlja	meine	čas.
I	want	have	friend.ACC	friend	must	have	for	me	time

'I want a friend. *The* friend must have time for me.'

Exophoric contexts are, likewise, not marked by a definite article:

(3.20) UKRAINIAN

Voda	zanadto	xolodna.
water	too	cold

'The water is too cold.'

Standard Russian. Russian behaves very much like Ukrainian. The following example illustrates that a noun which has already been introduced into the discourse and is then taken up for further elaboration in the narrative ('topic continuity', the typical function of definite articles), has to be left unmarked by any morphological means indicating definiteness/identifiability:

(3.21) RUSSIAN

Odnaždy	v	policii	byl	učitel'.	Vanja	znaet	učitelja.
One.day	in	police.office	was	teacher.NOM	Vanja	knows	teacher.ACC

'One day there was a teacher at the police office. Vanja knows the teacher.'

Belorussian. Belorussian does not have a definite article either. Thus sentences like the one below never contain an article:

(3.22) BELORUSSIAN

ën	napisaŭ	list	getym	aloŭkam
he	wrote	letter	this.INSTR	pen.INSTR

'He wrote the letter with this pen.'

In other words, we have a situation where the western European languages build a flank of languages with definite articles and the eastern European languages are languages without articles. In what follows, we will show that the zone between western and eastern European languages is one of a transition between a language system with a definite article and a language system without a definite article. More precisely, we will show that the languages in closest contact with Germanic and Romance languages—Polish, Sorbian, Czech, Slovenian, (Molise) Croatian, Kashubian—are also the ones developing definite articles. This represents a situation distinct from the one of the easternmost European languages, which, as we showed above, have nothing like a definite article. Thus we can speak of Polish, Sorbian, Czech, Slovenian, (Molise) Croatian, and Kashubian as forming a transitional zone between western and easternmost European languages with respect to the definite article.

The innovation in the eastern European languages of the transitional zone, which we believe to have been triggered or accelerated by language contact with western European languages, involves a preposed use of the demonstrative article as a definiteness marker in the same fashion in which western languages do it.

Polish. In various dialects of Polish—but not in the literary language—considerable use of the demonstrative pronouns, *ten* (M.SG), *ta* (F.SG), *to* (N.SG), is made for marking referents which have been previously mentioned in discourse:

(3.23) Colloquial Polish (Nitsch 1960: 113; Zygmunt Frajzyngier, p.c.)

No	jag	zawiezuja	budynek,	tag	na	pirsym	wengle
Well	when	build.PL.PRES	building	then	on	first	corner

tam	kuado	tam	jaki	pinionc,	na	pamiontko	i
there	put.PL.PRES	there	some	coin	for	memory	and

zeby	scescie	byuo	f	**tem**	budynku.
in.order	happiness	be	in	DEM	building

'When they begin to build a building they put some money on the first corner for the memory and in order for happiness to reign in **the** building'.

From the perspective of grammaticalization theory, colloquial Polish could then be regarded as a language variety with a minor use pattern of an incipient-stage definite article.

Sorbian.[8] Sorbian, spoken in eastern Germany, has a contact history with German of roughly one millennium. It appears to have proceeded

[8] Sorbian consists of two written languages, Upper Sorbian and Lower Sorbian. Whenever we simply use the term 'Sorbian', we refer to phenomena that concern both languages.

considerably further than Polish along the grammaticalization path from demonstrative to definite article: Sorbian has acquired major use patterns of an optional definite article on the model of German. For example, according to Šwela (1952: 135), in Lower Sorbian the proximal demonstrative *tón* 'this' is also used as a definite article under the influence of German. Lower Sorbian, in a similar way as Upper Sorbian, has done so by extending the use of its deixis-neutral demonstrative *tón* (M)/*ta* (F)/*te,to* (N)[9] to introduce the article. The definite marker appears to have undergone erosion, becoming unstressed in the same way as its German equivalent (Boretzky 1986: 17; Lötzsch 1996: 52–3).

The historical evidence indicates that this use of the demonstrative as definite article goes back at least as far as the sixteenth century:

> In einigen der ja nahezu ausnahmslos aus dem Deutschen übersetzten Texte der älteren Kirchenliteratur wird fast jeder Artikel mit den entsprechenden Formen von *tón (ten)), ta, te/to (to)* wiedergegeben. Lediglich bei Kontraktion mit einer Präposition, also in Fällen wie *im* statt *in dem*..., in denen der Artikel als selbstständiges Wort verschwindet, fehlt er auch im Sorbischen häufiger. So stehen den, in dem 1597 im Druck erschienenen obersorbischen Katechismus des Warichius... 359 Fällen, in denen der bestimmte Artikel in völliger Übereinstimmung mit dem Deutschen verwendet wird, lediglich 56 gegenüber, in denen er in der sorbischen Übersetzung fehlt, obwohl ihn das Original besitzt. Dabei handelt es sich in den meisten dieser 56 Fälle um solche, in denen der Artikel mit einer Präposition verschmilzt [In some of the texts of the older church literature, almost exclusively translated from German, almost every article is rendered with the corresponding forms of *tón (ten)), ta, te/to (to)*. It is absent in Sorbian more frequently only when contraction with a preposition is involved, that is, in cases such as *im* instead of *in dem*..., where the article disappears as an independent word. Thus, in the *Katechismus des Warichius*, published in Upper Sorbian in 1597,... the definite article is employed in 359 cases in total agreement with German, as opposed to 56 cases where it is absent in the Sorbian translation even if the (German) original has it. Still, most of these 56 cases concern instances where the article merges with a preposition.] (Lötzsch 1996: 52).

Compared to the German definite article, the Sorbian one is less grammaticalized. It is far less frequently used than its German equivalent and its use depends on contextual and situational factors. With the grammaticalization of the Sorbian demonstrative *tón* (M)/*ta* (F)/*te,to* (N) to a definite article, the erstwhile demonstrative has been 'strengthened', by adding, for example, the element *tu*-'here' to develop a proximal demonstrative and to distinguish the demonstrative from the definite marker (Lötzsch 1996: 52).

[9] These forms are taken from Upper Sorbian; Lower Sorbian has slightly different forms for the demonstrative (see Lötzsch 1996: 52).

There is a remarkable difference in the frequency of occurrence of the definite article in Upper Sorbian depending on whether the variety is standard or colloquial. As Faßke and Michalk (1981: 568) observe, German influence was strongest in older texts and in the modern colloquial language. While definite article uses tend to be avoided in the modern written language, the use of *tón* as a definite article shows hardly any constraints in modern colloquial speech. It has even been extended to contexts where it would not be used in German, such as in combination with proper nouns (e.g. *tón Budyšin*) or with a possessive phrase (e.g. *tón jeho bratr*).

The fact that the use of the demonstrative as a definite article in older written as well as in modern colloquial Sorbian is passed over with silence in Sorbian standard grammars is presumably due to the purist language policy characterizing the attitude of grammarians: since the oldest grammars of Sorbian, the article use is stigmatized as a 'detestable Germanicism' (*ein verabscheuungswürdiger Germanismus*; Lötzsch 1996: 52).

Czech. German influence also appears to have played some role in the fact that the Czech demonstrative (*ten*) assumed functions of a preposed definite article. The present situation is suggestive of an incipient category which has not acquired the ability to act as a resumptive anaphoric reference marker, not being recognized as a distinct category, being used only optionally as a definite article, and being discouraged in the written language (Berger n.d.: 462; Breu 1994: 54; Cummings, 1998). Likewise, Putzu and Ramat (2001: 128–9) state that in Czech, one may now find what they call 'an "articoloid" *ten*, which expresses direct and mediated anaphora, but does not function as a generic determinative or class indicator, as in the case of "The lion is the king of all animals"'. For a detailed description of definiteness in Czech, see Cummings (1998). He draws attention to the fact that *ten* is clearly less grammaticalized in literary Czech than in colloquial Czech:

> Evidence from the colloquial language shows that Czech *ten* is emerging as a definite article.... Like demonstratives and unlike articles, however, *ten* may not appear at every mention of a definite NP, and overuse of *ten* may not appear at every mention of a definite NP, and overuse of *ten* is condemned by normativists. The emergent category is strongly expressive, and as in literary Czech the boundaries between bare definiteness, neutral-deictic and anaphoric *ten*, and proximal demonstratives *tento, tenhle* 'this', *tamten* 'that' are very fluid (Cummings 1998: 589).

Where colloquial Czech differs in particular from literary Czech is that it uses *ten* not uncommonly with proper names (e.g. *v tom Brně* 'in Brno') and generic plurals. The following are examples of the Czech demonstrative that are suggestive of a definite article use pattern:

(3.24) CZECH

(a) John má auta. **Ta** auta jsou velká.
John has cars DEM cars are big
'John has cars. And the cars are big.'

(b) Chci vodu, ale **ta** voda musi by't čistá.
want water but DEM water must be clean
'I want water, but the water must be clean.'

Slovenian. Slovenian appears to provide a situation which is similar to that of Czech. Most likely under German influence, Slovenian has developed demonstratives that assume functions of a preposed definite article, and its use is also discouraged in the written language (Breu 1994: 54). But the demonstrative has definitely undergone grammaticalization into a definite article in the so-called Resian dialect of Slovenian (Duličenko 1998: 246), which is spoken by Slovenians living in the Italian Province Udine (Slovenian: *Videm*) and in the Valley of Resia. The ancestors of the Resian Slovenians settled down in the area of Venice in the eighth century, and they remained citizens of the Republic of Venice until 1797, after which they were subjected to the Habsburgs. In 1866, their territory was annexed to Italy; nowadays they live in ten villages in an enclave surrounded by Italians and Friulians, both fully-fledged article languages, and only part of their area has a common border with Slovenia.

Molise Croatian. A new use pattern appears to have arisen in the Slavic Croatian variety of Molise in southern Italy. Molise Croatian (or Molisean) has been strongly influenced by Southern Italian (Breu 1990*b*, 1992, 1994, 1996), and Italian influence is possibly also responsible for the fact that, as Breu (1996: 30) says, some Molisean speakers use demonstrative attributes for 'thematic-anaphoric' reference far more frequently than speakers of other Slavic languages would do. Still, the demonstratives have not turned into obligatory markers of definite reference, and on the basis of the details available it seems that they are to be located somewhere between a minor and a major article use pattern.

Kashubian. Kashubian, having a long history of contact with German, represents a situation similar to the one in the two Sorbian languages: the demonstratives *ten* and *nen* can be used as definite markers (Nau 1995: 114).

Serbian. Serbian is a language about which it has traditionally been accepted that the category of definiteness is only marked on the adjective (by means of special adjectival suffixes), and that the noun does not take a preposed article.

At first sight, this indeed seems to be true. In a sentence like the one below, which will require the use of the definite article in western European languages, Serbian would not use any morphological form to mark definiteness:

(3.25) SERBIAN

Ivan	ima	aute.	Auti	su	veliki.
John	has	cars	cars	are	big

'John has cars. The cars are big.'

If one takes into consideration colloquial language, however, there are indications that Serbian, too, could be on the way to acquiring a definite article, even though this might be a very incipient development. In the example below, our informant was asked to translate the sentence *The water is very cold* into Serbian. On the basis of what the standard grammars say on the ways of marking definiteness in Serbian, we expected that the translation equivalent in Serbian would contain the nominative form of the word for 'water', *voda*, with no preposed or postposed word form indicating referentiality. The translation elicited, however, involved the use of the demonstrative pronoun preposed to the noun, which is also the way in which Germanic languages, for instance, behaved when their definite articles were at earlier stages of development:

(3.26) SERBIAN

Ta	voda	je	mnogo	xladna.
this	water	is	very	cold

'The water is very cold.'

Macedonian. In Macedonian, the definite article is postposed and has achieved a highly grammaticalized status:

(3.27) MACEDONIAN (Julia Vuckovski, p.c.)

(a)

Toj	go	napiša	pismo-	**to**	so	ova	penkalo.
he	it	wrote	letter-	DEF.3.SG.N	with	this	pen

'He wrote the letter with this pen.'

(b)

Ivan	ima	avtomobili.	Avtomobili-	**te**	se	golemi.
Ivan	has	cars	cars-	DEF.PL	are	big.PL

'Ivan has cars. The cars are big.'

Bulgarian. Bulgarian has a fully grammaticalized suffixed definite article, for example:

(3.28) BULGARIAN

masa-	**ta**
table-	the.F.SG
'the table'	

Rumanian. Like all other Romance languages, Rumanian has a fully-fledged definite article. Unlike the Western Romance languages and in accordance with what is found in other Balkan languages except Greek, the article is postposed rather than preposed. Still, the Rumanian article is due to the same grammaticalization process as those of the Western Romance languages, being the result of a development from a distal demonstrative attribute (Latin *ille* M, *illa* F, *illud* N) to definite marker, for example Rumanian *capra* (< Latin *capra illa*) 'the goat', *omul* (< Latin *homine(m) illu*) 'the man' (Haarmann 1976*b*: 85).

Albanian. Like other Balkan languages except Greek, Albanian has a postposed article, but it is preposed when the noun is modified by an adjective. The article is documented already in the first Albanian texts of the sixteenth century (Haarmann 1976*b*: 85).

Finnish. The situation in Finnic languages appears to be comparable to that found in some Slavic languages: there are no articles, even though demonstrative attributes can be used in minor use patterns for definite reference. As a result of contact with Germanic languages, such minor patterns tend to gain in frequency and to be extended to new contexts. In this way, the Finnish demonstrative *se* is acquiring properties of an article. Laury's (1997) study of Finnish *se*, based on an examination of narrative data from three different periods during the last 100 years, suggests that *se* is acquiring the status of a definite article, particularly so for younger speakers. And in another detailed study, Juvonen (2000), while not entirely sharing Laury's interpretation, shows that among some individual speakers of Finnish, *se* has acquired the status of a definite category, being used consistently in anaphoric contexts (Juvonen 2000: 147).

Estonian. And much the same applies to Estonian (Nau 1995: 117ff; see also Haspelmath 1998: 283). Looking at six translations of the ode *An die Freude* by the German poet Friedrich Schiller into Estonian, Lehiste (1999) found that translators tended to use the demonstrative *see* as an equivalent for the German definite articles *der/die/das.*[10] Something very similar has been observed in early Finnish writings, where *se* tended to be used as a translation equivalent of definite articles (Nau 1995: 119).

10 Note, however, that translators were not consistent in their behaviour, and some would prefer to leave German articles untranslated.

On the basis of the data available, however, it seems doubtful whether article uses in these Finnic languages really qualify as major use patterns or instances of incipient categories.

Romani. A more advanced development appears to exist in the Indo-Aryan language Romani as spoken on the Balkans. As the description provided by Matras (1996: 60) suggests, Romani has grammaticalized a demonstrative inherited from its Indic past to a definite article. Matras adds that this happened under the influence of European languages, but it remains unclear which exactly these languages were and how far grammaticalization has proceeded.

Latvian. Latvian has a suffixal marking of definiteness but only on adjectives and numerals (Stolz 2004: 6):

(3.29) LATIVAN (Stolz 2004: 7)

Izdzirdu	maz-	**o**	puisēno	atbildam.
PREV[11].hear.PRET.1.SG	small-	DEF.ACC	boy.ACC	answer.PTCP

'I heard the little boy answer.'

Celtic languages. All living Celtic languages use a definite article having the status of a nominal prefix (Elmar Ternes, p.c.). The article in Breton is *a*C, where 'C' is a consonant whose exact shape depends on the initial phoneme of the following noun, (3.30a). The Welsh definite article is *y* before consonants except *h*, and *yr* before *h* and all vowels, (3.30b).

(3.30) BRETON (Ternes 1979: 217, 1992: 401)

(a)

an	ti	'the house'
ar	maen	'the stone'
al	leue	'the calf'

(b) WELSH (Thomas 1992: 291)

y	gath	'the cat'
yr	afon	'the river'

(c) IRISH (Ó Dochartaigh 1992: 54)

an	lámh	'the hand'

We are not aware of any viable etymology of this article, nor do we know when it arose.

The focus of our attention in this section was on articles in eastern European languages. As becomes clear from Map 3.1, there is a gradual geographical transition from languages with well-established articles in western and central Europe, through languages with incipient-stage and

[11] It is unclear what the gloss 'PREV' stands for.

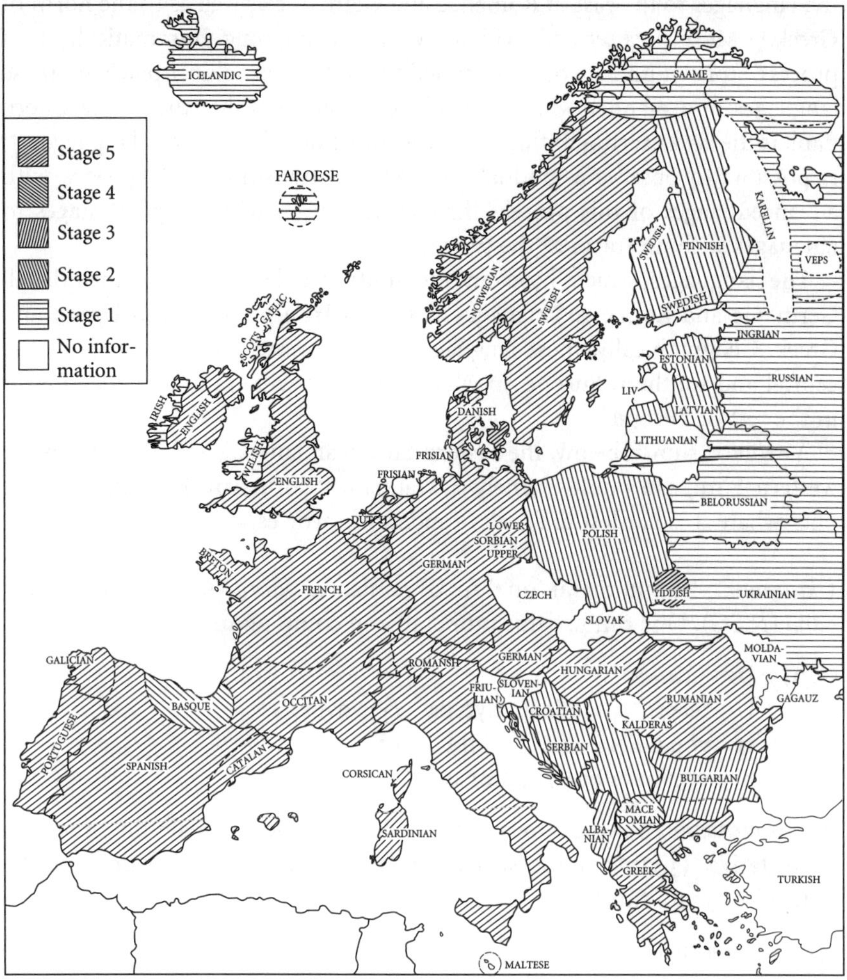

MAP 3.1. The definite article in European languages

intermediate-stage articles in those languages which are in immediate contact with western and central Europe, to languages with no articles in the easternmost part of Europe. The western influence is strongest in the southern part of the west–east demarcation line, with Romance and Greek presumably reinforcing each other's influence on eastern European languages.

3.3.3 *Indefinite articles*

In this section we argue that the Romance and the Germanic languages must have acted as models in the grammatical replication of the indefinite article in the languages to the east of Romance and Germanic as well as to the north of Greek.[12] More precisely, we will show that an ongoing grammaticalization process from numeral 'one' to indefinite article is taking place in these languages in a manner which unequivocally suggests that the southwestern flank is the area exerting influence in the direction of the eastern languages. It is possible to observe a gradual geographical transition of languages with advanced stages of this process through languages with incipient stages to languages with no traces of the process.

The languages which have an indefinite article in Europe include all Germanic and Romance languages as well as Hungarian (Finno-Ugric) and Greek. Geographically, these languages occupy western Europe, and in part central and southern Europe. In what follows we will examine the languages in the rest of Europe.

As will be shown below, the eastern European languages furthest from the western European ones—namely, Ukrainian, Belorussian, Russian—are the ones where it is hardest to speak of indefinite articles.

Ukrainian. The numeral 'one' in Ukrainian is *odin* (M.SG), *odna* (F.SG), *odno* (N.SG). One can use this numeral with count nouns:

(3.31) UKRAINIAN

U	tebja	odna	dytyna	čy	dvoe?
at	you.GEN	one	child	or	two?

'Do you have one child or two?'

It is impossible, however, to use *odin/odna/odno* adnominally in either the presentative, (3.32a), or the specific indefinite (3.32b), or the non-specific indefinite (3.32c) functions:

(3.32) UKRAINIAN

(a)

Kolys'	žyv	sobi	učitel'.
once.upon.a.time	lived	REFL	teacher

'Once upon a time there lived a teacher.'[13]

(b)

Odnogo	razu	učitelja	bilo	bačeno	v
one	time	teacher	was	seen	in

[12] Presumably, Greek also played some role, but we have no reliable information on its contribution to this process.

[13] Östen Dahl (p.c.) notes that phrases such as 'once upon a time...' tend to be heavily formulaic and to represent an earlier stage of a language; hence, they do not necessarily provide appropriate evidence.

policejskij diljanci.
police office
'One day there was a teacher at the police office.'

(c) Ja xoču mati druga.
I want have friend
'I want to have a friend.'

Belorussian. With respect to marking indefiniteness, Belorussian behaves in much the same way as Ukrainian. As the examples below show, no indefinite article is used in either presentative, specific indefinite, or non-specific indefinite contexts:

(3.33) BELORUSSIAN (Natalia Bugay, p.c.)
(a) Žyu byu stary...
lived was old.man
'Once upon a time there was an old man...'
(b) Učorau večar pryexau sused.
yesterday evening came neighbour
'A neighbour came last night.'
(c) Kali laska, kupi mne gazetu!
please buy me newspaper
'Buy me a newspaper, please!'

Russian. Russian is usually cited as one of the European languages where one can only speak of a very incipient stage of development of the indefinite article. It seems to be the case that one can hardly use the numeral 'one' as an indefiniteness marker apart from contexts involving headlines of scientific articles (3.34) or—sometimes—in presentative contexts (3.35):

(3.34) RUSSIAN (Schroeder to appear)
ob **odnom** slučae palatalizacii
of one case palatalization.F.SG.GEN
'of a (certain) palatalization phenomenon'

(3.35) RUSSIAN
Žyl da byl **odin** starik [...].
lived PTC was one old.man
'Once upon a time there was an old man [...].'

Note, however, that whereas examples like (3.35) seem unproblematic, some of our informants would not accept the use of the numeral 'one' as an indefiniteness marker in presentative contexts. In the following example, for instance, the use of *odin* 'one' is considered very doubtful:

(3.36) Russian (Alexandra Aikhenvald, p.c.)

?Žyl	da	byl	**odin**	car'[...].
lived	PARTICLE	was	one	king

'Once upon a time there lived a king [...].'

Whereas the easternmost European languages can hardly be said to have developed indefinite articles, those eastern European languages which are adjacent to western European ones (as well as to Hungarian, which, like West European languages, does have an indefinite article) manifest an ongoing development of the numeral 'one' into an indefinite article, whereby this process seems to be more advanced in some of them than in others.

Polish. In Polish, indefiniteness is either left unmarked (a noun without an indefiniteness marker may be interpreted as indefinite) or it is marked overtly by the form *jaki (ś)* 'some':

(3.37) Colloquial Polish (Nitsch 1960: 113; Zygmunt Frajzyngier, p.c.) = (3.23)

No	jag	zawiezuja	budynek,	tag	na	pirsym	wengle
Well	when	build.PL.PRES	building	then	on	first	corner

tam	kuado	tam	**jaki**	pinionc,	na	pamiontko	i
there	put.PL.PRES	there	some	coin	for	memory	and

zeby	scescie	byuo	f	tem	budynku.
in.order	happiness	be	in	DEM	building

'When they begin to build a building they put some money on the first corner for the memory and in order for happiness to reign in the building.'

In literary Polish, the preferred form is the adjective *pewien/pewna/pewni* 'certain'.[14] In colloquial Polish, however, one can sometimes find the numeral *jedyn* 'one' functioning as an indefinite article:

(3.38) Colloquial Polish (Nitsch 1960: 39; Zygmunt Frajzyngier, p.c.)

Byu	**jedyn**	gazda	v	Skočové	s	kunámi.
be.3SG.PAST	one	farmer	in	Skoczów	with	horses

'There was once a farmer in Skoczów with horses.'

[14] *Pewnie* (adverb) means either 'for sure' or 'perhaps', depending on stress. With heavy stress on the first syllable it means 'for sure' (Zygmunt Frajzyngier, p.c.).

Note, however, that even in colloquial Polish, the grammaticalization from numeral 'one' to indefinite article cannot be said to have proceeded beyond a minor use pattern of a presentative marker stage (i.e. stage 2), since very often no indefiniteness marker is used in presentative contexts at all, as the following example shows:

(3.39) COLLOQUIAL POLISH
Dawno, dawno temu, zyl krol [...].
long.ago long.ago lived king
'Once upon a time there lived a king [...].'

As for specific and non-specific indefinite contexts, there is no indefiniteness marker in either standard or colloquial Polish:

(3.40) POLISH
(a) Wczoraj wieczorem przyszed sasiad i musialem
yesterday evening came neighbour and I.had.to
przerwa prace.
stop work
'Last night a neighbour came and I had to stop working.'
(b) Prosz narysuj psa.
please draw dog
'Draw a dog, please!'

Sorbian. It is well-established that the numeral 'one' forms a major use pattern, functioning in a number of contexts as an indefiniteness marker in both Sorbian languages, replicating the grammaticalization of German *ein-* from numeral 'one' to indefinite article. The article in its masculine form *jedyn* of Upper Sorbian (Lower Sorbian *jaden*) has even undergone optional erosion, being unstressed and reduced to *jen* (Lower Sorbian *jan*) (Lötzsch 1996: 53). Moreover, Lötzsch (1996: 53) ascribes the same degree of development of the indefinite article as found in Bulgarian (and Macedonian), which we will show below to present a stage 3 indefinite article.

Whilst there can be hardly any doubt that the emergence of indefinite articles in Sorbian has been influenced by contact with German, article use in the Sorbian languages is portrayed as a distinct system that cannot be described as being a literal translation from German (see Nau 1995: 121).

Czech. Czech appears to have a firmly established stage 2/unsettled stage 3 indefinite article. The use of the numeral *jeden* 'one' as an indefinite article is unproblematic in cases where the noun phrase is to be taken up as a participant in subsequent discourse. The noun phrase may be the subject or the object of the sentence:

(3.41) CZECH

Byl	jednou	**jeden**	král…
was	once.upon.a.time	one	king

'Once upon a time there lived a king…'

(3.42) CZECH (Vaclav Blažek, p.c.)

Včera	jsem	potkal	**jednoho**	Afričana,	a	on	mi	řekl…
yesterday	am	met	one.ACC	African.ACC	and	he	me	told

'Yesterday I met an African and he told me…'

The sentences in which the numeral 'one' functions as an indefinite article often involve relative clauses:

(3.43) CZECH (Vaclav Blažek, p.c.)

Její	přítel	je	**jeden**	Španěl,	jehož	jsem	potkal
her	friend	is	one	Spaniard	whom	am	met
minuly	rok.						
last	year						

'Her friend is a Spaniard, whom I met last year.'

As becomes clear from the last example, the Czech numeral *jeden* can function as an indefinite article even when it precedes a nationality-denoting noun (this being one of the last environments a developing indefinite marker acquires, see Section 3.2 above) as long as the noun is characterized by topic continuity. Note, however, that the numeral 'one' cannot be used as a specific indefinite article in exophoric contexts:

(3.44) CZECH

Mohu	videt	auto,	ktere	prave	prijiždi	ke	mne […].
I.can	see	car	which	right	comes	towards	me

'I can see a car which is approaching me […] (said by a patient to an optician during a medical test).'

Slovenian. We have no conclusive data about the stage of development of 'one' into an indefinite article in Slovenian. All we know is that in Slovenian dialects and in colloquial Slovenian, one *can* use the numeral for 'one' *èn* (M.SG), *éna* (F.SG), and *éno* (N.SG) as an indefinite article (Svane 1958: 51ff.; Vincenot 1975: 150):

(3.45) SLOVENIAN (Ivan Duridanov, p.c.)

en	volovski	voz
one	bullock	carriage

'a bullock carriage'

There is at least one dialect of Slovenian, namely Resian Slovenian—spoken in Italy (see Section 3.3.2 above)—where one of the characterizing features of the noun phrase is that it is marked for indefiniteness by means of an indefinite article deriving from 'one' (Duličenko 1998: 247), but Duličenko does not give enough data on which we could determine what stage of development this indefinite article has reached. The standard variety of Slovenian has no indefinite article *èn/éna/éno* (Vincenot 1975: 150).

Serbian and Croatian. Whereas standard grammars remain silent on the use of the indefinite article *jedan/jedna/jedno* (which is identical in form with the numeral 'one'), colloquial speech seems to be a stage 2/stage 3 language variety. Thus our informants consistently translate the English indefinite article *a/an* by means of *jedan/jedna/jedno*, when asked to render presentative contexts:

(3.46) SERBIAN/CROATIAN
Bio jednom **jedan** kralj [...].
was once one king
'Once upon a time there was a king [...].'

Moreover, they accept as normal—but not obligatory—the use of *jedan/jedna/jedno* 'one' as an indefinite article in specific indefinite contexts in colloquial speech:

(3.47) SERBIAN/CROATIAN
Jedan čovek stoji na ćošku.
one man stands at corner
'A man is standing at the corner.'

Molise Croatian. Breu (1996: 30) mentions that this Slavic variety of southern Italy, in spite of having been shaped by a history of five centuries of intense contact with Italian, does not have an obligatory definite article. He does not mention indefinite articles, but the following example suggests that the use of the numeral for 'one' as an indefinite marker is not unheard of:

(3.48) MOLISE CROATIAN (Breu 1996: 31)
jena mala hiža
one big house
'a big house'

Kashubian. According to Nau (1995: 114), the Kashubian numeral *jeden* 'one' functions as an indefinite article; however, it is not clear how far the indefinite article has proceeded along the grammaticalization path.

Albanian. So far we have examined only those Slavic languages which are adjacent to the languages with well-established indefinite articles, that is, all Germanic, Romance languages as well as the Finno-Ugric language Hungarian. In addition to these Slavic languages, as we go south along the demarcation line 'west–south', there is one more, non-Slavic language which is geographically situated next to southwest European languages, and to the north of Greek (which, as mentioned already, is a language where articles have a long, documented history). This language is Albanian.

A preposed indefinite article *një* (deriving from the numeral 'one') turns out to be easily identifiable in Albanian dialects (Sasse 1992: 182ff). Here the indefinite article is used with all indefinite and specific noun phrases, irrespective of the pragmatic functions they have; in our terms, Albanian dialects represent a clear case of an established stage 3 situation. Thus Albanian dialects maintain a distinction between specific indefinite and non-specific indefinite nouns: the indefinite article *një* is generally used with specific indefinite noun phrases:

(3.49) ALBANIAN (Sasse 1992: 182)
Erdh **një** djaljë.
came one boy
'A boy came.'

The following examples show, however, that stage 4 has not been reached, since *një* cannot be used in contexts involving nouns in predicative use, (3.50), or with verbs like 'become', 'turn out to be', (3.51):

(3.50) ALBANIAN (Sasse 1992: 182ff.)
Koça ja djaljë.
K. is boy
'Koça is a boy.'

(3.51) ALBANIAN (Sasse 1992: 182)
Duall paljonjeri.
he.turned rascal
'He turned out to be a rascal.'

Let us turn now to northern Europe. Here, there are several non-Slavic languages which occupy a position adjacent to western European languages. These languages are Finnish, Estonian, Livonian, Latvian, and Lithuanian. For two of these five, Livonian and Lithuanian, we have no conclusive data. For the remaining three, however, there is enough evidence to suggest that the situation in these languages appears to be comparable to that found in some Slavic languages: there are no articles, even though a preposed numeral 'one' can be used in minor use patterns to mark indefiniteness. As a result of contact with Germanic languages, such minor patterns tend to gain in frequency and to be extended to new contexts. On the basis of the data available, however, it seems doubtful whether such uses in these languages really qualify as instances of incipient article categories.

Finnish. Colloquial Finnish may be undergoing an incipient grammaticalization of the numeral *yksi* 'one' into an indefinite article (Schroeder to appear). At this stage, *yksi* competes with adjectives expressing specific indefiniteness (*eräs, muuan* 'a certain'). In terms of our 5 stage grammaticalization path, the situation in Finnish is to be classified as no more than incipient stage 2 since, as the following example from a colloquial Finnish narrative shows, it is still often the case that no indefiniteness marker is used even in presentative contexts at the beginning of a spoken narrative:

(3.52) FINNISH (Laury 1997: 37)

Kuninkaan	ryytmoassa	ol	omenapuu
King.GEN	herb-land.INE	be.PAST	apple.tree

ja	siinä	ol	luvetut	omenat.
and	SE.INE	be.PAST	count-PAST.PTCP	apple.PL

Siitä	katos	aena	yöllä	yks	omena.
SE.ELA	disappear	always	night.ADE	one	apple

'There was an apple tree in a king's garden and it had apples which had been counted. Every night one apple disappeared from it.'

Note that in the above example the numeral *yks* 'one' is used only as a count word in the second sentence, but not as an indefinite article in the presentative context in the first sentence.

Estonian. Colloquial Estonian can use the numeral *üks* 'one' to mark indefiniteness in certain contexts (Schroeder to appear), and it seems to behave in a way very similar to Finnish, that is with an incipient stage 2 indefinite article. Looking at six translations of the ode *An die Freude* by the German poet Friedrich Schiller into Estonian, Lehiste (1999) found that translators tended to use *üks* as an equivalent for the German indefinite article *ein.* On the basis of our data, however, it is difficult to determine whether we are dealing here with a developing indefinite article.

Latvian. According to Schroeder (to appear), Latvian dialects seem to be on the point of developing an indefinite article *viens/viena* 'one'. It looks like these dialects have at least a stage 2 indefinite article; compare the beginning of a fairy tale from the standard variety of Latvian, (3.53)—where the indefinite pronoun *kāds* 'some' is used to introduce a major discourse participant—to its counterpart in nine Latvian dialects, in all of which *viens* 'one' is used instead of *kāds* 'some', (3.54).

(3.53) STANDARD LATVIAN (Schroeder to appear)

Sen-	os	laik-	os	**kād-**	am
Old-	LOC.PL.M.INDEF	time-	LOC.PL.M	some-	DAT.SG.M

vecit-	im	bij-	is	loti	gudr-	s
old.man-	DAT.SG.M	been-	NOM.SG.M	very	clever-	NOM.SG.M.NDEF

un	skaist-	s	dēl-	s
and	handsome-	NOM.SG.M.INDEF	son-	NOM.SG.M

'In the old days, a man had a very clever and handsome son.'

(3.54) NINE LATVIAN DIALECTS (Schroeder, to appear)

(i) Vaćijûs làikûs vînàm većeîsám b'ejś ćîži gudrys i smuks dâls.
(ii) Vacûs làikûs vînàm vec'eîsám bej's dyžàn gudrys i skàisc dâls.
(iii) Vacejûs làikûs vînàm većî'sàm biijs ćî'si gudrys i smuks dâls.
(iv) Vá: cuós làikuós viénàm vé: cisàm bijs sti: pri gudris un smú: ks dáls.
(v) Vecuôs laikuôs viênàm veceisàm bis varên gudris un skaisc dêls.
(vi) Vecuôs laikuôs viênam vecîtim bijs varen gudris un skaisc dêls.
(vii) Vecuôs laikuôs viênàm vecisam bîs dikt gûdrs ùn smuks dels.
(viii) Veces laikes viênåm vecåm viråm bijs varen gudrs un smuks dels.
(ix) Veces laikas viênam vecisam bîs brinum gu: drs un smuks dels.

Let us now turn to those languages which occupy a position intermediate between the languages we have just discussed, on the one hand, and the easternmost European languages, on the other. These languages are Rumanian, Bulgarian, and Macedonian.

Rumanian. The indefinite article *un/uno* (deriving from the numeral 'one') in Rumanian is highly grammaticalized: it is used not only in presentative, specific indefinite, and non-specific indefinite but also in predicative contexts:

(3.55) RUMANIAN (Schroeder, to appear)

Castorul	este	**un**	rozator.
bear.the	is	one	rodent

'The bear is a rodent.'

That Rumanian is a stage 5 language is not surprising at all since Rumanian is a Romance language, and it behaves very much like other such languages with respect to the extent to which it uses its numeral 'one' as an indefinite article.

Bulgarian. There exist enough examples in Bulgarian indicating that the language makes a consistent distinction between specific indefinite and non-specific indefinite noun phrases by means of marking the specific indefinite ones with the indefinite article *edin/edna/edno/edni* 'one', that is a stage 3 situation. One of the most convincing arguments for this involves the distinction between the so-called inferential mood (the referent is only inferred but not specific/known to either speaker or hearer) vs. the indicative mood (the referent is 'witnessed', and hence known to the speaker). Due to the formal marking of the inferential mood, it is possible to perform a test on the use of 'one' as an indefinite article in Bulgarian. In the first sentence below, the referent is known to the speaker (but not to the hearer), which is the reason why the verb is in the indicative, 'witnessed' mood. The numeral 'one' regularly takes on the function of the indefinite article in such cases:

(3.56) Bulgarian

Tova	stixotvorenie	go	napisa	**edna**	žena.
this	poem	it	wrote.3.SG.AOR.INDIC	one	woman

'A woman wrote this poem.'

In the next example, however, the referent of *žena* 'woman' is inferred but not known to either speaker or hearer, and the verb is in the so-called inferential mood: no use of *edna* 'one' as indefinite article is possible:

(3.57) Bulgarian

Tova	stixotvorenie	go	e	napisala	žena.
this	poem	it	is	write.F.SG.INFER	woman

'A woman (not a man) must have written this poem.'

Macedonian. Standard grammars of Macedonian mention no indefinite article. According to Hendriks (1976: 208), in the West Macedonian dialect of Radožda-Vevčani, however, the numeral 'one' may be used for the expression of specific indefinite reference in certain contexts. On the basis of the data we have collected,[15] we propose that at least the Macedonian spoken in the eastern part of the country has reached a stage 3 in the development of the indefinite article. In this variety of Macedonian, the

[15] With thanks to Julija Vuckovski (p.c.), whose variety of Macedonian is an eastern dialect near the border with Bulgaria.

numeral 'one' can be used as an indefiniteness marker not only in presentative contexts, see (3.58) below, but also in specific indefinite ones, see (3.59):

(3.58) Eastern Macedonian
Bil si edn'ška **eden** starec [...].
was PTCL once.upon.a.time one old.man
'Once upon a time there was an old man [...].'

(3.59) Eastern Macedonian
(a) Ivan saka da se žene za **edna** devójka so zeléni oči.
Ivan wants to REFL marry for one girl with green eyes
'Ivan wants to marry a girl with green eyes (i.e. a particular girl).'
(b) **Edén** čovék se približí do mene i me prašá [...].
one man REFL approached to me and me asked
'A man approached me and asked me [...].'

In non-specific indefinite contexts, no marker for indefiniteness is used, at least this seems to be the case most of the time:

(3.60) Eastern Macedonian
Ivan saka da se žene za devójka so zeléni oči.
Ivan wants to REFL marry for girl with green eyes
'Ivan wants to marry a girl with green eyes (i.e. not a particular girl).'

And yet, there are some non-specific indefinite contexts where the use of the numeral 'one' as indefinite marker is possible, even though not obligatory:

(3.61) Eastern Macedonian
Nacrtaj (**edno**) kuče!
draw (one) dog
'Draw a dog!'

In generic contexts, however, the use of the indefinite article seems to be ruled out:

(3.62) Eastern Macedonian
Učítel uleva u sobata, a ne učeník.
teacher enters in room.DEF and not pupil
'A teacher is entering the room, and not a pupil.'

Very much in the same way as Bulgarian, in this variety of Macedonian it is possible to also use the indefinite article in plural contexts involving specific indefinite reference:

(3.63) EASTERN MACEDONIAN
Edni amerikánci me zazboríja sinoka, i posle me zamolíja
one.PL Americans me chatted.up last.night and after.that me asked

da im go pokážam pato do železnička.
to them it show street to railway.station
'Certain/some Americans chatted me up last night, and then they asked me to show them the street to the railway station.'

It even turns out that the plural indefinite article deriving from 'one' may optionally be used in some generic contexts:

(3.64) EASTERN MACEDONIAN
(**Edni**) cvekínja se sekogaš prikladen poklon.
one.PL flowers are always suitable present
'Flowers are always a suitable present.'

In other words, in at least one variety of Macedonian, eastern Macedonian, the stage of development of the Macedonian indefinite article can be identified as stage 3.

The conclusion reached in a recent study by Weiss (2004: 139), that Macedonian is a language with a grammaticalized indefinite article which 'still is in *statu nascendi*', is most likely influenced by the fact that the author does not make a distinction between different functional and dialectal varieties. Note, however, that he too recognizes that:

[T]he impact of different functional varieties of Macedonian on the preference for *eden* as an indefiniteness marker is beyond any doubt: colloquial spontaneous speech is often described as being favourable to its expansive use, whereas formal speech tends to be more restricted (Weiss 2004: 140).

In a curious footnote, Weiss then points out an observation (reported in Friedman 2002) that 'in the editing of Macedonian for publication, there is a tendency in formal writing to eliminate article-like uses of *eden*', and that this practice parallels 'a similar ban on the indefinite article in earlier descriptions of Modern Greek "Katharevusa"' (Weiss 2004: 159).

To summarize, those eastern European languages which are geographically close to western European languages (e.g. Sorbian) as well as to both west European languages and the south European language Greek (i.e. Albanian, Bulgarian, Macedonian) are also languages with a clearly developing indefinite article, which may well represent a stage 2 or a stage 3 situation.

Breton. Observations similar to the ones we have just made on languages at the eastern fringes of SAE can also be made at the western fringes. The only living Celtic language having an indefinite article is Breton, which is uC, where 'C' is a consonant depending on the initial phoneme of the following noun, for example:

(3.65) BRETON (Ternes 1979: 217, 1992: 402)

un	ti	'a house'
ur	maen	'a stone'
ul	leue	'a calf'.

This article is said to have arisen as a result of roughly 1,500 years of contact with French, possibly a contact-induced grammaticalization of the Breton numeral *unan* 'one' (Elmar Ternes, p.c.).

Basque. Basque, as spoken in southwestern France, has had centuries of close contact with two Romance languages, first Gascon and later with French. As a result of this contact, Basque speakers developed their numeral for 'one', *bat*, into an indefinite article (Haase 1992: 59–61, 71; see also Sections 1.3, 7.2.1). As a specific marker, *bat* is occasionally attested since 1782. The further development into a non-specific article is a recent grammaticalization of Basque. Intense contact with its Romance neighbours was probably responsible for the fact that *bat* developed characteristics of a stage 4 article, in that it can be found in contexts involving participants whose referential identity neither the hearer nor the speaker knows. Consider the following example, where *bat* is used non-referentially:

(3.66) BASQUE, 1545 AD (Haase 1992: 60)

Balia	dikezit	senhar	gaixto	**bat**.
be.worth	POT.3.SG<1.SG.DAT.2.SG	husband	bad	one

'I will be worth a bad husband to you.'

Note that this example is taken from a sixteenth-century source, which suggests that the article is not a recent innovation. However, the article has not reached the same degree of grammaticalization that it has attained in its Romance model languages, in that it need not be used in some contexts where in Spanish or French the indefinite article would be obligatory.

Map 3.2 shows the areal distribution of indefinite articles in Europe. Overall, on the basis of those languages for which we were able to find data from dialectal and colloquial varieties, we can say that the closer a European language is to a Germanic or Romance language and/or to the south European language Greek, the more advanced the stage of the development from 'one' to indefinite article this language is likely to manifest. The more a

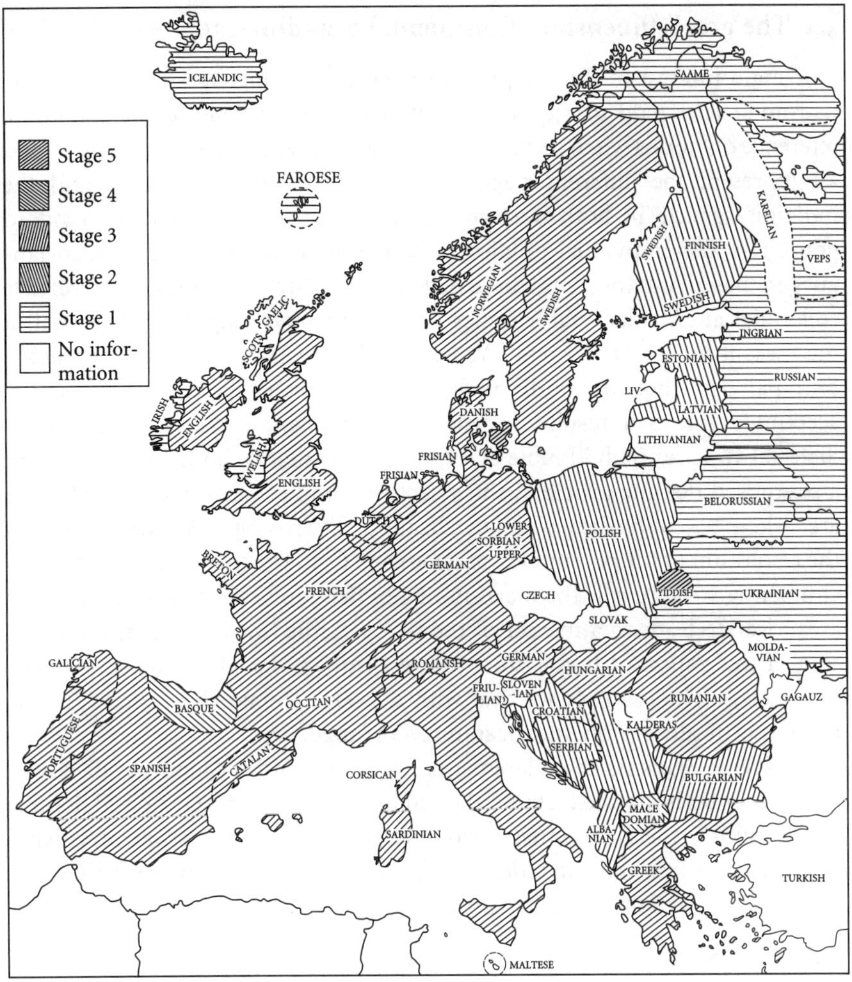

Map 3.2. The indefinite article in European languages

language is situated to the east of Europe, the greater the probability for that language not to have developed an indefinite article.

As this discussion shows, the growth and the general directionality of spread of articles in the languages concerned can be hypothesized to have been induced at least to some extent by contact. However, which language exactly provided the model for which language is in a number of cases unclear and requires further research.

3.4 The areal dimension: Continental Scandinavian

Our main interest in this chapter is to show how languages that previously had no articles tend to acquire use patterns to mark definite and indefinite reference on nouns when in contact with western SAE languages. Maps 3.1 and 3.2 represent the different stages of development of the definite and the indefinite article in both western European languages, based on standard grammars and individual publications, as well as in eastern European languages, based on the data discussed above, which in most cases reflects colloquial and/or dialectal varieties of the respective languages. The goal of the present section is different: We wish to demonstrate that grammaticalization patterns that are traditionally considered peculiar can be naturally accounted for as a result of dialectal areal phenomena. Thus European dialectal varieties with 'double determination'—that is, both a preposed and a postposed definite article in the adjective–noun phrase—are located in an area where two opposite grammaticalization patterns meet. We will show that the resolution of the potential conflict arising from the convergence of the two competing structures is the creation of a buffer zone, that is a zone where an areal overlap leads to a merger of the two patterns (for an excellent application of the notion of buffer zone to areal word order phenomena, see Stilo 1985, 2005). The example we deal with concerns the north of the SAE area, more specifically continental Scandinavian languages.

What distinguishes these languages from most of the languages discussed in this chapter is not the fact that they all have a fully grammaticalized definite article but that there are actually two different definite articles, one of which is preposed and free (*den*, *det*, *de*, homophonous with the demonstrative), see (3.67) below, while the other is suffixed (-*en*, -*et*, etc.), see (3.68):

(3.67) Danish, and marginally Norwegian (Dahl 2004: 148)
det stor-e hus
(DEM big house)
'the big house'

(3.68) Danish, and marginally Norwegian (Dahl 2004: 148)
hus- **et**
(house- DEF)
'the house'

Now, the preposed article is only used when the noun is preceded by an attribute. However, the extent to which these articles are grammaticalized differs from one language to another, and these differences exhibit a clear areal patterning. There are varieties of Scandinavian where, in appropriate contexts, definiteness is expressed essentially only by free preposed elements (like *the* in English) while in other varieties there are only suffixes, but there are also varieties where both co-occur, that is, where definiteness is marked twice[16]—a situation referred to variously with terms such as double determination or double articulation:

(3.69) SWEDISH AND MOST FORMS OF NORWEGIAN (Dahl 2004: 148)

det	stor-a	hus-	**et**
(DEM	big	house-	DEF)

'the big house'

Note that in canonical adjective–noun phrases (e.g. 'the white house') all standard languages use double determination except Danish, which uses only the preposed article (Dahl, p.c.); or rather, in Danish, the suffixed article is restrained whenever the prefixed article is used.

In a simplified format, Danish (marginally also Norwegian) uses suffixed articles in noun phrases which do not contain a preposed modifier but preposed articles when the noun phrase contains an adjective or a quantifier—that is, the two kinds of articles occur in complementary distribution. In Swedish (and most forms of Norwegian) on the other hand, there is typically both a preposed and a suffixed article in noun phrases containing preposed attributes. In other words, the preposed and the suffixed articles do not co-occur in Danish, whereas in Swedish the preposed article does not occur without the suffixed article.

The detailed description by Dahl (2004) reveals that—with the exception of Icelandic and Faroese—spoken Scandinavian varieties constitute a dialect continuum cutting across national boundaries. With reference to definite marking in adjective–noun combinations, there seems to be a clear areal distribution on the basis of relative degree of grammaticalization: Dahl (2004: 178) observes that there are two separate grammaticalization processes giving rise, respectively, to a suffixed- and a preposed-article area:

> In this perspective, it is natural to see 'double determination' as one possible outcome of the competition between two different grammaticalizing definite articles (Dahl 2004: 178).

Dahl (2004: 178) observes that the suffixed-article is historically the oldest in the area, having reached its fullest development in northeastern Scandinavia in the 'peripheral Swedish dialect area', with central and southern Sweden and

[16] There is even a third possibility that we will ignore here, namely marking definiteness by means of 'weak' endings of adjectives (Dahl 2004: 147).

Norway forming an intermediate zone, and Denmark displaying the most restricted use of the suffixed article. Conversely, the preposed article in the area is described by Dahl as a newcomer. It is in general use in southwest Jutland, decreasingly in the rest of Denmark, Norway, and southern and western Sweden, while in the north and east of the Baltic the use of the preposed article is weak, having left some areas virtually untouched.

The result of this areal distribution is that there is an intersection zone in the centre, where the two article areas overlap, hence where there is double determination, while at the southern borderline there appears to be a gradual transition towards a canonical SAE situation, where there are only preposed but no suffixed articles.

It remains largely unclear exactly what the historical processes were that contributed to this areal distribution in the Scandinavian dialect continuum. What is beyond reasonable doubt, however, is that this distribution correlates with differences in grammaticalization on the one hand and areal gradience on the other, in that there is both a south-to-northeast cline and a northeast-to-south cline with regard to relative degrees of grammaticalization. In view of these correlations, there is reason to hypothesize that language contact and grammaticalization must jointly have played some role in the diffusion of the two types of definite articles in continental Scandinavia.

3.5 Conclusions

The discussion in the present chapter may have shown, first, that the Europeanization of definite and indefinite marking on nouns has proceeded further than a superficial overview might suggest. Second, all developments that can be observed are in accordance with the unidirectionality principle: demonstratives acquired uses as definite markers and numerals as indefinite markers as a result of language contact—there is not a single case suggesting a reversed directionality whereby a definite article developed into a demonstrative or an indefinite article into a numeral for 'one'. Nevertheless, most of the developments surveyed represent early grammaticalizations. With the exception of Rumanian, which is after all a Romance language (and the south-eastern European languages Bulgarian, Macedonian, Albanian, and Modern Greek, with respect to the definite article), none has resulted in a conventionalized article used obligatorily, some are at the stage of advanced minor use patterns while others are suggestive of major use patterns or incipient categories, that is, of items whose categorial status tends to be controversial, as a rule ignored or condemned by conservative grammarians.

Note that replication of articles on the model of SAE was not restricted to the European continent; it also affected other languages as a result of the spread of European languages to other parts of the world. One such language is Pipil, an Aztecan language of El Salvador, which can be assumed to have lacked articles prior to its contact with Spanish but, as a result of this contact, has acquired what appear to be at least incipient categories of definite and indefinite reference markers on nouns. As the description by Campbell (1987: 272) suggests, the Pipil demonstrative *ne* and the numeral *se:* 'one' must already have played some role in minor use patterns associated with definite and indefinite reference, respectively; but in the course of intense contact with Spanish, they became nearly a complete match of Spanish articles (see Section 7.2.3).

Van Pottelberge makes the following important point:

> Eine Parallelentwicklung ist z.B. die Entstehung des Artikels in verschiedenen indogermanischen Sprachen. In der Ursprache fehlten Artikel. Sie erscheinen zuerst im Altgriechischen und viele Jahrhunderte später auch in den germanischen und romanischen Sprachen sowie im Armenischen (Campbell 1991: I.97). Das[s] dabei eine Sprache die andere beeinflusst hätte, wäre nachzuweisen und dürfte nicht vorausgesetzt werden, bloß weil alle diese Sprachen Artikel haben und in unterschiedlichen Phasen ihrer Geschichte tatsächlich miteinander in Kontakt standen [A parallel development can be seen for example in the rise of the article in various Indo-European languages. In the proto-language, articles were absent. They appear first in Ancient Greek and many centuries later also in the Germanic and Romance languages as well as in Armenian. That this is due to one language influencing the other needs to be proven and should not be taken for granted, simply because all these languages have articles and in fact have been in contact with one another in different phases of their history.] (Van Pottelberge 2005).

In accordance with this observation, there are good reasons to ask whether the developments described in this chapter might not have happened without language contact. Note further that, as we observed above, the grammaticalization from demonstrative attributes to definite articles and from 'one' to indefinite articles is a ubiquitous process, to be observed in many genetically and areally unrelated languages. It is therefore quite possible—at least in some of the cases discussed—that the rise of article-like uses was not contact-induced.

However, we argue that language contact was instrumental in either propelling or accelerating the grammaticalization of articles in the majority of the cases discussed, especially for the following reasons. First, this is overwhelmingly the conclusion reached by experts who have dealt in some detail with the languages concerned (e.g. Breu 1994; Lötzsch 1996). Second, there is sociolinguistic evidence to the effect that it is exactly those languages that are known to have had a long history of contact with article languages such as German, Italian, or Greek that exhibit strongly developed article use patterns—Sorbian Kashubian, Czech, Slovenian, Macedonian, and Bulgarian being cases in point. And third, there is also geographical evidence, as we saw with reference to the situation among the Slavic languages. There is hardly any discernable grammaticalization in the easternmost languages (Standard Russian, Belorussian, Ukrainian), and the more one moves west and south, the higher the degree of grammaticalization of articles becomes. Accordingly, Breu remarks with reference to the western fringes of the Slavic world:

> Auch in Dialekten der westlichen Peripherie treten Demonstrativpronomina mit Artikelfunktion auf. Wir finden solche Phänomene sowohl auf slovenischem als auch auf tschechischem und insbesondere auf sorbischem Gebiet. [. . .] In allen Fällen dürfte das deutsche Adstrat, das in weiten Bereichen auch Superstrat war, der Auslöser für das Auftreten artikelähnlicher Funktionen von Demonstrativa gewesen sein [In dialects of the western periphery as well there are demonstrative pronouns with article functions. We find such phenomena both on Slovenian and Czech, and especially on Sorbian territory. [. . .] In all the cases it should have been the German adstrate, which in large areas also was a superstrate, that was the trigger for the appearance of article-like functions of demonstratives.] (Breu 1994: 54).

This issue raises another question—one that is equally relevant to the subject matters discussed in other chapters, namely to what extent is the presence of the structures discussed here due to genetic inheritance rather than to language contact? In a number of cases there is no conclusive answer to this question, but in other cases there is. For example, the fact that all modern Romance languages have fully grammaticalized articles might suggest that they inherited this property from their common ancestor language. However, there are some observations that contradict such a hypothesis. First, there is the fact that most Romance languages use preposed definite articles whereas Rumanian has a postposed article. Postposed articles are a salient property of the Balkan sprachbund, to which Rumanian belongs. What this suggests is that there appear to have been factors other than genetic relationship that can be held responsible for the fact that Rumanian diverges from other Romance languages in the placement of the definite article. Second, there are at least two different channels of grammaticalization in the development of definite articles in Romance languages. The predominant channel involved the Latin distal demonstrative *ille* (M)/*illa* (F)/*illud* (N) 'that', giving rise, for example, to articles such as French *le* (M)/*la* (F). But there is a second channel, whereby Latin *ipse* 'self-same' was grammaticalized to a definite article in Sardinian and Balearean Catalan (Stolz 2004: 18). Once again, we are led to assume that genetic inheritance does not provide an exhaustive explanation for the presence of definite articles in the modern Romance languages.

To conclude, while language contact is probably not the only factor that can be held responsible, it was at least a contributing factor for the emergence of definite and indefinite markers in Slavic as well as in peripheral languages of Europe. What is required now is a more detailed analysis of historical textual data to determine the exact role played by contact in this process.

4

The Rise of Possessive Perfects

It is widely held that typological similarity between languages in contact facilitates or is even a requirement for grammatical transfer to happen (Weinreich 1953: 33; Johanson 1992: 210; but see also Thomason & Kaufman 1988). Possessive perfects in European languages have been adduced as an example of contact-induced grammatical transfer and as providing evidence in support of this hypothesis (Dahl 1990: 7;[1] Haspelmath 1998: 275). In fact, there is clearly a positive correlation between the presence of a transitive verb meaning 'have' and that of a possessive perfect in Europe. For example, languages such as French and German have both, while Russian or Welsh have essentially neither. This seems to suggest that what is replicated in language contact is constrained by a factor that may be called 'linguistic compatibility', that is, the relative degree of structural similarity among the languages involved. One of the goals of the present chapter is to test this hypothesis (see Section 4.5). Another goal is to look into the nature and limits of replication.

As we noted in Chapter 2, the rise and evolution of grammatical categories is a gradual process whereby discourse-pragmatically defined pieces of recurrent texts, referred to as use patterns, may eventually give rise to new functional categories. Friedman (2003) makes the following observation on this process:

> The process of the grammaticalization of pragmatic devices is itself reflected in dialectal variation. Thus pragmatically determined discourse functions constitute additional categories and isoglosses. A synchronic continuum from discourse-based variation through grammaticalization can be interpreted as reflecting the diachronic development of grammatical competition through language contact (Friedman 2003: 110–11).

In fact, this process has both a temporal and a spatial dimension, and areal distribution can mirror sequences of diachronic evolution, as we will see below in our discussion of the situation in Macedonia.

[1] We concur with Östen Dahl (p.c.) that the role of a transitive 'have'-construction is presumably more important if there is no external language pressure.

Haspelmath (2001: 1495) observes that possessive perfects exist in some way or other in all Romance and Germanic languages (English, Frisian, Dutch, German, Danish, Swedish, Norwegian, and Icelandic), in some Slavic languages (Macedonian, Bulgarian, Serbian/Croatian, Czech), in Greek, and Albanian, and he considers them to constitute one of the salient typological properties defining Standard Average European as a linguistic area, and Dahl (1996: 365) notes that a possessive perfect is rarely found cross-linguistically, being confined almost exclusively to Europe. There are a few exceptions however. A construction similar to the possessive perfect of Standard Average European appears to have existed in Hittite, where the verb *hark-* 'hold, have' formed a perfect/resultative construction in periphrasis with a participle, confined mainly to transitive verbs (Jacob 1994: 48). Note further that the transitive perfect of Georgian seems to be based on the Goal Schema [Y is to/ for X] (e.g. 'The letter is-written to-me'), using a passive participle, where the perfect has a quasi-passive structure, with the agent in the dative case (Haspelmath 2001: 1495). Besides, in addition to this perfect, there is also a colloquial possessive perfect in Georgian that uses the lexical verb 'have' plus the participle. Mention should also be made of the fact that in the languages of the Old World between western Europe and India there are further examples; languages that have been mentioned include Old Indian, Old Iranian, Old Armenian, Old Egyptian, and Chukchi (see e.g. Vendryes 1937; Benveniste 1952; Jacob 1998: 106).[2] What distinguishes these cases from the ones discussed here is that they do not exhibit any marked areal clustering.

The following discussion is largely confined to some morphosyntactic properties of the categories concerned. Thus, issues that have figured prominently in the relevant literature, such as the semantic development from possessive via resultative to perfect (anterior) and to past tense meanings (but see Section 4.2.2), or the relationship between 'have'- and 'be'-periphrasis are not considered here in any detail (but see, e.g., Pietsch 2004*a*; Cennamo 2005).[3]

4.1 Introduction

What we call the possessive perfect has been referred to by a wide range of labels, such as possessive construction, 'have'-perfect, Romance perfect, stative perfect, resultative past, resultative perfect, perfect II, and the like (see e.g. Vasilev 1968: 227–8). These labels appear to suggest that the possessive

[2] Zygmunt Frajzyngier (p.c.) reports that another non-European language, the Chadic language Hdi of northern Cameroon, has a possessive perfect construction, too.

[3] We wish to thank Andrii Danylenko, Bridget Drinka, Zygmunt Frajzyngier, Victor Friedman, and Ulrich Obst for helpful comments and insightful suggestions on a previous draft of this chapter.

perfect has been associated with a variety of different grammatical forms and functions. For present purposes we will define a possessive perfect as a grammatical construction having the form of a possessive (or 'have'-) construction, with the agent of the construction receiving the same case marking as the possessor, but differing from the possessive construction in that, instead of a possessee noun phrase (i.e. one denoting the item possessed), there is a verb appearing in a non-finite form typically referred to as the past participle or the past passive participle (PPP)[4]—we will refer to this verb as the PPP-verb.

Frequently, the agent of the perfect and the possessor form the clausal subject (encoded in the nominative case), as in (4.1), but this is not always the case. In the North Russian example (4.2), for instance, both appear in the genitive case headed by a locative preposition (*u*), while the patient (or undergoer or theme) and the possessee (= the item possessed), respectively, take the nominative case.

(4.1) ENGLISH
(a) I have a car.
(b) I have built a house.

(4.2) NORTH RUSSIAN (Timberlake 1976)
(a) U menja mašina.
PREP me.GEN car.NOM
'I have a car.'

(b) U menja postroen dom.
PREP me.GEN built house.NOM
'I have built a house.'

Constructions akin to possessive perfects abound in European languages. In this chapter, we are restricted to canonical instances of them—that is, cases such as (4.1b) and (4.2b) are included while related constructions like English *I have a house built* are excluded. Furthermore, in a number of European languages, possessive perfects coexist with 'be'-perfects, that is, constructions using 'be'-copulas as auxiliaries. The latter are ignored here, and it would also be beyond the scope of the present treatment to study how the two constructions interact, in particular how the presence of one construction affects that of the other.

[4] Note that our definition is semantically based. It thus differs from definitions relying on morphosyntactic criteria, such as the requirement that the possessive verb must be transitive (see e.g. Haspelmath 1998: 1495). As we will see below, this difference is not a trivial one, in that the latter definition would exclude a number of constructions built on the same pattern as other possessive perfects (Enfield 2003).

When referring to the constructions looked at in this chapter, therefore, we are ignoring a problem that is central to some other researchers, namely the fact that the term 'possessive perfect' is somewhat misleading. In quite a number of European languages, this construction has a meaning that has little in common with a perfect (or a present anterior); as we pointed out in Section 1.4, for example, if a speaker of a dialect of southern Germany uses the construction, saying, for example, *Ich habe es getan* (I have it done) then s/he is unlikely to mean 'I have done it' but rather 'I did it'.[5] We will see in Section 4.2.2 that the possessive perfect in European languages expresses a range of different—even if related—meanings.

4.2 Dynamic typology

By dynamic typology we mean a cross-linguistic classification of grammatical categories according to salient structural properties which can be related in a principled way to the evolution of these categories. With reference to possessive perfects, this classification concerns salient stages of grammaticalization to be observed in the rise and development of the constructions concerned.

4.2.1 *Morphosyntax*

We argue that possessive perfects evolved in the languages of Europe in the course of the last two millennia as a result of the grammaticalization of possessive constructions, more precisely of constructions for predicative possession of the 'have'-type (Heine 1997*a*). On the basis of their evolution and structural characteristics (Vincent 1982; Pietsch 2004*a*; Cennamo 2005), the following main stages can be distinguished. (Note that languages are listed only once with reference to the most advanced stage they have reached, which does not mean, however, that a particular stage does not maintain the usage possibilities of a previous stage. Note further that, for a number of languages, there are conflicting analyses, especially with regard to whether a given language belongs to stage 0 or stage 1.)

Stage 0 (possession schema). There is a possessive 'have'-construction but no possessive perfect. This is essentially the situation found in Standard Russian, Lithuanian, Finnish, and Welsh (see Section 4.4.5).

In addition to the possessive meaning, the construction may include a statal-possessive use pattern where the (implied) agent of the PPP-verb is the same as the possessor—hence where the resultant state expressed by the

[5] An anonymous reviewer draws our attention to the 'double perfect' in the Bavarian dialect of German, e.g., *Ich hab' das gemacht gehabt* (I have that made had) 'I have done that'.

PPP-verb was brought about by prior action of the possession (see Pietsch 2004*a*: 6). This use pattern is likely to be constrained by linguistic and/or sociolinguistic factors, in that it may be restricted to specific types of PPP-verbs, such as accomplishment verbs, and/or to certain groups of speakers, or to spoken (rather than written) registers of the language. But frequently there is ambiguity between the possessive and the statal-possessive interpretation. Thus, as the description by Vasilev (1968: 219) suggests, in the Finnish example of (4.3) the possessor may but need not be referentially identical with the agent associated with the PPP-verb (*aloitettua*).

(4.3) FINNISH (Vasilev 1968: 219)

minulla	on	viisi	aloitettua	rakennusta.
(1.SG.ADE	3.SG.PRES.be	five.NOM	begin.SG.PART.PPP	building.SG.PART)

'I have started five buildings' (or 'I have five started buildings').

However, the authors dealing with languages that exhibit a stage 0 situation point out that uses other than clearly possessive ones are either not common or not commonly accepted (Vasilev 1968: 219; Jacob 1994: 47). Stage 0 situations are sometimes described as being bi-clausal or bi-propositional, in that there are two predicates represented respectively by the possessive verb and the PPP-verbs, where the latter is embedded in the former.[6]

Stage 1. Possession is no longer the primary meaning of the construction; rather, there is now a major resultative use pattern where the subject of the possessive verb is no longer conceived as a possessor but rather typically as an agent referentially identical with that of the PPP-verb, and the construction expresses a state of affairs resulting from the completion of the action denoted by the PPP-verb (cf. Pietsch 2004*a*). Typically, this state of affairs still holds at the time of reference, but at a more advanced stage this may no longer be the case.

Stage 1 tends to be portrayed as a mono-clausal construction exhibiting many or all of the following properties:

(i) Only transitive verbs are allowed as main verbs.

(ii) The PPP-verb still has the structure of a modifier of the patient, agreeing with the patient noun phrase in case, number, and/or gender (if there are such morphological categories).

(iii) Nevertheless, the possessive verb tends to be interpreted as an auxiliary and the PPP-verb as the new main verb.

[6] Such an account is proposed by Harris (2003: 541ff) in her treatment of the French and German possessive perfects. While she admits that the possessive perfect is based on an earlier notion of possession, she argues that this process is suggestive of a development from a bi-clausal to a mono-clausal structure, where the PPP is interpreted by her as being historically the main verb of an embedded clause.

(iv) Both the possessive and the PPP-verbs tend to be associated with one and the same agent.

Typically, in stage 1 languages the patient (i.e. in many languages the accusative object) must be overtly expressed; some languages, however, have reached a more advanced development where the patient can be suppressed.

Stage 1 situations have many properties of incipient categories; they are widely found in Slavic, in particular in Serbian, Croatian, Czech, Slovak, Polish, Slovenian, Bulgarian, and some Ukrainian and Belorussian dialects—as far as the descriptions available suggest. Further examples are Modern Irish and Basque, and the Spanish *tener*-perfect as well as the Irish English (Hiberno-English) possessive perfect also belong here, even if some southern dialects appear to have stage 2 properties (Lukas Pietsch, p.c.).

Early uses of possessive perfects tend to reflect to some extent the possessive meaning of their genesis, to combine with telic PPP-verbs and to denote present states existing as the result of a previous action, that is, to be confined to resultative meanings. Gradually then, resultatives give rise to perfect (anterior) meanings, where past actions are presented as being relevant to the present situation (see Bybee *et al.* 1994: 68–9).

At a more advanced stage there will be uses of transitive main verbs where the presence of an object is implied but the object noun phrase is omitted (see Jacob 1994: 219 on Latin).

Stage 2. The main new properties are:

(i) Instead of being transitive, the main verb may be intransitive.
(ii) A possessive interpretation is now ruled out.
(iii) Agreement in number and gender between the main verb and the object gradually disappears, that is, the PPP-verb tends to be presented in one invariable form.
(iv) There is no more ambiguity, that is, there is only one agent, which can no longer be interpreted as a possessor.

The Portuguese and Galician *ter*-perfects, Breton, as well as the North Russian[7] perfect have salient properties of stage 2. Furthermore, the development of the Late Latin possessive perfect[8] does not seem to have proceeded beyond stage 2.

[7] Since North Russian has employed the Location Schema [Y is located at X] instead of the Action Schema [X has Y] (see Heine 1997a), the underlying subject is encoded as a locational phrase and the underlying object in the nominative case (see Vasilev 1968; Timberlake 1976 for details).

[8] That Latin did not proceed beyond stage 2 is suggested by the fact that well into the sixth century AD its possessive perfect was restricted to animate subjects, agreement between the main verb and the PPP was still the rule, and the use of intransitive verbs was rare (Jacob 1994: 210, 218).

The transition from stage 1 to stage 2 appears to involve an intermediate stage where there either is no direct object (= patient participant) or else where phrases resembling direct objects are accepted as equivalents for direct objects, for example where the patient participant has properties of both a complement and an adjunct. In the development of Romance, such syntactically ambiguous participants included quantifying and other adverbs which were structurally adjuncts but were somehow accepted as substitutes for direct objects (cf. Jacob 1994: 220), while in early German the extension from transitive to intransitive verbs started out with transitive verbs in absolute use and with verbs having a 'that'-complement (cf. Bybee & Dahl 1989: 71).

Stage 3. The possessive perfect is now fully established and no longer subject to constraints:

(i) Instead of human agents there may now be inanimate 'agents'.
(ii) There are no or hardly any restrictions on the kinds of verbs serving as main verbs.

The result may be that the possessive perfect is generalized to the extent that alternative perfects decline and disappear; however this is not always the case. Stage 3 is the situation found in most Romance and Germanic languages, but also in southwestern Macedonian.

Map 4.1 shows the areal distribution of the various stages of the possessive perfect in European languages.

4.2.2 *Meaning*

Our concern in this chapter is with the morphosyntactic evolution of the possessive perfect. There is also some research on the semantic evolution of perfects (e.g. Bybee *et al.* 1994; Breu 1994: 56–8; Thieroff 2000; Detges 2000; Pietsch 2004*a*), and in the present section we summarize the main lines of the latter evolution as far as it relates to the possessive perfect.

What emanates from this research is that this evolution involves—in the same way as the morphosyntactic evolution—a unidirectional gradual process encompassing a number of intermediate stages. The initial stage once again consists of a use pattern that we referred to in Section 4.2 as the possession schema, while the final stage bears little semantic resemblance to the initial stage, in that there is now a use pattern that is restricted to expressing past time reference. The following evolutionary scenario[9] is based on the works cited above (see also Section 1.4) but differs from them

[9] For a more fine-grained scenario, see Pietsch (2004*a*: 6–7).

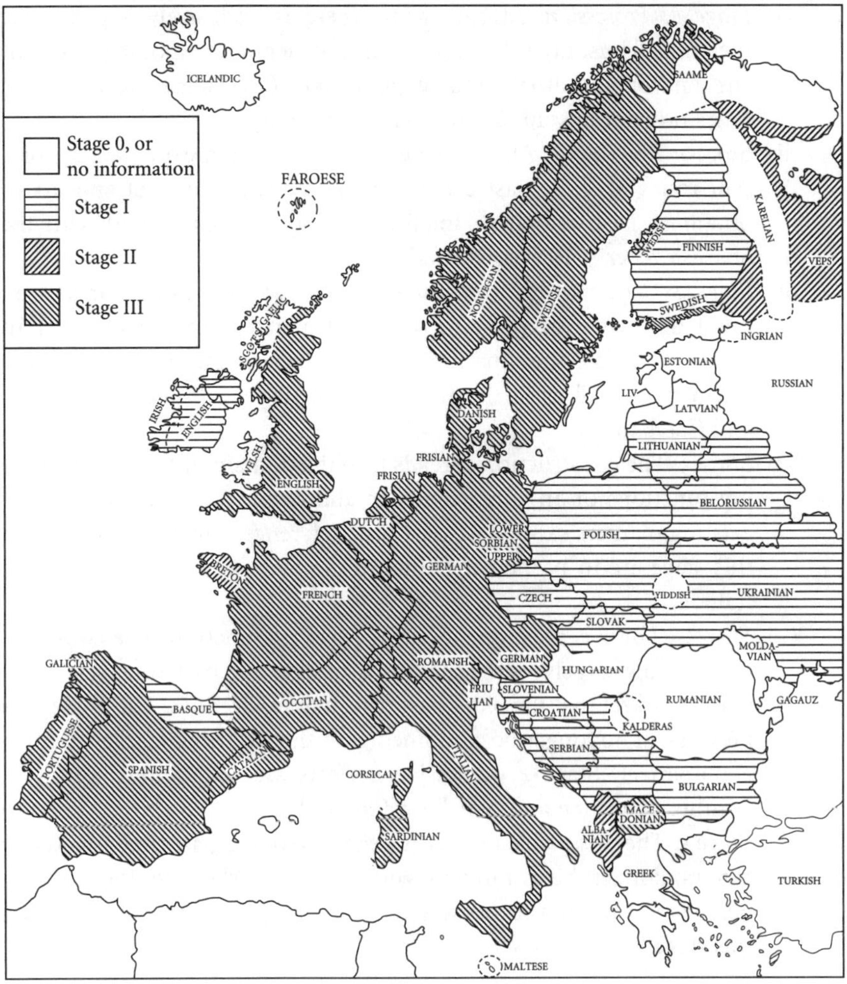

Map 4.1. The possessive perfect in Europe

in one important aspect: while those works are concerned generally with the development of tense–aspect marking, our interest here is specifically with that of the possessive perfect. Accordingly, the stages distinguished here do not exactly match those in Section 1.4,[10] and we look here only at languages having a possessive perfect category.

[10] Thus, the present stages 2 to 5 correspond to stages 0 to 3 in Section 1.4.

(i) *Stage 0: Possession.* At this stage, there is exclusively a possessive meaning. Thus, English *I have a car* may denote temporary, permanent, and/or any other kind of possession (see Heine 1997*a*), but it bears no relationship to tense–aspect marking.

(ii) *Stage 1: Resultative.* At this stage, the construction expresses the present result of some past event. This is the situation that appears to obtain in Irish and Irish English (see Section 4.4.3), and with the Spanish *tener* + PPP construction.[11]

(iii) *Stage 2: Perfect (= present anterior).* The construction expresses an event that occurred prior to the point of reference and has current relevance. This is the situation found in all Germanic languages except German, as well as in the Romance languages Portuguese, Spanish, and Catalan.

(iv) *Stage 3.* The construction spreads into the domain of the past, assuming functions of an aorist/preterite and competing with the already existing markers expressing past time reference. Languages exhibiting this stage are in particular Standard German, French, and Standard Italian.

(v) *Stage 4.* There is no more aorist or preterite function. The construction is now largely established as a marker for past time reference, with the effect that the older past time marker declines. The possessive perfect can no longer be combined with the past time marker to form a pluperfect. Stage 4 possessive perfects are found most of all in Southern German and Northern Italian dialects.

(vi) *Stage 5.* The possessive perfect is generalized as a past time marker. It can no longer be combined with future markers to form future perfects. None of the possessive perfects appears to have attained this stage.

These stages of functional evolution correlate to some extent with the morphosyntactic stages distinguished in Section 4.2.1, but the two must not be equated since there are a number of mismatches (see Section 4.2.3). The geographical distribution of the various functional stages exhibits a clear areal patterning (see Map 4.2): stage 1 is found only in Ireland (and in Spanish), while stage 2 is the situation to be encountered in the rest of northern and western Europe; it includes all Germanic languages except German, as well as the Romance languages Portuguese and Catalan. Within the centre of the stage 2 area there is the stage 3 area, surrounded by stage 2

[11] Detges (2000: 348) describes this Spanish construction as one that is well attested since the thirteenth century but shows no signs of turning into a perfect (stage 2).

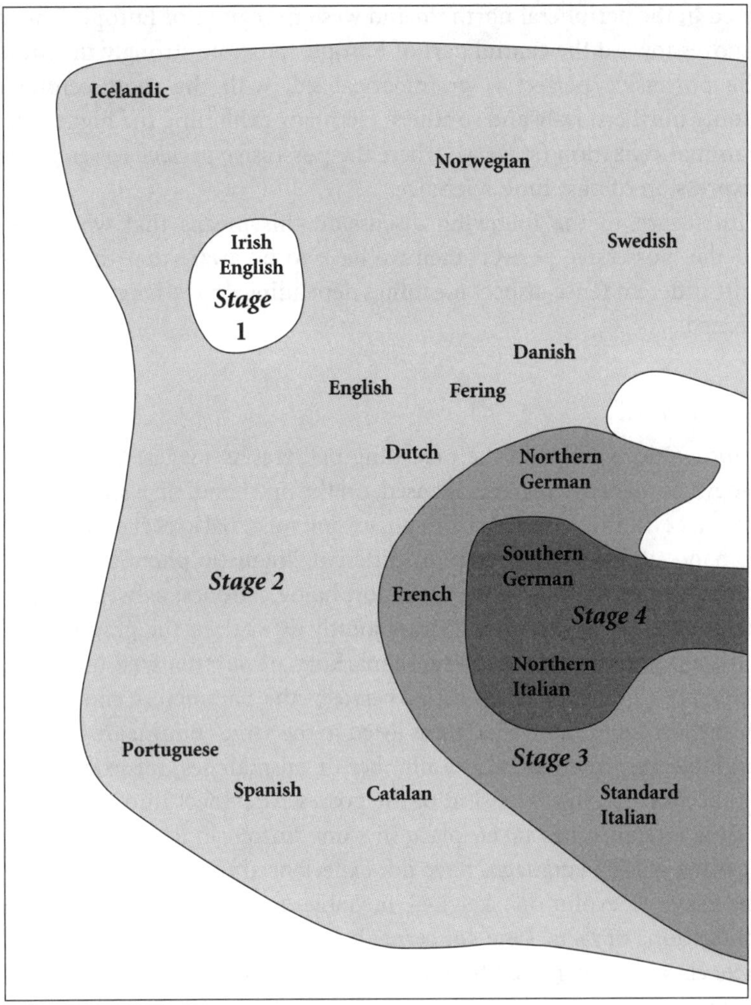

MAP 4.2. Stages in the semantic evolution of the possessive perfect (based on Thieroff 2000: 285)

languages. It includes Standard German (or Northern German), French, and Standard Italian (but not Northern Italian). The stage 4 area is geographically a centre within the centre, surrounded by stage 3 languages; it consists of Southern German and Northern Italian.

On the basis of this distribution, the following more general semantic development can be reconstructed (see Section 1.4 for a diachronic interpretation of this situation): the earliest stages of evolution (stages 1 and 2) are retained in the peripheral northern and western regions of Europe. The more one moves toward the central part of Europe, the more strongly the meaning of the possessive perfect is grammaticalized, with the most central area including northern Italy and southern Germany exhibiting the highest degree of grammaticalization (stage 4), where the possessive perfect serves primarily the expression of past time reference.

With regard to the following discussion this means that when we talk about the 'possessive perfect' then we have to be aware that this may refer to quite different tense–aspect meanings depending on the language or dialect concerned.

4.2.3 *Conclusion*

The observations made in the preceding paragraphs suggest that a dynamic typology of possessive perfects is based, on the one hand, on a straightforward conceptual evolution, leading from possession to verbal aspect schema. On the other hand, it involves a range of different linguistic phenomena, such as semantic, pragmatic, syntactic, and morphological ones, as well as different stages of evolution. The main factors jointly at work in the grammaticalization from possession to aspect–tense marking are summarized in Table 4.1.

There are significant correlations between the parameters and stages distinguished in Table 4.1, in that items listed in the same column are likely to co-occur. However, there are also a number of mismatches; for example, as we saw in Section 1.4, the extension of the possessive perfect into the domain of past time reference has taken place in some European languages at stage 3, while other stage 3 languages have not experienced this extension.

The scale of evolution sketched in Table 4.1 is based on a number of simplifications of facts. One concerns the nature of stages: rather than with discrete classes having fixed boundaries, we are dealing with continuum-like situations where a construction may still have the properties of a preceding stage while in other contexts it exhibits the properties of a subsequent stage, where context relates on the one hand to linguistic structures and on the other hand to sociolinguistic parameters such as speaker communities.

The continuum-like nature of the evolution is most conspicuous in the case of agreement between the PPP-verb and the patient noun phrase: the unidirectional development from full agreement to invariable PPP-verb is a gradual process that may start at stage 1 and extend beyond stage 2, that is, relics of agreement may still be found in stage 3 situations; as the history of the Romance languages shows, the loss of gender–number agreement proceeded gradually over more than fourteen centuries, and some agreement structures

TABLE 4.1. The main structural changes in the grammaticalization of possessive perfects

	Parameter/ Stage	0	1	2	3
a	Nature of subject	Possessor	Agent		Inanimate 'agent'
b	Possessive verb	Main verb	Auxiliary		
c	Properties of the PPP-verb	Modifier of patient, showing agreement with the patient	Main verb	Agreement with patient lost	
d	Valency of PPP-verb	Headed by patient	Patient may be suppressed	May be an intransitive verb	
e	Propositional meaning	Possession, resultant state	Resultative (possession irrelevant)	Perfect: Action completed in the past has current relevance	Past action
f	Propositional syntax	Main proposition + embedded proposition	(Embedded >) main proposition		

have survived in modern Romance languages (Jacob 1994), as the following Italian example illustrates:

(4.4) ITALIAN (Anderson 1997: 14)
Giovanni la ha accusata.
Giovanni her has accused.F.SG
('Giovanni has accused her.')[12]

The evolutionary scenario presented above is not the first one to be proposed; a number of alternative classifications have been suggested to describe the evolution of possessive perfects in terms of a limited set of stages (e.g. Vasilev 1968; Fleischman 1982*a*; Harris & Ramat 1987; Jacob 1994; Heine 1997*a*: 192–3; Squartini & Bertinetto 2000; Kuteva 2001: 40–2; Drinka 2003*a*). For example, in his discussion of Slavic languages, Vasilev (1968: 215) distinguishes between

[12] The translation is ours.

languages where the possessive perfect is confined to transitive verbs constructed as PPPs which agree in gender and number with the object (his type 3a), languages where the perfect is used with transitive verbs but an invariable PPP (his type 3), languages using intransitive verbs in addition with an invariable PPP (his type 2). His type 3a is suggestive of an early stage 1 and type 3 of an advanced stage 1 situation, while his type 2 is suggestive of our stage 2.

The scale in Table 4.1 agrees in its main points with earlier treatments but differs from them in one aspect: while previous works were devoted to the analysis of one particular language or group of closely related languages, the present work attempts to generalize across languages and genetic boundaries. The advantage this approach has *vis-à-vis* previous ones is that it allows for possessive perfects to be viewed as a more general phenomenon that is not restricted essentially to Romance and Germanic languages. The disadvantage inherent in such an approach is that it ignores many of the idiosyncratic developments characterizing individual constructions and languages.

4.3 Notes on history

In spite of all the historical records that are available, the history of possessive perfects in European languages is in larger parts still unclear, being characterized by controversies and contradicting theses, for example on whether there was a monogenetic or a polygenetic origin for these constructions: there are authors who argue for a single origin of possessive perfects in Europe (e.g. Vendryes 1937) while others maintain that the Germanic languages acquired their possessive perfects independent of Romance languages (Panzer 1984), and/or that speakers of North Russian developed their possessive perfect independent of other European languages (Maslov 1949). And even among authors arguing for a monogenetic origin, there is a wide range of views, especially on the question of which language was the ultimate donor. In view of this situation, the following discussion has to be taken with care.

4.3.1 *Hypotheses*

On the basis of the evidence that is available we propose the following hypotheses:

(i) The spread of possessive perfects across Europe is mainly due to language contact.

(ii) The diffusion of these constructions across languages did not involve borrowing, that is a transfer of form–meaning units, but rather the replication of a process whereby a possessive construction was grammaticalized to a construction marking aspect (and in some cases later on also tense).

(iii) In accordance with (ii), the process is unidirectional, conforming to the evolution sketched in Section 4.2.

Perfect (or anterior) categories found in the languages of the world have a limited number of conceptual sources (see Bybee *et al.* 1994). Among these sources, possessive constructions are rarely found; more importantly, however, possessive perfects resulting from a development as sketched in Section 4.2 are essentially only found in Europe. On typological grounds, therefore, it seems unlikely that such constructions arose independently in different European languages; rather, the rise of these constructions must have been due to historical factors. This leaves us with areal relationship as the most likely historical factor, and with (i) and (ii) as the most plausible hypotheses.[13] The possibility that the possessive perfect arose independently in two or even more European languages cannot entirely be ruled out. This, however, would not impair the gist of hypothesis (i), according to which language contact was a contributing factor in the spread of possessive perfects in European languages.

That the European possessive perfects are the result of grammaticalization processes has been demonstrated in a number of different works (e.g. Harris 1982; Vincent 1982; Bybee & Dahl 1989; Bybee *et al.* 1994; Jacob 1994; Pietsch 2004*a*). What this suggests is that the evolution was unidirectional; in fact, we are not aware of any author or any evidence suggesting that there has ever been a reversed development, for example leading from perfect aspect to possessive construction. Hypothesis (iii) can therefore be assumed to be fairly uncontroversial. So far, however, work has focused on Standard Average European languages, in particular on Romance languages (see e.g. Harris 1982; Vincent 1982; Jacob 1994). Languages spoken at the periphery of this linguistic area have received considerably less attention, and it is these languages that will be at the centre of our interest in this chapter.

4.3.2 *Latin and later*

According to a widespread view, the ultimate donor of European possessive perfects was Ancient Greek: According to Drinka (2003*b*), a new transitive periphrastic perfect formed with 'have' + active aorist participle is found in

[13] For Old Iranian and Old Armenian—both of which are spoken outside Europe—Benveniste (1952) argues that language contact is a highly unlikely factor for the development of the possessive perfect.

the writings of the fifth-century BC Tragedians, Sophocles and Euripides, as well as in Herodotus. Greek is said to have provided the model for Latin, with subsequent development of the construction in Romance and subsequently in other western European languages (Vendryes 1937: 92; Lockwood 1968: 115; Drinka 2003*b*: 123). This view is not uncontroversial though, especially in view of the fact that there are authors who argue that the possessive perfect developed independently in Germanic[14] and perhaps also in other languages (see Jacob 1994: 50 for a review).

The possessive perfect has its roots in early Latin, where it is attested with accomplishment verbs such as *coquere* 'to cook', *collocare* 'to gather', *claudere* 'to close', or *scribere* 'to write', while its use with stative verbs like *cognoscere* 'to know' was rare in early Latin but frequent from the classical period onward,[15] and activity verbs such as *dicere* 'to say' or *exquisire* 'to ask, examine' were rarely used prior to the Late Latin period.

In Classical Latin, the *habere* + PPP construction still had the appearance of a minor use pattern—that is, it was lexically severely restricted. However, since the classical period there are examples where there is reference identity between the subject of *habere* and the agent of the PPP,[16] and where *habere* could be interpreted as an auxiliary of anterior aspect (Cennamo 2005: 4).

As a result of a gradual process, the possessive perfect emerged in Late Latin as a distinct periphrastic active aspect category of stage 1. It denotes current relevance of a past event (= present anterior), spreading into narrative contexts, and being used interchangeably with the older synthetic perfect, eventually ousting the latter. And it exhibits a number of the traits of an advanced stage 1 situation (Cennamo 2005: 2, 5): there are examples where the object participant could be omitted (4.5a), and where there is no more agreement between the object and the PPP (4.5b).

(4.5) LATE LATIN (Cennamo 2005)

(a)

de	ea	re	supra	scriptum	habemus.
About	this.ABL	thing.ABL	above	write.PPP.N.SG	have.PRES.1.PL

'(As) we have written above on the matter.' (Vitr. 91, 14)

(b)

haec	omnia	probatum	habemus.
this.PL	all.PL	experience.PPP.N.SG	have.PRES.1.PL

'We have experienced all these things.' (Orib. *Syn.* 7, 48)

14 Evidence for a separate origin includes the observation that 'have'-constructions are said to have been widespread in languages which were not in direct contact with Latin or the Romance languages, such as Old English, Old Saxon, Proto-Scandinavian, and Old Norse (Panzer 1984: 116).

15 In Ciceronian Latin, *habere* was found with verbs such as 'learn', 'discover', 'persuade', and 'compel' (Harris 1982: 47).

16 Such reference identity is found in early authors such as Cato (Cennamo 2005: 4).

In the sixth century there were more examples of transitive verbs without agreement, and eventually the construction was extended to intransitive PPP-verbs, thus becoming a stage 2 construction[17] (cf. Bybee & Dahl 1989: 72).

According to Haspelmath (1998: 285), possessive perfects diffused across Europe at the time of transition between antiquity and the Early Middle Ages. In Iberian languages, *habere* was superseded by later reflexes of Latin *tenire* 'to hold' as a possessive verb, and possessive perfects based on *tenire* emerged fairly late. The Spanish *tener*-perfect gradually arose from the thirteenth century onwards, and, at the present time, it is confined to transitive verbs, that is, it did not proceed beyond stage 1.[18] The Portuguese *ter*-perfect on the other hand has reached stage 2: it has spread to intransitive verbs (Vincent 1982: 92). In Catalan, the *tenir*-perfect appears to have had a short lifespan: it is attested as a resultative from roughly 1600 up to the eighteenth century, and since around 1700 occasionally as a past tense marker, but the grammaticalization process was discontinued around 1800 (Steinkrüger 1995: 57).

No conclusive evidence is available on when Albanian developed a possessive perfect, owing to the complete lack of significant textual data for Albanian prior to the mid-sixteenth century, at which time the 'have'-perfect is established (cf. Demiraj 1985: 84). The fact that 'have' as a perfect-forming auxiliary is more widespread in Tosk Albanian than in Geg Albanian is suggestive of contact, as is the very significant and very old Latin component.[19] In other words, there is no conclusive evidence for an external model for the possessive perfect in Albanian, but the possibility that Latin was the donor cannot be ruled out.

That possessive perfects spread via replication from Romance languages to Germanic is the most plausible hypothesis on typological grounds, and this hypothesis is maintained in some way or other by a number of authors (see e.g. Vasilev 1968: 227; Drinka 2003*a*, 2003*b*). However, there remain a number of problems. It is unclear, in particular, when and how such a transfer should have taken place, and which languages exactly were involved in the process. Moreover, the internal situation within Germanic does not seem to provide

[17] Cennamo (2005: 10) finds only the following example of an intransitive agent in the seventh century:

sicut	parabolatum	habuistis.
as	speak.PPP.N.SG	have.PERF.2.PL

'As you (PL) have said (lit.: spoken).' (Form. Merkel. 260, 7)

[18] As Detges (2000) has shown, the Spanish *tener* + PPP is not what is commonly assumed to be a resultative construction but rather what he calls 'Resultative II', where the state of affairs concerns the current result of an action but where the subject referent is the agent of a past event.

[19] With thanks to Victor Friedman (p.c.) for pointing out this argument to us.

strong evidence for this hypothesis. Gothic and Old High German had a transitive 'have'-construction involving an object modified by a PPP which agreed with the object noun in gender and number.[20] This construction is suggestive essentially of Stage 0, where a possessive interpretation is always possible while an aspectual interpretation is not, cf. (4.6).[21]

(4.6) OLD HIGH GERMAN (Tatian; Critchley 1983: 137)

phîgboum	habêta sum	giflanzôtan	in	sînemo	wîngarten.
fig.tree	he.had	planted	in	his	vineyard

'He had a fig-tree, planted in his vineyard.'

That this grammaticalization represents an early stage in the evolution of the construction is suggested by the fact that in Old High German there were two possessive verbs competing as auxiliaries: *habên* and *eigan* (Lockwood 1968: 115). By Notker's time, approximately 1000 AD, fairly clear instances of a stage 1 perfect can be found, in that instead of object noun phrases, reflexives could be used, and the construction was extended to intransitive verbs, even if many instances of the new usage pattern were still open to a possession interpretation. At this stage, the transition from participial modifier of the object noun phrase to main verb is also revealed by the fact that, when used in the perfect construction, the PPP lost in adjectival properties: instead of the adjectival negation prefix *un-* 'un-', the negation of the perfect is expressed with the negative particle *niht* 'not'[22] (Harris 2003: 543–4). To conclude, German appears to have turned into a stage 2 language by around 1000 AD. But it is only since the fifteenth century that the new perfect was grammaticalized to the extent that it could be used with *haben* 'have' as its main verb (e.g. *hat gehabt* 'has had').

In English, the rise of the possessive perfect goes back to the earliest stages of Old English, where it was used only in possessive contexts as an early stage 1 construction associated with resultative uses (Bybee *et al.* 1994: 68):

(4.7) OLD ENGLISH (Mitchell 1985; cited from Anderson 1997: 13)

hu	Þu	me	hæfst	afrefredne.
how	you	me	have	comforted.M.SG.ACC

('How you have comforted me.')[23]

[20] The evidence in Gothic, however, is not entirely clear. For example, Lockwood (1968: 114–15) remarks that a possessive perfect was unknown in Gothic (*c.* 350 AD).

[21] Conceivably, however, (4.6) was a literal translation from Latin (Lockwood 1968: 115).

[22] There is an additional property characterizing the grammaticalization of the German possessive perfect: while at stage 1 there were two possessive verbs, *haben* and *eigan*, the use of the latter verb was discontinued with the transition from stage 1 to stage 2, that is, *haben* became the only perfect auxiliary (Harris 2003: 543).

[23] No translation is provided by the authors.

An advanced stage 1 possessive perfect must have existed, however, in North Germanic from the Runic Scandinavian languages to Edda; some of the examples show a lack of gender–number agreement, and the object could be omitted (Panzer 1984: 123).

On the basis of such observations, it would seem that the hypothesis of a transfer of possessive perfects from Romance to Germanic cannot be taken to be the last word on this issue.

4.4 The periphery

Our main interest in this chapter, however, is not with Romance and Germanic languages, most of which have fairly strongly grammaticalized stage 3 possessive perfects, but rather with the languages spoken at the periphery of the Romance- and Germanic-speaking territories. The development in these languages tends to be described as being contact-related; the prevailing hypothesis is summarized appropriately by Drinka (see also Breu 1994: 54):

> What is interesting to note is that just in those areas where Slavic and other non-western European languages come in contact with languages using HAVE as an auxiliary, a HAVE-type auxiliary has tended to appear (Drinka 2003*a*: 6).

In the following sections we will test this hypothesis. Our main concern will be with Slavic and Celtic languages.

4.4.1 *Slavic languages*

In spite of all the research that has been carried out on the possessive perfect, the situation in many Slavic languages is still far from clear, especially with reference to which stage a given construction has attained. We have come across quite a number of controversial classifications on this issue, and the following generalizations therefore have to be taken with care.

Introduction. Old Church Slavonic (863–950 AD) had a past passive participle formed exclusively from transitive verbs, but it had no possessive perfect (Friedman 1976: 97).[24] The situation in modern Slavic languages tends to be portrayed as one where the presence of a possessive perfect is the exception rather than the rule. Table 4.2 summarizes this situation with reference to the types distinguished in Section 4.2. Note that in quite a number of cases, there are alternative analyses of the situation in the language concerned.

[24] Friedman (1976: 97) refers to this construction as an analytic one being 'midway between a true perfect and an adjectival construction', occurring in Bulgarian and Serbian.

TABLE 4.2. Types of possessive perfect in Slavic languages

Language	Stage 0	1	2	3
Standard Russian	+			
Polish	+	+		
Ukrainian (dial.)	+	+		
Belorussian (dial.)	+	+		
Czech	+	+		
Slovak	+	+		
Upper Sorbian	+	+		
Slovenian	+	+		
Serbian	+	+		
Croatian	+	+		
Bulgarian	+	+		
Southern Thracian Bulgarian	+	+	+	
North Russian	+	+	+	
Southwestern Macedonian	+	+	+	+

The data presented in Table 4.2 show that possessive perfects in Slavic languages are not nearly as strongly grammaticalized as they are in Romance and Germanic. With the exception of southwestern Macedonian,[25] we have found no stage 3 possessive perfect in Slavic languages. Two language varieties have developed a stage 2 perfect: Southern Thracian Bulgarian, and North Russian, while other language varieties exhibit a less strongly grammaticalized, stage 1 possessive perfect, and Standard Russian does not exhibit any noteworthy grammaticalization. In the remainder of this section we will illustrate the information summarized in Table 4.2. For reasons to be outlined below, North Russian and Southwestern Macedonian will be discussed separately.

An overview. The situation in Standard Russian is suggestive of a stage 0 situation, although stage 1 use patterns can be found in colloquial Russian. Thus, examples such as the following have been reported:

(4.8) COLLOQUIAL RUSSIAN (Vasilev 1968: 219)
u nego vsë prigotovleno.
(at he.GEN all prepare.PPP.SG.N)
'He has prepared everything.'

[25] Note that Southwestern Macedonian overlaps with Standard Macedonian since the latter is based on western dialects.

Such use patterns, however, do not appear to be commonly accepted with a possessive perfect interpretation (Vasilev 1968: 219).[26]

Polish is said to have a stage 1 resultative strongly associated with possession (of the kind 'I have a written book'; Jacob 1994: 47), illustrated below:

(4.9) POLISH (Vasilev 1968: 219)
mam miejsce zamówione na dzisiejsze widowisko.
(have.1SG.PRES seat reserve.PPP on today show)
'I have reserved a seat (lit.: 'a reserved seat') for today's show.'

According to Vasilev (1968: 226), the Polish possessive perfect has been influenced by German, and Weinreich notes:

> In Silesia, the German verbal construction *haben* + past participle has been reproduced in Polish to function as a past tense: *ja to mam sprzedane* 'I have sold it', after *ich habe es verkauft* [...] (Weinreich [1953] 1964: 41).

The two Sorbian languages[27] are said to lack an established possessive perfect, even if it is claimed (Danylenko 2001*b*: 5) that 'mostly colloquially' there is one in both Lower and Upper Sorbian. In fact, (Upper) Sorbian has an advanced stage 1 possessive perfect construction, [*měc*' 'have' + DO + PPP] (Faßke und Michalk 1981: 224–32), which is used with transitive verbs (and a very limited number of intransitive verbs; for details see Faßke und Michalk 1981: 228–9). The direct object (= patient noun) agrees in case–gender–number with the PPP:

(4.10) (UPPER) SORBIAN (Faßke und Michalk 1981: 225)
Jan ma polo zworane.
(Jan have.3.SG.PRES field.ACC.NEUT.SG plow.PPP.ACC.NEUT.SG)
'Jan has plowed the field.'

In some cases, the patient noun may be omitted, whereby the PPP takes the accusative singular neuter form:

(4.11) (UPPER) SORBIAN (Faßke und Michalk 1981: 229)
mam kazane.
have.1.SG.PRES say.PPP.ACC.SG.NEUT
'I have said.'

[26] However, it can be used in the sense, e.g., that he did not prepare it himself, or at least alone (Dahl, p.c.).

[27] Sorbian consists of two written languages, Upper Sorbian and Lower Sorbian. Whenever we simply use the term 'Sorbian', we refer to phenomena that concern both languages.

The possessive perfect in (Upper) Sorbian has characteristics of an incipient category of stage 1: it is used frequently in colloquial speech and in various dialects. The same construction appears rather rarely, however, in the written language, and whenever it is used, it is not stylistically neutral. Moreover, it can sometimes be interpreted as having a possession meaning rather than a perfect meaning. In the following example, the context—as well as the word order—indicate that the verb *měješe* 'had' is used as a full lexical, possession-denoting verb (Faßke und Michalk 1981: 232):

(4.12) (UPPER) SORBIAN (Faßke und Michalk 1981: 232)

Horbank	měješe	w	pincy	hišc'e
(H.	have.3.SG.PAST	in	cellar	still
blešu	wina	schowanu.		
bottle.ACC	wine	hide.PPP.ACC)		

'Horbank still had a bottle of wine hidden in the cellar.'

The following example suggests that the possessive perfect also occurs in dialects of Ukrainian; we appear to be dealing with an advanced stage 1 construction, where the object can be deleted:

(4.13) UKRAINIAN DIALECTS (Danylenko 2001*b*: 21)

u	nas	(pole)	vyorano.
at	we.GEN	field.ACC.SG.N	plough.PPP.SG.N

'We have ploughed (the field).'

Note that this is only a dialectal use. There exist other dialects in the Ukraine where the structure [*u* 'at'+ GEN + ACC + PPP] has a possessive meaning and does not imply that the possessor (the sentential subject) is also the agent of the action in the participle:

(4.14) WESTERN UKRANIAN, Bukovina dialect (Natalia Bugay, p.c.)

U	nas	(pole)	vyorano.
at	we.GEN	field.ACC.SG.N	plough.PPP.SG.N

'We have a ploughed field'/'We have our field ploughed.'

(4.15) WESTERN UKRANIAN, Bukovina dialect (Natalia Bugay, p.c.)

U	mene	lekcija	vidrukuvana	na	sin'omu	paper'.
at	I.GEN	lecture.SG.F	print.PPP.SG.F	on	blue	paper

'I have the lecture printed out on blue paper.'

Overall, it seems that in most cases the past is used in Ukrainian in order to express anterior meaning:

(4.16) UKRANIAN (Danylenko and Vakulenko 1995: 61)

Jakyj	ty	buv,	takyj	ty
what.NOM.M	you.NOM	be.PAST.M	such.NOM.M	you.NOM

zalyšyvsia.
remain.PAST.M
'You have remained as you were.'

Passive-anterior meaning is expressed by a specialized construction [ACC + PPP.SG.N]:

(4.17) UKRANIAN (Danylenko and Vakulenko 1995: 62)

My	pryjšly,	bo	nas	poklykano.
(we.NOM	come.PAST.PL	because	we.ACC	call.PPP.SG.N)

'We came because we had been called.'

Danylenko (2001*b*: 21) points out that in Belorussian dialects one comes across examples of the possessive perfect parallel to the ones in Ukranian, see (4.14) above.

According to Isačenko (1974: 73), Czech has developed from possession to a very productive construction ['have' + accusative noun + perfective past participle], rapidly spreading in the colloquial varieties. Breu (1994: 55) concedes that Czech has a possessive perfect but hastens to add that it does not appear to have achieved any marked degree of grammaticalization. Example (4.18) illustrates this construction, which is suggestive of a stage 1 situation, used with transitive verbs and agreement between PPP and object. Tommola (2000: 464) gives further examples of the Czech possessive perfect.

(4.18) CZECH (Bybee & Dahl 1989: 70)

Maš	výčištěné	zuby?
have.you	cleaned.PL	teeth

'Have you brushed your teeth?'

According to Vasilev (1968: 226), the possessive perfect in Czech has been influenced by German. In fact, Garvin (1949: 84) had reported earlier that Czech replicated the German 'have'-perfect by using its verb for 'have, own' with the passive participle, even though there was already a perfect formed with the auxiliary 'to be' plus past participle. But the new construction has traits of a conclusive perfect, differing from the already existing one by 'differentiating what in English would be the contrast of "I've got it done" and "I've done it".'

Much of what we observed on Czech also applies to Slovak: it appears to have a weakly grammaticalized stage 1 possessive perfect whose rise is said to have been influenced by German (Vasilev 1968: 226). The following is an example:

(4.19) Slovak (Vasilev 1968: 219)
lóžu už máme kúpenú.
(theatre.box already have.1.PL.PRES buy.PPP)
'We have already bought a (theatre) box.'

In Slovenian, Vasilev (1968: 218) found what he calls a type 3a perfect, that is, a transitive possessive perfect formed by means of PPP-verbs agreeing with the object in gender and number, for example:

(4.20) Slovenian (Vasilev 1968: 219)
imam pismo že napisano.
(have.1.SG.PRES letter.SG.NEUT already write.PPP.SG.NEUT)
'I have already written the letter.'

The Slovenian construction tends to be portrayed in the literature as resultative, being strongly associated with a possessive function (of the kind 'I have a written book'; Jacob 1994: 47), and Breu (1994: 55) says that Slovenian has a possessive perfect which, however, does not appear to have reached any marked degree of grammaticalization.

Both Serbian and Croatian present stage 1 situations, where the possessive perfect is said to be strongly associated with a possessive function (Jacob 1994: 47). Accordingly, Breu (1994: 55) says that Serbian/Croatian has a possessive perfect which does not appear to have attained any marked degree of grammaticalization. Vasilev (1968: 218) found what he calls a type 3a perfect, that is, a transitive possessive perfect formed by means of PPP-verbs agreeing with the object in gender and number in both Serbian and Croatian:

(4.21) Serbian, Belgrad (Vasilev 1968: 218)[28]
imam kupljene cipele.
(have.1.SG.PRES buy.PPP.PL shoe.PL)
'I have bought shoes.'

(4.22) Croatian, Zagreb (Vasilev 1968: 218)
imamo plaćen račun.
(have.1.PL pay.PPP.SG.M bill.SG.M)
'We have paid a bill.'

[28] Elvira Veselinović (p.c.) observes, however, that this example is an instance of stage 0, that is, that it constitutes a possessive rather than a perfect construction.

The areal impact on the development of the possessive perfect is demonstrated by the fact that Vasilev (1968: 220) found an advanced stage 1 possessive perfect among Croats living in Burgenland, where they are surrounded by Germans. This construction is of Vasilev's type 3, the PPP-verb no longer exhibits agreement with the object.

The Bulgarian possessive perfect is described as a recent category still being in a process of development (Vasilev 1968: 229), and Breu (1994: 55) says that the possessive perfect of Bulgarian has 'a dialectal appearance'. As early as Old Bulgarian, historical documents abound with occurrences of the structure ['have' + direct object + PPP], where the PPP was used as an adjectival modifier of the direct object. Examples of a stage 1 possessive perfect are found since the end of the nineteenth century, that is, two centuries after the possessive perfect had developed in Macedonian. Modern Bulgarian is an advanced stage 1 language; the following examples illustrate the various structures found in this language (for more details, see Kuteva 2001: 40–2): Example (4.23a) is an instance of the possession stage 0, while (4.23b) illustrates the transitional (ambiguity) situation, where the subject can be interpreted either as a possessor or an agent. In (4.23c), the subject is unambiguously the agent and the participle is reinterpreted as the main verb. Finally, example (4.23d) suggests that Bulgarian has reached an advanced stage 1 situation, in that the patient (object) can be omitted.

(4.23) Bulgarian (Kuteva 2001: 40–2)

(a) Imam tezi lekcii.
have.1.SG these lectures
'I have these lectures (i.e. the materials for the lectures).'

(b) Imam gi napisani.
have.1.SG them write.PPP.PL
'I have them written.'

(c) Imam napisani tezi lekcii.
have.1.SG write.PPP.PL these lectures
'I have written these lectures.'

(d) Imam sgotveno.
have.1.SG cook.PPP.SG.N
'I have cooked.'

But Bulgarian has not proceeded to stage 2, in that the construction may not be used with intransitive main verbs (Kuteva 2001: 42).

According to some authors, the possessive perfect in Bulgarian is the result of language-internal development; according to other authors it is due to contact with Western European languages. However, it seems much more natural to assume that Macedonian is the major factor for the development of the Bulgarian possessive perfect for the following two reasons (Friedman 1976: 98–101):

(i) The southeast Bulgarian dialects of Thrace and Strandža—where the possessive perfect occurs with transitive verbs and non-agreeing neuter participles—could represent continuations of the southeast Macedonian dialects of Northern Greece rather than separate Bulgarian developments. The Thracian Bulgarian dialects border on the easternmost Macedonian dialects of Northern Greece (the Strandža dialects are directly to the north and east of Thrace), and so these dialects can be said to represent the furthest extent of the Macedonian possessive perfect.

(ii) The dialects of Macedonia north and east of the river Vardar have essentially the same characteristics with regard to the possessive perfects as the neighbouring Bulgarian and Serbian dialects.

Data on Southern Thracian Bulgarian are scanty; but on the basis of Vasilev's description (Vasilev 1968: 216–18) we will assume that, at least in the varieties spoken around Xanthi (West Thrace) and Malkara (East Thrace), there is a fairly well-established and commonly used possessive perfect of stage 2. Example (4.24a) is suggestive of a stage 1 situation, where a transitive verb is used and the main verb shows agreement with the object (= patient; Vasilev's type 3a). Example (4.24b) exhibits stage 1, where there is a transitive verb but no more agreement (Vasilev's type 3), and (4.24c) illustrates a stage 2 situation, where an intransitive verb is used (Vasilev's type 2).

(4.24) SOUTHERN THRACIAN BULGARIAN (Vasilev 1968: 217)

(a)

tŭva	pčela	e	imam	fatena	tva	l'ato.
(this	bee.SG.F	ACC.F	have.1.SG.PRES	catch.PPP.SG.F	this	summer)

'This bee I've caught this summer.'

(b)

meč(ka	n'amam	ubijenu.
(bear.NOM	not.have.1.SG.PRES	kill.PPP.SG.N)

'I've killed no bear.'

(c)

tugava	ošte	nemax	xodeno	na	kasabata.
(then	still	not.have.1.SG.PAST	go.PPP.SG.N	on	town)

'At that time I had not yet gone to town.'

Vasilev (1968: 223–5) assumes that it was influence from Greek that can be held responsible for the rise of a stage 2 perfect in Southern Thracian Bulgarian.

However, this is not the only analysis offered in the literature: it has also been proposed that Macedonian could have influenced the Southern Thracian possessive perfect (Mladenov 1935).

North Russian. North Russian differs drastically from contemporary Standard Russian in having a stage 2 possessive perfect. Unlike other Slavic languages, however, it is not based on the Action Schema of possession [X has Y] (see e.g. Vasilev 1968; Timberlake 1976; Panzer 1984).[29] Example (4.25a) shows that possession in North Russian is encoded by the Location Schema [Y is located at X]. Example (4.25b) is representative of the bridging stage 1, where Standard Russian only allows for a possessive interpretation (4.25b, i) while North Russian has a perfect interpretation in addition (4.25b, ii). That the North Russian possessive perfect has reached stage 2 is suggested by the fact that it can be used with intransitive verbs (4.25c). The erstwhile prepositional phrase, expressing the underlying agent, appears to have acquired subject properties to the extent that it can be conjoined with canonical subjects (4.25d) and used in an absolutive construction with the object being omitted. Accordingly, Vasilev (1968: 220) finds in North Russian examples for both his types 2 (invariable participle, intransitive verb) and 3 (invariable participle and transitive verb) of a possessive perfect. Note further that in some dialects the subject properties of the agent include agreement between the agent and the main verb (= participle; Koptjevskaja-Tamm & Wälchli 2001: 690). However, the North Russian possessive perfect has not reached stage 3, in that it may not be used with inanimate nouns (except for metaphorically transferred animacy; Timberlake 1976).[30]

(4.25) North Russian (Vasilev 1968: 220–1; Timberlake 1976; Panzer 1984: 120)

(a)

U	menja	mašina.
PREP	me.GEN	car.NOM

'I have a car.'

(b)

U	menja	postroen	dom.
PREP	me.GEN	built	house.NOM

(i) 'I have/had a house built.' (No necessary subject identity)
(ii) 'I have built a house.'

[29] Concerning the terms Action Schema and Location Schema, see Heine (1997*a*).

[30] Under the influence of the written language, the North Russian possessive perfect is said to be receding (cf. Vasilev 1968: 229).

(c) U menja odna zima xožena.
PREP me.GEN one winter.NOM.F.SG walked.PART.F.SG
'By me one winter was walked (to school).'[31]
U nego v gorod uechano.
(PREP he.GEN PREP town has.travelled)
'He has travelled into the town.'
U nego uechano.
(PREP he.GEN has.travelled)
'He has driven away.'

(d) U menja zabyto, a Stepanida pomnit.
PREP me.GEN forgotten but St. remembers
'By me it's been forgotten, but Stepanida remembers.'[32]

In addition to North Russian, this construction based on the Location Schema is also said to exist in some western central dialects of Russian.

This construction is almost unknown in Old Russian (Danylenko 2001*b*: 20). The rise of the North Russian possessive perfect, and the fact that no such perfect evolved in Standard Russian, is attributed to the influence from Northern Germanic languages (Breu 1996: 31). There is, in fact, a pronounced history of contacts between Scandinavian languages and North Russian. During the eleventh century especially, most extensive and intensive contacts existed between Russia and Scandinavia (Lägreid 1984: 100)—a fact which might account for the advanced grammaticalization that the North Russian possessive perfect has attained. There are also, however, authors who have proposed Finno-Ugric influence as the source for the North Russian possessive perfect. For example, according to Vasilev (1968: 226), the North Russian possessive perfect has been influenced by Finnish (see also Veenker 1967: 137ff).

This North Russian example raises a more general question, namely how close a construction in the model language has to be to that of the replica language in order to be recruited for replication—in other words, is it really plausible that a locative construction of North Russian was conceived by its earlier speakers as being equivalent to the transitive 'have'-constructions of the presumed model language or languages? We argue that this question can be answered in the affirmative, for the following reasons: first, the North Russian example is not an isolated case; essentially, the same situation exists in Celtic languages, and especially in Breton, as we will see in Section 4.4.2. And second, as has been demonstrated in Heine and Kuteva (2005), grammatical

[31] Translation as provided by Timberlake (1976).
[32] ibid.

replication is first and foremost a conceptual rather than a morphosyntactic process, and in the present case we would be dealing with a conceptual transfer from a possession schema to an aspect schema. Thus, irrespective of the fact that there remain many questions on whether or how North Russian speakers acquired their possessive perfect via language contact, on the basis of evidence from many cases of grammatical replication worldwide, it would seem plausible that quite divergent morphosyntactic structures in different languages can be considered as equivalent by the speakers concerned as long as the concepts expressed by these structures are the same.

Macedonian. The areal dimension. That Macedonian is exceptional among the Slavic languages in having a fully-fledged possessive stage 3 perfect akin to that of Romance or Germanic languages has been pointed out time and again in the relevant literature. Breu (1994: 54–5) observes that, unlike the situation found in other Slavic languages, the Macedonian possessive perfect has even entered the written language. However, the situation turns out to be slightly more complex than it tends to be described in most works.

That Macedonian has developed a stage 3 possessive perfect is suggested by the presence of the following properties: (a) the construction is used both with transitive and intransitive verbs (especially in the southwestern-most Macedonian dialects); (b) the PPP-verb has turned into an invariant form, that is, agreement with the direct object is lost in certain varieties; and (c) the subject has been extended from human to inanimate referents (in all Macedonian dialects south and west of the Vardar River):

(4.26) MACEDONIAN (Friedman 1976: 99)
Nožov me ima isečeno.
(knife me have.3.SG.PRES cut.PPP.SG.N)
'This here knife has cut me.'

However, what is subsumed under the label 'Macedonian' refers to a number of varieties differing from one another in substantial typological properties. These differences exhibit a clearly areally defined pattern (Friedman 1976). Table 4.3 summarizes the areal distribution of salient properties of the Macedonian possessive perfects.

The data summarized in Table 4.3 suggest, first, that the claim that Macedonian has a fully developed possessive perfect needs to be qualified. There are varieties of Macedonian[33] that do not comply with such a claim: Northeastern Macedonian exhibits a construction that is very different from the possessive

[33] Standard Macedonian is based on West-Central dialects of Macedonian (Victor Friedman, p.c.).

TABLE 4.3. Structural properties of the possessive perfect in different varieties of Macedonian

Stage	Construction	Area of use
1	[*ima* + object] + PPP, with the PPP agreeing with the object, and having characteristics of both an adjectival modifier and a main verb	Northeastern Macedonian, Serbian, and literary Bulgarian
2	In addition to transitive verbs, intransitive ones can be used	Most eastern Macedonian dialects, as well as Strandža and Thracian dialects of southeast Bulgarian
3	The participle no longer shows agreement; instead of human subjects, there may be inanimate ones	All Macedonian dialects south and west of the Vardar River

Source: Friedman 1976; see also Drinka (2003*a*, 2003*b*).[34]

perfect of Southwestern Macedonian, for instance. Second, the linguistic structure of the possessive perfect in Macedonian can be described more appropriately in terms of areal parameters. There is a geographical continuum extending from northeastern Macedonia, where there is hardly a grammaticalized possessive perfect (= stage 1) to Southwestern Macedonia, where there is a fully grammaticalized possessive perfect (= stage 3). And third, this areal patterning correlates with diachronic development and, hence, can be, and has been, accounted for with reference to historical factors. As the data presented by Friedman (1976) suggest, there was a wave of innovation giving rise to a stage 3 possessive perfect in southwestern Macedonia, gradually spreading northeast.

The authors who have dealt with this situation seem to concur that it is the result of language contact whereby Southwestern Macedonian received its possessive perfect from other languages and the construction subsequently spread to other varieties of Macedonian. However, which exactly these languages were, or how the process of replication took place, is not entirely clear. Vasilev (1968: 226) observes that Southwestern Macedonian is in contact with Greek, Aromunian,[35] and Albanian, and that this can be related to the fact that Southwestern Macedonian has almost entirely replaced the earlier Slavic perfect by the 'Romance perfect'. Similarly, Breu (1994: 55) draws attention to contacts with Aromunian and Albanian,[36] and Panzer

[34] Discussion is confined to the possession schema; that is, we are ignoring the alternative 'be'-construction discussed by Friedman (1976) and Drinka (2003).

[35] Gołab (1959) is the first detailed argumentation on the Aromunian origin of the Macedonian possessive perfect.

[36] 'Das gilt insbesondere für den Kernbereich der Neuerung, das südwestliche makedonische Sprachgebiet, dort wo sich noch heute makedonische und aromunische Bevölkerung stark mischt.

(1984: 118) hypothesizes that the Macedonian perfect is a result of Balkan-Romance substratum influence.

Whichever contact language it was that played a decisive role for the possessive perfect to develop in Macedonian, one thing is clear: Old Church Slavonic (863–950 AD)—which for our purposes can be taken as representing the ancestral language from which Macedonian is descended—had no possessive perfect. It had, instead, a well-developed 'be'-perfect and pluperfect paradigm in which a resultative past participle (ending in *-l*) was used. A characteristic of Old Church Slavonic relevant to the present discussion is that it had a rich system of participles, both active and passive. In Macedonian, the present active participle (ending in *-ki*) was transformed into a verbal adverb. Besides, the present passive participle (ending in *-m*) and the past active participle (ending in *-(v)š*) disappeared. In contradistinction to these, the past passive participle (ending in *-n/-t*) gained ground and extended its use from transitive verbs only to intransitive ones. The result was that there developed a common participial form based on the past passive participle in *-n/-t*. This form now became neutral with respect to voice (Koneski 1965: 153). Moreover, the *-n/-t* participle became the verbal adjective in Macedonian used like any adjective. It was about a century later that the first case of the Macedonian possessive perfect appeared in textual evidence (Friedman 1976: 97). The earliest example attested comes from a 1706 manuscript from the monastery of Krnino (Koneski 1965: 171) and involves a past participle of transitive verbs with gender–number agreement between patient noun and past participle:

(4.27) MACEDONIAN OF 1706 (Koneski 1965: 171)

[...] imamŭ	go	aforesanŭ
(have.1.SG.PRES	he.ACC.SG.M	excommunicate.PPP.SG.M
i	prokletŭ [...].	
and	curse.PPP.SG.M)	

'[...] I have excommunicated and cursed him [...].'

In other words, in its earliest attested uses, the Macedonian possessive perfect is suggestive of an early stage 1 construction, where the past participle had characteristics of both an adjectival modifier and a main verb (Friedman 1976: 97). It is justifiable to regard the 'neutralization' (with respect to voice) of the erstwhile past passive participle in *-n/-t* as an important factor for the early possessive perfect structure to further advance in its grammaticalization. The reason is this: the *-n/-t* participle had already started moving away from its

Allerdings kann gerade hier auch mit albanischer Adstratwirkung gerechnet werden, da das Albanische ebenfalls ein HABEN-Perfekt aufweist.' (Breu 1994: 55).

initial passive meaning—due to its extension of use to also encompass intransitive verbs—so it could not have been very difficult for it to get an 'active' reinterpretation whereby the past participle no longer encodes an action performed on the patient by some outside agency but an action performed by the sentential subject. Furthermore, the very same neutralization of the *-n/-t* past participle must also have facilitated the extension of use of the possessive perfect in contexts with intransitive verbs.

Discussion. Wherever there is a stage 1 or stage 2 situation in Slavic languages, it is language contact that has been held responsible for this state. For example, Breu observes:

> Einige slavische Sprachen an der Peripherie haben unter Kontakteinfluß ein analytisches HABEN-Perfekt entwickelt, das allerdings in den Adstratsituationen nicht den grammatischen Status der Geberspachen erreicht hat. Der Aufbau hat aber durch die Nachbildung der periphrastischen Konstruktion begonnen [Some Slavic languages of the periphery have developed an analytic HAVE-perfect under contact influence, which however has not reached the status of the donor languages. But the construction has begun with the imitation of the periphrastic construction.] (Breu 1996: 31).

Vasilev (1968: 226) maintains that the possessive perfect in Czech, Polish, Polabian, and Kashubian has been influenced by German, while those of Macedonian and Thracian were induced by contact with Greek (Vasilev 1968: 224ff).

According to Vasilev (1968: 221), the Slavic stage 1 possessive perfects showing gender–number agreement between the PPP-verb and the object (= his type 3) can be explained as resulting from a development internal to Slavic, whereby the past passive participle was used commonly as a nominal attribute, agreeing with the noun in number and gender, with 'have' as the main verb. Thus, the following Bulgarian example is said to be compatible with the syntactic rules of Slavic languages:

(4.28) BULGARIAN (Vasilev 1968: 221)

včera	imaxme	varena	riba.
(yesterday	have.1.PL.PAST	cook.PPP.SG.F	fish.SG.F)

'Yesterday we had cooked fish.'

In fact, Slavic languages provide good structural prerequisites for a possessive perfect to evolve: as has been pointed out by some authors (e.g. Vasilev 1968; Panzer 1984) there are structures not unlike such an aspect construction; for example, Ukrainian and Belorussian from the fourteenth century and Polish from the fifteenth century onward developed an impersonal active construction involving a neuter *n/t*-participle with an accusative object, although without an agent (Panzer 1984: 118).[37]

That Slavic possessive perfects are the result of a grammaticalization of already existing structures appears to be uncontroversial. It would seem, however, that internal development was not the only factor to be held responsible for this fact; rather, that process appears to have been induced by language contact, for the following reasons:

(i) This is the conclusion drawn by most of the specialists (but see Maslov 1949; Vasilev 1968: 221).
(ii) In the oldest attested Slavic language, Old Church Slavonic (863–950 AD), whose oldest texts (or copies of such) date back to the ninth century and which for these purposes can be taken to represent Common Slavic, we know that there was a perfect and it was not of the possessive type, whereas all the relevant languages were in contact with languages that did have possessive perfects.[38] All Slavic languages that can be shown to have had a longer history of contact with languages having a fully-fledged possessive perfect have at least a stage 1 possessive perfect, while the more geographically remote Russian has not.[39]
(iii) On the basis of crosslinguistic observations (that is, the fact that possessive perfects are rarely found outside European languages), it appears unlikely that a possessive perfect would have evolved independently in many different languages.

What may seem surprising, however, is that the development in Slavic languages did not lead further to possessive perfects of the kind found in Germanic or Romance languages. The Macedonian example suggests the following:

(i) Contact-induced grammaticalization proceeds gradually and is more likely to affect immediate neighbours rather than languages or dialects spoken at some distance from one another.
(ii) Grammatical categories are not transferred wholesale from one language to another; rather they are adopted as use patterns confined to specific contexts.[40]

[37] Note, however, that according to Shevelov (1991: 201), this construction arose in Polish, after which it spread to East Slavic.

[38] We do not always have precise documentation, for the actual contact languages, but we do so for related varieties that allow us to draw such conclusions.

[39] For example, Breu observes: 'Daneben finden wir an der Peripherie des slavischen Sprachraums auch andere Perfektbildungen und zwar mit dem Hilfsverb HABEN' (Breu 1984: 54).

[40] For an alternative grammatical transfer process, see Friedman (1994).

(iii) Accordingly, transferred categories are not adopted in their entirety but rather in some reduced form.
(iv) This reduced form differs from the model category in that it constitutes a less grammaticalized form of that of the model category.
(v) Accordingly, contact-induced transfer appears to be constrained by principles of grammaticalization. If the model language has a category composed of a grammaticalization chain A>B>C, then the replica language is likely to adopt a reduced part of the process, which is A>B, and apparently never B>C.

That contact-induced grammaticalization does not lead to a transfer of fully-fledged grammatical categories but rather proceeds in the form of a step-by-step grammaticalization is suggested, perhaps most clearly, by the spread of the possessive perfect in Macedonian.

4.4.2 *Celtic languages*

There is no evidence to suggest that in their earliest stages, Celtic languages had anything corresponding to possessive perfects in other European languages. The development and present situation of possessive perfects is summarized in Table 4.4.

There are no indications that there was a possessive perfect in Middle Irish (eleventh to seventeenth centuries), and this situation is also characteristic of earlier and present-day Welsh. From the early seventeenth century onwards, Modern Irish developed a possessive perfect based on the Location Schema [Y is at X], using the preposition *ag* 'at', which first developed into a possession schema [X has Y], illustrated in (4.29a). The latter again gave rise to a possessive perfect,[41] involving a process that is, conceptually, strikingly similar to that found in North Russian (see pp. 165–7), but unlike the latter it did not reach a stage 2 structure. Example (4.29b) illustrates the early stage 1 situation of Irish, where the construction is ambiguous, as indicated by the different translations. Note that the possessor/agent is an optional constituent: It can be omitted, in which case there is a statal passive function, (4.29c).

(4.29) Modern Irish (Pietsch 2004*a*: 10)
(a) Tá litir agam.
is letter at.1.SG
'I have a letter.'

[41] Cf. Harris (1984), who observes that the Irish possessive perfect, referred to by him as 'PII', 'is realized as a possessive construction which incorporates a verbal adjective as object complement (possession in Irish is expressed prepositionally as "object-of-possession is at possessor")' (Harris 1984: 319).

TABLE 4.4. Morphosyntactic changes leading from possessive to perfect schema in Celtic languages

Stage	Construction	Languages
0	There is a locative construction expressing predicative possession only	Old Breton, Middle Irish, Modern Welsh
1	(a) Only transitive verbs are allowed as main verbs. (b) The main verb appears as a modifier of the patient. (c) The main verb has the structure of a PPP. (d) There is frequently ambiguity in the meaning of the main verb, in that it can be understood to refer either to a state or a state resulting from an action. (e) Similarly, there tends to be ambiguity with regard to the agent of the construction, which can also be understood to be a possessor.	Modern Irish
2	In addition to transitive verbs, intransitive ones can be used	Modern Breton
3	There can now be inanimate agents	—

PPP = past passive participle or some language-specific equivalent of it. Languages are listed only once with reference to the most advanced stage of grammaticalization they exhibit.

(b) Tá an litir scríofa agam.
is the letter to.write.PPP at.1.SG
(i) 'I have the letter written.'
(ii) 'I have written the letter.'
(iii) 'The letter has been written by me.'

(c) Tá an litir scríofa.
is the letter to.write.PPP
'The letter has been written.'

The central meaning of the Irish possessive perfect is still a statal-possessive one, 'and it is only in the process of being extended marginally into the domain of a true anterior, for instance by allowing indefinite-past usage' (Pietsch 2004*a*: 11; see also Harris 1991: 205–6). It has not proceeded beyond stage 1, that is, it is used with transitive verbs, while neither intransitive verbs nor inanimate agents are allowed. Furthermore, its structure can still be analyzed as bi-clausal: Harris (1991: 205–6) analyzes sentences such as (4.30) 'as a complex statal construction consisting of a matrix clause indicating possession and an embedded clause containing the object NP, i.e. along the lines of [She has [the boat sold]].'

(4.30) MODERN IRISH (Harris 1991: 205)
Tá an bád díolta aici.
(is the boat sold at.3.SG.F)
'She has sold the boat.'

Like the Macedonian possessive perfect (see pp. 167–70), the Irish one is suggestive of an areally defined continuum on the basis of its relative degree of grammaticalization:

> Broadly speaking, Irish dialects can be described in terms of a south-to-north dialect continuum, with Munster (south-western) dialects at the one end, Connacht at an intermediate position, and Donegal (Ulster) dialects—bordering in many respects on Scots Gaelic—at the other .... Within this continuum, it is consistently the southern dialects, especially Munster, that shows signs of stronger grammaticalization of the participial perfect construction (Pietsch 2004*a*: 12).

Whereas in Ulster Irish the construction can be described as an early stage 1 perfect, limited to transitive PPP-verbs with affected patients, in the southern dialects it has been grammaticalized to stage 2, being extended to intransitive verbs. There are two different ways in which the change from stage 1 to stage 2 is achieved: either by leaving the syntactic subject slot empty (4.31a), or by assigning the agent the role of a subject, cf. (4.31b) (Pietsch 2004*a*: 12–13).

(4.31) MODERN IRISH, southern dialects (Pietsch 2004*a*: 12–13)
(a) Tá scríte agam chuige.
is written at.1.SG to.3.SG.M
'I have written to him.'
(b) Tá an coileach glaoite.
is the cock crowed
'The cock has crowed.'

The grammaticalization from possessive to aspectual meaning in Irish tends to be viewed as being due to conceptual transfer from English, but there are no details on the exact modalities of such a transfer.

Breton is separated from the British Isles and has been in contact with French for roughly 1500 years (Ternes 1998: 286). In Old Breton no possessive perfect appears to have existed, but Middle Breton (eleventh to seventeenth centuries) has a possessive perfect, based on the Goal Schema [Y exists to/for X] that was grammaticalized to a construction of predicative possession (e.g. *am eus* ('is to me') 'I have'), which again developed into a possessive perfect (*gwelet am eus* 'I have seen'; Vendryes 1937), where a nominal modifier, encoded in the perfect participle, developed into the main verb.

Modern Breton has a well-established stage 2 possessive perfect. Example (4.32a) illustrates the possessive construction, while (4.32b) is unambiguously an instance of a stage 2 perfect, as is suggested by the use of an intransitive verb (see also Ternes 1979: 220).

(4.32) MODERN BRETON (Press 1986: 139; Elvira Veselinović, p.c.)

(a)

Ur	velo	c'hlas	am	eus.
(a	bicycle	blue	have	1.SG)

'I have a blue bicycle.' (Lit. '[to] me is a blue bicycle.')

(b)

Kousket	am	eus.
sleep	have	1.SG

'I have slept.'

The possessive perfect of Modern Breton tends to be portrayed as having been influenced by, or even to be a conceptual replica of French, being characterized by an attempt to literally translate the French perfect. This hypothesis is supported by the fact that the use patterns of the Breton possessive perfect are similar to those of the French possessive perfect. For example, both languages use a 'be'-perfect in (4.33a) but a possessive perfect in (4.33b).[42]

(4.33) MODERN BRETON (Elvira Veselinović, p.c.)

(a)

Aet	eo.	cf. French	Il	est	allé.
go.PPP	is		he	is	go.PPP

'He has gone.' — 'He has gone.'

(b)

Me	am	eus	komprenet.	cf. French	j'	ai	compris.
I	have	1.SG	understand.PPP		I	have	understand.PPP

'I have understood.' — 'I have understood.'

4.4.3 *Irish English (Hiberno-English)*

Irish English (Hiberno-English) has several different perfect constructions; with reference to the phenomena studied here, it can be defined as one of Europe's peripheral languages with regard to the structure of its possessive perfect (referred to in the relevant literature as the 'PII'), illustrated in (4.34).

[42] The equivalence relation is however not complete. For example, the copula verb 'be' uses the 'be'-perfect in Breton but the possessive perfect in French (Elmar Ternes, p.c.).

(4.34) THE POSSESSIVE PERFECT OF IRISH ENGLISH (Harris 1984: 307)
She's nearly her course finished.

While Standard English has a fully-fledged stage 3 possessive perfect, Irish English has a weakly grammaticalized stage 1 possessive perfect. Accordingly, it differs from the former in a number of properties, such as the following:

(4.35) PROPERTIES OF THE IRISH ENGLISH PII (Harris 1984: 307, 311–12)
(a) It only occurs in transitive sentences.
(b) The participle is placed after the direct object.
(c) It is used only with dynamic verbs (*do*, *write*, *spend*, etc.), not with stative verbs (*know*, *recognize*, *resemble*).
(d) It resembles the possessive 'have'-construction and is best analyzed as a complex construction consisting of a main verb *have*-clause and a subjoined clause containing a participle, i.e. something along the lines of [I have [my dinner eaten]].
(e) Rather than a perfect (anterior), it appears to be essentially a resultative construction, focusing on the state rather than a past event that gives rise to a present state. Accordingly, adverbials which focus on an anterior event are excluded.
(f) The scope of negation can be either the whole construction (4.36a) or the subjoined clause alone (4.36b):

(4.36) IRISH ENGLISH (Harris 1984: 312).
(a) I haven't even it made.
(b) I've a loaf not touched.

While contrasting sharply with Standard English, the Irish English possessive perfect agrees with the corresponding construction of Modern Irish in all the major properties listed in (4.35). Consider the following example, where (4.37a) provides an Irish sentence, (4.37b) a translation of it into Irish English and (4.37c) into Standard English.

(4.37) IRISH (Harris 1991: 205 = 1984: 319)
(a) Tá an bád díolta aici.
be.NON-PAST the boat sold at.her
(b) 'She has the boat sold.'
(c) 'She has sold the boat.'

This striking typological congruence is in need of explanation. Harris (1984: 320) argues that features similar to the ones listed in (4.35) for Irish English are well attested in earlier forms of British English, hence, that the Irish

English construction reflects an earlier state found in the history of British English, more precisely, that it is a retention of the older English split perfect:

> The modern English perfect is generally agreed to derive historically from an older transitive 'split' perfect which consists of a 'have' form and an EN-participle placed after the object noun phrase. This construction is often interpreted as referring to a state of completion ('I had him in a state of being bound'). The 'have' of this older perfect is usually assumed to be a full lexical verb denoting possession and the participle to be a complement of the object noun phrase (Harris 1984: 321).

An alternative hypothesis would be that the typological congruence of the Irish and the Irish English possessive perfects is due to language contact, but Harris (1984: 320) observes that 'the evidence for substratum interference is ambiguous to say the least'. In the absence of more detailed information, one may adopt Harris's position according to which the Irish English possessive perfect reflects an earlier state of some variety of British English. Assuming that this position is historically correct, the following questions arise: (a) Why among all the many varieties of modern English is it only Irish English that lacks a stage 3 perfect? (b) Why has Irish English retained the earlier construction? (c) Why is essentially the same stage 1 perfect found in Irish, considering the fact that Irish English and Irish share a history of over 300 years of intense language contact, leading to a number of grammatical replications in Irish English, as Harris (1984; 1991) himself admits?

The only convincing answer to this question, we argue, is that contact with Irish must have played some role in shaping the structure of the Irish English possessive perfect. This answer is not incompatible with the hypothesis proposed by Harris; and it is in line with what is found in other situations of language contact, where external influence and internal development tend to reinforce one another.

That contact was in fact involved in this case is argued for by Pietsch (2004a). Based on the analysis of a large corpus of eighteenth- and nineteenth-century text material and of other documents that exist on the history of Irish English, he observes that there was an early construction, the 'conclusive perfect', where the patient (= object) is under the control of the agent (= subject), the state predicated of the patient has been brought about through the agent, and the resultant state is evaluated as a positive accomplishment desired and attained by the agent, as in example (4.38b) from 1817. This construction, which was available in the varieties of the original British settlers in Ireland, was gradually grammaticalized from a bi-clausal towards a mono-clausal construction, and towards a more general perfect pattern where the notion of possession no longer played any role in the agent's accomplishment, as in (4.38b).

(4.38) IRISH ENGLISH (Pietsch 2004*a*: 14, 16)
(a) we **have** some good brick Houses **erected** and a Clever Brick meeting House for Friends.
(WrightJ04, 1817)
(b) they **have** 150 tons **sold** for the farmer Bailie, & not a pound made of it.
(BrownW07, 1821)

As the detailed discussion by Pietsch (2004a) suggests, there is in fact reason to assume that this grammaticalization was influenced by the presence of a comparable Irish construction: rather than drawing on the established stage 3 perfect of English, Irish learners of English appear to have opted in favour of the English 'conclusive perfect' since it offered a more immediate equivalent of the existing Irish participial construction, using the latter as a model for grammatical replication. This contact hypothesis is supported by the fact that grammaticalization affected primarily groups of speakers in whose linguistic environments there was still a strong element of Irish/English bilingualism.

4.4.4 *German in the USA and Australia*

German has a well-established stage 3 possessive perfect (see above), but in this language the grammaticalization of the possessive perfect has not really reached its theoretical endpoint. It has not been extended to all verbs, for example, with intransitive verbs such as *geschehen* 'to happen', it may not be used; instead, the 'be'-perfect must be used, see (4.39). As a result of their contact with English, speakers of Pennsylvania German have extended the use of the possessive perfect at the expense of the 'be'-perfect; the former is now used with all transitive and most intransitive verbs. A mechanism that appears to have contributed to this process of context extension (see Section 2.3) is that speakers of Pennsylvania German tend to equate their verbs with corresponding English verbs and to use the possessive perfect whenever the latter is required by the relevant English verb. For example, the verb form *geschehne* 'happened' takes the possessive perfect since the corresponding English verb form *happened* does so too, see (4.40).

(4.39) HIGH GERMAN
Was ist geschehen?
what is happened
'What has happened?'

(4.40) PENNSYLVANIA GERMAN (Enninger 1980: 344)

Nau	hoeret	moll	ihr	liewe	Leute,	was	geschehne	hott
(now	listen	once	you	dear	people	what	happened	has
zu	derre	Zeit.						
at	that	time)						

'Now listen, dear people, what has happened at that time.'

In Sauk County Low German of Wisconsin, context extension appears to have been even more dramatic—to the extent that the 'be'-construction has been given up completely in favour of the 'have'-construction (Eichhoff 1971: 53).

Similarly, among Germans living in Australia, *haben* 'have' is generalized as the perfect auxiliary on the pattern of English (Clyne 1972: 76).

What is remarkable about these cases of contact between German and English is that it suggests that grammatical replication does not relate to the grammatical categories *per se* but is an epiphenomenal product of the replication of properties associated with lexical categories—in this case with lexical verbs. Still, replication is in accordance with directionality characteristic of grammaticalization, in that context extension, for example from transitive to intransitive verbs, results in an increased degree of grammaticalization of the possessive perfect in these German varieties.

4.4.5 *Other peripheral languages*

One noteworthy case of a possessive perfect is found in Albanian, dating back at least to the sixteenth century (Demiraj 1985: 84), perhaps it is much older. It has the properties of a stage 2 possessive perfect (see Section 4.3.2), but perhaps, especially in Tosk Albanian, even a stage 3 possessive perfect (Victor Friedman, p.c.). The possibility that Latin provided the model cannot be ruled out, but there is no conclusive evidence for an external model.

According to Haase (1992), Basque has replicated the Latin-Romance possessive perfect via contact-induced grammaticalization, using the verb *ukan* 'have' plus the transitive participle as a complement to form a recent perfect, for example:

(4.41) BASQUE (Haase 1992: 92)

ikus-	i	dut.
see-	PTCP	PRES.3.SG<1.SG

'I have seen.' (Lit. 'I have it seen')

The category is restricted to transitive main verbs, while intransitive verbs use the same periphrasis with the verb *izan* 'be' as an auxiliary (Haase 1992: 92–3).

Minor use patterns that appear to be on the verge from stage 0 to stage 1 are found in Finnish and Lithuanian. Both are strongly associated with a 'possessive function' (of the kind 'I have a written book') and it is not entirely clear whether they really constitute aspectual categories (Vasilev 1968: 219; Jacob 1994: 47). Nevertheless, perfect-like structures have been documented, compare (4.3) for Finnish, or (4.42) for Lithuanian.

(4.42) LITHUANIAN (Vasilev 1968: 219)[43]
aš turiu užsakytas knigas.
'I have ordered books.'

4.5 Conclusions

In the preceding paragraphs, we have investigated the genesis and evolution of the possessive perfect. There exist three theoretical possibilities for the development of this construction. First, the development of a possessive construction into a perfect structure may be a universally motivated but language-internal phenomenon. Whereas it is difficult to point to convincing evidence in favour of such a hypothesis, it is easy to come up with an argument against it: the fact that possessive perfects are rarely attested outside the European continent makes this hypothesis fairly implausible (see Ramat 1998: 232–3).

A second theoretical possibility would be for the possessive perfects in modern European languages to simply reflect a genetically inherited pattern from Indo-European. An argument in favour of this hypothesis would be the existence of a possessive perfect structure in Hittite as well as in Old Indian, Old Iranian, or Old Armenian (Benveniste 1952; Jacob 1998: 106). There are two counterarguments to this hypothesis. First, there are some non-Indo-European languages, Finnish and Basque, that have also developed a possessive perfect, even if a weakly grammaticalized one. The second counterargument can be seen in the existence of more than one pattern serving as structural templates of the possessive perfect (Drinka 2003*a*). Thus, if the possessive perfects in European languages were *exclusively* the result of genetic inheritance, then in all the European languages where the possessive perfect developed we should expect to see the same initial structure—that is, [NOM + 'have' + ACC + PPP]—developing into the possessive perfect. But the facts we come across are different: along with the grammaticalization from [NOM + 'have' + ACC + PPP] to possessive perfect, there is another

[43] No glosses are provided by the author.

structure, [('at' + GEN) + NOM/ACC + PPP][44] that grammaticalizes into a possessive perfect construction.

The third possibility is to hypothesize that language contact played some role in the development of the possessive perfect in European languages. An argument in favour of this hypothesis is the geographical distribution of the grammaticalization developments mentioned above, [NOM + 'have' + ACC + PPP] > possessive perfect and [('at' + GEN) + NOM/ACC + PPP] > possessive perfect: Each of them took place in geographically contiguous languages, and it is only in those areas where Slavic and other non-western European languages came in contact with languages using 'have' as an auxiliary for their perfects that a 'have'-type auxiliary has tended to appear in the perfect construction (Drinka 2003*a*: 6).

In spite of the fact that the history of European languages is, comparatively speaking, well documented, the evidence adduced in the present chapter is to some extent circumstantial, that is, in many of the cases discussed we lack appropriate historical data. Major issues concerning the origins and the spread of the possessive perfect are still unresolved. In the specialized literature, the most frequent hypotheses proposed involve either Latin or Greek or—alternatively—drift, that is, parallel development of the possessive perfects found in Europe, as well as language contact as the cause for the appearance of the Germanic possessive perfect under Romance influence; however, linguists still disagree about the conclusiveness of the evidence that Latin received it from Greek, or that Germanic languages received it from Romance (see Jacob 1994: 52, Drinka 2003*a*, 2003*b*, for discussion).

Nevertheless, it is hoped that the hypotheses presented here are plausible, at least more plausible than alternative hypotheses that have been proposed. Our hypotheses are based, first, on whatever historical information is available, second, on the geographical distribution of the linguistic phenomena examined and, third, on cross-linguistic generalizations made within the framework of grammaticalization theory (e.g. Heine & Kuteva 2002). These observations suggest, first, that language contact must have been involved in the diffusion of the possessive perfect and, second, that in all cases we have examined contact-induced change was in the direction from less to more grammaticalized constructions. We do not wish to exclude the possibility that language contact may also lead to a development in the opposite direction,

[44] Andrii Danylenko (p.c.) points out that there are additional structures which can be regarded as the structural templates for possessive perfects in European languages, e.g. Lithuanian [GEN + invariable PPP] as well as Old Church Slavonic ['at' + LOC + NP + invariable PPP]. Note that Karskij (1956: 317) also gives an example—from sixteenth-century Belorussian—of a possessive perfect whose structure is ['at' + LOC + NP + invariable PPP].

but we hypothesize that such a development would be fairly unlikely and, hence, in need of explanation.

The observations made above also suggest that contact-induced grammatical replication is severely constrained by principles of grammaticalization. This means, first, that the transfer of a grammaticalization process from the model language M to the replica language R is unlikely to be complete, that is, we will expect R to exhibit a less advanced stage of grammaticalization than M—even if after an extended period of intense contact the replica construction can become largely indistinguishable from the model construction.

It would seem that these observations can be of help in reconstructing other cases of grammatical change. For example, if we observe that languages X and Y have undergone the same process of contact-induced grammaticalization but that the process has reached a more advanced stage in X than in Y, then it can be hypothesized that the transfer is likely to have proceeded from X to Y rather than the other way round. As we just observed, however, R may, and is likely to, attain the same degree of grammaticalization as M given enough time, in which case this hypothesis is no longer relevant.

The findings made support to some extent the 'linguistic-compatibility' hypothesis discussed in the introduction to this chapter, according to which the relative degree of structural similarity among the languages involved plays some role in constraining grammatical replication: languages that are genetically closely related and structurally alike are more likely to share the same kind of possessive perfect. At the same time, these findings also suggest that linguistic compatibility does not constitute a salient constraint for diffusion: languages such as Breton, North Russian, and Macedonian have acquired a possessive perfect, while fellow Celtic and Slavic languages, respectively, have not (or at least not to nearly the same extent); more research is required on this issue.

5

From Comitative to Instrumental Forms

Another characteristic of Standard Average European languages can be seen in the fact that they do not formally distinguish between comitative and instrumental adpositions or case forms (henceforth: comitatives and instrumentals), that is, they use the same form for both.[1] Thus, in both (5.1a) and (5.1b) there is an adverbial phrase introduced by *with*, but while *with* can be paraphrased by *together with* in its comitative use of (5.1a), in its instrumental use of (5.1b) a possible paraphrase of *with* would be *by means of*.

(5.1) ENGLISH
 (a) She danced **with** her son.
 (b) She cut the bread **with** a knife.

We will say that in languages such as English there is a comitative–instrumental case polysemy or, as Stolz *et al.* (2006) prefer to say, there is case syncretism. While examples of such polysemy are also found in other languages, they are far less common outside Europe than within Europe. Another force leading to the gradual Europeanization of peripheral languages can, in fact, be seen in a strategy whereby comitative markers are grammaticalized to instrumental markers—with the result that the use of comitative markers is extended to present instrumental participants, as we hope to demonstrate in the present chapter.

5.1 Typology

Comitatives tend to exhibit the following structural properties (see Stassen 2000: 18; Stolz 1998; 2001[2]):

[1] In the present chapter we have benefited greatly from the work of Thomas Stolz and his associates Cornelia Stroh and Aina Urdze. Some of this work is available in print, other parts are still unpublished (especially Stolz, Stroh, & Urdze 2006). We wish to express our gratitude to these colleagues for their extraordinary cooperation.

[2] Additional characteristics of comitatives are proposed in the following definition by Stolz (2001: 591): 'A relationship between two participants of a verbal predication is labelled comitative if two

(i) They have typically human referents denoting a companion; in some languages, inanimate referents are excluded from comitative marking.
(ii) They are peripheral rather than core participants and are treated syntactically as adverbial phrases.
(iii) They may be marked by a variety of different forms, in particular by adpositions, case affixes, clitics or any combination thereof.[3]
(iv) They are suggestive of a universal grammatical concept in that all languages appear to have some structure for marking comitative participants, even if that structure may also be used to express other additional functions (cf. Stassen 2000: 21).

Instrumentals normally share properties (ii), (iii), and (iv) with comitatives, although not (i), but they exhibit the following additional properties:

(v) They are inanimate and manipulable.
(vi) Prototypical situations involving instrumentals require three participants: an agent (i.e. the one who deploys the instrument), the instrument itself, and a patient (see Stolz 2001: 591).

Thus, the two functions are sufficiently conceptually and morphosyntactically different to understand why in the majority of the world's languages they are coded by different grammatical forms. Nevertheless, a number of languages exhibit a comitative-instrumental polysemy, that is, in such languages the same marker is used for both case functions. However, this does not seem to be the prevailing situation cross-linguistically, as has been established by Stolz (1996*b*) and Stolz *et al.* (2006). On the basis of a survey of 323 languages of worldwide distribution, these authors propose a threefold typological distinction in the marking of comitatives and instrumentals in the languages of the world, which is summarized in (5.2).

(5.2) A CROSSLINGUISTIC TYPOLOGY OF COMITATIVE AND INSTRUMENTAL marking according to Stolz (1996*b*), Stolz *et al.* (2006)
Type A (*the incoherent type*): Comitative and instrumental receive different markings.
Type B (*the coherent type*): Comitative and instrumental receive the same marking.

participants have the same macrorôle, while their degree of involvement in the situation described by the verbal predicate is not absolutely symmetrical. The relationship is one of accompaniment: one of the participants is the accompanee, the other the companion.'

[3] There are some languages where the comitative marker can be head-marked, being incorporated into the predicate (Stassen 2000: 19).

Type C (the mixed type): Two different kinds of case marking exist in a given language, one expressing comitative–instrumental syncretism while the other is restricted to either comitative or instrumental marking.

Table 5.1 summarizes some results of this survey. As this table suggests, it is only roughly one-quarter of the world's languages that clearly exhibit a polysemy pattern (= type B), while nearly two thirds of the languages use separate markings for the two case functions (type A).

A contrasting situation is found in Europe, as Table 5.2 shows: roughly half of all European languages use the same marking for comitatives and instrumentals (type B), while only one-third of the languages clearly distinguish the two morphologically (type A). The difference is even more dramatic if one turns to the internal situation within Europe: The vast majority of SAE languages have a type B polysemy; this applies to all Romance languages (e.g. Italian, French, Spanish, Gascon) and Germanic languages (e.g. English, German, Danish, Swedish). Peripheral languages, on the other hand, are less likely to use the same marking for comitatives and instrumentals, as we will see in Section 5.3.

Stolz and his associates use this typology on the one hand to describe the structural diversity that they observe in the languages of the world; on the other hand, it also serves to propose a diachronic scenario on the evolution of comitative/instrumental markings. In a simplified format, this scenario can be described as in (5.3).

(5.3) A SCENARIO OF THE EVOLUTION OF COMITATIVE AND INSTRUMENTAL MARKINGS (based on Stolz *et al.* 2006)
Type B > type C > type A > type B

The evolution hypothesized in (5.3) is cyclic, in that it may, and frequently does, proceed from type B via C and A back to type B. But it is also

TABLE 5.1. Types of marking used for comitatives and instrumentals

Type	Number of languages	Percentage
Type B	79	24.5
Type C	35	10.8
Type A	209	64.7
Total	323	100

Sample: 323 languages of worldwide distribution.

Source: Stolz 1996*b*: 127.

TABLE 5.2. Types of marking used for comitatives and instrumentals in Europe

Type	Number of languages	Percentage
Type B	25	49.0
Type C	10	19.6
Type A	16	31.4
Total	51	100

Sample: 51 European languages.

Source: Stolz 1996*b*: 128).

unidirectional; while the possibility cannot be excluded that there are languages that do not conform to this scenario, there is massive diachronic evidence in its support. As we will see below, this scenario is immediately relevant for the diachronic typology of European languages.

5.2 Notes on history

Reconstruction work on the earliest situation of Indo-European languages suggests that there was a type B situation, that is, there was polysemy expressed by a case suffix, the so-called inflectional instrumental. Subsequent developments in Europe were, on the one hand, shaped to some extent by the gradual decline of case inflections that affected many languages of this family; on the other hand, it was also shaped by a process going in the direction of a type C situation, where a new marking for the comitative evolved, typically involving a preposition, even if the older case marking may still have been available for this purpose.

This was also roughly the situation in the classical European languages, Greek and Latin. In Ancient Greek, the instrumental was marked by the dative case form. This option was also available for the comitative, but with this function the preposition *syn* 'with' tended to be used in addition; alternatively, there was the preposition *metà* governing the genitive case used for the comitative. This preposition was extended to the instrumental function, and in the early Byzantine period, between the sixth and the eleventh centuries, *metà* (reduced to *me* via erosion) had established itself as a polysemous type B marker in Greek.

In earlier Latin, the instrumental was coded by means of the ablative case suffix. The comitative function of *cum* 'with' was the original one, to be found throughout the history of the language, while the instrumental function of *cum* is only marginally attested in Catullus (i.e. in Classical Latin). The first examples of instrumental *cum* are reported to have occurred in authors from the provinces of the empire, who often employed vulgar forms, and it became fairly common in Late Latin, with clear attestations by the fourth century AD (Michela Cennamo, p.c.).

Processes gradually leading from a hypothesized early type B situation (= polysemy) to a later type C and finally to a type A situation (= distinct markings) are found in other early Indo-European languages of Europe. Written records from Old Church Slavonic show that the instrumental was expressed by means of the instrumental case suffix:

(5.4) OLD CHURCH SLAVONIC (863–950 AD; Mirčev 1963: 51)
sã dr'zitŭ t'n'koju stæniceju.
REFL hold thin.INSTR wall.DIM.INSTR
'holds itself by means of a thin little wall (of each little cell—of a honey-comb—"holding itself" to the neighbouring cells)'.

To express comitativity in Old Church Slavonic there existed a comitative preposition, *să* 'with', which was used with nominals marked for the instrumental case in order to express accompaniment 'together with'. In addition to this, the preposition *să* 'with' could also be used with nominals marked for the genitive case. But in terms of the typology of Stolz *et al.* (2006; see (5.2) above), Old Church Slavonic can be described as being a type C language, since the instrumental was still used occasionally for comitative participants.

In both Old Irish and Gothic, the use of the bare instrumental was already limited, giving way to the use of prepositional phrases. The development in Old Norse/Old Icelandic, Gothic, and Old Saxon appears to have been similar to that of Old High German. The development in Old High German can be sketched as follows: in the eighth and ninth centuries, the inflectional instrumental was still used with a relatively high text frequency, even if attested only for masculine and neuter nouns. Already early on, the preposition *mit* 'with' had been used as a 'prepositional support'. In the tenth century, the instrumental case was replaced by the dative case, but nominal word forms inflected for the instrumental are still attested occasionally in the eleventh century. Around the turn from the ninth to the tenth century, Old High German had completed the whole cycle sketched in (5.3), ending in a type B polysemy pattern, where *mit* was used for both comitative and instrumental participants. By the turn from the eleventh to the twelfth century, a type B polysemy had established itself in the Germanic languages.

But Germanic languages were not the first to acquire a fairly stable type B polysemy; rather, this process had occurred centuries earlier in the Romance languages. When the Latin case system collapsed, the ablative case suffix was no longer available to mark the instrumental function. The emerging

Romance languages were characterized by the presence of a type B polysemy, and they have remained so for their entire documented history: all modern Romance languages exhibit the polysemy.

In the rise of polysemy in the Balkans, Middle Greek as well as early Rumanian, emerging out of Balkanic Vulgar Latin, were centuries ahead of the Slavic languages, Bulgarian and Macedonian, and may have contributed to the latter acquiring the polysemy, even though this process might have happened anyway after the loss of the inflectional case system in these two South Slavic languages.

On the basis of these overall developments, Stolz and associates observe that 'the spread of the B-type in early Medieval Europe could be understood as a wave of innovation triggered by Romance-Greek-Germanic-Celtic language contacts' (Stolz *et al.* 2006: 414). These authors are careful to add however that, given our present state of knowledge, this hypothesis must of necessity remain conjectural.

5.3 Peripheral languages

Table 5.3 summarizes the forms used in a number of peripheral European languages to express comitatives and instrumentals. We will now look at the languages listed there in turn. Note that Slavic languages are treated here as 'peripheral', even though they are SAE languages according to the convention we proposed in Section 1.2.7, the reason being that, with reference to the problem that is the subject of the present chapter, Slavic languages behave like peripheral languages.

Slavic languages. Russian consistently distinguishes between comitatives and instrumentals. The comitative participant is encoded by means of the instrumental case suffix plus the preposition *s* in addition, (5.5a), whereas the instrumental only takes the instrumental case suffix, (5.5b):

(5.5) RUSSIAN

(a) Ja pojdu v kino s mamoj.
I go in movies with mom.INSTR
'I'll go to the movies with my mom.'

(b) Ja narezal xleb etim nožem.
I cut bread this.INSTR knife.INSTR
'I cut the bread with this knife.'

The instrumental was marked by a single form, that is the instrumental case suffix, at earlier stages of the Russian language, as can be seen from the following example from the end of the sixteenth century:

TABLE 5.3. Comitative and instrumental case markers in Slavic and some peripheral European languages

Family/branch	Language	Comitative	Instrumental
Slavic	Russian	*s* N-INSTR	N-INSTR
	Belorussian	*z* N-INSTR	N-INSTR
	Ukranian	*z* N-INSTR	N-INSTR
	Polish	*z* N-INSTR	N-INSTR
	Bulgarian	*s* N	s N
	Macedonian	*s* N	*s* N
	Sorbian	*z* N-INSTR	z N-INSTR
	Croatian	s N-INSTR	N-INSTR
	Molise Croatian	s N-INSTR	s N-INSTR
Baltic	Lithuanian	*Su* N-INSTR	(*su*) N-INSTR
	Latvian	*ar* N-ACC.SG	*ar* N-ACC.SG
Finnic	Finnish	N-GEN *kanssa*	N-ADE
	Estonian	N-*ga/ka*	N-*ga/ka*
	Livonian	N-*[kõ]ks*	N-*[kõ]ks*
	Sami	N-*(gu)in*	N-*(gu)in*
Ugric	Hungarian	**N-*val***	**N-*val***
Celtic	Welsh	*â* N, *gyda(g)* N	*â* N
Basque	Basque	N-*ekilan*	N-*(e)z*

Inflections are marked by a dash added to the relevant form. *Abbreviations*: ACC = accusative, ADE = adessive, GEN = genitive, INE = inessive, INSTR = instrumental case, N = noun, SG = singular

(5.6) SIXTEENTH-CENTURY RUSSIAN (Kabal'nye knigi 1594–1599, Feoktisova 1961: 203, Panzer 1984: 126)

(a) [...] pleči u sebja — skazalŭ — vŭ
(shoulders at himself — said — in)

livomŭ nožemŭ koloto [...].
(left knife.INS stab.PPP.NEUT.SG)

'[...] and his own shoulders—he said—stabbed on the left (shoulder) with the knife [...].'

Just like in Russian, in Belorussian, too, a comitative preposition, the phonological form of which is *z*, plus the instrumental case suffix encode comitative participants, see (5.7) below, whereas the instrumental category is expressed only by the instrumental case suffix, cf. (8):

(5.7) BELORUSSIAN (Natalia Bugay, p.c.)

Jana priexala **z** mamaj.
she came with mother

'She came with her mom.'

(5.8) BELORUSSIAN (Natalia Bugay, p.c.)
Ën napisau list getim aloukam.
he wrote letter this.INS pencil.INS
'He wrote the letter with this pencil.'

The situation in Ukranian is the same as in Russian and Belorussian: there is a comitative preposition, *z*, plus an instrumental case suffix for marking the comitative on the one hand, (5.9), and just the instrumental case suffix for marking the instrumental, on the other, (5.10):

(5.9) UKRAINIAN (Natalia Bugay, p.c.)
Vona priïxala z mamoju.
she came with mother.INS
'She came with her mom.'

(5.10) UKRAINIAN (Natalia Bugay, p.c.)
Vin napisav lista cim olivcem.
he wrote letter this.INS pencil.INS
'He wrote the letter with this pencil.'

Likewise, Polish consistently distinguishes between marking comitatives and instrumentals. Thus, in example (5.11a), the comitative participant has a double marking: an instrumental case suffix plus the preposition *z*, whereas the instrument in (5.11b) is marked simply by means of the instrumental case suffix. Both case roles use the instrumental case suffix, but the comitative is distinguished by adding a preposition.

(5.11) POLISH (Lötzsch 1996: 56)
(a) Ja mówię z przyjacielem.
(I speak with friend.INSTR)[4]
'I speak with my friend.'
(b) Ja pracuję ręką.
(I work hand.INSTR)
'I work with my hand.'

Essentially, the situation in Polish is the same as the one found in Russian, Ukrainian, and Belorussian, which consistently distinguish between comitatives and instrumentals: all four languages use the instrumental case suffix for both comitative and instrumental participants, but comitative participants additionally take the comitative preposition.

In the South Slavic language Bulgarian, one and the same form, the preposition *s (săs)*, is used to code both the comitative and the instrumental, (5.12):

[4] Glosses are ours; no glosses are provided by the author.

(5.12) BULGARIAN

(a) Tja dojde s brat si.
she came with brother her
'She came with her brother.'

(b) Toj otvori vratata s tozi ključ.
he opened door.the with this key
'He opened the door with this key.'

This comitative–instrumental polysemy, however, is an innovation. This does not mean that there was no preposition 'with' in Old Bulgarian (= Old Church Slavonic): the Modern Bulgarian form *s (sŭs)* can easily be traced back to the Old Bulgarian preposition *sŭ*. However, in Old Bulgarian, the preposition *sŭ* 'with' did not mark the instrumental. Old Bulgarian had an elaborate case system (which almost disappeared by the end of the fourteenth century) and the instrumental case was one of the cases. So, just like in Russian, Ukranian, Belorussian, and Polish, in order to mark instrumental meaning, only the instrumental case suffix was used. The comitative preposition *sŭ* was used to mark 'togetherness', 'co-location' with concrete entities. Written records from Old Bulgarian indicate that with abstract entities, the comitative preposition could also be used—in order to express manner, (5.13)—but this use was not obligatory in all cases, (5.14):

(5.13) OLD CHURCH SLAVONIC (Mirčev 1963: 183)
I pridoša naprasno sŭ straxom veliem
and came.they all.of.a.sudden with intimidation great

mnjašte ustrašiti ego, xotjašte da bežit ot mjasto
thinking frighten him wanting to force.out from place

togo stogo [...].
this.ACC sacred
'And they came all of a sudden with many threats, thinking that they will frighten him, because they wanted to force him to leave this/the sacred place [...].'

(5.14) OLD CHURCH SLAVONIC (Codex Suprasliensis 441, 19–20; Kuteva 1998)
kyimŭ li poušteniemŭ stojati xotěxǫ za
what.INS Q bravery.INS stay.INF want.3PL.PAST for

mrĭtvĭca [...].
dead.man
'with what bravery would they have taken sides with the dead man [...].'

That the comitative marker—the preposition *sŭ*—was extending its function to mark manner also is a grammaticalization development attested across genetically and geographically remote languages (Heine and Kuteva 2002), and it is not surprising that we should be able to come across evidence for this development also taking place in Old Bulgarian. What is relevant to us here is that the frequently observed, universal grammaticalization development *comitative* > *instrumental*, has—to the best of our knowledge—not been attested in Old Bulgarian.

Just like Bulgarian, Macedonian marks both comitatives and instrumentals by means of the comitative preposition (*so*) only, (5.15) and (5.16), respectively:

(5.15) MACEDONIAN (Friedman 1977: 140–1)
Po kratko vreme se vrati vo Skopje [...]
after short time REFL returned in Skopje
so eden drugar, Zoran.
with one friend Zoran
'After a short time, he returned to Skopje [...] with a friend, Zoran.'

(5.16) MACEDONIAN (Friedman 1977: 140)
Pioneri patuvaat **so** voz.
pioneers travel with train
'The pioneers are travelling by train.'

Both Upper Sorbian and Lower Sorbian have a comitative–instrumental polysemy, using the preposition *z*(*e*) 'with' both as a comitative and an instrumental marker, (5.17).

(5.17) UPPER SORBIAN (Lötzsch 1996: 56)
(a) Ja rěču **z** přećelom.
(I speak with friend.INSTR)
'I speak with my friend.'
(b) Ja dźěłam **z** ruku.
(I work with hand.INSTR)
'I work with my hand.'

As Lötzsch (1996: 56) argues convincingly, Sorbian, as a result of nearly one millennium of intense contact with German, has replicated the German comitative–instrumental polysemy by grammaticalizing the comitative preposition *z(e)* 'with' to an instrumental marker—with the effect that this preposition is now used obligatorily for both comitative (5.17a) and instrumental participants (5.17b). Thus, Sorbian has acquired a property that unites it with SAE.

And the same appears to apply to Slovenian, which has developed a comitative–instrumental polysemy generally attributed to German influence (Stolz 2001: 601).

Croatian displays the Slavic pattern that we illustrated with example (5.11) from Polish, distinguishing the comitative and instrumental by means of the preposition *s*, (5.18a). But there is one variety of Croatian that has experienced the same development as Sorbian and Slovenian. This is Molise Croatian, or Molisean, the language of the Croatian minority of Molise, southern Italy, which has a history of 500 years of contact with Italian (Breu 1996: 26–8). In the same way as Sorbian and Slovenian, this Slavic minority has extended the use of its comitative preposition *s* to also mark instrumental participants. Accordingly, a Standard Croatian instrumental phrase, as in (5.18a), is expressed in Molisean as in (5.18b) on the model of Italian, (5.18c).

(5.18) Instrumental marking in Standard Croatian, Molisean, and Italian (Breu 1996: 26).

(a) STANDARD CROATIAN nožem 'with a knife'
(knife.INSTR)

(b) MOLISE CROATIAN **s** nožem 'with a knife'
(with knife.INSTR)

(c) ITALIAN **con** un coltello 'with a knife'
(with a knife)

In this way, Molisean speakers, like Sorbian or Slovenian speakers, established structural isomorphism in a double sense: first, they introduced a comitative–instrumental polysemy identical to the one of the model language and, second, they introduced a preposition where the model language also has a preposition.

To conclude, there is an immediate correlation between language structure and the sociolinguistic factor of language contact: those Slavic communities that are known to have had a long history of intense language contact with the SAE languages German and Italian, that is Sorbian, Slovenian, and Molisean, have acquired a comitative–instrumental polysemy via grammaticalization, while Slavic languages such as Polish, Ukranian, Belorussian, and Russian, that do not have such a history, have retained the Slavic case distinction.

On account of this situation it comes as no surprise that it is exactly those Slavic languages or varieties that appear to have replicated article uses from

German or Italian (see Chapter 3) that have also acquired a comitative–instrumental polysemy on the model of the same languages.

Baltic languages.[5] Written documents suggest that, in the sixteenth century, Lithuanian distinguished morphologically between comitative and instrumental marking (Stolz *et al.* 2006: 417). In Modern Lithuanian, instrumental relations can be expressed simply with the instrumental inflection, as in (5.19a), but even prototypical instrumental relations can be expressed by the preposition *su* plus the instrumental case inflection, as in (5.19b). The construction in (5.19b) is an innovation but is gaining ground to the detriment of that of (5.19a).

(5.19) LITHUANIAN (Stolz 2001: 604)

(a)

Seniau	rugius	piautuv-ais	piaudavom.
formerly	rye.ACC.PL	sickle-INSTR.PL	cut.FREQ.1.PL

'Formerly, we used to harvest rye with sickles.'

(b)

Nue̊jo	arti	Jonelis	smilčių
go.away.3.PRET	plough.INF	Jonelis.NOM	sand.GEN.PL
su	savo	žagrel-	e.
with	his	plough-INSTR	

'Jonelis went to plough sandy ground with his plough.'

As the description by Stolz (2001: 604) suggests, Lithuanian represents the first step on the way from comitative to instrumental marking, where the comitative preposition *su* is added to the instrumental phrase as a reinforcing device. Using the structure [*su* + INST] for optionally marking instrumental relations in this way is an innovation in Lithuanian, leading to a situation where comitatives and instrumentals are no longer formally distinguished.

The next step in this general evolution is represented by Latvian (Stolz 2001: 604). In this language, the preposition *ar* is the uncontested marker of both comitative and instrumental (Stolz 2001: 594–5); the preposition governs the accusative case suffix in the singular and the dative suffix in the plural. The comitative–instrumental polysemy, however, has not always been there: in Old Latvian there appears to have been distinct marking for comitatives and instrumentals, where the instrumental was expressed inflectionally and the comitative by the preposition *ar.* As in Lithuanian, the prepositional phrase with *ar* started as a reinforcing use pattern of the morphological instrumental. Subsequently, the prepositional pattern ousted the simple morphological instrumental (Stolz 2001: 600–1). With the generalization of the preposition

[5] The following is a brief summary of the detailed analysis presented by Stolz (2001) and Stolz *et al.* (2006).

ar to mark instrumentals, the formerly distinct morphological instrumental case was marginalized, gradually disappearing from the Latvian case paradigm of both nouns and pronouns, but surviving in relics in the modern literary language and in some highly lexicalized relics. Thus, Latvian is suggestive of an evolution that was similar to the one that appears to have taken place in Sorbian, Slovenian, and Molise Croatian.

Note that the present situation of Latvian is not an entirely new one in this language; rather, it is similar to what can be assumed to have been the case in the earlier history of the language, where there was also case polysemy:

> by the introduction of the preposition *ar*, the inherited Indo-European morphological instrumental, which covered both comitative and instrumental functions, first was split up in two distinct categories, viz. a prepositional comitative and an inflectional instrumental, before the new comitative took over the entire functional domain of the original instrumental (Stolz 2001: 601).

Finno-Ugric languages. Since the sixteenth century, when written documents became available, Finnish has had separate markings for comitative and instrumental (Stolz *et al.* 2006: 417). The comitative is expressed either by the (more literary) inflectional *-ine-*, obligatorily followed by a possessive suffix, or by the postpositional phrase with *kanssa* (Stolz 2001: 603). Prototypical instrumental relations are encoded by the polyfunctional adessive case, which also encodes possession and local relations (Stolz 2001: 602). Sami on the other hand has a comitative–instrumental polysemy: the comitative case suffixes *-in* and *-guin* encode both comitatives and instrumentals (for details, see Stolz 2001: 599–600). The rise of this polysemy was possibly induced by contact with Norwegian and Swedish,[6] but there is no concrete evidence to substantiate this hypothesis (Stolz 2001: 604; see below).

Estonian has been a type B language since at least the sixteenth century, where the comitative case suffix *-ga* is used for both comitatives and instrumentals (Stolz 2001: 599–600). That Estonian *-ga*, unlike its Finnish cognate *kanssa*, has developed a comitative–instrumental polysemy 'is most convincingly explained by the long presence of a German upper class in former Livland' (Stolz 2001: 603; cf. Nau 1995: 136–7), presumably also by Swedish influence. This polysemy can be traced back to the earliest documented stage in the development of Estonian. In the sixteenth century, the adposition *kaas* had both comitative and instrumental functions, and this did not change when *kaas* underwent decategorialization and erosion, turning into the case

[6] Stolz (2001: 609) hypothesizes that the comitative–instrumental polysemy in Sami is due to 'the partial Germanicization in northern Scandinavia.'

suffix *-ga* in the seventeenth and eighteenth centuries. On account of the etymology of this marker, Stolz *et al.* (2006, ch. 13) hypothesize that this case suffix is the result of a development from noun to affix, as sketched in (5.20), and that the polysemy stage encountered in the sixteenth century was preceded by a situation where *kaas* was exclusively a comitative adposition.

(5.20) The grammaticalization of the Estonian case suffix *-ga* (Stolz *et al.* 2006, ch. 13)
kansa 'people, crowd' (noun) > *kaas* 'with' (adposition) > *ka* > *-ga* (suffix)

With reference to the growth of the comitative-instrumental polysemy, Stolz observes:

> We are also positive that the Germanicization of the comitative–instrumental distinction goes beyond the language boundaries of Estonian. Latvian—sharing the same Germanic superstrate with Estonian for several centuries—has also remodelled its formerly incoherent system in terms of coherence (Stolz 2001: 604).

Hungarian appears to have had a comitative–instrumental polysemy since the twelfth century. As Stolz *et al.* (forthc.; fn. 320) note, in the first piece of written Hungarian, a late twelfth-century funeral speech, there was an inflectional case marker that covered both functions. And this polysemy is also found in modern Hungarian, see (5.21).

(5.21) Hungarian (John Haiman, p.c.)

(a)

A	fi-	á-	**val**	lakik.
DEF	son-	3.SG.POSS-	with	live.3.SG.PRES

'She lives with her son.'

(b)

Egy	ceruzá-	**val**	ír.
one	pencil-	with	write.3.SG.PRES

'I am writing with a pencil.'

While Hungarian has a long history of language contact with German, we are not aware of any information to the effect that the presence of this polysemy is contact-induced.

Celtic languages. What we observed in the languages of Europe's eastern periphery applies in a similar fashion to Europe's western periphery. Welsh has an inherited polysemy, where the preposition *â* (or *ag*)[7] is used for both comitative and instrumental functions. But there is also a specialized

[7] The preposition *â* is etymologically related to the Irish conjunction *ac* 'and'.

comitative preposition, *gyda(g)*, which emerged in the sixteenth century, being composed of the the noun *cyd* 'union, junction' and the preposition *â/ag*. *gyda(g)* appears to be gaining ground at the expense of *â/ag* (Stolz 1998; Stolz *et al.* 2006).

Basque. Basque has an instrumental (*-(e)z*) and a comitative (*-ekin, -ekilan*) case suffix, although the latter can also be used for the former case function. While there is a traditional case distinction, Basque as spoken in southwestern France has replicated the comitative–instrumental polysemy of its Romance model languages Gascon and French, whereby the comitative suffix *-ekin/-ekilan* was grammaticalized to also express the instrumental function, with the effect that the replica language now has the same polysemy as the model languages (Haase 1992). A similar development has taken place in Basque varieties spoken in Spain, where Spanish was the model language (see Hurch 1989: 14ff for details). In these varieties as well, the instrumental case suffix *-(e)z* is a declining category; nevertheless, it can still be used to present instruments or means, (5.22a). But in many contexts it tends to be replaced by the comitative, as in the present context (5.22b), since the model language would use the comitative–instrumental preposition in this context, as in (5.23).

(5.22) BASQUE (Hurch 1989: 14)

(a)	kotxe-	**z**	'with a car'		
	car-	INSTR			
(b)	kotxe-	a-	r-	**ekin**	'with the car'
	car-	the-	*r*-	COM	

(5.23) SPANISH (Hurch 1989: 15)

con	el	coche	'with the car'
with	the	car	

However, the situation in Spain turns out to be more complex. Spanish uses three prepositions for presenting instrumental participants: *por, con*, and, under certain circumstances, the locative preposition *en*. For each of these prepositions there is a corresponding Basque case suffix, viz. *-gatik* (cause, for Spanish *por*), *-ekin* (comitative), and *-an* (inessive locative). Now, in accordance with which preposition Spanish speakers would use in the relevant context, the instrumental suffix tends to be replaced with the corresponding Basque case suffix. In other words, the complex pattern of instrumental marking to be found in Spanish was replicated in Basque by developing three different case categories in the direction of an instrumental function, at least in specific contexts.[8] Thus, grammaticalization was responsible for the rise of a diffuse situation where a fairly transparent case, the instrumental -*(e)z*, is being given up and where there is no longer a one-to-one correspondence between form and meaning in the marking of the instrumental function.

5.4 The growth of polysemy

What we noted in the preceding paragraphs is that there is a process to be observed in a number of peripheral as well as Slavic languages whereby a distinction between comitative and instrumental marking is given up in favour of a case polysemy. This process is induced, at least to some extent, by contact with SAE languages, Stolz (2001: 604) calls it 'the Germanicization of the comitative–instrumental distinction' in Circum-Baltic languages. In all cases concerned it exhibits the same structure: a comitative case marker is also extended to mark instrumentals, the end result being polysemy in case functions.

These observations on Slavic, Baltic, Finnic languages, and Basque suggest that there was a unidirectional evolution whereby the use of comitative markers was also extended to mark instrumentals. There does not appear to be any counterexample to this evolution, which is sketched in Table 5.4. Table 5.4 represents a highly simplified depiction of the overall process; for a detailed description and model, see Stolz *et al.* (2006).

Note that comitative markers themselves are likely to be historically derived from other concepts, as the situation in Finnic languages illustrates. The Sami comitative marker -*(gu)in* is etymologically identical with modern Sami *guoibmi* 'comrade'. Presumably because of its relatively recent grammaticalization to a case marker, -*(gu)in* has not yet been fully integrated into the morphological paradigm (Stolz 2001: 599). For both the Finnish postposition *kanssa* and the Estonian case suffix -*ga/ka* an evolution can be reconstructed whereby a noun *kansa(ssa)* '(in the) people/ethnos' developed into a comitative postposition (Finnish *kanssa*, Estonian *kaas*), subsequently into a comitative, and eventually into a comitative–instrumental marker (Estonian -*ga/ka*). Stolz (2001: 600) therefore concludes that 'Sami -*guin* and Estonian -*ga*

[8] Note that whereas the Spanish markers for cause, comitative, and locative, that is, *por*, *con*, and *en*, respectively, are preposed, the corresponding forms in Basque, -*gatik*, -*ekin*, and -*an* are postposed. The best explanation for this—we propose—is the internal systemic organization of the Basque language: it is reasonable to assume that the 'formulas of equivalence' that Basque speakers establish involve the prepositional forms of the model language, Spanish, on the one hand, and the well-established case suffixes for the expression of cause, comitative, and inessive locative in their own language, on the other.

Table 5.4. The evolution from comitative to instrumental marking in peripheral and Slavic languages

Stage	Structure	Languages	Typology of Stolz *et al.* (2006)
0	Comitatives and instrumentals have different case expressions.	Polish, Ukranian, Belorussian, Russian, Finnish	Type A
1	The comitative marking is extended to also present instrumental participants, e.g. as a reinforcing, emphasizing use pattern.	Lithuanian, Welsh, Basque	Type C
2	The comitative marking is generalized as an instrumental marker; there is now comitative–instrumental polysemy. The instrumental survives in specific contexts, e.g. in idiomatic expressions, or in folk literature.	Sorbian, Slovenian, Molise Croatian, Latvian, Estonian, Sami	Type B

Source: based on Stolz 1996b; Stolz *et al.* forthc.

go back to nouns which designate (societal institutions of) human beings'[9] (see also Heine & Kuteva 2002: 91–2 for additional evidence for this grammaticalization).

5.5 Evidence for directionality

The assumptions made in the preceding section crucially depend on two main hypotheses, one concerning directionality, to be discussed in the present section, and the other relating to the role of language contact in grammatical change, which is the topic of Section 5.6.

According to the first hypothesis there is a unidirectional development from comitative to instrumental case markers. This hypothesis has been proposed independently in two different lines of research: on the one hand, the hypothesis is based on findings made within the paradigm of (synchronic) cognitive linguistics (Lakoff & Johnson 1980); on the other hand, it is based on cross-linguistic observations made by students of grammaticalization (Heine

[9] According to Nau (1995: 133), the Finnish comitative postposition *kanssa* goes back to a reconstructed noun **kansa* 'companion, comrade, compatriot'. Originally, Finnish *kanssa* and Estonian *-ga/ka* are said to be derived from a German loanword which is lexically represented in the noun *kansa* meaning 'people' in Finnish and 'spouse' in Estonian (Koptjevskaja-Tamm & Wälchli 2001: 681).

et al. 1991). But this hypothesis has been challenged by Nau (1995: 128), who claimed that comitative markers can be diachronically derived from instrumental markers. Heine and Kuteva (2002: 86) therefore conclude that more diachronic evidence is required to establish that there is a unidirectional development from comitative to instrumental markers. Note that two of the three examples adduced by Nau to substantiate her claim relate to complex comitative markers which each contain an instrumental suffix plus some additional morpheme, and she argues that these examples are suggestive of directionality from instrumentals to comitatives. It commonly happens that old comitative markers ('with') are reinforced by an additional marker (meaning something like 'together with'), while the instrumental marker retains the simple form; we dealt with cases illustrating this process in Section 5.3.

In the meantime, some pieces of evidence for a unidirectional evolution from comitative to instrumental markers have become available. This evidence concerns, first, historical observations made on the languages concerned. To give an example that was mentioned in the introduction to this chapter (Section 5.2): the Latin preposition *cum* 'with' was originally a comitative marker, attested throughout the history of the language. The instrumental function arose later, marginally attested in Classical Latin, and it is only from the fourth century AD onwards that there are clear attestations of it. In a similar fashion, case expressions such as Sorbian *z*(*e*), Molise Croatian *s*, Bulgarian *s*, Macedonian *s*, Lithuanian *su*, Latvian *ar*, Estonian *-ga*, or Basque *-ekilan* can be shown to have been used first as comitative markers before their use was extended to mark instrumentals. More recently, this hypothesis has been corroborated by reconstruction work carried out in Indo-European and other languages (Luraghi 2001; Stolz 2001).

Second, evidence for the unidirectional evolution from comitative to instrumental marking also comes from the contextual analysis of case marking. Earlier stages tend to survive in specific contexts, such as subordinate clauses, frozen (idiomatic) expressions, or oral literature. Modern Latvian has comitative–instrumental polysemy, but this polysemy is the historical result of the extension of the comitative preposition *ar* to also mark instruments. The earlier state is retained in Latvian folk songs (Dainas), where comitative and instrumentals are still distinguished in that the instrumental is primarily encoded by the pure instrumental case (Koptjevskaja-Tamm & Wälchli 2001: 681).

Conversely, we are not aware of any convincing example showing a reverse directionality, that is, where an instrumental marker turned into a comitative marker—irrespective of whether or not such a case involved language contact.

5.6 Evidence for contact

According to the second hypothesis, the grammaticalization of comitatives as instrumentals was contact-induced in the languages examined here.

Our claim that the rise of a comitative–instrumental polysemy in these languages is due to language contact is based on the following observation (see Heine & Kuteva 2005: 1.4). Suppose that language L1 has a certain structure S1 which corresponds to structure S2 in language L2. Suppose further that some speakers of L1 who have been in close contact with speakers of L2 have S2 rather than S1. In such a case we hypothesize, *ceteris paribus*, that the presence of S2 in L1 is the result of contact influence of L2 on L1. The following example from the situation in Lithuania illustrates this procedure. As we observed in Section 5.3, in Lithuanian the preposition *su* in combination with the instrumental case suffix encodes the comitative, but this structure is also optionally used to mark instrumentals. Russian and Polish consistently distinguish the two case functions, using the preposition *s* (Russian) or *z* (Polish) for comitatives while absence of the preposition marks instrumentals. Now, speakers of Russian and Polish dialects in Lithuania often also use the preposition for instrumentals (i.e. the preposition *s* in the case of Russian and *z* in the case of Polish). Thus, as in Lithuanian, the comitative preposition is added as an optional constituent of the instrumental construction in these two Slavic languages—at least as far as they are spoken in Lithuania (Koptjevskaja-Tamm & Wälchli 2001: 681). We therefore hypothesize that the Russian and Polish speakers concerned are replicating the polysemy structure they found in Lithuanian.

As Stolz *et al.* (2006: 415) note, the history of Slavic languages is telling: it is Slavic languages that are known to have had a history of intense contact with languages exhibiting a comitative–instrumental polysemy that also acquired this polysemy. These languages are on the one hand Sorbian, Slovenian, and Molise Croatian; on the other hand they are the South Slavic languages Bulgarian and Macedonian, which were part of the Balkan sprachbund configuration with its general type B situation. Accordingly, the Slavic languages without such a contact history, such as Russian, Belorussian, and Ukrainian, did not acquire a type B status. We therefore adopt the hypothesis of the authors who have dealt with these languages in some detail (Lötzsch 1996: 56; Breu 1996: 26–8) in assuming that the presence of a comitative–instrumental polysemy in these Slavic languages is due to contact-induced grammaticalization.

There is an additional reason for adopting this hypothesis: As we noted in Section 5.3, it is exactly those Slavic languages that appear to have replicated articles from German or Italian that also acquired a comitative–instrumental polysemy on the model of these very languages, whereas Slavic languages such as Russian, Belorussian, and Ukrainian have neither of these structures.

Since the grammaticalization from comitatives to instrumentals is cross-linguistically a widespread process, we cannot rule out the possibility that this process may have happened anyway in languages such as Sorbian, Slovenian, or Molise Croatian, or in the Russian or Polish varieties spoken in Lithuania, and that contact simply contributed to accelerating this process, rather than triggering it. But even if this were so, this would not invalidate the hypothesis that contact was a contributing factor in these cases of grammatical change.

The situation is more difficult to assess in the case of the Baltic languages and Basque since there is no contrasting situation of the kind just examined. However, as has been pointed out by the authors concerned (e.g. Hurch 1989; Haase 1992; Stolz 2001), these languages have also experienced a long history of contact with other languages, namely Spanish, Gascon, and French in the case of Basque, and German and Swedish in the case of the Baltic languages, and the extension of the comitative to mark instrumentals as well did not happen prior to these contacts. With reference to the growth of a comitative–instrumental polysemy (i.e. the coherent type B) in the Baltic language Latvian and the Finnic language Estonian, Stolz concludes:

> Rather, coherence was introduced into Latvian and Estonian via the Germanic languages which served as a common superstrate since the early days of the German Knights. Latvian and Estonian have not become similar in structure because of direct contact between them. Their similarity has been brought about more indirectly by way of being exposed to the pressure of exactly the same coherent prestige languages, viz. (Middle) Low German, German, and Swedish. (Stolz 2001: 607)

We therefore follow these authors in arguing that, in the case of these languages as well, contact-induced change provides the most plausible hypothesis.

5.7 Conclusions

Our analysis thus confirms the hypothesis proposed by Stolz (2001) according to which the extension of comitative markers to also mark instrumentals in Estonian (as well as Livonian), Sami, and Latvian is both unidirectional and contact-induced. Koptjevskaja-Tamm and Wälchli comment on this situation in the following way:

Stolz'[s] conclusion is that the complete merger of instrumental and comitative functions in Estonian, (Livonian), Sami and Latvian is likely to be the result of the Germanic influence on these languages, even though the Latvian situation could in principle be accounted for by internal factors (the weak morphological distinctiveness of the instrumental case). Interestingly, the Latvian merger finds parallels in the Slavic languages Slovenian and Sorbian, where it has most probably arisen because of German influence (Koptjevskaja-Tamm and Wälchli 2001: 681).

As elsewhere in this work, we argue that internal and external motivations of grammaticalization are not only not mutually exclusive, rather that they tend to reinforce one another. Quite plausibly, the extension of the Latvian comitative preposition *ar* to also mark instrumental participants may have been internally motivated, but it is likely that it was also influenced, if not triggered, by language contact.

It is hoped that the present chapter has demonstrated that the comitative–instrumental polysemy characterizing Standard Average European languages provided another attractive model for speakers of other languages. Accordingly, whenever speakers of any of the peripheral languages lacking such a polysemy entered into a situation of intense and extended contact with an SAE language, the almost predictable result was that the former developed in the direction of the latter, creating use patterns where instrumental participants are expressed by means of comitative forms, and in a number of peripheral languages such use patterns have become an obligatory component of grammatical categorization, resulting in case syncretism. In the same way as we saw in preceding chapters, the dynamics underlying this 'Europeanization' process is constrained by principles of grammaticalization, in particular by the unidirectionality principle.

6

From Question to Subordination

Among the cognitive processes leading to a gradual merger of European languages there is one that in some way or another figures in most discussions on Europe as an areal unit. It concerns the extension of forms used for expressing questions to mark relations within the clause or across clauses, that is, a conceptual transfer from the domain of interpersonal functions, relating to the interaction between speakers and hearers, to the domain of textual functions, relating to the organization of texts—more specifically to the way in which nominal participants and their connections are presented in discourse.

In the present chapter we will deal with two contrasting instances of what one might wish to call the question-to-syntax strategy. The main effect of this strategy in the languages of Europe is that it gives rise to new modes of clause subordination (Sections 6.2–6.4); additionally, it appears to have contributed to the emergence of one type of comparative constructions, to be discussed in Section 6.5.

6.1 The rise of complement, adverbial, and relative clauses

One of the puzzles surrounding grammatical polysemy in Europe concerns the fact that in the majority of European languages one and the same form is used to present word questions (6.1a), complement clauses (6.1b), and relative clauses (6.1c):

(6.1) ENGLISH
- (a) **Who** will come?
- (b) We don't know **who** killed her.
- (c) The man **who** killed her was not her husband.

We will not be concerned here with the question of whether the various uses of *who* in example (6.1) constitute—synchronically— a case of polysemy, that is, of 'related' meanings, or of homonymy, that is, of 'unrelated' meanings. However, there is little doubt that these uses can be defined as cases of heterosemy (Lichtenberk 1991), that is, that the different uses of *who* are etymologically related in that they share the same historical origin. On the basis of what we know about the history of English there is little doubt that the use of *who* in (6.1a) is temporally prior, that is to say that *who* was first used as a question marker before it was put to other uses, such as serving as a marker of complement clauses (6.1b) or of restrictive relative clauses (6.1c) (see Section 6.4.1 on this issue). Nevertheless, for the sake of convenience we will refer to cases such as (6.1) as instances of interrogative–subordination polysemy.[1]

Cross-linguistically, few languages exhibit such a polysemy pattern. It may therefore be surprising that in Europe many languages do: it is found in all Romance and Slavic languages, as well as in some Germanic languages, in Modern Greek, Hungarian and Georgian. As a result, Haspelmath (1998: 281–2) therefore considers it to be a property of Standard Average European (SAE). The questions that arise are in particular the following:

(i) Why does such a polysemy exist in the first place?
(ii) If it is due to historical factors, is it the result of genetic inheritance?
(iii) Why is it found almost everywhere in Europe but is fairly uncommon elsewhere?

The answer to question (i) appears to be uncontroversial: all the available evidence suggests that this polysemy is the result of a grammaticalization process whereby a grammatical marker originally used to introduce questions was extended to introduce subordinate clauses as well; we will return to this issue in Section 6.4.1. Question (ii) can—at least in part—be answered in the negative. Since it is found in European languages that appear to be genetically unrelated, such as Indo-European languages on the one hand and Hungarian and Georgian on the other, genetic relationship can be ruled out as the only, or the decisive factor in the spread of the polysemy. And there is also an obvious answer to (iii): the fact that this polysemy is found throughout Europe but rarely elsewhere (but see Nadkarni 1975 for examples from India) suggests that it is the result of language contact—more specifically of contact-induced grammaticalization. That this hypothesis is empirically sound can be demonstrated by looking at languages that do not belong to the core of SAE but are known to have had a history of intense contact with SAE languages. Such languages are likely to exhibit a similar kind of polysemy,

[1] In doing so, we are aware that the different uses of *who* in (6.1) do not meet all the criteria that are widely held to be definitional properties of polysemy, such as the requirement that members of a polysemous set should belong to one and the same grammatical category.

and for some of these languages it is possible to reconstruct details of the process that led to the rise of this polysemy.

Our first example concerns Basque (see also Section 6.3 below). In this language, a finite relative clause precedes its head; there is no relative pronoun, but the verb takes a suffix marking it as subordinate. However, a new relativization strategy has been used in certain parts of the Basque-speaking area under the influence of Spanish, in that the Basque question marker *zein* 'which?' (also 'who?' in places) is being used as an equivalent of the Spanish interrogative pronouns and *zein* has been grammaticalized to a relative clause marker (Trask 1998: 320). Relative clauses introduced by *zein* are documented in texts since the seventeenth century, but as a rule only in translations (Hurch 1989: 21). As we noted above, the new form does not replace the earlier structure; rather, *zein* is added to the existing relative construction[2]—with the result that there is now double marking on post-nominal relative clauses.

With reference to the questions raised above, the following answers can be given. The rise of polysemy of the Basque item *zein* is due to a process whereby the use of this item was extended from question marker to additionally mark clause subordination. Genetic relationship can be ruled out as a contributing factor; all the available evidence (Hurch 1989; see also Haase 1992) suggests that this process is the result of the grammatical replication of a Romance marker. Basque is not the only non-Indo-European language, however, that has replicated the European strategy of using interrogatives as relative clause markers.

Balkan Turkish provides another example for the contact-induced interrogative-to-relative grammaticalization (Matras 1998*b*: 94–6). One of the functions of Standard Turkish converbs is to express what corresponds to relative clauses in other languages, involving an attributive construction preceding the head noun. More recently, this construction is being replaced in Balkan Turkish by a finite-clause construction based on the grammaticalization of the interrogative *ne* 'what?' referring back to the head noun. For example, in West Rumelian Turkish dialects spoken in Macedonia the interrogative *ne* 'what?' has been grammaticalized to a relativizer modelled on Macedonian *što*, and in a similar fashion the use of Turkish *ne zaman* 'when?' also turned into a relativizer on the model of Macedonian *koga* and Albanian *kur* 'when', thereby eliminating participial constructions. Furthermore, the use of Turkish *niçin* 'why' was extended to serve as a reason marker 'because', thereby replicating colloquial usages of Macedonian *zošto/zašto*, Albanian *pse*, etc. (Friedman 2003: 64–5).

[2] But see alsoTrask (1998: 320).

As in other cases of grammatical replication, the interrogative-to-subordination process did not start from zero but is suggestive of a transition from minor to major use pattern (see Section 2.2). Speakers of Ottoman Turkish appear to have known an interrogative use pattern serving at least as a complementizer, as suggested by (6.2), where *nekim* introduces an object complement clause; and this pattern has its parallels in modern Standard Turkish.

(6.2) OTTOMAN TURKISH (Matras 1998*b*: 96)

nekim	siz	dilersenüz	edevüz.
what.CONJ	2.PL.NOM	wish.COND.2.PL	do.OPT.1.PL

'We shall do whatever you wish.'

The transition from minor to major use pattern in Balkan Turkish entailed in particular the following changes. First, it introduced a new construction where the relative clause appears to be added to the main clause as a kind of afterthought, (6.3). Accordingly, the new use pattern started out as a pragmatically marked structure rather than as a subordinating construction. Second, the interrogative-based relative use pattern entirely replaces the earlier gerundial or converbal relative construction in this Turkish dialect. Third, it also replaces Turkish converbs in adverbial clauses, drawing on the same semantic specifiers as the respective interrogatives, (6.4). Fourth, it is in accordance with the general drift to be observed in Balkan languages leading from non-finite to finite constructions of clause subordination. And fifth, it has been grammaticalized to the extent that it includes uses as a marker of headed relative clauses, (6.3).

(6.3) BALKAN TURKISH (Matras 1998: 94)

eski	konuşma	**ne**	onlar	konuşurlar.
old	speech	REL	3.PL.NOM	speak.HAB.3.PL

'It is an old language that they speak.'

(6.4) BALKAN TURKISH (Matras 1998: 95)

ben	ne	kadar	**ne**	bilirim	birinci	geldi	Yahudi.
1.SG.NOM	REL	much	REL	know.HAB.1.SG	first	come.PAST.3.SG	Jew

'As far as I know the Jews came first.'

While there seems to be little doubt that the rise of the new use pattern was contact-induced, there is no information on which of the Balkan languages exactly provided the model (but see Friedman 2003: 64–5). Note that in neighbouring Indo-European Balkan languages, for example Slavic languages, there were appropriate models for the interrogative-to-subordination strategy, and that the Balkan Turkish use pattern exhibits a functional configuration that is essentially identical to that of the neighbouring Indo-European Balkan languages.

Note also that in some varieties of Balkan Turkish it is not only the neighbouring Indo-European languages on the Balkan Peninsula that have influenced relative clause formation, but also Persian, at least partially. A careful investigation (Tufan forthc.) of one particular variety of Balkan Turkish—the one spoken in Gostivar, Macedonia—shows that for most positions of the accessibility hierarchy (Keenan & Comrie 1977), Gostivar Macedonian Turkish follows the Macedonian model. For one position, however—the indirect object—the relative clause construction is structured in a way which is neither Standard Turkish nor Macedonian; rather, it follows the model of Persian, a language with which Standard Turkish has been in contact for centuries. The idea that Persian has influenced Turkish in relative clause formation is not new (Adamović 1985: 260, cited after Matras 1998*b*: 94). What is new is the recognition that this influence has left a trace in such a high-contact variety of Turkish as Gostivar Macedonian Turkish, which has otherwise been predominantly modelled on the Slavic variety of Gostivar Macedonian.

Nevertheless, the Balkan Turkish *ne*-construction differs remarkably from the constructions of these neighbouring Indo-European languages in that it lacks what Matras calls 'a well-developed, pre-planned hypotaxis' (Matras 1998*b*: 95). This fact is far from surprising—rather, it is to be expected: being the result of a fairly young process of grammaticalization, the construction still exhibits properties of its genesis as a pragmatically motivated construction devoid of syntactic constraints such as involving hypotaxis. Furthermore, as we observed in Chapter 2, replicated categories, at least in their early stages of replication, tend to be less grammaticalized than their model categories.

In most cases, the replication of the interrogative-to-relative strategy does not lead to replacement, that is, to the loss of an existing structure. But this does not apply to this Balkan Turkish example, as we saw above: the interrogative-based relative use pattern appears to be replacing the earlier Turkish gerundial or converbal relative construction as well as Turkish converbs in adverbial clauses.

6.2 A four-stage scenario of grammaticalization

We will now formulate—very tentatively at this stage of research—a hypothesis which is compatible with all the data on WH-relativization that we have been able to collect so far. The term interrogative marker (IM) refers to a paradigm of linguistic forms typically, but not confined to, distinguishing the ontological categories listed in Table 6.1. We will ignore here other ontological categories, such as quantity (*how many/how much?*), reason (*why?*), etc., because they tend to receive complex morphological expressions.

On the basis of the cross-linguistic evidence available, the following major stages of grammaticalization from IM to marker of clause subordination can be hypothesized:

(i) *Stage 1.* The IM is used to present word questions (6.5a). Stage 1 differs from all other stages in that it may, and for the most part does, involve mono-clausal sentences, while all other stages require clause combining.

(ii) *Stage 2.* The use of the IM is extended to introduce indefinite subordinate clauses (6.5b). Depending on the ontological category of the IM involved, these may be complement or adverbial clauses. Thus, the human ('who?') and the inanimate ('what?') IMs are likely to be grammaticalized to complementizers; in the case of all other ontological categories, IMs tend to grammaticalize into indefinite adverbial clause markers.

(iii) *Stage 3.* In addition to indefinite clauses, the IM now introduces definite subordinate (complement or adverbial) clauses, which may also be interpreted as headless relative clauses (6.5c); but it is not used for headed relative clauses.

(iv) *Stage 4.* In addition to definite non-headed relative clauses, the IM now introduces headed relative clauses (6.5d).

(6.5) ENGLISH
(a) **Who** came?
(b) I don't know **who** came.
(c) You also know **who** came.
(d) Do you know the woman **who** came?

TABLE 6.1. Salient interrogative categories (IMs)

Ontological category	English example
Human	*who?*
Inanimate	*what?*
Space	*where?*
Time	*when?*
Manner	*how?*
Attributive	*which?*

TABLE 6.2 Stages in the evolution from interrogative to relative clause marker

Stage	Function of interrogative marker
1	Marking word questions
2	Introducing indefinite complement or adverbial clauses
3	Introducing definite complement or adverbial clauses
4	Introducing headed relative clauses

Table 6.2 summarizes these stages.

The stages discussed above are not discrete entities, rather there are intermediate stages which can be interpreted with reference to either the preceding or the following stage, and which are crucial for the process to proceed from one stage to another. For instance, the following example in (6.6) can be interpreted with reference to either stage 2, paraphrased in (6.6a), or to stage 3, paraphrased in (6.6b).

(6.6) ENGLISH

What he wrote was not of much help to us.

(a) 'Whatever he wrote, it was not of much help to us.'

(b) '(The letter) he wrote was not of much help to us.'

We noted above that distinctions between IMs of different ontological categories are ignored here. For our general purposes, this may be justified; in a more fine-grained analysis, however, this procedure turns out to be too simplistic. Grammaticalization is a process that starts out in one specific context and is gradually extended to more and more contexts, and subsequently to classes of contexts. Now, each of the ontological categories distinguished in Table 6.1 can be viewed as constituting a distinct kind of context, and each can exhibit a different grammaticalization behaviour.

This may be illustrated with the situation in German. In accordance with Table 6.1, German can be classified as a stage 3 language, that is, it exhibits all stages except stage 4. This classification is justified on the basis of the observation that neither the human (*wer* 'who?'), nor the inanimate (*was* 'what?') or the time IM (*wann* 'when?') may be used as a marker introducing headed relative clauses. Accordingly, sentence (6.7a) is not well-formed, at least not in the High variety of German (this does not apply to some dialects of southern Germany, where the process is more advanced). But a different situation is found with the manner IM (*wie* 'how?'), which can clearly be used as a relative clause marker, as in (6.7b).

(6.7) GERMAN

(a) *Der Mann, **wer** gestern gestorben ist, war sein Vater.
the man who yesterday died is was his father
'The man who died yesterday was his father.'

(b) Ich mag nicht die Art, **wie** du deine Frau behandelst.
I like not the manner how you your wife treat
'I don't like the way you treat your wife.'

The situation is more complex in the case of the space IM (*wo* 'where?'), which is accepted by some speakers and/or in some contexts but rejected otherwise. Accordingly, in examples such as the following there will be disagreement among native speakers of High German as to whether it is well-formed or not.

(6.8) GERMAN

?Ich kenne nicht die Straße, **wo** du wohnst.
I know not the street where you live
'I don't know the street where you live.'

What these observations suggest is that grammaticalization has affected the various IMs in different ways: whereas the human, the inanimate, and the time IMs are still solidly stage 3, the space IM appears to be somewhere in between stages 3 and 4, and the manner IM has reached the final stage 4.

6.2.1 *A survey*

In Section 6.1 we provided two examples to establish that there appears to be a process of 'Europeanization' whereby SAE languages served as models to replicate the interrogative-to-subordination process—and consequently the polysemy pattern uniting question and subordination markers—in peripheral languages of Europe. In the present section, we will look in more detail at a number of peripheral European languages that are hypothesized to have grammaticalized IMs to markers of clause subordination.

Basque. We have already briefly discussed this language in Section 6.1. Basque has a fully grammaticalized scale extending from stage 1 to stage 4, involving in particular the question markers *non* 'who?', *zer* 'what?', *nun* 'where?', *nola* 'how?', and *zein* or *zoin* 'which?'. The following are examples of stages 1, 2, and 4.

(6.9) BASQUE (Haase 1992: 123, 149, 152) Stage 1

(a) **Zer** ari da?
what PROG PRS.3.SG
'What is he doing?'

(b)

Ba-	dakizü,	**zer**	de-	n?	Stage 2
ENZ-	know.PRS.3.SG<2.SG	what	PRS.3.SG-	SR	

'Do you know what he/she/it is?'

(c)

Hiri	bat	ba-	zen,	**zoin**-	tan	Stage 4
town	one	ENZ-	PRT.3.SG	which-	TRN.INE	
ez	bait-	zen	eliza-	rik.		
NEG	SR-	PRT.3.SG	church-	PART		

'There was a town where there was no church.'

As we observed in Section 6.1, constructions using interrogatives for clause subordination are not recent ones. By 1782, *nun* 'where?', *nola* 'how?', and *çoinh* (= *zoin*) 'which?' appear to have been established as markers of adverbial and relative clauses (see Haase 1992: 151–2). There is little doubt that the constructions are the result of replication from Romance languages, which is also reflected in the fact that these constructions are called by experts of the language the 'Romance subordination type'. It may therefore come as no surprise that they do not appear to be very popular among modern Basque speakers:

In der heutigen Sprache ist der Gebrauch solcher Konstruktionen zurückgegangen; auch in geschriebener Sprache werden sie vermieden, da sie zu romanisch erscheinen [In the present-day language, the use of such constructions has receded; in the written language as well they are avoided since they appear to be too much of the Romance type.] (Haase 1992: 153).

Accordingly, the informants that Haase consulted during his research in the Basque-speaking territory of France rejected the use of the 'Romance subordination type'.

Romani. (Vlach dialect of Romani or Romanes). Under the influence of Balkanic languages, the Kelderaš/Lovari variety of the Vlach dialect of Romani has grammaticalized its interrogative markers *k*- and *s*-, both inherited from its Indic past, to relative clause markers, thereby replacing the earlier Indic constructions of marking relative clauses (Matras 1996: 65–6). In a detailed treatment of the 'Balkanization' of Romani, Matras (1998*b*: 97–8) observes that the modern Romani relativizers and adverbial conjunctions derive historically from interrogatives, replacing the left-branching exposition that is likely to have characterized relativization at an earlier state of Romani's history as an Indo-Aryan language.

Romani has gone through the whole range of grammaticalization, in that the question words *kon* 'who?', *so* 'what?', *kaj* 'where?', *kana* 'when?', and *sar* 'how?' have been grammaticalized to markers of complement clauses, adverbial clauses, and relative clauses. The following examples illustrate the various stages.

(6.10) ROMANI (Romanes, Vlach dialect; Matras 1996: 66ff, 73)
(a) [. . .] **sar** te phenav, [. . .]? Stage 1
how COMP say.1.SG
'[. . .] how shall I say [. . .]?'

(b) Tu žanes **kon** sas kodo kaj tu mardan les? Stage 2
you know.2.SG who was this where you beat.2.SG him.ACC
'Do you know who it was whom you hit?'

(c) Mukhlas štare šavoren **kana** voj mulas. Stage 3
left.3.SG four.OBL childen.ACC.PL when she died.3.SG
'She left four children behind when she died.'

(d) Si jekh gažo **kaj** žutil ame. Stage 4
is one man who help.3.SG us
'There is a man who helps us.'

Outside Europe. With the spread of European languages to other parts of the world, the interrogative-to-subordination replication has been extended to other continents, such as the Americas. The North Arawak language Tariana of northwestern Brazil is in close contact with Portuguese, the official language of Brazil, and has been influenced by the latter in various ways (Aikhenvald 2002). One way in which this influence is reflected concerns a process that is strikingly similar to what happened in the Basque and Romani cases just examined: young and innovative speakers of Tariana recognize that in Portuguese interrogative pronouns are also used as relative clause markers and these speakers, therefore, also use their interrogative pronouns as markers of clause subordination on the pattern of the model language Portuguese. In doing so, they retain their own relative construction and simply add their interrogative pronoun (e.g. *kwana* 'who?')—exactly in the way that Basque speakers do. Accordingly, instead of (6.11), which is characteristic of a traditional speaker, they use (6.12).

(6.11) TARIANA (North Arawak; Aikhenvald 2002: 183)
ka-yeka-kani hĩ kayu-na na-sape.
REL-know-PAST. DEM:ANIM thus-REM.P.VIS 3.PL-speak
REL.PL
'Those who knew used to talk like this.'

(6.12) YOUNGER TARIANA SPEAKERS (North Arawak; Aikhenvald 2002: 183)
kwana ka-yeka-kani hĩ kayu-na na-sape.
who REL-know-PAST. DEM:ANIM thus-REM. 3.PL-speak
REL.PL P.VIS
'Those who knew used to talk like this.'

This Tariana example is suggestive of stage 3; there is no evidence that grammatical replication proceeded further to stage 4.

That language contact can have the effect that a language proceeds from stage 3 to a stage 4 structure is suggested by the following examples. The SAE model of extending the use of interrogative pronouns to markers of headed relative clauses appears to have been applied among Yiddish bilinguals in the USA. These bilinguals identified English *who*, the interrogative pronoun for human referents, with their corresponding interrogative pronoun *ver* 'who?' and introduced it as a relative clause marker on the model of the English relative clause marker *who*, cf. (6.13).

(6.13) YIDDISH OF AMERICAN BILINGUALS (Weinreich [1953] 1964: 30)

der	mentš	**ver**	is	do.
(the	person	who	is	here)

'The man who is here.'

Examples where a stage 3 structure was extended in a situation of language contact to a stage 4 structure can also be found among German immigrants in the USA. As we saw above, High German lacks a stage 4 situation, that is, interrogatives such as *wer* 'who?' are not used as markers of headed relative clauses. But these immigrants tend to extend the German interrogative pronoun *wer* 'who?' to uses as a relative pronoun where it would not be used in High German. Thus, in the following example, taken from German as spoken by bilinguals in Gillespie County, Texas, and Dubois County, Indiana, *wer* introduces a headed relative clause:

(6.14) GERMAN–ENGLISH BILINGUALS OF TEXAS AND INDIANA (Salmons 1990: 459)

[...] verheirat mit en(somebody mit einer, **wer** kein deutsch, eng ..., gesprochen hat, [...].

'[...] married to one ... somebody with one, that didn't speak any German, [...].'

The replication of the interrogative-to-subordination strategy does not necessarily lead to replacement of an existing structure, as we noted above; Pipil, an Aztecan language of El Salvador provides an additional example. The language can be reconstructed back as having known a number of different ways of signalling relativization (Campbell 1987: 258–60). First, it appears to have employed juxtaposition without any subordination, second, it used a 'generic' subordinator (which is *ne* in modern Pipil but can be reconstructed to *in* in Proto-Nahua), and third, there were the markers *a*[:]*kin* for animate referents and *tlein* for inanimate referents, being arguments of the matrix verb and serving as nominal heads in headless relative sentences. These structures are still found in Pipil, although juxtaposition has been almost completely eliminated. But new structures have been introduced as a result of language contact with Spanish. One concerns the Spanish relative marker *que*, which has been borrowed as *ke*. The second involves replica grammaticalization: the Pipil interrogative word *ka(h)* 'who, what?', illustrated in (6.15a), was grammaticalized to a relative clause marker, (6.15b). In roughly the same fashion, the Pipil interrogative word *tay/ta:* 'what?' was grammaticalized to a complementizer, exactly equivalent to Spanish *que/lo que* 'that, that which', which is now a constituent of the subordinate clause, (6.15c).

(6.15) PIPIL (Aztecan, Uto-Aztecan; Campbell 1985: 114–16; 1987: 259–60)

(a) **ka:** uni.
'Who is it?'

(b)

ni-	ki-	miktih	ne	mistun	**ka**	ki-	kwah	ne	tu:tu- t.
I-	it-	killed	the	cat	that	it-	ate	the	bird- ABSOL

'I killed the cat which ate the bird.'

(c)

k-	ita	**ta:**	ki-	chiwa	nemi	ne	i-	siwa:-	w.
it-	see	what	it-	do	is	the	his-	wife-	POSS

'(He) sees what his wife is doing.'

A similar situation is found in the fellow Aztecan language, Nahuatl, which can be seen as another 'victim' of the SAE expansion (Langacker 1975; Karttunen 1976; Hill & Hill 1986: 276–88): what were interrogative particles serving as indefinite pronouns of main clauses appear to have 'come to be identified with the interrogative-looking relative pronouns of Spanish and reanalyzed into the subordinate clause' (Karttunen 1976: 151). In this way, the Nahuatl interrogative particles *tlen* 'which', *aquin* 'who', and *canin* 'where' were used as equivalents of the Spanish pronouns *qui*, *que*, and *donde*, respectively. Thus, the Nahuatl sentence (6.16) appears to have been influenced by a corresponding Spanish structure as illustrated in (6.17).[3]

(6.16) NAHUATL (Karttunen 1976: 151)

In	cizhuanton	**aquin**	ocualhuicac	atl	omocuep	ichan.
the	girl	who	it.brought	water	returned	her.home

'The girl who brought (us) water went home.'

(6.17) SPANISH (Karttunen 1976: 151)
La muchacha **que** nos trajo agua volvió a casa.
'The girl who brought us water went home.'

[3] This reconstruction is, however, not uncontroversial: while some attribute this change in Nahuatl to universal/internal developments, others maintain that it can be interpreted meaningfully only if one assumes language contact (see Karttunen 1976: 152).

In both these Aztecan languages, grammatical replication has reached the final stage 4, in that it has led to a marker of headed relative clauses. Still, as in Pipil, the Nahuatl structure replicated from Spanish has not replaced the earlier structure of relative clause marking; rather, 'a Spanish relative clause type has been added to but has not supplanted the surface manifestation of an earlier Na. [Nahuatl; a.n.] relative clause structure' (Karttunen 1976: 153).

In addition to the diffusion of Portuguese and Spanish in the Americas there is another direction of diffusion of an SAE language and its interrogative-to-subordination strategy, namely the spread of Russian to other languages of the former USSR, which Comrie summarizes in the following way:

> many languages of the USSR have recently developed or are in the process of developing subordinating conjunctions, either borrowing them directly from Russian or calquing them on the structure of Russian conjunctions ... for instance by using interrogative pronouns to introduce relative clauses, or to introduce time clauses, like Russian *kogda* 'when', which, like English *when*, can introduce both questions and time clauses (Comrie 1981: 12–13, 85).

The process described by Comrie involving Russian as a model language appears to be essentially the same as that observed in Latin American languages such as Tariana, Pipil, and Nahuatl on the model of Portuguese and Spanish. First, there are two competing strategies, namely direct borrowing of interrogative forms and grammatical replication via the creation of categories corresponding to the model categories by using the grammatical means available in the replica languages. Second, what Comrie refers to as 'calquing' can be assumed to be the same mechanism as the one described in the American languages, that is the one we proposed to call replica grammaticalization. And third, the process appears to have involved both relative clauses, headless relative clauses, and adverbial clauses.

What all these examples of contact-induced change from interrogative to subordinating structures may have shown is that the situation in the various languages examined differs considerably with regard to the extent to which the grammaticalization process has proceeded. Table 6.3 sketches the main stages that can be distinguished on the basis of the data available.

6.2.2 *A grammaticalization area on the Balkans*

In concluding this section, we wish to draw attention to the fact that there are also regionally confined processes in Europe leading to the grammaticalization from interrogative to subordinating structures. For example, in a monographic treatment of adverbial subordinators in the languages of Europe, Kortmann (1998*b*: 498–500) found that the languages of the Balkan sprachbund all employ

TABLE 6.3. Stages in the evolution from interrogative to subordination in peripheral languages

Stage	Status of the old category	Status of the new category	Languages
A	The old use pattern is the only really acceptable one	Incipient stage of grammaticalization: there is a contact-induced new use pattern confined to specific groups of speakers, being portrayed as 'bad language' by conservative speakers	Tariana
B		The new use pattern is accepted side-by-side with the old construction	Basque, Pipil, Nahuatl
C	The old use pattern declines	The new use pattern is the preferred one, being used more frequently and in more contexts than the old one	Balkan Turkish, Balkan Romani
D	The old use pattern disappears, perhaps surviving in frozen relics	The new use pattern is the only acceptable one	Kelderaš/Lovari Romani

a subordinator incorporating an interrogative quantifier 'how much?' for adverbial subordinators expressing degree ('inasmuch as, insofar as') as their exclusive or one of their primary meanings, for example Albanian *me sa* ('with how.much'), Bulgarian *do-kolkoto* ('until/up.to-how.much.REL'), Rumanian *după cît* ('according.to-how.much'). In addition to the uncontroversial Balkan languages, this structure is also found in Serbian/Croatian, Hungarian, Italian, Polish, Russian, and Latvian (but also in Udmurt and Armenian).

We hypothesize that this evidence is suggestive of an area of grammaticalization,[4] for the following reasons. The geographical distribution of this property makes it plausible to assume that language contact was involved in its spread. That we are dealing with a grammaticalization process is suggested by the fact that it appears to be another instance of a development whereby interrogative pronouns grammaticalize to markers of clause subordination, including

[4] A grammaticalization area consists of a group of geographically contiguous languages that have undergone the same grammaticalization process as a result of language contact (Heine & Kuteva 2005: 5.2).

relative clause markers and complementizers. The present case, where a quantifying interrogative—typically in collocation with some adpositional or other element—assumes the function of a comparative subordinator, can be seen as a special instance of this conceptual transfer from interrogative to subordinating structures, arising and spreading in one specific region of Europe. But, like the other grammaticalization areas characterizing the Balkan sprachbund, this area is not restricted to Balkan languages (see Heine & Kuteva 2005).

6.3 Notes on history

The interrogative–subordination polysemy characterizing SAE languages has a long history in Europe. In Latin there was a fully grammaticalized polysemy, where interrogative markers were used in the same way for marking indefinite (6.18a) and definite complement clauses (6.18b), as well as for headed relative clauses (6.18c).

(6.18) LATIN (Plautus)

(a) Miser est **qui** amat. Stage 2
poor is who loves
'Someone who is in love is to be deplored.'

(b) **Quod** credidisti reddo. Stage 3
what you.have.lent I.return
'What you have lent (me) I return (it to you).'

(c) (Eae) litterae **quas** mihi scripsisti mihi jucundissimae fuerunt. Stage 4
these letters which me you. rote me most.pleasant. ones were
'The letters that you wrote me were very pleasant to me.'

All modern Romance languages have a fully grammaticalized polysemy as well, but the extent to which this is due to genetic relationship, that is, to direct inheritance from Latin, or to areal diffusion is not entirely clear. In Classical Latin, the question words and corresponding relative markers were only slightly differentiated, but in the early history of French and other Romance languages they became increasingly different (Harris & Campbell 1995: 309).

Germanic languages. Whereas the polysemy has a history of well over two millennia in Romance, it is a more recent phenomenon in Germanic, and it seems plausible to assume that the Germanic languages acquired the polysemy as a result of contact with Romance languages. Accordingly, Thomason and Kaufman observe:

The use of the words **who/which/what** (originally only interrogative/indefinite in Germanic) in restrictive relative clauses is found in several Germanic languages, but it is limited to formal usage, and seems clearly to be modeled on French or Latin usage (Thomason and Kaufman 1988: 320).

This use did not remain restricted to specific sociolinguistic categories such as formal usage, as the case of English demonstrates, where the interrogatives have been fully grammaticalized to stage 4 markers across sociolinguistic variables. However, as we would predict on the basis of generalizations on grammatical replication (Heine & Kuteva 2005, ch. 3), grammaticalization in the Germanic languages has not attained the level of development that it has in Romance languages. For example, it has not generally reached the stage 4 situation characteristic of the Romance languages.

Proto-Germanic does not seem to have known any interrogative–subordination polysemy. Stage 3 uses of definite complementizers are documented in both Old High German[5] and Old English, at least in written communication, see (6.19). Such uses first occur in translations from Latin, hence it is possible that they were induced by contact with Latin (Lockwood 1968: 246).

(6.19)	(a)	Old High German:	inu ni lârut ir **hwaz** David teta.
	(b)	Old English:	ne rǣdde ge þæt **hwæt** David dyde.
	(c)	Latin:	non legistis quid fecerit David.
			'Have ye not read what David did?'
			(Lockwood 1968: 245–6)

Whilst there are a few examples of interrogative pronouns in Old High German that came close to representing relative clause markers, they were confined to translations from Latin. Interrogatives such as *hwer* 'who' and *hwelîh* 'which' remained restricted to stage 2 and stage 3 uses, while demonstratives and the demonstrative adverb *dâr* 'there' were grammaticalized to relative clause markers.

Only centuries later did simple interrogative pronouns appear as relatives (Lockwood 1968: 246). It was, in particular, the German locative interrogative *wo* 'where' which intruded the domain of the older relative clause marker *da*, and the two were in competition for some four centuries, until about 1800 *wo* was accepted as the established norm, and in a similar fashion, the neuter interrogative *was* 'what' replaced the older demonstrative-based relative *das* in a number of contexts, especially when referring to indefinite antecedents (Romaine 1984: 450).

[5] By the ninth century, the interrogatives *hwer* 'who' and *hwelîh* 'which' tended to be preceded (and followed) by *sô* to form stage 2 and stage 3 complementizers in Old High German, but *sô* was later on reduced to *s*, and in the fourteenth century it disappeared entirely (Lockwood 1968: 246–7).

In spoken German of many areas, *was* was extended to all contexts. Originally confined to introducing peripheral (oblique) complements, *wo* was extended in some German dialects, such as Alemannic, to mark core participants as well, and in these dialects it has acquired full status as a stage 4 relative marker, (see 6.20). In the early nineteenth century, *was* intruded a context that until then had been reserved for *das*, namely that of introducing adjuncts and referring anaphorically to entire clauses (Fleischer 2004: 233–4).

(6.20) LOW ALEMANNIC OF BASLE (Fleischer 2004: 225)

Dä	Ma,	**wo**ni	im	s	Mässer	gä	ha
the	man	REL.I	him	the	knife	given	have

'the man to whom I have given the knife'

Early in the fifteenth century, the interrogative adjective *welch* 'which' appeared as a relative clause marker:

> This was a new construction, unknown to older German. It was a creation of chancery style, most likely in imitation of French *lequel* or Latin *qui*, originating in the Netherlands towards the end of the thirteenth century (Lockwood 1968: 248).

But unlike *wo* and *was*, *welch* appears to have developed straight from the interrogative stage 1 to the final relative stage 4. In the nineteenth century, *welch* almost drove the demonstrative-based relative marker *der* out of the written language (Lockwood 1968: 247–9).

A similar development appears to have taken place in English. In Old English, the declinable demonstrative *Þæt* (neuter form), the indeclinable demonstrative particle *Þe*, and the locative adverb *Þær* 'there' were used as relatives. In Middle English, *Þe* was gradually supplanted by *Þat* (< *Þæt*) and simultaneously the interrogative pronouns ancestral to *who*, *which*, etc. emerged as relatives, and *Þat* tended to be confined to restrictive relative clauses. Romaine observes that '[T]he transition from interrogative to relative pronoun began in types of indirect questions where the interrogative character of the pronoun became weakened, and the pronouns so used were generalizing relatives' (Romaine 1984: 449). Example (6.21) from early Middle English illustrates the stage 2 situation, where the new interrogatives still had the meaning 'whoever', 'whatever', 'whichever', etc., being used at first as generalizing relatives in a generic sense.

The new pronominal *wh*-relativizer started with indirect objects and possessives before it spread to subjects (Hopper & Traugott 2003: 203). While *whose* and *whom* were in use since the earliest part of Middle English, *who* was the last to establish itself as a relative, appearing in the first half of the fifteenth century in a strictly relative use in a few stereotyped closing phrases of letters

(Romaine 1982: 62). The interrogative *which* developed into a relative clause marker around the same time as the etymologically identical German reflex *welch* 'which', that is, in the fifteenth century (Lockwood 1968: 248).

(6.21) EARLY MIDDLE ENGLISH (*Wooing of Lord* 275; Mustanoja 1960: 192; Romaine 1982: 61)
Hwam mai he luve treweliche **hwa** ne luves his broÞer.
'Whom may he love truly, who (-ever) does not love his brother.'

In Scottish English, a similar grammaticalization from interrogative to relative clause marker took place in the same way as in Middle English. In the period roughly between 1375 and 1500, the *quh*-forms (*quhilk*) do not appear to have been an integrated part of spoken Middle Scots. But these forms, to be replaced later by the English *wh*-forms, began to encroach upon the relativizer *that* (or *at*) in Middle Scots. Encroachment of *quhilk* on *that*, more pronounced in prose than in verse, reached its peak in the late sixteenth century, when *that* was still the most frequently used relative in restrictive function but the interrogative-derived *quhilk* had become the most frequent form found in non-restrictive clauses. Like its English counterpart *who*, the Middle Scots nominative form *quha* was not used in the early development from interrogative to relative (Romaine 1982: 70–2).

Whilst there is no compelling evidence, it is believed that the evolution from interrogatives to relatives was originally prompted by Latin influence (Bergs & Stein 2001) and strengthened in Middle English under French influence (Mustanoja 1960: 191; Romaine 1982: 61).

The development in Dutch exhibits the same overall structure: Old Dutch used demonstrative pronouns as relativizers, and the interrogative pronouns *wiens* and *wier* began to be used along with the demonstratives in Middle Dutch. Unlike the situation in German and English, however, the Dutch interrogatives remained limited to genitive and oblique positions (Romaine 1984: 451).

To conclude, in the course of the last millennium, the interrogative-to-subordination strategy increasingly replaced the demonstrative- and locative-based forms used for clause subordination in Germanic languages and, as the available evidence suggests, Latin and French models must have played some role in this development, even if other factors may have been involved as well.

Slavic languages. A second diffusion centre of the polysemy must have existed in eastern Europe. In Old Bulgarian, that is, Old Church Slavonic, there existed several ways of marking relative clauses. First, there were the old relative pronouns *iže, jaže, ježe* which were built out of the so-called anaphoric **yo*-pronoun plus the emphatic particle *že*, (see 6.21).

(6.21) OLD BULGARIAN (Mirčev 1963: 168)
oče našŭ **ježe** jesi na n[e]be[se]x' [. . .].
(father.VOC our REL be.2.SG.PRES on skies)
'You, our father, who are in heaven [. . .].'

These were lost fairly early, around the end of the Old Bulgarian period. Second, there were prenominal, participial syntagms which functioned as relatives:

(6.22) OLD BULGARIAN (Mirčev 1963: 236)
ljubjai d[u]šǫ svoju pogoubitŭ ja.
(love.PRES.PART soul POSS.REFL destroy.3.SG.PRES it)
'He who loves his soul will destroy it.'

Third, there were interrogative words used as stage 4 relatives (Mirčev 1963; Večerka 1993). Two of these were identical with interrogative adverbs for time *jegda* 'when' and place *k'de* 'where', cf.

(6.23) OLD BULGARIAN (Mirčev 1963: 235–6)
(a) vŭ to že vremja, **jegda** svjatyja mŭčaaxa
(in this PTCL time when saints torture.3PL.PAST
běaše studen' velika.
be.3SG.IMPF cold great)
'At that time when they were torturing the saints it was very cold.'
(b) vedy mesto, **k'de** živetŭ svjatyi
(knowing place where live.3SG.PRES saint)
'knowing the place where the saint lives'

Another group of interrogative words were identical with the adjectival interrogatives for property *jakŭ/kakŭ, jaka/kaka, jako/kako* 'what kind of', whereby the form *jako/kako* also functioned as the adverbial interrogative for manner ('how'). They could either be followed by the emphatic particle *-že* (most probably due to the influence of the model upon which the old relative pronoun was built, as in (6.24), or they could stand on their own (6.25).

(6.24) OLD BULGARIAN (Mirčev 1963: 235)
bŭdetŭ bo togda skrŭb' velie, ja**kŭ**-že
(be.3SG.FUT PTCL then sadness great what.kind.of-PTCL
nestŭ otŭ načęla v'sego mira.
be.3SG.PRES from beginning whole world)
'Because then there will be a great sadness, such as there has never been in the whole world.'

(6.25) Old Bulgarian (Mirčev 1963: 235)

rizy	ego	l'štę štę	sę	běly
(shirt.PL	his	became.gleaming	REFL	white.PL
sělo ěko	sněgă,	**ěcěxŭ**	ne	možetŭ
very how	snow	what.kind.of.PL	NEG	be.able.SG.PRES
gnafei	na	zemi	tako	uběliti.
bleacher	on	earth	so	bleach.INF)

'His clothes became gleaming, very white, such that no bleacher on earth could ever bleach them.'

Interrogative pronouns for entities, that is 'who?', 'what?', have also been attested as relative markers in Old Bulgarian.

It was as late as Middle Bulgarian that interrogative pronouns developed into proper relative pronouns. Some of them were used with the emphatic particle -*že* attached to them, (6.26), while others stood on their own (6.27).

(6.26) Middle Bulgarian, 1342 (Mirčev 1963: 169)

xrisovuli	**koi-**	že	prinesošǫ	sę
(documents	who-	PTCP	having.moved	REFL)

'documents which were brought'

(6.27) Middle Bulgarian, 1277 (Mirčev 1963: 169)

drom,	**koi**
(road	who)

'road which'

There are also examples—dating back to the fourteenth century—where the interrogative pronoun could be used as a relative marker with the old relative pronoun *iže* attached to it:

(6.28) Middle Bulgarian (Mirčev 1963: 169)

něs	rodivyi	sę	**kto**	
(carry.3.SG.PRET	the.new-born	REFL	who	
iže	možet	obnaxoditi	silǫ	b[o]žjo.
REL	can.3.SG.PRES	find.INF	power	God's)

'carried the new-born one who can find God's power.'

In an increasing number of cases, however, the interrogative pronouns were followed by the particle -*to*, which is historically derived from the demonstrative pronouns *tŭ* (M), *ta* (F), *to* (N). Later, in Modern Bulgarian, the form for the neuter gender singular *to* replaced the other two forms and came to be attached to all forms of the interrogatives for entities:

(6.29) Modern Bulgarian

(a) mŭžŭt, **koj-** to dojde, beše [. . .].
man.the who.M- DEM.N came was
'the man who came was [. . .].'

(b) ženata, **koja-** to dojde, beše [. . .].
woman.the who.F- DEM.N came was
'the woman who came was [. . .].'

(c) deteto, **koe-** to dojde, beše [. . .].
child.the which.N- DEM.N came was
'the child which came was [. . .].'

The above pattern of building the relative pronoun out of the interrogative plus the demonstrative for the neuter gender singular *to* got spread to all ontological interrogative categories (for place, time, property, manner) in Modern Bulgarian. Note, however, that there are still a number of Bulgarian dialects where the particle *-to* is not used, and it is only the interrogative that functions as a relative pronoun.

The interrogative–subordination polysemy has been generalized in all modern Slavic languages; the following examples are restricted to stage 4 instances of interrogative markers used as headed relative clause markers.

(6.30) Interrogative-derived relative clause markers in Slavic languages

(a) Czech
Dum, **wekterym** bydlím [. . .].
house in which.LOC live.1.SG.PRES
'The house in which I am living [. . .].'

(b) Lower Sorbian
Muž **kótarego-** zh viźiš, jo moj brat.
man who.ACC- zh see.2.SG.PRES is my brother
'The man whom you see is my brother.'

(c) Upper Sorbian
Knihu **kotru-** zh čitam, napisa Gogol.
book.ACC which- zh read.1.SG.PRES wrote Gogol
'The book that I am reading is written by Gogol.'

(d) Polish
Boga **który** nie przemówi.
God.GEN who NEG say
'God, who is not going to talk.'

(e) Russian

Kniga,	**kotor-**	uju	ja	tol'ko	što	pročla,
book	which-	SG.F.ACC	1.SG	just	read	
okazalos'	interesnoj.					
turned.out	interesting					

'The book which I just read turned out to be interesting.'

(f) Serbian/Croatian

Žena	**koja**	čeka [. . .].
woman	who	wait

'The woman who is waiting [. . .].'

(g) Slovak

Videl	otca,	**ktorého**	uzh	niekol'ko	dni
see.3.SG.PAST	father.ACC	who.ACC	already	several	days
nebolo	doma.				
wasn't	home				

'He saw (the) father who hadn't been at home for several days.'

(h) Slovenian

Človek,	**katerega**	vidiš,	je	star.
man	who.ACC	see.2.SG.PRES	is	old

'The man whom you see is old.'

To conclude, there appear to be at least two centres of innovation of the interrogative–subordination polysemy in Europe: Romance on the one hand and the Slavic languages on the other. And it seems that it was these two centres that can be held responsible for the diffusion of the polysemy via contact-induced grammaticalization, affecting other SAE languages such as Germanic languages, but also peripheral languages such as Basque, Romani, and Balkan Turkish.

The German dialect area lies sandwiched between these two centres of early interrogative–subordination polysemy, and it appears to have been influenced by both centres. In the west, as well as in High German, it was Latin and French that provided convenient models, whereas eastern dialects of German were exposed to Slavic languages. Thus, Fleischer remarks on the interrogative-derived relative clause marker *was* 'what' in Yiddish and the Lubica (Leibitz) dialect of German, spoken some 250 kilometres northeast of Bratislava, the capital of Slovakia:

One particular instance, however, *was* + resumptive personal pronoun, occurs only in the Lubica linguistic island and in Yiddish, and this particular subtype occurs in the Slavic languages, too . . . . The Lubica linguistic island is in the Slovak language area, where this type occurs, and the same holds for the main Slavic contact languages of Yiddish. I think, thus, that this subtype, uninflected *was* in conjunction with a resumptive personal pronoun, might best be explained as contact-induced (Fleischer 2004: 235).

6.4 Discussion

6.4.1 *Evidence for directionality*

That the polysemy between question and subordination markers that we are concerned with here is the result of a unidirectional process from the former to the latter has been claimed independently by a number of authors (Lehmann 1984; Thomason & Kaufman 1988: 320; Schafroth 1993; Matras 1996: 64; Kortmann 1998*b*: 554; Le Goffic 2001; Heine & Kuteva 2002); accordingly, in the preceding sections we tacitly assumed that this is a commonplace in European linguistics. Still, to our knowledge, it has never been proven. In the present section we will now look for evidence substantiating that there is in fact a unidirectional evolution from question markers to markers of clause subordination while the inverse is unlikely to happen, that is, we do not expect complementizers or relative clause markers to develop into question markers.

The first piece of evidence relates to the morphosyntactic structure of the markers concerned. In a number of languages, interrogatives are morphologically unmarked, being used in their basic form, while the corresponding subordinators exhibit a marked structure, consisting of the interrogative plus some additional element. For example, in Georgian the interrogative *ros* 'when?' has given rise to the temporal subordinator *roca* 'when', where it is combined with *ca* 'and, also, even' (Kortmann 1998*b*: 555–6). In a similar fashion, the Bulgarian markers occur in their basic form when used as interrogatives (6.31a) but take the demonstrative suffix -*to* when serving as subordinators (6.31b).

(6.31) BULGARIAN

(a) **Koj** šte dojde?
who will come
'Who will come?'

(b) Štastliv e **koj-** to ima pari.
happy is who- *to* has money
'He who has money is happy.'

Second, when used as interrogatives, the markers occur in mono-clausal sentences, while as subordinators the markers are—by definition—restricted to complex sentences. There is a common pathway of grammaticalization whereby linguistic expressions, such as adverbs, adpositional phrases, or demonstratives, are first used in mono-clausal sentences before they develop into markers of clause subordination, that is, turn into markers of complex sentences (see Heine & Kuteva 2002 for examples), while a process in the opposite direction is fairly unlikely to occur. Accordingly, it is plausible to assume that the subordinators are historically derived from interrogatives rather than the other way round.

Third, in a number of languages interrogatives exhibit more ontological distinctions than the subordinators. For example, as Table 6.4 shows, all six ontological categories of English that we are concerned with in this chapter are lexically distinguished as interrogatives, namely human (*who*), inanimate (*what*), space (*where*), time (*when*), manner (*how*), and attributive (*which*), but only four of these are distinguished as subordinators. This is compatible with a general characteristic of grammaticalization: the specialization of a limited number of means for expressing a particular grammatical function out of a larger number of competing structures.

Fourth, in addition to ontological categories, subordinators frequently also exhibit a decrease in distinctions of gender, animacy, number, and case compared to the corresponding interrogatives (see Fleischer 2004 for examples); in the terminology of grammaticalization theory, again, subordinators exhibit specialization (Hopper 1991), in that the variety of formal choices narrows and an increasingly smaller range of forms assumes a more general (grammatical) meaning. In addition, subordinators also exhibit decategorialization (see Section 1.5.1), in that they exhibit fewer morphological distinctions than the corresponding interrogatives.

Finally, there is also diachronic evidence. This evidence is of two kinds. First, there are historical reconstructions, as we saw in our discussion of Germanic languages (see also Lehmann 1984: 389–93). Similar observations

TABLE 6.4. Ontological distinctions in interrogative and relative clause constructions in English

Ontological category	English example	Interrogative	Relative clause marker
Human	*who?*	+	+
Inanimate	*what?*	+	−
Space	*where?*	+	+
Time	*when?*	+	+
Manner	*how?*	+	−
Attributive	*which?*	+	+

can be made in the peripheral languages of Europe. That the markers for complement, adverbial, and relative clauses in Romani (Romanes) were question markers (*kon* 'who?', *so* 'what?', *kaj* 'where?', *kana* 'when?', *sar* 'how?') prior to being grammaticalized for purposes of clause combining is suggested, for instance, by the fact that they can be traced back to the Indo-Aryan interrogative stems **k*- and **s*-. The use of these Romani question markers as subordination markers cannot be traced back to the pre-Balkanic history of the language, hence it must be the result of contact with languages of the Balkan sprachbund (Matras 1996: 65).

Second, there are also attested cases of language change suggesting this directionality. One such case concerns Germanic languages such as English, Dutch, and German, where there is historical evidence that the relevant markers served as interrogatives long before their use was extended to mark clause subordination (see Section 6.3). Another case concerns Basque, where it is fairly uncontroversial that markers such as *zer* 'what' and *zoin* (or *zein*) 'which' served as interrogatives prior to assuming functions as subordinators (Trask 1998: 320; Hurch 1989: 21). A third case concerns a non-European language, the North Arawak language Tariana of northwestern Brazil: as we saw in Section 6.2, there is an ongoing process whereby young and innovative speakers of Tariana use their interrogative pronouns as markers of relative clauses on the model of Portuguese, their official language (Aikhenvald 2002: 183).

To conclude, there is sufficient evidence to assume that there is a unidirectional development from interrogatives to subordinators, while there is no evidence for the reverse directionality—that is, we are not aware of any case where a subordinating form gave rise to a question word.[6] On the basis of these observations, we are in a position to refute another possible hypothesis, according to which the interrogative–subordinator polysemy was always there, that is, that there was no directionality from the one to the other. Such a hypothesis is not supported by any of the data discussed above.

6.4.2 *Evidence for contact*

The observations made above also shed light on another issue that is even more crucial to the subject matter of this book, namely the role played by language contact in the development of the interrogative–subordinator polysemy. This issue entails the following questions:

[6] Note, however, that this does not apply to coordinating markers: alternative conjunctions ('or') can be the source for markers of polar (yes–no) questions (see Heine & Kuteva 2002: 226–7).

(6.32) QUESTIONS ON CONTACT
(a) How did this polysemy arise?
(b) How did it spread across languages?
(c) Was language contact involved in the spread?

While our concern is essentially with (6.32c), all three questions are relevant in some way to our discussion. Question (6.32a) is hard to answer; on the basis of the evidence available, it would seem that the polysemy cannot be reconstructed back to any of the ancestral languages of Europe, not even to Proto-Indo-European, even though it is found in various branches of Indo-European, including Indo-Aryan languages; we will return to this question in Section 6.4.3. With regard to question (6.32b), there is reason to assume that a genetic relationship played some role in the diffusion of the polysemy; for example, its presence and overall structure in the Romance languages is most likely to be due, at least to some extent, to genetic inheritance from their ancestor Latin.

There is no entirely satisfactory answer to question (6.32c). Still, as the preceding discussion has established, there is reason to argue that language contact was a contributing factor in the creation of the polysemy: neither Basque nor the West Rumelian Turkish dialects of Macedonia, Balkan Romani, Pipil, Nahuatl, or Tariana would be expected to have the polysemy on account of their overall structure and genetic affiliation. In all these cases, SAE languages must have provided an attractive model for replication of the grammaticalization from interrogative to subordinating functions.

Whilst the interrogative–subordinator polysemy has a history of well over two millennia in Romance, its evolution in the Germanic languages is far from clear. However, there are reasons to adopt the hypothesis proposed by Thomason and Kaufman (1988: 320) in assuming that grammatical replication played a crucial role. These reasons are: first, the function of interrogatives as markers of clause subordination is clearly less grammaticalized in Germanic languages than it is in the Romance languages. And second, while the polysemy can be reconstructed back to Proto-Romance and Latin, there is no convincing evidence that it existed in Proto-Germanic.

6.4.3 *On the transition from interrogative to subordination marking*

The development of interrogative markers into relative clause markers has been a puzzle to linguists for quite some time. The following remark summarizes what appears to be the widely-held opinion on this issue:

It is well known that relative pronouns sometimes take the form of interrogative pronouns. Why this development should take place in only certain kinds of relative clause is obscure. Why the development should take place at all is still more obscure (Schwartz 1971: 141).

In this section, we are confronted with two of the questions raised above, namely: How did the process arise in the first place (6.32a)? How did it spread from one language to another (6.32b)? We will deal with them in turn.

Genesis. There have been suggestions in the literature that if a relative clause marker is formally related to an interrogative marker, then the relative clause marking has resulted from the grammaticalization of questions. For example, Hopper and Traugott (1993: 96) admit that a relative sentence such as (6.33a) 'could with very little change be distributed over two parts of a discourse', as in (6.33b).

(6.33) ENGLISH (Hopper & Traugott 1993: 196)
(a) The sheep which he stole was Squire Trelawney's prize ram.
(b) Which sheep did he steal?—The sheep was Squire Trelawney's prize ram.

However, these authors are careful to explicitly point out that 'there is rarely evidence that relative clauses derive directly from the grammaticalization of questions' (ibid.: 196). Harris and Campbell (1995: 284) draw attention to what they call a 'marker/structure fallacy', according to which the historical sources of subordination markers do not necessarily imply the sources of the structures of which these markers are a part; accordingly, the etymology of the subordinator does not always reveal the structure of the syntactic source. This is an important observation; there are, in fact, a number of attested cases where in a situation of language contact, one language just adds an appropriate subordinator replicated on the model of another language to an already existing construction of subordination (see Heine & Kuteva 2003, 2005 for examples). The main argument adduced by Harris and Campbell is that, at least in the history of English, there is no historical evidence for the marker-plus-structure hypothesis:

> If relative clauses that make use of relative pronouns that derive from Q-words developed from independent questions, we would expect to find these questions in attested forms of English during this change. But there is no evidence that questions were involved in this change; rather, the facts suggest that the Q-words began to replace the demonstratives and particles found in the existing relative clause structure (Harris & Campbell 1995: 284–5).

But there are alternative positions. Lehmann (1984: 252, 385) argues that the explanation of the formal similarity between relative pronouns and interrogative pronouns is to be sought in more comprehensive relations that still need to be identified. He goes on to propose that the development of relatives formally related to interrogatives (which for European languages, all go back to the Indo-European **kwi*- element) crucially involves a correlative structure (*das korrelative Diptychon*) of the type exemplified in (6.34).

(6.34) German

Wer	das	weiß,	**der**	bekommt	einen	Preis.
Who	that	knows	he	gets	a	prize

'Whoever knows that will get a prize.'

Lehmann hypothesizes that the correlative structure, which is important for the emergence of the **kwi*- relative sentence in languages such as Latin, fronts the clause with the **kwi*- element and postposes the clause with the correlating element which refers anaphorically to the nucleus in the **kwi*- clause. Moreover, he argues that the **kwi*- element in the fronted clause is an indefinite rather than an interrogative element. Later on, the indefinite element **kwi*- grammaticalizes into a relative marker and from this point onwards it can also be used in relative sentences involving a definite nucleus. Once the **kwi*- element has grammaticalized into a relative marker, the **kwi*-relative clause comes to occupy a second position in the correlative structure and thus becomes a postposed, postnominal relative clause. Note that Lehmann (1984: 372) points out that it cannot be proved that a *post*nominal relative sentence has developed out of a *pre*posed relative clause in case there were no earlier postnominal variant of a relative sentence.

The following cross-linguistic fact is also suggestive of the problem inherent in analysing a postnominal relative clause as deriving out of the preposed WH-clause in a correlative structure: in no language does a WH-form occur as a relative clause marker within a *pre*posed relative clause. Thus Schwartz (1971: 155) reports on the non-occurrence of the following sequences in natural languages:

(6.35) Cross-linguistically non-attested structures according to Schwartz (1971: 155; where N = noun, S = sentence)

(a) *[...WH...] N
S

(b) *[...WH] N
S

(c) *[WH...] N
S

In other words, languages do not seem to tolerate WH-words as relative clause markers either in the middle or at the end or in the beginning of a preposed relative clause. This fact certainly does not buttress an argumentation in favour of the derivation of a postnominal relative clause out of a preposed WH-clause in a correlative structure.

On the basis of all these observations, one is led to conclude that there are still many problems surrounding the process from interrogative to subordinate structures. While there is little doubt that it was question words that represented the earliest stage of development, there are several possible ways in which this process may have happened. One concerns the replication of a grammaticalization from question word to subordination marker, another way concerns a process from interrogative to subordinate propositions. The latter was discussed in the form of a four-stage scenario of grammaticalization in Section 6.2, since all the stages are synchronically attested and, hence, may well have played a role in the evolution of the relative clause structure.

In accordance with the latter scenario, the evolution from interrogative to relative clause marker is due to a strategy whereby recurrent interpersonal communication structures used for presenting questions are used as conceptual templates for expressing relations between clauses (see Table 6.2). At stage 1, an interrogative structure of the form (6.36a) serves as a template to express the relationship between a main clause and a complement clause (6.36b), where *who* has the function of an object complement clause marker (stage 2). While *who* introduces an indefinite complement in (6.36b), it can be assumed to be a definite complement in (6.36c), which can also be interpreted as a headless relative clause (stage 3). Finally, at stage 4, the erstwhile interrogative can be headed by a noun phrase (6.36d).

(6.36) ENGLISH
- (a) I don't know: **who** came?
- (b) I don't know **who** came.
- (c) You also know **who** came.
- (d) Do you know the woman **who** came?

This scenario is in line with the one proposed by Matras (1996: 66), according to which there is a promotion (*Beförderung*) of interrogatives from markers combining speech acts in a question–answer schema to conjunctions combining propositional constituents of one and the same utterance within a complex speech act. In a similar fashion, Mustanoja (1960: 191) argues that the transition from interrogative to relative pronoun in Middle English began in types of indirect questions where the interrogative character of the pronoun became weakened before the pronouns turned into relative clause markers.

Diachronic evidence for this scenario comes from Germanic languages like German or English, where the interrogatives appear to have served first to introduce complements before developing into markers of headed relative clauses (see Section 6.3). But there is also diachronic evidence from other Indo-European languages that interrogative structures gave rise to subordinating constructions. For example, the Latin interrogative *quārē* 'why?' developed into the French subordinating conjunction *car* 'because, for', and this grammaticalization is explained in the following way. In colloquial speech, speakers use rhetorical questions which they answer themselves instantly. In this way, an utterance of the kind 'He left. Why? His father died' was subsequently reinterpreted as 'He left because his father died', where the interrogative 'why?' was reinterpreted as a reason conjunction, reanalysed as part of the second clause, which thereby turned into a subordinate clause (Hermann 1943: 4). But more research on the transition from interrogative (or indefinite) to clause subordination marking is required.

Diffusion. The second question that we need to look into concerns the way the 'polysemy' pattern was transferred from one language to another. What exactly is it that speakers of peripheral languages such as Basque, Pipil, or Nahuatl replicated from SAE languages—a polysemy pattern, where one and the same item, used, for example, as both an interrogative and a relative or complement clause marker, was copied from the model language, or a gradual process of grammaticalization? On the surface it would seem that the former process was involved, since in all languages concerned we observe a polysemy pattern. There are, however, cases that can be interpreted as supporting an analysis in terms of a gradual process in accordance with the four-stage scenario proposed above. Such cases involve usage patterns which can be interpreted alternatively with reference to interrogative and to clause-subordinating functions. We hypothesize that this process starts out with cognition, perception, and/or utterance verbs serving as main clause predicates, especially when these verbs are negated. Grammaticalization has the effect that direct-speech clauses involving such verbs come to be reinterpreted as complement clauses.

Irish English (or Hiberno-English or Anglo-Irish) appears to present such a case. This variety of English is usually portrayed as having been heavily influenced by the Celtic language Irish (or Gaelic) and, in fact, a number of structures of Irish English are suggestive of contact-induced grammaticalization on the model of Irish (see Heine & Kuteva 2005; Pietsch 2004*a*, 2004*b*; Pfaff 2004). One of these structures concerns complement clauses that seem to have evolved on the model of Irish interrogative clauses. Van Hamel (1912: 280) observes that after cognition, perception and utterance verbs, subordinate clauses are presented as interrogative clauses on the pattern of Irish, as in the examples listed in (6.37):

(6.37) IRISH ENGLISH ('Anglo-Irish'; van Hamel 1912: 280)
I don't know is it here she is coming?
Do you think could she be the widow Casey?
Wait till you see is he the lad I think him to be.

Now, when the direct-speech clause constitutes a word question, the interrogative word may be reinterpreted as a complement clause or headless relative clause marker. A possible example is provided by the Arawak languages of the Upper Rio Negro region in Brazil, where the use of interrogative pronouns has been extended to what Aikhenvald (2002: 166) calls indirect or oblique questions. The following example from Baniwa illustrates this use pattern.

(6.38) BANIWA (North Arawak; Aikhenvald 2002: 166)

wasa	wa-	kapa	**kwaka**	khedza-	ʒi	i-	aʒa-	kawa.
let's.go	1.PL-	see	who	quick-	REL	INDF-	fly-	INTR

'Le'ts go and see who is quick in flying.' (i.e. who flies quicker)

Aikhenvald (2002: 166) mentions that this use pattern is the result of influence from Língua Geral, a creolized variety of the Tupí-Guaraní family; Língua Geral was the lingua franca of the Upper Rio Negro region until recently.

The following example from the Dravidian language Kannada can be viewed as presenting a case of 'overuse' of this interrogative-to-relative strategy, in that speakers used simultaneously a word question (WH-question) and a polar (yes–no) question to create a relative clause construction[7] (see Nadkarni 1975 for details). The former is constructed by means of question words such as *yāva* 'which?' in (6.39a), while the latter takes a clause-final element *ō* instead, (6.39b). Now, if these two interrogative constructions are combined, a relative clause construction results, (6.39c).

(6.39) KANNADA (Dravidian; Nadkarni 1975: 674, 676)

(a)

yāva	mudukanu	pēpar	ōdutta	iddāne.
(which	old.man	paper	reading	is)

'Which old man is reading a newspaper?'

(b)

mudukanu	pēpar	ōdutta	iddān-	ō.
(old.man	paper	reading	is	Q)

'Is the old man reading a newspaper?'

[7] There is a second relative construction in Kannada which is ignored here (see Nadkarni 1975: 674).

(c)	[yāva	mudukanu	pēpar	ōdutta	iddān-	ō]	avanu	ḍākṭaranu	iddāne.
	which	old.man	paper	reading	is	**Q**	that	doctor	is

'The old man who is reading a newspaper is a doctor.'

This grammaticalization from a combined interrogative construction to a relative construction was replicated in the Saraswat Brahmins dialect of the Indo-Aryan language Konkani in the course of a history of at least four centuries of contact, leading to total isomorphism in the syntax of this relative construction between these two genetically unrelated languages (see Nadkarni 1975).

That in the contact-induced transition from interrogative to subordinator there may be an intermediate stage is suggested by the following examples of contact-induced change, where a question word (e.g. 'who?') is used in contexts where its interrogative function is backgrounded and where it expresses the notion of an indefinite pronoun (e.g. 'whoever?'). Speakers of the Aztecan language Nahuatl appear to have identified their interrogative particles serving as indefinite pronouns of main clauses with the interrogative-looking relative pronouns of Spanish and, consequently, reinterpreted them as markers of the subordinate clause (Karttunen 1976: 151). That such a process involves an intermediate stage where the item concerned can be interpreted alternatively as an indefinite pronoun or as a headless relative clause marker or complementizer is suggested by the following sentence, taken from a Nahuatl letter written in 1554. Whereas Langacker (1975) interprets the phrase *in tlen* as an indefinite pronoun of the main clause (6.40a), Rosenthal (1972) treats it as a relative pronoun (6.40b):

(6.40) NAHUATL, AD 1554 (quoted from Karttunen 1976: 150)

	Huel	topan	quichihuazque	in	tlen	quinequi.
(a)	[well	us.on	it.do.will.PL	ART	thing]	[it.want.PL]
						Langacker (1975)
(b)	[well	our.on	they.it.will.do]	[the	what	they.it.want]
						Rosenthal (1972)

'Well for us they will do what they want.'

Another example involving non-European languages comes from a contact situation in northwest Brazil, where the North Arawak language Tariana has replicated a number of structures of East Tucanoan languages (Aikhenvald 2002). In the following example, Tariana speakers use their interrogative pronoun *kani* 'where?' in the meaning of 'wherever' apparently on the model of East Tucanoan languages; hence, the corresponding sentence in Tucano has the same structure as this Tariana sentence, where instead of *kani* the Tucano interrogative *no'ó* ('where', 'wherever') is used:

(6.41) TARIANA (North Arawak; Aikhenvald 2002: 165)

kani	nuha	nu-	a-	mi	nuha-	nuku
where	I	1.SG-	go-	NOMIN.LOC	I-	TOP.NON.A/S

di-	pinita-	naka.
3.SG.nf-	follow-	PRES.VIS

'He follows me wherever I go.' (Lit. 'where my going he follows me.')

Aikhenvald summarizes what we take to be suggestive of a process from interrogative to indefinite pronoun and finally to complementizer thus:

The use of interrogative pronouns in Tariana relative clauses with an indefinite meaning—similar to English 'whoever'—is indicative of East Tucanoan influence (Aikhenvald 2002: 165).

6.5 Case marking: the rise of standard markers in equative and similative constructions

Essentially the same cognitive transfer process from question markers to markers used for the organization of texts has also affected other structures of European languages. In the present section we will be concerned with one of these structures, specifically with the way comparisons are conceptualized, more precisely with comparisons concerning sameness or similarity between the items compared. Discussion is based on the seminal work by Haspelmath and Buchholz (1998), even if our interpretation differs in minor details from theirs.

Following these authors, we will distinguish between equative and similative constructions or, in short, between equatives, illustrated in (6.42a), and similatives in (6.42b).

(6.42) ENGLISH (Haspelmath & Buchholz 1998: 278)
(a) Robert is **as** tall **as** Maria.
(b) He sings **like** a nightingale.

We also adopt the terminology proposed by these authors, that is, we will call *Robert* and *He* the comparee (also called the item of comparison), the first *as* the parameter marker (degree marker), *tall* and *sings* the parameter (gradable property), the second *as* and *like* the standard markers, and *Maria* and *nightingale* the standard (of comparison).

Our interest here is exclusively with the way the standard is expressed. The reason for ignoring the parameter marker in this survey is the following: unlike Haspelmath and Buchholz (1998), who are concerned with the entire structure of equative and similative constructions, we are concerned here with reconstructing the conceptual nature of certain functional categories of European languages, which in the present section is the standard marker.

Note that parameter markers are restricted in their occurrence in a number of ways. First, they are not found on similative constructions,[8] second, while standard markers are usually an obligatory component of equatives, parameter markers are not: there are a number of languages, in Europe and elsewhere, that do without parameter markers; European languages not using parameter markers include Albanian, Bulgarian, Modern Greek, Serbian, Croatian, and Italian (Haspelmath & Buchholz 1998: 292),[9] (see 6.43). And third, in a number of languages, such as English, German, Dutch, Yiddish, Portuguese, Spanish, Catalan, Friulian, Russian, Slovak, Slovenian, Czech, and Lithuanian, the use of the parameter marker is optional or even disallowed when the standard is a generic noun (Haspelmath & Buchholz 1998: 310), (see 6.44).

(6.43) ITALIAN (Haspelmath & Buchholz 1998: 279)

Mia	sorella	è	alta	**come**	me.
my	sister	is	tall	how	I

'My sister is as tall as I.'

(6.44) GERMAN

Er	ist	(so)	dumm	**wie**	ein	Ochs.
he	is	so	stupid	like	an	ox

'(He is as stupid as an ox.' *or* 'He is stupid like an ox.'

Haspelmath and Buchholz (1998: 278, 313) argue that equatives differ from similatives in that the former express equal extent or quantity while the latter express equal manner or quality. However, it would seem that equatives can also express equal manner or quality. We will assume rather that equatives typically involve 'adjectival' qualities relating to size, quantity, manner, etc., while similatives concern qualities relating to activities that are presumed to be characteristic of the standard referent. Thus, the equative construction in (6.45a) relates to the quality expressed by *schlecht* 'bad(ly)', while the similative construction in (6.45b) relates to the quality of the action of *tanzen* 'dance' associated with the standard. However, this is an issue that is not relevant to our discussion.

[8] According to Haspelmath & Buchholz (1998: 314), Hungarian is an exception in also having a parameter marker on the similative.

[9] Haspelmath & Buchholz (1998: 291) point out that the distribution of these languages lacking a parameter marker shows a clear areal patterning.

(6.45) German

(a) Paul tanzt so schlecht **wie** sein Bruder.
Paul dances so badly as his brother
'Paul dances as badly as his brother.'

(b) Paul tanzt **wie** sein Bruder.
Paul dances like his brother
'Paul dances like his brother.'

Manner interrogatives that serve as conceptual sources for standard markers may be mono-morphemic pronouns, such as German *wie* 'how?'. But they may also go back to manner adverbial phrases meaning '(in) which way/manner/kind?'. The Georgian standard marker *rogorc* is based on a word meaning 'manner': < *ra gvar(a)-c(a)* 'what kind', and in most Romance languages, the Latin standard marker *quam* 'how?' was replaced by the phrase *quo modo* 'in what way?', later on reduced to *comme* (French), *come* (Italian), *como* (Spanish, Portuguese), and the like (Haspelmath & Buchholz 1998: 331, 292–3).

6.5.1 *On the conceptual source of the standard marker*

In accordance with the present discussion, these authors invoke a grammaticalization perspective to account for the nature and structure of a prevalent type of equative and similative marking in European languages. They observe that the standard markers in what they call SAE languages are 'based' on relative clause markers:

> Semantically, the derivation of equative constructions from relative clauses is very plausible. The only syntactic difference between correlative equatives and correlative relatives is that everything but the standard is elliptically omitted from the relative clause (Haspelmath & Buchholz 1998: 288).

Thus, they hypothesize that there was a kind of 'stripping' process leading from relative to standard constructions. As this citation appears to indicate, their notion 'based on' is meant as implying a diachronic derivation process. That this is so is also suggested by the fact that these relative-based standard markers are 'originally interrogative-based' (ibid.: 326). Thus, the scenario they propose can be summarized as in (6.46):

(6.46) Interrogative pronoun > Relative clause marker > Standard marker

The evidence adduced for this scenario is as follows. The authors maintain that the standard markers cannot be based directly on interrogative markers because there are languages that distinguish relative pronouns from interrogative pronouns, for example Greek (*pos* 'how?' vs. *ópos* 'how (relative)') and Bulgarian (*kak* 'how?' vs. *kak-to* > *kato* 'how (relative)' (Haspelmath & Buchholz 1998: 331); note also that the standard markers found in Scandinavian languages, such as Swedish, Norwegian, and Danish *som*, are also used as relative particles. Furthermore, they argue (ibid.: 288) that 'in any event relative clauses are the diachronic sources of certain types of comparative constructions', although they do not give examples. But there are questions that hypothesis (6.46) raises, such as the following:

(i) If relative clause markers provide the source for standard markers in many European languages, why is it only interrogative-derived relative markers that are used for this purpose—that is, why are there no demonstrative-derived relative markers (e.g. *that*), considering that demonstrative attributes form another common source for relative clause markers in European languages?

(ii) Why are there essentially only manner interrogatives ('how?')[10] that figure as standard markers in equative and similative constructions—that is, why did other interrogatives that were grammaticalized to relative clause markers, such as English *what, which, where, when, why*, not give rise to standard markers?

There is an alternative hypothesis on the rise of standard markers. According to this hypothesis, standard markers in equative and similative constructions are immediately derived from manner interrogatives qualifying adjectives and verbs, that is, instead of (6.46) there is (6.47).

(6.47)	INTERROGATIVE MARKER	>	(a)	relative clause marker
		>	(b)	standard marker

Evidence for (6.47) comes, on the one hand, from answers to the questions just raised: (i) If standard markers were derived from relative clause markers then it remains unclear why it was never demonstrative-derived relatives that gave rise to standard markers. (ii) And it also remains unclear why it was essentially only manner interrogatives that turned into standard markers. That standard markers are derived from manner interrogatives is suggested by the following observations. Manner interrogatives provide the most immediate pronominal template to refer to qualities expressed by adjectives and verbs, (6.48).

[10] There are a few exceptions, e.g. the French interrogative-derived marker *que*, which is the standard marker in equative constructions (although not in similative constructions) and also a relative pronoun; see Haspelmath & Buchholz (1998: 293) for discussion.

(6.48) English
How tall is he?
How does he sing?

Accordingly, in replies to manner questions, manner markers provide the most obvious option for presenting the standard in equative (6.49a) and similative propositions (6.49b).

(6.49) German

(a) **Wie** dumm ist er? (Er ist dumm) **Wie** ein Ochs.
how stupid is he he is stupid how an ox
'How stupid is he?' '(He is stupid) Like an ox.'

(b) **Wie** arbeitet er? (Er arbeitet) **Wie** ein Roboter.
how works he he works how a robot
'How does he work?' '(He works) Like a robot.'

In a similar fashion, manner interrogatives are the most obvious choice for serving as manner complementizers, as in the following English example:

(6.50) English
I don't know **how** he sings.

Finally, if one were to decide on hypothesis (6.46) then the question would arise why—to our knowledge—there is no language where expressions for the standard of comparison in equative or similative constructions clearly have the structure of a relative clause. To be sure, grammaticalization theory would predict that, in the development from relative to standard expression, all elements that are irrelevant to the new function tend to be eliminated, as Haspelmath and Buchholz (1998: 288) argue. However, one might expect that—given the large number of European languages that are presumed to have undergone this development—there would be some languages where the earlier structure has been retained, at least to some extent.

We do not wish to decide on which of these hypotheses is correct; what is beyond reasonable doubt, however, is that standard markers are historically derived from manner interrogatives—irrespective of whether there was an intermediate stage where they served as relative clause markers.

6.5.2 *Areal patterning*

Standard markers derived from manner interrogatives are found in most Slavic and Romance languages, on the Balkans, and in Germanic except for Scandinavian, as well as in Hungarian, Romani, and Georgian. Thus, they form a compact geographically defined unit, as can be seen in Map 6.1, and Haspelmath and Buchholz therefore conclude:

As far as we know, this construction is not at all widespread in non-European languages, and it must therefore be considered as an important characteristic feature of the European *Sprachbund*, a Europeanism, a defining feature of SAE (Haspelmath & Buchholz 1998: 290).

MAP 6.1. Markers of standard of comparison derived from manner interrogatives in equative and/or similative constructions (based on Haspelmath & Buchholz 1998)

The only non-European language in the sample of these authors also having this feature is the Indo-Aryan language Punjabi (Haspelmath & Buchholz 1998: 286).

In accordance with this evidence, we hypothesize that we are dealing with a conceptual transfer from the domain of interrogation to that of syntactic relations, whereby pronouns denoting manner questions were grammaticalized to case markers introducing the standard of comparison in equative and similative constructions. And, on the basis of the areal distribution of languages having experienced this grammaticalization process, we furthermore hypothesize that this transfer was to a large extent contact-induced.

The question then is: What was the centre of diffusion? Ramat (1998: 231) observes that 'the canonical SAE equative construction is of Indo-European origin'; it is already well attested in Latin:

(6.51) LATIN (Ramat 1998: 231)

Soror	mea	**tam**	pulchra	est	**quam**	tu.
sister	my	so	pretty	is	as	you

'My sister is as pretty as you.'

In the absence of any detailed historical evidence, one is led to hypothesize that, as in the case of the grammaticalization from interrogative to clause subordination (Section 6.2), Latin and the Romance languages provided at least one major model for the spread of interrogative-based equative and similative constructions.

6.6 Conclusions

In this chapter we have been dealing with a fairly dramatic cognitive process, leading from the domain of interpersonal functions, more specifically that of questions, to the domain of textual functions, namely that of syntactic relations. We argued that, in most languages of Europe, there was a conceptual shift from interrogative marking as illustrated in (6.52a) to other markings introducing subordinate clauses, as in (6.52b), or noun phrases, as in (6.52c).

(6.52) GERMAN

(a)

Wie	tanzt	Paul?
how	dances	Paul

'How does Paul dance?'

(b)

Ich	weiß	nicht,	**wie**	Paul	tanzt.
I	know	not	how	Paul	dances

'I don't know how Paul dances.'

(c) Paul tanzt **wie** sein Bruder.
Paul dances like his brother
'Paul dances like his brother.'

Such a process is not unheard of in languages outside Europe; but, whereas in Europe it can be observed in language after language, it is rarely encountered in other parts of the world. Its spread within Europe appears to be due partly to genetic relationship, as Ramat (1998: 236) observes; to quite some extent, however, it is also suggestive of areal diffusion, that is, of language contact.

The grammaticalization paths discussed in the preceding paragraphs differ in a number of ways from one another. First, the transfer from interrogative to syntactic marking involved a range of ontological notions in the case of clause subordination, such as person ('who?'), (inanimate) object ('what?'), place ('where?'), time ('when?'), manner ('how?'), etc., while the evolution of standard markers concerned essentially only manner interrogatives. Second, it concerned the rise of new kinds of clauses on the one hand and of noun phrases on the other.

The evolution from interrogative sentences to syntactic structures of clause subordination is a complex one, and more detailed research is required to reconstruct the conceptual patterns underlying this evolution. On the basis of the diachronic evidence that is available, it would seem that independent internal development, genetic relationship, and drift (parallel development) may all have played some role in this evolution. But what the observations made in this chapter suggest is that, in a number of cases, this evolution was triggered or favoured by language contact, that is, that Romance languages in particular and to a lesser extent Slavic languages as well provided a model for replication in other SAE languages, such as Germanic languages, as well as in a number of peripheral languages.

7

Europe's Periphery

7.1 Introduction

Europe is a geographically compact region; with reference to language contact, however, Europe might be said to constitute a much larger, and diffuse entity. As a result of the spread of European languages to other parts of the world, cross-linguistically a fairly unusual situation has evolved in the course of the last five centuries, where contact has affected languages that are spoken far beyond the geographical confines of the European continent, giving rise to new patterns of areal linguistic relationship and new typological profiles on virtually all continents, some of them uniting European with non-European languages. These patterns are the subject of the present chapter.

The chapter will deal with two different kinds of situations. On the one hand, our concern is with languages that have come under the influence of Standard Average European (SAE) languages and as a result have experienced what we refer to as changes in their typological profiles. These are cases of L2>L1 transfer, where SAE languages provided the model of replication for L1 speakers of peripheral languages. We will discuss such cases in Section 7.2, where we will be concerned in particular with the question of which grammatical concepts of SAE languages do provide particularly attractive models to be replicated in other languages.

On the other hand, our interest is with L1>L2-transfer, and more specifically with the way SAE languages originally used as L2 were the target of replication on the model of other languages serving as L1—in some cases with the effect that an SAE L2 itself acquired a new typological profile. The reader is referred to the literature on pidgin and creole languages, which is rife with examples of this kind of transfer, commonly referred to as 'substrate influence'. What will be highlighted in our discussion, and the subject of Section 7.3, are some salient processes of grammatical replication, centring around the question of what the grammatical concepts are that SAE languages are likely to adopt from other languages.

The term 'change in typological profile' will be used as a technical term in the following discussion; with it we refer—in accordance with the theme of this book—to cases where a language as a result of grammatical replication experiences a number of structural changes to the effect that that language is structurally clearly different from its state prior to language contact. Typically, these changes are in the direction of the model language, thus making the two languages structurally more equivalent—a process that in contact linguistics tends to be described as 'convergence'. However, as we will see below, this is not necessarily the case.

7.2 Towards a European typological profile

The main theme of this book is to study how language contact may affect the typological orientation of a given language. In the preceding chapters we were concerned with a wide range of European languages and with individual properties being affected by language contact. In the present section, we will deal with the question of what 'Europeanization' means with reference to one particular language.

To this end, we discuss the situation of a number of languages that can be said to be located in peripheral regions and to contrast typologically with the languages of the SAE area. One of these languages, Basque, has a history of over a millennium of interaction with Indo-European languages, and much the same applies to some Slavic minorities with reference to German, while our third case, the Pipil language of San Salvador, has been in contact with Europe for a considerably shorter time span and, while not being spoken in Europe, it can nevertheless be considered to be a peripheral language of the European diffusion area.

That areal diffusion in general and grammatical replication in particular do not necessarily constitute a one-way process will be shown in Section 7.3.1, where we provide examples demonstrating that one and the same language can be at the same time a model and a replica language.

7.2.1 *Basque*

In all the various areal classifications of European languages that have been proposed more recently, Basque occupies a fairly peripheral position, contrasting genetically and structurally with all SAE languages. Thus, Haspelmath (2001: 1493) classifies Basque as a marginal European language exhibiting very few Europeanisms and, in a similar fashion, Kortmann (1998*a*; 1998*b*: 507ff) treats Basque as a language of Europe's linguistic periphery.

While these classifications are well-founded, being based on solid linguistic evidence, in the present section we will try to show that Basque nevertheless moved considerably towards SAE, and that contact-induced grammaticalization was one of the main factors in this process. Basque speakers have had most intense contacts with Spanish; but our discussion is confined essentially to Basque varieties spoken in southwestern France, for which there exists a detailed analysis (Haase 1992).

For centuries, these Basque varieties have been influenced by two Romance languages, Gascon and later French, to the extent that there is now a wide range of semantic and morphosyntactic equivalence relations, resulting in a certain degree of structural isomorphism; Ross (2001: 146) therefore views this as a case of metatypy.[1] We will provide a few examples to illustrate how contact-induced grammaticalization contributed to the growth of equivalence relations; the reader is referred to the seminal study by Haase (1992) for additional examples.

Nominal structure. A paradigm case concerns the rise of an indefinite article, which Basque speakers appear to have introduced as a result of centuries of close contact with Gascon and later with French (see Sections 1.3, 3.3.3). In doing so, they developed their numeral for 'one', *bat*, into an indefinite article.[2] Occasional uses of *bat* as a specific marker were attested as early as 1782. There are incipient uses as a non-specific marker as early as 1545, but the grammaticalization as a non-specific article is clearly a recent innovation of Basque. While the Basque article exhibits a high degree of grammaticalization, it is still less grammaticalized than its equivalents in the Romance model languages. Concerning the marking of definiteness in Basque, see Section 1.3.

Another example relating to noun phrase morphology concerns the rise of a comitative–instrumental case polysemy on the model of the three Romance languages; we have dealt with this issue in Section 5.3. Basque is a language rich in case inflections, distinguishing at least fourteen case suffixes. This paradigm includes both a comitative and an instrumental suffix. The languages with which Basque is or has been in contact—Spanish, Gascon and French—like most other European languages (see Stolz 1996*b*), have a comitative–instrumental polysemy, that is, Spanish *con*, Gascon *dab*, *dambe*, and French *avec* are used for both comitative and instrumental participants. As a result of

[1] Metatypy can be defined as the wholesale restructuring of a language's semantic and syntactic structures as a result of language contact, leading to a new typological profile in the replica language on the one hand, and to a large degree of direct intertranslatability between the model and the replica language on the other (see e.g. Ross 1996: 182).

[2] Haase describes this process thus: 'Anders ausgedrückt: *bat* und frz./gask. *un* sind im Bereich der Zahlwörter *Übersetzungsäquivalente.* Wie in anderen Fällen von Übersetzungsäquivalenz, die wir später noch kennenlernen werden, kann sich nun der Funktionsbereich von *bat* auf alle die Fälle ausbreiten, in denen in den Modellsprachen *un* gebraucht wird, also auch auf die Signalisierung von Indefinitheit' (Haase 1992: 59).

these contacts, Basque is in a process of giving up this distinction: wherever in the model languages[3] the comitative–instrumental preposition is used to present instrumental participants, Basque uses its comitative case suffix *-ekin* (or *-ekilan*) for instrumentals. The instrumental case suffix *-(e)z* can still be used to some extent to present instruments or means, but in most contexts it tends to be replaced by the comitative case since the model language would use the comitative–instrumental preposition in this context, as Spanish does. In other words, the instrumental case is gradually being replaced in these Basque varieties by the comitative suffix—that is, in an attempt to establish equivalence with the model languages, the comitative–instrumental polysemy of the model languages is replicated in Basque by grammaticalizing the comitative to also present instrumental participants (see also below).

But semantic replication also has a morphosyntactic effect increasingly affecting the Basque case system: on the model of the Romance prepositions, Basque is gradually developing a set of postpositions via the grammaticalization of relational nouns. Thus, by grammaticalizing relational nouns such as *buru* 'head' or *baita* 'interior', Basque is acquiring a set of complex postpositions modelled after corresponding complex prepositions in the Romance languages; for example, the Basque postposition *-ri/-ra(t) buru-z* (DAT/DIR head-INSTR) 'in the direction of' is modelled after the Gascon preposition (*de*) *cap a* ((from) head at) 'in the direction of' (Haase 1992: 73–5);[4] for a paradigm of equivalences in complex adpositions, see Haase (1992: 80).

Grammaticalization induced by contact with Romance languages has also affected the system of (self-standing) personal pronouns. First, it has filled a gap in the deictic paradigm by producing a new personal pronoun: while Gascon and French have third person pronouns (Gascon *eth* 'he', *era* 'she'; French *lui* 'he', *elle* 'she'), Basque has not. In order to develop an equivalent third person pronoun and thereby bring their paradigm in line with that of the model languages, Basque is grammaticalizing its identity pronoun[5] *ber-* 'same, -self' to a third person pronoun (Haase 1992: 135–7).[6]

[3] Note that the influence of Gascon on Basque was not unilateral; rather, it appears that Basque has also acted as a model language for Gascon (see Haase 1997).

[4] Haase (1992: 81) refers to this process as the creation of translational equivalents via loan translation (see Section 2.6).

[5] It would seem that the 'identity pronoun' corresponds largely to what König and Siemund (2000) would call an intensifier.

[6] That this is a process of grammaticalization is suggested by the fact that, first, we are dealing with a unidirectional development: cross-linguistically there are a number of languages where intensifier ('-self') or identity forms ('the same') have given rise to personal pronouns, while there is no evidence of a development in the opposite direction. Second, this development can be described in terms of desemanticization (see Section 2.3), whereby the specific intensifier or identity semantics is bleached out—with the effect that third person reference is the only semantic function that is left.

Second, language contact affecting the personal pronouns of Basque has also had a somewhat peculiar effect: instead of establishing an equivalence relation, the opposite is found, as the following example suggests (Haase 1992: 134). It seems that, at an earlier stage, Basque was using *hi* as a second person singular pronoun and *zu* for second person plural. Since Roman times, the Romance languages have had a second person distinction between an informal/familiar form (etymologically derived from Latin *tu*) and a formal/polite form (*vos*), which is the result of the extension of the second person plural pronoun (*vos*) to serve as a formal/polite second person singular pronoun. Early Basque speakers appear to have replicated this distinction by extending the meaning of their plural pronoun *zu* to a use as a polite second person singular pronoun (a new plural pronoun *zu-ek* was formed by adding the plural marker *-ek*). But the meaning of the Basque pronouns changed: *hi* became restricted to highly familiar second person reference while *zu* turned into the general marker of second person address—with the effect that there is no longer an equivalence relation between Basque and the Romance languages. In addition, *hi* does not clearly correspond to the modern reflexes of Romance *tu*, nor does *zu* correspond to either *tu* or *vos*; rather, *zu* can be used for both in many contexts.

What this suggests is that speakers aiming to establish an equivalence relation with their model language may actually achieve the contrary. Instead of creating a structural one-to-one correspondence between the two languages concerned, a situation arises where by the paradigms of grammatical categories are hardly more mutually compatible than they were prior to language contact.

That this is not an exceptional case can be illustrated with the following example. As we observed above, Basque has replicated the comitative–instrumental polysemy of the model languages Gascon and French whereby the comitative suffix *-ekin/-ekilan* was grammaticalized to also express the instrumental function, with the effect that the replica language now has the same polysemy as the model language (Haase 1992). A similar development has taken place in Basque varieties spoken in Spain, where Spanish is the model language (see Hurch 1989: 14ff for details). In these varieties as well, the instrumental case suffix *-(e)z* is a declining category. However, the situation in Spain turns out to be more complex, in that grammaticalization was responsible for the rise of a complex situation where there is no longer a one-to-one correspondence between form and meaning in the marking of the instrumental function (see Section 5.2).

Verbal structure. Within the verbal system, the same kinds of replication can be observed, leading in the direction of what Haase (1992: 158) calls a

'Romance TAM system'. Consider the following examples. Gascon has grammaticalized a progressive aspect based on the Location Schema [X is at doing Y], illustrated in (7.1); Basque speakers have done the same on the pattern of Gascon, using a nominalizer (*-tze*) instead of the Gascon infinitive marker (subsequently grammaticalizing the progressive further into an imperfective; Haase 1992: 93), see (7.2).

(7.1) GASCON (Romance; Haase 1992: 93)

èste	a	her	quaucòm
be	at	do.INF	something

'be in the process of doing something'

(7.2) BASQUE (Haase 1992: 93)

kanta-	tze-	n	dut.
sing-	NOMIN-	INE	PRES.3.SG<1.SG

'I sing.'

Furthermore, Basque has replicated the Latin-Romance possessive perfect via contact-induced grammaticalization, using the verb *ukan* 'have' plus the transitive participle as a complement to form a recent perfect (Haase 1992: 92–3; see Section 4.4.5).

With regard to verbal derivation, the Basque verb *egin* 'to do' appears to have been grammaticalized to some extent to a causative marker, used in a participial form, on the model of Gascon *har* + infinitive or French *faire* + infinitive:

(7.3) BASQUE (Haase 1992: 125–6)

[...]	ber-	e-	k	lei[h]o	bat-	eta-	(r)at	jautz-
	IDN-	ART.P-	ERG	window	one-	TRN-	DIR	descend-
	i	[eg]in	eta [...]					
	PTCP	do.PTCP	and					

'[...] they must take them (down) to a window and [...]'

That contact-induced grammaticalization may lead to subtle changes of meaning and context generalization (Bybee *et al.* 1994) can be shown with the following example.[7] Basque has a set of nine 'modal operators' two of which express ability or possibility: *ahal* 'be able to' and *ezin* 'not to be able to' (Haase 1992: 111). The forms corresponding semantically to *ahal* in the model languages are the modal verbs Gascon *poder* and French *pouvoir*, while the equivalents of *ezin* consist of these verbs plus a negation marker: Gascon *poder*

7 The following interpretation differs from that proposed by Haase (1992: 121) in detail but not in substance.

pas, French *ne pas pouvoir*, that is, a structure [NEG + 'be able to']. In an attempt to replicate the situation in the model languages, where no distinction is made between positive and negated ability, Basque appears to have generalized the use of *ahal* to be compatible with the negation marker *ez*, that is, Basque speakers have given up the constraint whereby *ahal* was replaced by *ezin* whenever negation was involved. The result is that *ezin* is gradually being replaced by *ez ahal* (NEG 'be able to'), in accordance with the model provided by Gascon and French, that is, Basque is losing one of its modal operators.

This process can be interpreted in a number of different ways. For example, it may be understood to be an instance of what has been called 'unpacking', where the synthetic expression *ezin* is replaced by the analytic phrase *ez ahal*. Our proposal to treat it as an instance of grammaticalization rests on the observation that *ahal* has gone through two interrelated grammaticalization processes: first, it underwent extension (or context generalization), whereby its use was extended to contexts formerly reserved for *ezin*, and second, it also underwent desemanticization in that it lost some of its semantic distinctiveness, acquiring a more general meaning—one that is compatible with the use of a negation marker. In accordance with what commonly happens in grammaticalization, the form being lost tends to survive in specific contexts: the use of *ezin* is retained in nominalized subordinate clauses (Haase 1992: 121).

Restructuring of a special kind has affected the negative imperative of Basque. In the model language, Gascon, it is expressed with the subjunctive, even though otherwise the subjunctive is restricted to subordinate clauses. In Basque, the subjunctive (SB) also occurs in main clauses, and whenever it does, it may be associated with the imperative of Gascon. On account of the structural difference between the Gascon and the Basque subjunctive, Basque speakers add an optional subordinator (SR) to mark the negative imperative, (7.4).

(7.4) BASQUE (Haase 1992: 106)

Haurr-	a-	k,	etzizte-	la	jin!
child-	ART-	PL	NEG.SB.2.PL.PRS-	SR	come

'Children, don't come!'

The sentence. Developments within the Basque verbal system have also had an impact on participant marking. Basque has traditionally had no passive category, but in an attempt to replicate the Gascon and French passive it is grammaticalizing the resultative aspect for this purpose, adding the intransitive participle form *izan* (the agent being suppressed):

(7.5) Basque (Example taken from the weekly *Herria*; Haase 1992: 102)

Adolfo	Villoslada	...	libra-	tu-	a	izan	da.
Adolfo	Villoslada	...	free-	PTCP-	ART	be.PTCP	PRES.3.SG

'Adolfo Villoslada [a kidnapped industrialist] has been freed.'

And Basque has also taken the next step in replicating a Romance-type passive: following the Gascon model, which uses either of the prepositions *de* or *per* to present an agent, it has chosen the ablative-partitive case suffix-*(r)ik* to introduce an agent:

(7.6) Basque (Haase 1992: 132)

A(b)antxü	xakür	bat-	eta-	(r)ik	ausiki	izan
almost	dog	one-	TRN-	ABL/PART	bite.PTCP	be.PTCP

tzün.
PRT.3.SG.2.AL

'He was almost bitten by a dog.'

Clause combining has been shaped to quite some extent by the grammaticalization from interrogative pronoun to relative and complement clause marker in a number of languages that have been in contact with SAE languages (see Chapter 6). Language contact in Spain affected the marking of relative clauses. In Basque, a finite relative clause precedes its head; there is no relative pronoun, but the verb takes a suffix marking it as subordinate. However, for some generations now, a new relativization strategy has been used in certain parts of the Basque-speaking area under the influence of Spanish. The question marker *zein* 'which?' or 'who?' was used as an equivalent of the Spanish interrogative pronouns and *zein* was grammaticalized to a relative clause marker (Trask 1998: 320). This grammaticalization of *zein* has been documented in texts since the seventeenth century but as a rule only in translations (Hurch 1989: 21). The new form does not replace the earlier structure; rather, *zein* is added to the existing relative construction (but see also Trask 1998: 320), with the result that there is now double marking on post-nominal relative clauses.

It would seem that Basque (at least as spoken in southwestern France) has gone one step further in having developed a fairly productive type of relative clause on the model of Romance languages. Thus, the following construction used in the written language corresponds in its major properties to that of many SAE languages: the relative clause is postnominal, has inflecting relative pronouns introducing the relative clause, and the pronoun is resumptive, signalling the head's role within the relative clause (Haspelmath 1998: 1494–5).

(7.7) Basque (Haase 1992: 152)

Hiri	bat	ba-	zen,	zoin-	tan	ez	bait-
town	one	ENZ-	PRT.3.SG	which-	TRN.INE	NEG	SR-

zen	eliza-	rik.
PRT.3.SG	church-	PART

'There was a town where there was no church.'

But it was not only relative clauses that were affected by what we referred to in Chapter 6 as the rise of the 'Romance subordination type' and the interrogative-to-subordination grammaticalization: Basque speakers in France have used a range of question words, such as *non* 'who?', *zer* 'what?', *nun* 'where?', *nola* 'how?', and *zoin* 'which?', to replicate complement and adverbial clauses from Gascon and French; the following example illustrates the resulting structure.

(7.8) Basque (Haase 1992: 149)

Ba-	dakizü,	zer	de-	n?
ENZ-	know.PRS.3.SG<2.SG	what	PRS.3.SG-	SR

'Do you know what he/she/it is?'

The various innovations discussed above did not all enter Basque at the same time, rather they were spread over quite a number of centuries; Table 7.1 gives an indication of the chronological profile involved. What this table suggests in particular is that there may have been two major waves of replication: one falling in the period prior to 1600 and a second affecting modern, twentieth-century Basque.

Table 7.1. Approximate chronology of replications in Basque

Kind of replication	Proto-Basque	16th century	18th century	20th century
'Do' > causative marker	–	–	–	+
Comitative > instrumental	–	–	–	+
Rise of passive	–	–	–	+
Rise of third person pronoun	–	–	–	+
Status of verbal modal operators	–	–	–	+
Complex postpositions	(–)	(+)	(+)	+
Rise of indefinite article	(–)	(+)	(+)	+
Romance TAM system	(–)	(+)	+	+
Interrogative > subordination	(–)	+	+	+

Source: Haase (1992: 158).

To conclude, contact-induced grammaticalization was one of the main factors responsible for changes leading to an increase in intertranslatability between the replica language Basque and the Romance model languages. Via these model languages, Basque has acquired a number of features characterizing SAE[8] even if, on the surface, this fact is not yet reflected in its overall profile of grammatical categorization.

7.2.2 *Slavic minorities in central Europe*

There appear to be two main sociolinguistic settings shaping the 'Europeanization' of languages. On the one hand, it is lingua francas serving as models, being used as media of higher education, and transmitted mainly via written discourse—a paradigm case being Latin, to a minor extent also Greek. In this case, geography is of secondary importance, what matters most of all is the spread of these languages in specific domains of communication, such as religion and education. On the other hand, it is contact between geographically contiguous speech communities that triggers replication. While in such contact situations formal education, religious instruction and the like may play some role as well, it is oral day-to-day interaction among neighbouring peoples and dialects that is central.

An example of the second kind is provided by language contact between Germans and speakers of Slavic minority languages spoken in eastern Germany or close to the German-speaking territory. Such minority languages are in particular Upper Sorbian and Lower Sorbian—spoken, respectively, in Upper and Lower Lusatia of eastern Germany, Kashubian—spoken on the left bank of lower Vistula, Poland—and Slovincian, spoken until the middle of the twentieth century in the parishes of Schmolsin and Grossgarde of northwestern Poland, but now possibly extinct. In the course of this contact, these Slavic languages have been massively influenced by German where grammaticalization played a not insignificant role.

A typological characteristic of German can be seen in the presence of a number of passive-like use patterns where the main verb is encoded in the past perfect participle (PPP) and the auxiliary is either one of the verbal items *bekommen*, *kriegen*, or *erhalten*, all meaning 'to get, receive', *will haben* 'wants to have', *gehören* 'to belong to', *sich lassen* 'to let oneself', etc. The following examples illustrate the first two of these constructions.

[8] Among the features we discussed in this section are the presence or emergence of an indefinite article, a 'have'-perfect, and of relative clauses with an introducing pronoun. These are all features that Haspelmath (2001) proposes to be diagnostic of SAE but finds to be absent in Basque.

(7.9) STANDARD GERMAN

(a) Klaus bekommt heute die Haare geschnitten.
Klaus gets today the hair cut
'Klaus has his hair cut today.'

(b) Klaus will heute die Haare geschnitten haben.
Klaus wants today the hair cut have
'Klaus wants his hair to be cut today.'

As the evidence volunteered by Lötzsch (1969; see also Nau 1995: 96ff) suggests, these constructions have been replicated in the neighbouring Slavic languages—a process that also involved borrowing. The German verb *kriegen* 'get, receive' was borrowed in the form *krynuś* (or *krynuć* or *kry(d)nyć*) in all colloquial varieties of Sorbian, and as *krëgac* in Slovincian. What is technically known as the German dative, indirect, or recipient passive, where any of the verbs *bekommen, kriegen,* or *erhalten* 'get, receive', serve as auxiliaries and the main verb appears in the past perfect participle, was replicated in both Upper and Lower Sorbian, first attested in Sorbian in 1814, where Sorbian speakers used their verb *krynuś* in the creation of the passive. However, as Nau (1995: 107) argues, Sorbian speakers did not borrow *krynuś* as a passive auxiliary but rather as a lexical verb, and they grammaticalized the borrowed verb in a way similar to the way German speakers had done earlier with *kriegen,* (7.10), where there is a structurally corresponding German translation in (7.10a) and a free English translation in (7.10b).

(7.10) UPPER SORBIAN (Lötzsch 1969: 105)
Pón … jo krynył ten młun zapisany.
(then … is gotten the mill registered)
(a) 'Dann … hat er die Mühle eingetragen gekriegt.'
(b) 'Then … he's got the mill registered.'

In examples such as (7.10), replica grammaticalization concerned a borrowed item. But the same replication process also took place involving an inherited Sorbian verb: Upper Sorbian *dóstać* or *dostaś* 'get' was also grammaticalized to an auxiliary of the dative passive around the same time as *krynuś,* first attestations dating back to 1811 (Nau 1995: 107):

(7.11) UPPER SORBIAN OF 1811 (Lötzsch 1969: 105)
Ta holca […] hłowu wotćatu dósta.
(the girl head.FEM.ACC.SG cut.off.FEM.ACC.SG got)
(a) 'Das Mädchen … bekam den Kopf abgeschnitten.'
(b) 'The girl … had her head cut off.'

In modern written Sorbian, the Sorbian verb *dóstać* or *dostaś* 'get' has replaced *krynuś* as the passive auxiliary. From its earliest attestations, the Sorbian construction shows roughly the same advanced stage of grammaticalization as the corresponding German indirect passive—with one exception: whereas in German the past perfect participle form of the main verb does not exhibit agreement with the object noun, this is not the case in Sorbian, where the (*-n-*, *-t-*) participle agrees with the object noun in gender, case, and number.

The same process has taken place in Slovincian, where the German dative passive was replicated by grammaticalizing the lexical verb *krëgac* 'get' in combination with the main verb encoded as a participial form to a dative passive echoing the structure of the corresponding German use pattern (Lötzsch 1969: 108). And a similar situation has been reported from Kashubian, where the German dative passive also provided the model for a passive-like use pattern. However, the lexical verb recruited for grammaticalization was not a borrowed one but rather the inherited Slavic verb *dostac* 'get' (Lötzsch 1969: 108).

Much the same transfer of a grammaticalization process has led to the introduction of a passive-like modal use pattern in these Slavic languages on the model of German. There is a weakly grammaticalized pattern in German, exemplified above in (7.9b), where the modal *wollen* 'want' in combination with the main verb in the past perfect participle and *haben* 'have' as a second auxiliary expresses the notion 'want to have something done'. Essentially the same kind of modal passive has developed in Sorbian, illustrated in (7.12), where once again (7.12a) is a corresponding German translation while (7.12b) is a free English translation.

(7.12) SORBIAN (Lötzsch 1969: 107)

Što	ceš	měč	nowe	kupjene [...]?
(what	want.2.SG.PRES	have	new	bought)

(a) 'Was willst du Neues gekauft haben [...]?'
(b) 'What new (things) do you want to have bought [...]?'

A similar use pattern has been observed in Slovincian, where there is a passive-like modal use pattern apparently modelled on the German pattern, (7.13).

(7.13) SLOVINCIAN (Lötzsch 1969: 108)

[...]	na-ca	mjìe̯c	kùo̯ko̯š	vu̯	vařuo̯nē.
	(she-wanted	have.INF	chicken	?	cooked)

(a) '[...] sie wollte ein Huhn gekocht haben.'
(b) '[...] she wanted to have a chicken cooked.'

Another area where these Slavic minority languages developed new use patterns on the model of German concerns compounding. For example, there is a productive compounding pattern in German consisting of an object noun headed by a following infinitival verb,[9] for example German *Staubwischen* (dust.to.wipe) 'dusting'. Slavic languages do not have an immediate structural equivalent, but Hinze (1969) argues that speakers of Slovincian have replicated the German use pattern, using the grammatical means available in their own language but copying the German word order arrangement. This use pattern, documented in Slovincian since 1856, is illustrated in (7.14), where the Slovincian structure is said to be structurally equivalent to the German translation (7.14a). It involves mostly purpose phrases, where the Slovincian preposition *do* appears to be used as a fairly regular equivalent of the German preposition *zum* ('to the').

(7.14) SLOVINCIAN (Hinze 1969: 64)

Ga	te	tåfle	na sǫ	f'in	zrivǫne	tei̯	to	je	dó	xleba	pječeńå.
(when	the	potatoes	are	fine	grated	then	this	is	for	bread	baking)

(a) 'Wenn die Kartoffeln fein gerieben sind, dann ist das *zum Brotbacken*.'

(b) 'When the potatoes are delicately grated then that is for baking bread.'

To conclude, there is a German-dominated region of areal influence, whereby speakers of Slavic minority languages, some of them having had a history of up to 1,000 years of contact with German, developed grammatical structures for which there is no immediate equivalent in Slavic languages. The replication processes resulting from these contact situations were illustrated above with examples involving specifically German passive-like constructions and noun–verb compounding. But there are also more global replication processes, suggesting that local contact-induced changes in these Slavic languages can be viewed as manifestations of a more general process of Europeanization.

One of these processes concerned the grammaticalization of articles. While we have no information on the situation in Slovincian, there is robust evidence to show that both Upper and Lower Sorbian have created definite and indefinite article forms on the model of German; we discussed these cases in Chapter 3. And a similar situation is found in Kashubian, where the

[9] Hinze (1969: 64) calls this the German *Kompositionstyp Substantiv + Verbalabstraktum*.

demonstratives *ten* and *nen* can be used as definite markers, and the numeral *jeden* 'one' functions as an indefinite article (Nau 1995: 114).

The rise of a possessive perfect is another similar case, presumably also replicated from German: as we saw in Chapter 4, in both Upper and Lower Sorbian there is an incipient category of a perfect-like construction built on a verb for 'have'. That both the articles and the possessive perfects in Sorbian are not as highly grammaticalized as they are in German is in accordance with the observation made time and again in the preceding chapters, according to which replicated categories are generally likely to be less grammaticalized than their model categories.

7.2.3 *Pipil*

As we observed in the introduction to this chapter, Europe's linguistic influence extends far beyond the geographical boundaries of this continent. An example from the Americas is provided by Pipil, a Uto-Aztecan language of El Salvador, belonging to the Nahua subgroup of Aztecan. The language is now nearing extinction; the remaining few hundred speakers are all Pipil-Spanish bilinguals, and for many of them Spanish is the dominant language. Accordingly, Pipil's more recent linguistic history is shaped primarily by its interaction with an SAE language, Spanish. While Pipil is a moribund language, Campbell (1987: 254) argues that the changes to be discussed below are not due to processes associated primarily with language death, and our analysis corroborates this hypothesis. The following account is based primarily on Campbell (1987) and Harris and Campbell (1995).

Nominal structure. Prior to their contact with a European language and culture, Pipil speakers did not dispose of conventionalized devices for marking definite or indefinite reference of nouns. Later developments are summarized by Campbell thus:

> Today, Pipil nouns occur with both definite (*ne*) and indefinite (*se:*) articles, quite parallel to Spanish. While in pre-Conquest times such constructions were not unheard of, the definite had a much more demonstrative ring to it (like 'that [one]') and the indefinite was not an article at all but rather the numeral 'one'. ... Their usage has come to be nearly a complete match of Spanish articles (Campbell 1987: 272).

These observations suggest, first, that Pipil speakers have drawn on universal strategies for developing the reference markers concerned: definite articles are almost invariably derived from demonstrative attributes, while indefinite articles are most likely to be grammaticalized forms of the numeral 'one' (Heine & Kuteva 2002). Second, both grammaticalizations were at least to some extent influenced by contact with Spanish. And third, the two reference markers differ in the extent to which language contact contributed to their evolution: while the indefinite article *se:* appears to be a novel creation arising in the period of Pipil-Spanish contacts, the grammaticalization of the definite article *ne* can be assumed to have started prior to these contacts, that is, replication involved not the genesis but at best the further development of an incipient category. Finally, the result of the process summarized by Campbell had the effect that Pipil achieved a higher degree of equivalence, and hence of intertranslatability, with the model language Spanish.

Prepositions. Pipil had neither prepositions nor postpositions in pre-Conquest times, using relational nouns instead. More recently, however, it has developed these relational nouns into a set of prepositions on the model of Spanish: 'Under Spanish influence, some Pipil relational nouns shifted both in form and function to become true prepositions of the Spanish type' (Harris & Campbell 1995: 126). Table 7.2 summarizes the process concerned.

The effect that this process had on the structure of Pipil is summarized by Harris and Campbell in the following way:

> The borrowed category 'preposition' is totally at odds with the former 'system' (not just the 'norms'), and is not 'structurally compatible' with the typological grain of the language (Harris & Campbell 1995: 127).

As we will see below, the preposition *wan* has been further grammaticalized on the model of Spanish.

However the replication process has gone even further. One of the emerging prepositions listed in Table 7.2, *pal*, has been grammaticalized into a periphrastic genitive equivalent of Spanish *de* 'of'. The following example illustrates the resulting use pattern:

(7.15) Pipil (Aztecan, Uto-Aztecan; Harris & Campbell 1995: 126)

Kinekit	kikwat	ne	nakat,	ne	ihyak	nakat	**pal**
they.want	they.eat	the	meat	the	stinking	meat	of
ne	masa:t.						
the	deer						

'They want to eat the meat, the stinking meat of the deer.'

Table 7.2 The grammaticalization of relational nouns to prepositions in Pipil

Relational noun		Preposition	
-(i)hpak	'on, upon, over, on top of'	pak	'on'
-pal	'possession'	pal	'of'
-wan	'with'	wan	'with'

Source: based on Harris and Campbell (1995: 126–7).

From verbal to adjectival use pattern. Pipil has a category of past participial forms, marked by *-tuk*, which formerly functioned only in verbal constructions, as in (7.16a). Apparently, Pipil speakers established an equivalence relation between their category and the Spanish participle, which functions not only in verb forms (*ha roto* 'has broken') but also often as adjectives (*el vidrio roto* 'the broken glass'). On the basis of the model provided by Spanish, the use of the Pipil past participial forms has been extended to new contexts, bearing an adjectival function in addition (glossed PERF by Campbell 1987: 265), as in (7.16b).

(7.16) PIPIL (Aztecan, Uto-Aztecan; Campbell 1987: 265)

(a) ki- chiw- tuk.
it- do- PAST.PARTICIPIAL
'S/he has done it.'

(b) kabál uksi- tuk ne wahkal.
exact ripe- PERF the gourd
'The gourd was just ripe.'

Verb structure. According to Campbell (1987: 272), language contact also contributed to the rise of a progressive aspect of the type found in the model language Spanish:

> Pipil has a 'progressive' verbal construction formed with *nemi* 'to be' + finite verb (e.g. *nemi ni-ta-kwa* [is I-OBJ-eat] 'I am eating'). Among all the Nahua varieties, a progressive of this form is found only in Pipil. A progressive construction formed with a verb meaning 'to be' (as in English 'I *am* eating' or Spanish *estoy comiendo*) may develop independently, as it did in Pipil. However, the frequency and usage matches that of the Spanish 'progressive' so exactly that Spanish influence is clear (Campbell 1987: 272).

More than some other cases discussed in this section, this is a case where contact does not provide an entirely convincing hypothesis. First, as acknowledged by Campbell, we are dealing with a fairly widespread grammaticalization process which may, but need not, have involved contact. And second, the Pipil construction differs in one essential aspect from the corresponding model category: while in Spanish the main verb appears in a non-finite form, this is not the case in Pipil. Nevertheless, there are reasons to adopt Campbell's hypothesis on the basis of the arguments presented by him, suggesting that language contact had at least the effect of achieving isomorphism with regard to frequency of use.

Another example relating to the tense–aspect domain concerns the rise of a de-allative future. Campbell (1987: 267–8; see also Harris and Campbell

1995: 148–9) observes that Pipil speakers tend to use a 'go-to'-future which these authors attribute to the influence of the local Spanish de-allative future (*lo voy a hacer* 'I'm going to do it'). Once again, we seem to be dealing with the replication of a grammaticalization process that has a universal base but appears to have been influenced by language contact. In the same way as we observed in the preceding case of the progressive, replication did not lead to structural isomorphism, in that what appears in Spanish as a non-finite main verb corresponds to a finite verb in Pipil. Thus, there appears to be a more general process whereby Pipil speakers replicated the conceptual schema, rather than the morphosyntax, of a grammaticalization process leading from location or motion schemas to categories of aspect and tense in the replica language.

The sentence. Traditionally, Pipil has no formal means for coordinating clauses, that is, clause-conjoining ('and') is not formally marked. Pipil has a 'relational noun' *-wan* which requires a possessive pronominal prefix as a modifier, thus having the appearance of a possessed noun (Campbell 1987: 256). Another effect of the impact with an SAE language can be seen in the development of structures for noun phrase and clause combining under the influence of Spanish (see Table 7.2): Pipil speakers grammaticalized the relational noun-*wan* 'with' to a preposition *wan* 'with', and *wan* has further developed into a noun phrase-conjoining conjunction 'and', and eventually to a coordinating conjunction 'and', that is, its use has been extended to also conjoin clauses. Accordingly, in the course of less than five centuries, Pipil changed from a language of limited coordination with no true coordinate conjunctions and with restricted modes of parataxis and hypotaxis to one that has come to resemble the structure of Spanish in a number of ways (Campbell 1987: 258).

Relative clauses. Pipil has also developed new structures of clause subordination as a result of language contact with Spanish. Grammaticalization had the following effect in particular: the Pipil interrogative word *ka(h)* 'who, what?' appears to have been grammaticalized to a relative clause marker, and *tay/ta:* 'what?' to a complementizer, exactly equivalent to Spanish *que/lo que* 'that, that which', which is now a member of the subordinate clause; see Section 6.2 for more details.

Purpose clauses. Another example illustrating the rise of new forms of clause combining is provided by the development of the relational noun *-pal* 'possession' to a subordinating conjunction of purpose (*pal* 'in order to, so that'; see Table 7.2):

(7.17) Pipil (Aztecan, Uto-Aztecan; Campbell 1987: 264)

ni-	mu-	kets-	ki	ni-	k-	tatia	ti-	t	**pal**
I-	REFL-	arise-	PRET	I-	it-	burn	fire-	ABSOL	so
ni-	mu-	tutu:nia.							
I-	REFL-	heat							

'I got up to light (the) fire in order to warm myself.'

The grammaticalization of nouns to adpositions and eventually to conjunctions constitutes cross-linguistically a common process (see Heine & Kuteva 2002 for examples); note that this Aztecan language also has grammaticalized its relational noun -*wan* 'with' to an adposition and eventually to a (coordinating) conjunction used for clause conjoining (see above). As Campbell (1987: 263–4) shows, there is also little doubt that the grammaticalization of -*pal*, like that of -*wan*, is the result of a replication on the model of Spanish; note that both have undergone decategorialization, which had the effect that both items lost the ability to take possessive pronominal prefixes. What makes -*pal* a special case is that in addition to grammaticalization it also involved phonological similarity: the Spanish item *para* 'for, in order to' provided not only the conceptual but also the phonetic model for this innovation, especially since there is no *r*/*l* distinction in native Pipil words.

Campbell (1987: 264) provides another example suggesting that phonological factors contributed to shaping contact-induced grammaticalization in Pipil. On the model of Spanish *sólo* 'alone, only', Pipil has grammaticalized its relational noun -*se:l* 'alone' to an adverb *se:l* 'alone, only', presumably influenced by the phonetic similarity between the two items. Decategorialization had the effect that possessive prefixes used with the relational noun are no longer required with the adverb, and decategorialization was accompanied by desemanticization. The Pipil item underwent a fairly widespread semantic process from 'alone' to 'only' (see Heine & Kuteva 2002: 41–3), thereby replicating the polysemy of the Spanish model.

The Spanish subjunctive. Campbell (1987: 266–7) remarks that Spanish has a grammatical category 'subjunctive' while Pipil lacks such a category. But Pipil speakers appear to be aiming to replicate the Spanish category, using two of their own categories for this purpose: the conditional (-*skiya*) and the imperative (*x*(*i*)-, 2.SG, and *ma:*). Note that the Spanish subjunctive expresses notions of both deontic and epistemic modality, while the Pipil examples provided by Campbell all relate to deontic modality. The data provided do not make it entirely clear to what extent Pipil speakers were successful; what they suggest, however, is that there appears to be an attempt to establish an equivalence relation with the Spanish category.

Impersonal. Pipil once had a number of passive suffixes which have survived only in frozen verb stems. The only modern equivalent to a passive is an impersonal construction where the subject is not specified other than by a grammaticalized form of the third person plural pronoun (-*t*), for example:

(7.18) PIPIL (Aztecan, Uto-Aztecan; Campbell 1987: 272)

nech-	tawilih-	ke-	t	ne	pe:lu.
me-	give-	PRET-	PL	the	dog

(a) 'They gave me the dog.' (b) 'I was given the dog.'

This construction and its diachronic status are described by Campbell in the following way:

> It is quite clear that the widespread usage of third-person plural forms for impersonal utterances, which have replaced totally the former passive constructions, has been stimulated by the similar Spanish employment of third-person plural forms as impersonals (cf. *Comen pescado en Japón* 'they eat fish in Japan', 'fish are eaten in Japan'). Nevertheless, while extremely rare, similar examples are not unknown from CN [Classical Nahuatl; a.n.] texts. Thus, it is not clear whether this construction owes its origin in Pipil to Spanish (with CN having undergone an independent development) or whether Pipil, like CN, had the construction and came to replace other passives/impersonals with it because of its similarity to Spanish (Campbell 1987: 273).

This suggests that the grammaticalization of a third person plural pronoun to a marker of an impersonal construction, a cross-linguistically common process (Heine & Kuteva 2002), was not necessarily triggered by language contact, but that contact nevertheless played a role in the process. In any case, grammaticalization is still in its initial stage, where the source meaning has not entirely been bleached out.

In concluding we may mention that replication has also affected the morphophonology of Pipil. The final stage in grammaticalization concerns grammatical forms that are desemanticized to the extent that they cease to exist as meaningful units, that they are lost, and/or that they merge with other forms and become inseparable appendages of the latter. As Campbell (1987: 274) argues, this stage can also be observed in Pipil as a result of contact-induced replication of the Spanish model. The Pipil 'absolutive' suffix -*ti* (-*t* after vowels) occurs whenever a noun bears no other affixes, that is, it is absent with possessed nouns. With a few roots, the absolutive suffix has lost its grammatical status, in that it appears to have become a frozen part of the nominal root, for example *-a:pan-ti* > *a:panti* 'irrigated field'. Campbell accounts for this change in the following way:

Local Spanish has borrowed the Pipil forms with the absolutive reflected in the loan. These borrowed Spanish forms, in turn, seem to have influenced native Pipil words to establish a root more like the Spanish version, e.g., *-awa-t* ['bud'; a.n.] is in local Spanish *aguate*, *-kal-tsun-ti* ['beam, roof pole'; a.n.] is *calsonte*. Thus, even here, the boundary loss seems to be caused by Spanish influence (Campbell 1987: 274).

This loss of the absolutive suffix as a distinct unit appears to have been a more complex process, involving on the one hand the reinterpretation of an existing form via contact-induced replication and borrowing on the other.

7.2.4 *Discussion*

As we pointed out in Section 7.1, a central question to be answered in the preceding paragraphs was to determine which grammatical concepts of SAE European languages provide particularly attractive models to be replicated in other languages. Our comparison of the overall results of transfer from Romance languages to the non-Indo-European peripheral languages Basque (Section 7.2.1) and Pipil (Section 7.2.3), and from German to Slavic minority languages (Section 7.2.2) suggests that there are in fact some concepts that can be said to provide attractive models, triggering some strikingly similar processes in the direction of SAE languages, and affecting all major domains of language structure.

Among the grammatical concepts that have been replicated in all three types of languages there are articles: all languages created new articles of some kind. Basque is the only language that has replicated an indefinite article but not a definite one. Note that Basque traditionally has a suffix *-a* that has been described by Bascologists as a definite article. As a matter of fact, *-a* is not a definite marker but rather what Haase (1992: 54) calls an individualizer; however, its function overlaps with that of a definite marker (see Section 1.3). Conceivably, this is the reason why Basque differs from Sorbian, Kashubian, and Pipil in not having replicated both articles from its Romance model languages.

Also, the adpositional structure of SAE appears to have attracted contact-induced grammaticalization, in that speakers of Basque and Pipil changed existing structures in the direction of their SAE model languages. In a similar fashion, the verb phrase was affected, leading to new structures for expressing tense and aspect, such as a progressive aspect or a possessive perfect. Replication also extended to sentence structure, where SAE passives appear to have played some role as a model. And, finally, it was the SAE strategy of recruiting interrogative forms for marking clause subordination that was exploited in both languages in some way.

To conclude, language contact led to new modes of reference tracking, of presenting participants in the clause, of describing the aspectual and temporal contours of events, and of combining clauses. And the strategy employed was essentially the same in all languages, namely using forms and constructions having a fairly concrete meaning and developing them into more abstract grammatical use patterns and categories. In fact, most cases discussed in Sections 7.2.1, 7.2.2, and 7.2.3 concern instances of well documented processes of grammaticalization, that is, changes based on universal strategies of grammatical development.[10] This means that these processes could as well have happened without language contact. What language contact appears to have achieved is to initiate or accelerate grammatical change, or both.

As elsewhere, we were confined here to only one explanatory parameter. But this does not mean that there were no other factors at work. One factor that we came across in the examples above concerns phonetic similarity, which appears to have contributed for example to the grammaticalization of the Pipil relational noun *-pal* 'possession' to a subordinating conjunction of purpose on the model of Spanish *para* 'for, in order to', or of the Pipil relational noun *-se:l* 'alone' to an adverb *se:l* 'alone, only' on the model of the polysemous Spanish item *sólo* 'alone, only'. Another factor discussed by Campbell (1987: 277–8) is 'gap filling'.

In conclusion, we may say that Basque, Sorbian, Pipil, etc. are experiencing a gradual 'Europeanization' of their structure, leading to a changed typological profile in the sense defined in Section 7.1. But none of the languages has changed to the extent that it now represents a new language type, clearly different from the one it exhibited prior to language contact or being distinctly typologically similar to the respective model languages. Accordingly, Trask (1998: 319) maintains that there is virtually no observable tendency for Indo-European morphological features to be transferred into Basque, and Comrie observes:

> Basque certainly doesn't seem to borrow many bound morphemes from Romance, nor to change its overall morphological typology (i.e. it retains a rich nominal morphology, also a rich verb morphology but virtually restricted to a few auxiliary verbs). In the nominal system, there is some shifting of the content of morphological categories under contact. And in the verb, it is largely the development of periphrastic constructions (Bernard Comrie, p.c.).

Note also that Campbell (1987: 276) concludes with reference to Pipil that in spite of all the influence that Spanish has had, 'the basic pattern of the

[10] In the relevant literature there are also a few cases of borrowing, that is, of transfer of linguistic forms. In line with the general theme of this volume, such cases are not considered here.

language has remained unaltered and scarcely any attested syntactic phenomenon has been fully lost or replaced.'

What appears to have happened is—to use the wording of Campbell (1987: 271)—a change 'in spirit' to conform to the norms of the model language, and this spirit is of a special kind: rather than replacing conventionalized grammatical categories by corresponding model categories, speakers of the replica languages activate marginal patterns or develop new use patterns that are interpreted as being equivalent to corresponding model patterns, using these patterns more frequently and in more contexts, and adapting the meanings expressed by them to meanings and categories found in the model languages.

7.3 Towards a non-European typological profile

Section 7.2 was concerned with L2>L1 transfers, it was meant to demonstrate that peripheral languages are gradually 'Europeanized' via contact with SAE languages. In the present section we wish to demonstrate that there also processes in the opposite direction, that is, L1>L2 transfers—especially in situations where SAE languages lack a significant body of native speakers. To this effect we will rely on evidence from contact situations between SAE languages and languages spoken outside Europe, even if there is some evidence from contact situations within Europe, as we will see in Section 7.3.1. In Sections 7.3.2 and 7.3.3 we will deal with two cases of 'de-Europeanization', both involving English. We will, however, not provide a full account of this process; rather, we will be satisfied with providing evidence to establish, first, that a change towards a new typological profile has in fact taken place and, second, that this change crucially involved contact-induced grammaticalization, even if this was not the only mechanism to be held responsible for change.

7.3.1 Introduction

Processes such as the ones sketched in the preceding sections may give the impression that we are dealing with a one-way process from one language—typically a pragmatically dominant language (Matras 1998*a*: 285) or dominant code (Johanson 1992, 2002*a*)—to a dominated code. This, however, is not the case; not infrequently, replication processes may also proceed from the dominated to the dominant code, in particular when speakers transfer structures of their L1 to their L2. There are, in fact, a number of cases showing that grammatical replication may proceed in both directions. For example, Austronesian languages such as Tigak appear to have provided a model for replication in the lingua franca Tok Pisin, but Tok Pisin also served as a model for Tigak (Jenkins 2002); note further that in situations of language contact between Turkic and Iranian languages, both served at the same time as model and as replica languages (see Soper 1987).

In the following we will show that replication can in fact be reciprocal. Our concern will be with peripheral, dominated, languages and the way their speakers have used their L1 to shape their L2. More importantly, however, we will argue in this section that in the same way as SAE languages have shaped the structure of peripheral languages, they themselves have been shaped by the latter under appropriate sociolinguistic circumstances. Once again we are concerned with peripheral languages located on the European continent, but the main bulk of our data comes from overseas, where SAE languages spread as vehicles of cross-cultural and cross-linguistic interaction and were exposed to alternative models of conceptualization and linguistic expression and, as a result of this exposure, changed their typological profile in the direction of local model languages.

Basque as an L1 model language. In Section 7.2.1 we saw how the Basque language has been affected by contact with its Romance neighbours. But transfer in general and grammatical replication in particular were not entirely a one-directional. While Basque served as a replica language *vis-à-vis* Spanish, French, and Gascon (see e.g. Hurch 1989; Haase 1992, 1997) it also acted as a model language for Spanish speakers in the Basque Country. In the present section we provide a couple of examples to illustrate this; the reader is referred to Cárdenas (1995) for a more detailed treatment.

There is a widespread grammaticalization process whereby demonstrative pronouns may develop into personal pronouns (see e.g. Heine & Kuteva 2002). Basque does not have third person personal pronouns, and in south-western France, Basque speakers are developing their identity pronoun *ber-* 'same, -self' into a third person pronoun, as we saw in Section 7.2.1. Basque speakers in Spain may use demonstratives to function as third person pronouns and, as the description by Cárdenas (1995: 245) suggests, Spanish speakers in the Basque country have replicated this grammaticalization strategy, using their proximal demonstratives where Basque speakers would use demonstrative pronouns. Thus, in example (7.19), such Spanish speakers use the demonstrative *este* 'this' on the model of Basque *honek*, instead of the Standard Spanish personal pronoun *el* 'he'.

(7.19) Spanish in the Basque Country (Cárdenas 1995: 245)

(a) Basque: *Honek* kontrakoa uste du.
(Lit.: '*This* thinks the opposite.')

(b) Basque-influenced Spanish: *Este* opina lo contrario.
(c) Standard Spanish: *El* opina lo contrario.
Meaning: '*He* thinks the opposite.'

Another example concerns object agreement in Basque. Cárdenas (1995: 248–9) argues that in an attempt to replicate this structure, Spanish speakers in the Basque country use an unstressed pronoun coreferentially with an overt direct object nominal when the latter is human and definite—the pronouns employed for this purpose being the dative pronouns (*le*, plural *les*). Accordingly, these Spanish speakers use an object pronoun in (7.20b) on the model of Basque, (7.20a), where the corresponding Standard Spanish sentence (7.20c) has no object pronoun.[11]

(7.20) SPANISH IN THE BASQUE COUNTRY (Cárdenas 1995: 248)
(a) Basque: *Jon* parkean ikusten $d_i$ut.
(b) Basque-influenced Spanish: Le_i veo *a* $Juan_i$ en el parque.
(c) Standard Spanish: Veo *a* $Juan_i$ en el parque.
Meaning: 'I see John at the park.'

That the use of personal pronouns is extended to new contexts, in some cases thereby giving rise to personal agreement, appears to be a fairly common instance of extension (see Section 2.3) occurring in situations of language contact.

Amazonian languages as L1 model languages. A different kind of situation concerns the impact of Indian languages of the Americas on SAE languages. While there is no information on how Spanish was affected by its use by Pipil speakers, there are some data on another Romance SAE language spoken in the Americas: in the Vaupés region of northwest Brazil, the L2 Portuguese is the target of replication on the model of local Indian languages such as Tucano and Tariana (L1), leading to the emergence of new grammatical use patterns in the lingua franca Portuguese. Aikhenvald observes:

> The main characteristic of spontaneously produced discourse in Portuguese is an attempt to find an equivalent for grammatical distinctions found in the languages of the Vaupés. This makes the Indians' Portuguese in some ways richer than the standard language (Aikhenvald 2002: 313).

In fact, one effect of this impact is that in the variety of the European language as spoken by speakers of Tucanoan and Arawak languages, new use patterns and functional categories are created. The reader is referred to Aikhenvald (2002: 314–18) for discussion, a few examples may suffice here.

[11] For a related example from the contact situation between Spanish and Nahuatl, see Section 2.2.

The North Arawak language Tariana of northwest Amazonia has an obligatory paradigm of four clitics marking tense and evidentiality, distinguishing between visual, non-visual, inferred, and reported evidence. Tariana speakers use Portuguese, the official language of Brazil, as an important lingua franca, but Portuguese has no grammaticalized categories marking evidentiality. In using Portuguese, Tariana speakers tend to replicate their evidentiality system by drawing on lexical expressions of Portuguese, using them more frequently and developing them into incipient categories for which there is no equivalent in Standard Portuguese (Aikhenvald 2002: 117–27, 315–16). Thus, Tariana speakers tend to grammaticalize the Portuguese expressions *eu vi* 'I saw', *eu tenho prova* 'I have proof', or *eu tenha experiência* 'I have experience' to visual evidentials, *eu escutei* 'I heard' and *eu senti* 'I felt' to non-visual evidentials, *parece* 'it appears, it seems' to an inferred evidential, and *diz que* 'it is said that' to a reported evidential.

Another kind of replication involves the use of stance verbs to specify the posture of a referent, distinguishing, for example, whether an action is carried out while standing or sitting. To this end, Tariana speakers employ specifying expressions in their use of Portuguese, thereby creating a use pattern that is uncommon in both Standard Portuguese and Vernacular Brazilian Portuguese. Thus, speakers of Vaupés Portuguese would be specific about the position taken to carry out some specific action, as in (7.21), while (7.22) would be typical of Standard Portuguese and Vernacular Brazilian Portuguese.

(7.21) PORTUGUESE SPOKEN BY TARIANA IN NORTHWEST BRAZIL
(Aikhenvald 2002: 316–17)

Tava	urinando	em	pé.
be.PAST.3.SG	peeing	in	foot

'(He) was peeing standing.'

(7.22) STANDARD PORTUGUESE

Estava	urinando.
be.PAST.3.SG	peeing

'(He) was peeing.'

A final example illustrating the restructuring of Portuguese on the model of Amazonian languages in the Vaupés concerns the valency behaviour of verbs. Aikhenvald (2002: 317) reports that speakers in the Vaupés region of northwest Brazil tend to replicate the verbal structure of their own language by using many intransitive verbs transitively in their variety of Portuguese. Thus, in their use of Portuguese, the verb *cahir* can mean both 'fall' and 'fell', or *arder* can mean 'burn (intr.)' and 'cause to burn'.

To conclude, even if—superficially—dominant European languages such as Spanish, Portuguese, English, and French tend to act as 'donors' when in contact with other languages, they may as well be 'receivers'. In the following sections we will look at some more dramatic effects of L1>L2 replication. To this end, we will leave the European continent and look at the fate of an SAE language, English, in two different regions of the world. These regions are Southeast Asia (Section 7.3.2) and West Africa (Section 7.3.3), and each of these regions highlights a different manifestation of areal forces, the former leading to a new nominal and the latter to a new clausal profile. Our discussion is restricted to grammatical replication, that is, we will ignore other factors that also played some role in the grammatical changes concerned, such as pidginization and creolization.

7.3.2 *Singlish*

In 1819, the first British trading post was established in Singapore, which was inhabited predominantly by Malays. Today, English is one of the official languages of Singapore, along with Malay, Mandarin, and Tamil; together with Malay it is the main means of communication across ethnic groups. While Chinese account for a little under 80 per cent of Singapore's population,[12] nearly 70 per cent of the current generation of children are said to be native speakers of English (Gupta 1994: 27). Singlish, a short hand for Colloquial Singaporean English (or Singaporean Colloquial English), is a basilectal, low-prestige variety of English (Platt 1975), mainly used as L2 although it has acquired a substantial number of native speakers. While Formal Singaporean English bears a close resemblance to the standards of British and American English (henceforth referred to as 'Standard English'), Singlish does not; rather, it:

> exhibits many of the characteristics of an Asian language. More specifically, Singlish shares many of the features of the other languages spoken in Singapore, primarily Cantonese, Teochew and Hokkien Chinese, and Singaporean and Bazaar Malay. Phonetically, Singlish is syllable timed, with greatly reduced syllable structure and, possibly, lexical tone: a newcomer to Singapore, hearing it for the first time, is likely to mistake it for Chinese (Gil 2003: 469).

The following account is restricted to the noun phrase of Singlish (Gil 2003). The overall changes from a variety that can be assumed to have been fairly similar to varieties of British Standard English to present-day Singlish mainly involved two kinds of processes. One, that we will not discuss further,

[12] According to Debra Ziegeler (p.c.), this is a high estimate; the number of Chinese is declining whereas the Malay population is increasing.

concerns pidginization:[13] The morphology of Singlish is characterized by the fact that many of the inflections of Standard English are either optional or completely absent (Gil 2003: 469). But pidginization was not complete, in that the grammatical markers of Standard English have frequently survived as optional markers, coexisting with newly arising functional categories (see Gil 2003 for details).

Conceivably, pidginization was enhanced by the fact that in the languages that contributed to the rise of Singlish there are no immediate equivalents for many of the grammatical markers of English. For example, with the loss of obligatory markings on the noun phrase, Singlish nouns have come to resemble nouns in East Asian languages such as Cantonese, Hokkien, Mandarin, and Malay in being unmarked for number and (in)definiteness. Thus, the noun *apple* in (7.24a) can be understood to refer to a singular, plural, or mass entity, and it can be understood to be either definite or indefinite.

The second kind of changes involved what we propose to call contact-induced grammaticalization, whereby Singlish created a catalogue of new functional categories. One new set of categories concerns articles: while the inherited articles *the* and *a*(*n*) did not disappear but survived as optional markers, Singlish speakers have drawn on a universal strategy to create new articles by grammaticalizing the numeral *one* to an indefinite and the distal demonstrative attribute *that* to a definite marker (Gil 2003: 474; see our discussion in Chapter 3). Accordingly, indefiniteness can be expressed either as in (7.23b) or (7.23c), and definiteness either as in (7.23d) or (7.23e). As would be expected in the early stages of grammaticalization, the new categories have not (yet) become obligatory ones, and they have retained their earlier meaning—with the effect that they are frequently ambiguous between their ungrammaticalized numeral or demonstrative and their grammaticalized article meanings.

(7.23) SINGLISH (Gil 2003: 472–4)[14]

(a)	Geraint eat apple.	'Geraint ate an/the apple(s).'
(b)	Geraint eat an apple.	'Geraint ate an apple.'
(c)	Geraint eat one apple.	'Geraint ate an apple.'
(d)	Geraint eat the apple.	'Geraint ate the apple.'
(e)	Geraint eat that apple.	'Geraint ate the apple.'
(f)	Geraint eat that apples.	'Geraint ate the apples.'

[13] With the term pidginization we refer to a process whereby a language in a situation of contact loses a large part of its lexicon, most of its inflectional and derivational morphology, and a number of its phonological distinctions, and its use is restricted to a limited range of domains of human interaction.

[14] Gil does not provide translations of his Singlish examples. The translations are therefore ours based on the information available.

The rise of the new indefinite marker *one* might be an instance of replica grammaticalization since virtually all the languages with which Singlish is in contact (Cantonese, Hokkien, Mandarin, as well as Singaporean and Standard Malay) use their numeral 'one' as a marker of indefiniteness (Gil 2003: 502). The contact-induced nature of the definite article *that* is less clear; but it is fairly obvious that it is fully grammaticalized in some contexts. For example, constructions such as the following do not seem to allow for the use of demonstrative categories, hence *this* may not be used in (7.24a), whereas the definite markers *the* and *that* can, (7.24b) and (7.24c).

(7.24) SINGLISH (Gil 2003: 486)
(a) *Ah Chew buy the house this expensive one.
(b) Ah Chew buy the house that expensive one. 'Ah, Chew bought the expensive house.'
(c) Ah Chew buy the house the expensive one. 'Ah, Chew bought the expensive house.'

On the surface, the new articles are functionally identical with their Standard English equivalents; as a matter of fact however they are not: while the new indefinite article *one* indeed has singular reference (7.23b), the new definite article *that* is transnumeral, that is neutral with respect to number, hence it can cooccur with plural head nouns, as in (7.23f). However, when in combination with a head noun, which—as observed above—is equally transnumeral, there is a non-plural interpretation—that is, *that apple* in (7.23e) can refer to a singular or a mass concept but not to a plural concept.

Gil (2003: 474–5) points out that such a determiner non-plurality effect, as he refers to it, is not really common, but it is also found in Singaporean Malay (although not in Standard Malay). For example, both the noun *epal* 'apple' and the distal demonstrative *itu* 'that' are transnumeral, but in combination they are not transnumeral but rather non-plural, that is, *epal itu* can only refer to singular or mass concepts. In order to express plurality, the noun has to be marked for plurality via reduplication:

(7.25) SINGAPOREAN MALAY (Gil 2003: 475)

epal-	epal	itu
apple-	apple	that

'the/those apples'

Thus, Singaporean Malay exhibits the same structure as Singlish and, on account of this situation, there is reason to suggest that Singlish has replicated the determiner non-plurality effect from Singaporean Malay.

A quite different kind of replication process that Singlish experienced concerns the grammaticalization parameter of context extension, that is, the generalization of a given use pattern to new contexts (see Section 2.3). In Standard English, the numeral *one* may serve to pronominalize nominal modifiers such as demonstratives and adjectives, for example *this one*, *the big one*. This pattern has been further grammaticalized in Singlish, in that it has been extended to a wider range of contexts—with the effect that it has assumed, for example, the function of turning some constituents that cannot serve as arguments into arguments. Gil argues that, unlike its Standard English cognate, *one* in Singlish is not a proform but is what he calls a reifier. Accordingly, *one* may not only turn adjectives (7.26a) but also possessor NPs (7.26b), locative adverbial phrases (7.26c), and even clauses (7.26d) into object complements.[15] In accordance with the general typological format of Singlish, *one* in this use pattern is transnumeral and unmarked for (in)definiteness,[16] that is, it can have singular, mass, plural, definite, and/or indefinite referents.

(7.26) Singlish (Gil 2003: 480)

(a)	Ah[17] Chew buy expensive one.	'Ah, Chew bought an/the expensive one.'
(b)	Ah Chew buy Jamil one.	'Ah, Chew bought (the) one of Jamil.'
(c)	Ah Chew buy in Jurong one.	'Ah, Chew bought (the) one in Jurong.'
(d)	Ah Chew buy yesterday Lisa choose one.	'Ah, Chew bought (the) one that Lisa chose yesterday.'

This use of *one* appears to be a replication of corresponding particles in what Gil calls the Singaporean substratum languages of Singlish, namely Cantonese *ge*^{33}, Hokkien *e*^{24}, Mandarin *de*, Singaporean Malay *yang*, and Bazaar Malay *mia*: in the same way as Singlish *one*, these particles are transnumeral, and they are reifiers rather than proforms, even if there are also a small number of differences in the use of the various particles.

But the reifier *one* appears to have undergone a further grammaticalization process, developing into what in the relevant literature is referred to as a

[15] For comparative convenience, we have replaced some of the technical terms used by Gil (2003) with more commonly used labels. For example, Gil refers to 'nouns' as thing words and to 'adjectives' as property words.

[16] Debra Ziegeler (p.c.) proposes to discuss this issue in terms of specificity rather than of (in)definiteness.

[17] The particle *ah* has been described variously as a filler or an optional interrogative tagmeme expressing tentative attitude and also serving to punctuate speech (Gil 2003: 482).

pragmatic particle. The exact function of the particle is largely unclear; in the following sentence it conveys the meaning 'I am the one who asked you' (Gil 2003: 481).

(7.27) SINGLISH (Gil 2003: 481)
I ask you one.

Once again, this appears to be an instance of grammatical replication since it has clear parallels in a number of the substratum languages of Singlish: reifiers such as Cantonese *ge*[33], Hokkien *e*[24], and Bazaar Malay *mia* exhibit a usage similar to Singlish *one.*

In addition to this transnumeral reifier which is unmarked for (in)definiteness, Singlish speakers have created a second reifier, *that one*, which differs from *one* essentially in the fact that it is definite. Accordingly, whereas *one* in (7.26d) can have either indefinite or definite reference, *that one* in (7.28) can only be definite.

(7.28) SINGLISH (Gil 2003: 480)
Ah Chew buy yesterday Lisa choose that one.
'Ah, Chew bought the one that Lisa chose yesterday.'

The collocation *that one* has developed into a conventionalized construction marker, where nothing can intervene between the two elements, and *that* may not be replaced with *this.* While we interpret the *one*-construction as an extension of a Standard English pattern, the *that one*-construction has no analogue in Standard English; it is a new grammaticalization from pronominalized demonstrative to what we interpret as a marker turning nominal modifiers into arguments, that is, into definite object complements. That this is another instance of grammatical replication is suggested by the following observation:

> Resembling nothing in Standard English, Singlish *that one* would appear to be a calque on the Hokkien construction *hit*[4]*e*[24], consisting of the distal demonstrative *hit*[4] plus reifier *e*[24]. Like *that one*, the Hokkien construction *hit*[4]*e*[24] is unmarked for number, marked as definite, and forms a closely-knit constituent—as evidenced by the fact that it may form a single tone group with respect to the rules of tone sandhi (Gil 2003: 483).

But the development of *one* (indefinite) and *that one* (definite) into markers of argument status has a profound effect on relative clause formation—that is, structures involving clausal postnominal modifiers—in Singlish. The following examples are confined to a clausal modifier that we have already seen in (7.28), where (7.29a) illustrates the indefinite use (*one*) and (7.29b) the definite one (*that one*).

(7.29) Singlish (Gil 2003: 484)

(a) Ah Chew buy house yesterday Lisa choose one.
'Ah, Chew bought a house that Lisa chose yesterday.'

(b) Ah Chew buy house yesterday Lisa choose that one.
'Ah, Chew bought the house that Lisa chose yesterday.'

Once again, there is no corresponding pattern in Standard English, while there are counterparts for these clausal reified modifiers in all Singaporean substratum languages, which are therefore likely to have provided the model for Singlish, such as Cantonese *ge*^{33}, Hokkien *e*^{24}, Mandarin *de*, Singaporean Malay *yang*, and Bazaar Malay *mia*—even if the reified modifiers are prenominal in all these languages except for Singaporean Malay, where the modifier has the same position as in Singlish (Gil 2003: 484–5). Alsagoff and Lick (1998: 129)[18] give the following examples of relative clause formation in the substratal languages as compared to Singlish and Standard English:

(7.30) Singlish (Alsagoff and Lick 1998: 129)
That boy pinch my mother one very naughty.
'That boy who pinched my mother is very naughty.'

(7.31) Malay (Alsagoff and Lick 1998: 129)

Budak	itu	yang	mencubit	ibu	saya	sangat	jahat.
child	the	*yang*	pinch	mother	my	very	naughty

'That boy who pinched my mother is very naughty.'

(7.32) Mandarin (Alsagoff and Lick 1998: 129)

Nie	wode	mama	de	neige	nanhaizi	hen	huaidan.
pinch	my	mother	*de*	that	child	very	naughty

'That boy who pinched my mother is very naughty.'

(7.33) Hokkien (Alsagoff and Lick 1998: 129)

Ngiap	wa-e	laubu	e	hi-le	tabo	gina	jin	pai.
pinch	my	mother	*e*	that	boy	child	very	naughty

'That boy who pinched my mother is very naughty.'

(7.34) Cantonese (Alsagoff and Lick 1998: 129)

Mit	ngo	mama	ge	go-go	namzai	ho	kuai.
pinch	my	mother	*ge*	that	boy	very	naughty

'That boy who pinched my mother is very naughty.'

Moreover, Alsagoff and Lick (1998) show that Singlish relative clauses are extremely elaborate grammatical structures, which contradicts the commonly

[18] Note that, unlike (Gil 2003), Alsagoff and Lick (1998) treat *one* in Singlish as a form having both a nominalizing—that is, 'reifying'—and a pronominalizing (anaphoric) function.

taken standpoint that new varieties of English are simplified versions of their superstrate language. Thus, there are three ways to render the Standard English relative sentence *The man who sells ice-kachang has gone home already* in Singlish. One of them coincides with the major relativization strategy as it occurs in Standard English, using a WH-word as a relative pronoun:

(7.35) SINGLISH (Alsagoff and Lick 1998: 131)
The man [who sell ice-kachang] gone home already.

The second one demonstrates the substratal influence on Singlish: it involves the use of the obligatory form *one*:

(7.36) SINGLISH (Alsagoff and Lick 1998: 131)
The man [sell ice-kachang one] gone home already.

That it is substratal influence that underlies the use of *one* in relative clauses in Singlish is also suggested by the similarity in syntactic positioning: both in Singlish and in Mandarin, for instance, the relative construction marker (*one* in Singlish, and the particle *de* in Mandarin) follows the relative clause, whereas in Standard English it is the other way round:

(7.37) SINGLISH (Alsagoff and Lick 1998: 134)
The fruit [they grow] ONE very sweet.

(7.38) MANDARIN (Alsagoff and Lick 1998: 134)
[Tamen zhong] DE shuiguo hen tian.
they grow *de* fruit very sweet
'The fruit that they grow is very sweet'.

(7.39) STANDARD ENGLISH
The fruit THAT [they grow] is very sweet.

The third relativization strategy in Singlish involves a double marking of the relative clause construction: the WH-relative pronoun—taken from Standard English—and the form *one*, which, as shown above, is the result of substratal influence:

(7.40) SINGLISH (Alsagoff and Lick 1998: 131)
The man WHO [sell ice-kachang] ONE gone home already.

The existence of such doubly marked sentences in Singlish shows that there can be combined structures from both L1 and L2; this results in a highly marked, and complex structure.

To conclude, what in the wording of Gil (2003: 470) used to be 'a characteristic European language' has turned into 'an equally typical exemplar of an

East Asian language'—in other words, Singlish has, as a result of contact, acquired a new typological profile, to the extent that Debra Ziegeler (p.c.) claims for it the status of a Sino-Tibetan language. While the data that we were able to access suggest that grammatical replication has contributed to an increase in structural equivalence between this English-based variety on the one hand and the Sino-Tibetan, Austronesian and other languages spoken in Singapore on the other, it also produced non-equivalence. For example, as the description by Gil (2003) and Alsagoff and Lick (1998) aptly show, the coexistence of inherited, largely optional, English morphology and of newly created functional categories on the model of East Asian languages has given rise to a mixed situation of highly complex marking, and to a type of language that contains some cross-linguistically unusual structures, and it is also responsible for the fact that Singlish stands out typologically both against Standard English and against its Asian model languages.

That the Singlish case is not unique in situations of L1>L2 replication where SAE languages are exposed to languages outside Europe has been pointed out in quite a number of studies. Templates of grammatical categorization characterizing European languages turn out to be vulnerable when being exposed to alternative models of categorization. As we saw in this section, typological properties such as the rigid singular–plural distinction characterizing SAE languages are readily abandoned whenever there is a contrastive way of number marking in the local L1. Another example is provided by Central Pomo, a Pomoan language of California spoken 100 miles north of San Francisco. Number marking on non-human nouns is not normally specified in this Indian language and, accordingly, speakers of this language tend to transfer their conceptualization of number into their L2 English by omitting English plural inflections (Mithun 1992: 106).

7.3.3 *Nigerian Pidgin English*

The fate that SAE languages may suffer when exposed to language contact can be demonstrated with another example illustrating the significance of grammatical replication. Our example concerns the fate of English[19] along the coast of West Africa.

Whilst the first British trading contacts with the West African coast date back to 1553, more intense contacts arose in the seventeenth century, and since roughly 1680 there has been a contact language on the Gold Coast based on an English lexicon and, in the nineteenth century, a number of pidginized

[19] There is some debate on which variety or varieties of English may have been involved; for the present purposes, this issue is largely—although not entirely—irrelevant.

varieties of English emerged along the coast of West Africa (Huber 1999). Our main interest here is with the varieties spoken in the coastal belt between Ghana and Nigeria and exposed to intense contacts with a wide range of languages mostly belonging to the Kwa and Benue-Congo branches of the Niger-Congo family, such languages including Yoruba, Fon, Ewe, and Akan.

In the course of more than two centuries of contact, English experienced fairly drastic changes, giving rise to what is more generally dubbed West African Pidgin English, but what actually consists of a range of different, although largely mutually intelligible, varieties derived from English.[20] There are a number of processes that contributed to this change, most of all what is commonly described as pidginization; in accordance with the general theme of this work, our interest here is with only one of these processes, namely contact-induced grammaticalization. Accordingly, we will ignore all other kinds of processes, in particular processes relating to pidginization and creolization[21]—even if it is far from easy to clearly distinguish between all these processes. We are confined to a few examples demonstrating that speakers in West Africa used the same kind of strategies in creating new grammatical categories in English as their L2, using their first languages (L1) as a model[22]—in much the same way as speakers in Singapore or other parts of the world did.

The examples discussed below are taken from the variety spoken in southern Nigeria, usually called Nigerian Pidgin English (or, in short, Nigerian Pidgin), which is clearly the most important West African pidgin variety, spoken by an estimated 40 million people as an L2 and by roughly one million as an L1, and for which there exists a detailed grammar (Faraclas 1996), and examples from African languages are taken from Ewe, with which the present authors are most familiar. Nevertheless, these examples concern processes that can also be observed in pidgin English varieties of other parts of West Africa, especially in the coastal belt between Ghana and Cameroon (see Huber 1996, 1999). Evidence to the effect that we are dealing with contact-induced

[20] The term '(genetically) derived' is not uncontroversial; in the literature of creole linguistics, terms such as 'English-lexicon' or 'English-lexified' languages tend to be used instead. What we refer to with that label is that the majority of items of the basic vocabulary and of the markers used to express grammatical functions in West African Pidgin varieties are etymologically derived from English, and also that the majority of word order arrangements used in day-to-day interaction and in narrative discourse can be related to corresponding forms and structures of English, rather than of any other languages.

[21] In the literature on pidgin/creoles, the varieties looked at here tend to be referred to as 'English-lexifier pidgins and creoles.'

[22] In the relevant literature, this phenomenon tends to be described as 'substratum influence' (see e.g. Lefebvre 1998).

replication is based mainly on the fact that the linguistic properties discussed are absent in Standard English and most other varieties of English, but are widely found in the languages of the communities in which Nigerian Pidgin and related varieties of English are spoken.

Most of the African languages that have influenced these varieties are verb-serializing, and in the course of its contact with these African languages, this variety of English has replicated this mode of syntactic organization. Accordingly, Faraclas offers the following description of Nigerian Pidgin, which would apply in much the same way to many of the African languages spoken as L1 in the region where Nigerian Pidgin English arose and spread:

> Verb phrases may be strung together in serialized verb constructions. Verbs in serialized verb constructions usually share the same sentential subject, which precedes the first verb in the series and is not repeated thereafter. Each verb in a serialized construction may normally take its own object(s), adverbials and ideophones (Faraclas 1996: 75).

But in addition to adopting a new syntactic mode, the speakers of Nigerian English also replicated the grammaticalization processes characterizing their L1 model languages, as we will now demonstrate.

Our first example concerns the marking of clausal participants. Where other languages would use case inflections or adpositions to present peripheral participants of the clause, verbs in serial constructions tend to be used in West African languages for encoding case relations. This strategy was replicated by speakers of Nigerian English, in that a number of verbs were grammaticalized to some extent to case markers on the model of local languages such as Yoruba, Fon, Ewe, or Akan. Accordingly, speakers of Nigerian Pidgin may use the verb *tek* 'take' (< *take*) for instrumental (7.41a) and a number of other participants, such as time in (7.41b), *giv* 'give' (< *give*) for benefactive participants (7.41c), or the motion verbs *go* 'go' (< *go*) and *kom* 'come' (< *come*) for directed motion, (7.41d).

(7.41) NIGERIAN PIDGIN (Faraclas 1996: 76–9, 171)

(a) A tek nayf ko̱t dì nyam.
(I take.FACT knife cut the yam)
'I cut the yam with a knife.'

(b) A tek nayt ko̱t dì nyam.
(I take.FACT night cut the yam)
'I cut the yam at night.' (Lit. 'I took the night cut the yam.')

(c) A bay nyam giv yù.
(I buy.FACT yam give you)
'I bought you the yam.'

(d) A gò tek dì chudren go maket.
(I FUT take the children go market)
'I will take the children to the market.'

The corresponding constructions in West African languages are illustrated in (7.42), where the erstwhile verbs *tsɔ́* 'take', *ná* 'give', and *yi* 'go' have largely equivalent functions as case markers.

(7.42) Ewe (Kwa, Niger-Congo; Westermann 1930: 131, 134; own data)
(a) wó- tsɔ- a agblenú ŋlɔ- a agble.
(they- take- HAB hoe hoe- HAB field
'One hoes a farm with a hoe.' (Lit. 'They take a hoe, hoe field.')
(b) é- tsɔ dɔme ɣeɣí yi aƒé.
(s/he take belly empty go home)
'He went home without eating.' (Lit. 'S/he took empty belly went home.')
(c) Me ƒle te ná wo.
(I buy yam give you)
'I bought you yam.'
(d) Wó- tsɔ- n- ɛ̀ yi Kéta.
(they- take- HAB- him go Keta)
'One carries him to Keta.'

To express comparisons of inequality, Standard English uses either the adjectival inflection *-er* (e.g., *Jennifer runs faster than Eloise*) or the particle *more* (*Jennifer is more beautiful than Eloise*) plus the standard marker *than*. In Africa, the primary means for this grammatical notion is provided by the Action Schema (Heine 1997*b*; Heine & Kuteva 2002: 123–6), whereby comparisons are expressed using a lexical verb meaning 'exceed, surpass' or 'pass' as the standard of comparison, that is, where *Jennifer runs faster than Eloise* would be rendered as 'Jennifer runs fast exceeds/surpasses/passes Eloise'. This conceptual template is typically African, in that most African languages use it, whilst outside Africa it is rarely found as the major schema for encoding the comparative of inequality. In Nigerian Pidgin English, this African schema has become the primary means of expressing the comparative of inequality, as example (7.43) illustrates.

(7.43) Nigerian Pidgin (Faraclas 1996: 110)
A big pas yu.
(I be:big pass you)
'I am bigger than you.'

That this is not an isolated case is suggested by the fact that other comparative concepts as well are expressed in this variety of English in the same way as they are in (West) African languages. The notion of a superlative, for example *John is the biggest* is cross-linguistically expressed by a number of different conceptual notions; in Africa, the prevailing notion is by using an expression of the form 'John is big, surpasses all' (Heine 1997*b*: 124ff). This is exactly what is found in Nigerian English, (7.44).

(7.44) Nigerian Pidgin (Faraclas 1996: 110)
Audu big pas o̱l.
(Audu be:big pass all)
'Audu is (the) biggest of all.'

Exactly the same constructions are found in West African languages, as (7.45) shows, where (7.45a) corresponds to (7.43) and (7.45b) to (7.44).

(7.45) Ewe (Kwa, Niger-Congo; own data)
(a) Me lolo wú wo.
(I be:big surpass you)
'I am bigger than you.'
(b) Kofí lolo wú wó kátã.
(Kofi be:big surpass them all)
'Kofi is the biggest of all.'

Comparisons of equality (e.g. *John is as big as you*) have a variety of means of expression in the languages of the world (see e.g. Haspelmath & Buchholz 1998); in West African languages one way of expressing this functional notion is by grammaticalizing a verb meaning 'reach' to an equative marker, whereby something like 'John reaches you in bigness' is used to express 'John is as big as you'; for example, in the Kwa language Ewe, the phrase *de nu* 'reach the end' has been grammaticalized to an equative marker, (7.46). Nigerian Pidgin appears to have replicated this grammaticalization, using *rich* 'arrive' (< *reach*) to form an equative construction (7.47).

(7.46) Ewe (Kwa, Niger-Congo; Westermann 1930: 141)
alégèlia ɖé- wo lolo de- a núkpui nu.
(rat some- PL be.big reach- HAB bristly.rat end)
'A few rats are as large as the bristly rat.'

(7.47) Nigerian Pidgin (Faraclas 1996: 78, 112)
A gò big rich yu.
(I FUT be.big reach you)
'I will be as big as you.'

To conclude, mechanisms used in Standard English to express comparative concepts have been replaced in the English-based Nigerian Pidgin with a West African strategy whereby verbal concepts ('defeat', 'pass', 'reach', etc.) are grammaticalized to comparative markers.

But the serial verb construction has also affected the system of marking verbal aspect: the verb *want* appears to be a proximative marker ('be about to', expressing imminence, as Faraclas says), cf. (7.48), presumably on the model of West African Kwa languages that show a similar grammaticalization, as the Ewe example in (7.49) illustrates.

(7.48) NIGERIAN PIDGIN (Faraclas 1996: 78, 205)
A want wo̱sh plet.
(I want.FACT wash dish)
'I am about to wash (the) dishes.'

(7.49) EWE (Kwa, Niger-Congo; Heine & Kuteva 2002: 312)
tsi dí bé ye- a dza.
water want that LOG- IRR fall
'It is about to rain.' (Lit.: 'Water wants to fall.')

Furthermore, the verb *finish* has developed into a completive marker (7.50), again presumably on the model of West African languages, (7.51). Note that in both cases, the grammaticalized verb is placed in the same position: 'want' precedes the main verb while 'finish' follows it.

(7.50) NIGERIAN PIDGIN (Faraclas 1996: 78)
Wì cho̱p dì nyam bèlèfûl finish kpakpa.
(we eat.FACT the yam be.full finish IDEO)
'We ate up all the yams until we were full.'

(7.51) EWE (Kwa, Niger-Congo; Westermann 1930: 133)
me- ɖu- i vɔ.
(I- eat- it finish)
'I have eaten it up.'

That these structures are replications of corresponding structures in African languages spoken along the West African coast is suggested by the fact that they simultaneously concerned two different kinds of processes, namely restructuring on the one hand and grammaticalization on the other. Restructuring (see Section 2.4) is negatively defined as contact-induced grammatical change not involving grammaticalization, whereby an existing structure is rearranged or replaced with some other structure; with reference to the variety of English looked at here, it had the effect that an existing SAE mode of syntactic organization was replaced with a new mode, namely that of verb serialization. But in addition it also involved a series of grammaticalizations, whereby lexical structures were recruited to create a range of new functional categories.

We observed in Section 7.3.2 that Gil (2003: 470) portrays the development of Singlish as one leading from 'a characteristic European language' to 'an equally typical exemplar of an East Asian language'; in a similar fashion we may conclude that in the present case the result is 'an equally typical exemplar of a West African language'. As a result of contact, Nigerian Pidgin English has acquired a typological profile that contrasts with that of Standard English and mirrors the verb-serializing profile of West African languages in structure, although not in form. As in the case of Singlish, the lexical material that was grammaticalized to functional categories is essentially all derived from English. And once again, this new profile is, on the one hand, due to universal processes of grammaticalization and, on the other hand, to the specific linguistic situation obtaining along the West African coast, where languages are spoken that are characterized by a fairly analytic-isolating morphosyntax and by verb serialization as important means for structuring linguistic discourse. Accordingly, choice among the universally available options of grammaticalization was constrained in Nigerian Pidgin English by the models that the speakers of this variety of English found in their L1, leading to the rise of serial verb constructions and to new modes of marking syntactic relations and other grammatical functions. In a number of cases, the new structures replaced the old SAE structures; in other cases, the two co-exist side by side—with the effect that the grammar of Nigerian English, like that of Singlish, is more complex than is widely assumed.

7.4 Conclusions

The present chapter was designed to demonstrate that SAE languages are both 'donors' and 'receivers', and Section 7.2 focused on the former and Section 7.3 on the latter role. A central question that we were concerned with in Section 7.3 was what kind of grammatical concepts it is that SAE languages are likely to adopt when in contact with other languages. It goes without saying that the answer that we can offer is severely limited by the kind of data that we were able to access. With regard to the structure of nouns, a perhaps surprising outcome in Singapore can be seen in the readiness with which the SAE template of obligatory marking of number and definiteness was abandoned in favour of an East Asian mould of a more economic, pragmatically determined way of optional encoding of grammatical information. Our West

African example led to a perhaps equally surprising observation, namely that an SAE language acquired a new architecture for organizing syntactic relations within the clause.

As we saw in this chapter, Europe's linguistic periphery goes far beyond the geographical limits of the continent: as a result of the expansion of European languages such as English, Spanish, Portuguese, French, etc., it includes essentially the whole world. We were therefore not confined to language contact within Europe; rather, we were also dealing with the question of how European languages react when being confronted with non-European languages in order to test our hypothesis that grammatical replication is a cross-linguistically uniform process.

It is hoped that the cases discussed in this chapter have made it clear, first, that contact-induced grammaticalization played an important role in the rise of new typological profiles, second, that this mechanism was shaped significantly by areal factors, that is, by contact between different languages and, third, that European languages when in intense contact with languages in other parts of the world, and where they are spoken primarily as L2's, may lose much of what makes up an SAE profile and acquire new profiles reflecting, although not being identical to, those of the languages with which they interact.

As elsewhere in this book, we were confronted on one side with grammaticalization as a universal phenomenon, but on the other side as a phenomenon that is constrained by the particular linguistic situation characterizing language contact.

8

Conclusions

The central theme of this book was to find out whether Europe qualifies as a linguistic unit. We noted in the introductory chapter that it is possible on the basis of the quantitative evidence provided by Haspelmath (2001) to argue that there is in fact a geographically defined linguistic area—one that includes languages such as Spanish and English but excludes Basque and Irish, or that includes Hungarian but not the fellow Finno-Ugric language Finnish (Section 1.2). At the same time, we also drew attention to the problems surrounding previous work on areal taxonomy in Europe carried out in frameworks of discrete categorization. Our subject matter was more complex: rather than searching for a discrete areal typology in terms of a set of distinct properties, we were concerned with the processes leading to the gradual 'Europeanization' of the languages spoken in Europe. We saw that there is a continuous development whereby linguistically and/or geographically more peripheral languages gradually acquire new use patterns and categories on the model of languages such as French, German, English, or Italian—a process that involves both internal development and contact effects in concert. This development, which concerns different domains of grammar such as the coding of reference (Chapter 3), tense–aspect (Chapter 4), case (Chapter 5), and clause combining (Chapter 6), led to or is leading towards a new typological orientation of the languages concerned.

Research on grammatical change in the languages of Europe and the role played by language contact within it has given rise to a wide range of hypotheses and controversies, centring in particular around dichotomies such as the following: Was a given change internally or externally motivated? Did it involve universal forces or is it the result of particular historical events? Can it be described by means of traditional methods of historical linguistics or does it require alternative methods that take care of the special conditions characterizing human behaviour in situations of language contact?

The findings presented in this book suggest that there are no straightforward answers to these questions. The processes that we discussed have both internal and external motivations, they have been the result of an interplay of universal and idiosyncratic developments, and neither the conventional tools of historical linguistics, such as the comparative method, nor the theoretical concepts developed in recent research on second language acquisition provide a satisfactory basis for understanding why European languages underwent the kind of processes they did. Internal motivation can be seen in the fact that the grammaticalization processes that we described are language-internal, they do not involve, for example the borrowing of linguistic material. External motivation means that there was some other language, sometimes more than one language, that provided the model for sparking off or accelerating these grammaticalization processes. Since grammaticalization is a universally defined process, this means that there is a universal component. At the same time, there is also an idiosyncratic component in that, in many cases, speakers may choose among the various use patterns that are available in the replica language which of them is most suitable to be recruited for grammaticalization. Note however that in some cases, choice is severely limited; for instance, in the grammaticalization of indefinite articles there usually is only one option, namely drawing on a numeral for 'one' in attributive function.

Since grammaticalization is essentially a unidirectional process, these findings suggest that the processes leading to the gradual 'Europeanization' of peripheral languages are to some extent predictable within limits. For example, given that there is a language exposed to intense contact over an extended period of time with an SAE model language, then that language is likely to acquire a new typological orientation. Assuming that that language lacks salient properties characterizing SAE languages, then we will predict on the basis of the observations that were made in the course of this book that the language is likely to undergo processes in the following directions:

(i) it will grammaticalize a demonstrative attribute and the numeral 'one' into definite and indefinite articles, respectively (see Chapter 3);
(ii) it will develop a perfect aspect–tense category based on an expression for predicative possession (Chapter 4);
(iii) it will develop a comitative–instrumental polysemy by extending the use of the comitative marker to express instruments (Chapter 5);
(iv) it will extend the use of question words to mark clause subordination (Chapter 6).

The result of these processes will not necessarily be spectacular: there will be new minor use patterns, or major use patterns built on existing minor patterns (Section 2.2), but the overall architecture of grammatical categorization tends to remain unaffected. However, there is reason to speak of a new typological profile: grammatical functions are no longer expressed the way they were prior to language contact, and existing modes of expressing grammatical concepts may gradually give way to new modes arising as a result of language contact. And in some cases there will be more dramatic effects, in that new functional categories will emerge, such as the possessive perfects in Macedonian and North Russian.

A question that permeates all the discussions of the preceding chapters is how language contact affects the structure of the languages concerned. We have witnessed some dramatic structural effects in Chapter 7, but they concerned, for the most part, situations where European languages interacted as lingua francas with languages in other parts of the world, such as southeast Asia or West Africa. Within Europe, structural transformations were, on the whole, modest. For example, Basque speakers created a number of new use patterns and categories on the model of Romance languages; however, on the surface, their language has largely retained the grammatical architecture it had prior to these contacts.

Nevertheless, it is hoped that our discussions have shown that contact between SAE and peripheral languages had some impact on the structure of the latter. For example, Slavic languages are commonly understood to characterize a language type without articles, lacking a grammaticalized distinction between definite and indefinite reference. As we saw in Chapter 3, this situation has changed in some Slavic languages spoken along the western periphery of the Slavic-speaking world: languages such as Upper Sorbian and Lower Sorbian have acquired a typological property that sets them off from their fellow Slavic languages in the east and unites them with Germanic and Romance languages. As grammaticalization theory would predict, the article categories that were created in these Slavic languages have not attained the degree of grammatical elaboration characterizing their German models. However, examples like this one show that language contact can be responsible for structural innovations in domains of grammar that are considered by some to be impervious to change.

Contact-induced language change tends to be described in terms of 'convergence' or structural equivalence. As our discussion in the previous chapters may have shown, such a view is not without problems if applied to the languages of Europe: replication does not necessarily lead to structural equivalence, for the following reasons. First, grammatical replication does not entail that speakers employ exactly the same conceptual schema they find in the model language. Our example of possessive perfects in Chapter 4 may illustrate what is meant with this claim: speakers of North Russian or Breton appear to have replicated the SAE strategy of using a possessive concept (e.g. *He has blue eyes*) to develop a verbal aspect category, a perfect (*He has eaten*); in doing so, however, they used the particular grammatical construction available to them—with the effect that the morphosyntactic structure of the perfect in North Russian is different from that commonly found in SAE languages, in that the agent in the perfect construction has the properties of a locative participant while the patient (undergoer) has the properties of a sentence subject. Thus, conceptual replication of functional categories may have unusual and unpredictable results, giving rise to new morphosyntactic structures in the replica language that have no analogue in the model language.

A second reason can be seen in the specific nature of grammaticalization. Replicated categories are generally (although not necessarily) less grammaticalized than the corresponding model categories. What this means is that frequently there is a fully-fledged functional category used obligatorily in the model language, whereas the replica language has a weakly grammaticalized equivalent—one that is not used obligatorily and may even be rejected by prescriptive grammarians. We saw a number of examples in Chapter 3, where we discussed the evolution of articles. In languages such as Sorbian, Czech, and Slovenian, the use of articles is largely optional and articles are not generally recognized as distinct grammatical categories. In this respect, they contrast with articles in the presumed model language German, where articles are used obligatorily and constitute generally recognized paradigms in grammatical descriptions of any kind. Much the same observation was made in other chapters, for example in Chapter 4, where we saw that possessive perfects in quite a number of replica languages are far from being what one might wish to call structural equivalents of the corresponding perfects in the model languages. What this means is that quite commonly we are confronted with situations where the grammatical structure of the replica language is of a different nature than that of the model language.

Third, what is seemingly a development towards 'convergence' may actually have the opposite effect, leading to 'non-convergence'. We had a number of examples of this kind in the preceding chapters. One example concerned Basque (Section 7.2.1), where the replication of the second person distinction between an informal/familiar form based on the singular pronoun and a formal/polite form based on the plural pronoun on the model of Romance languages led to a complex situation of marking social relations that is hard to reconcile with the distinction characterizing the Romance model languages: instead of creating a structural one-to-one correspondence with the model languages, a situation was created in Basque where the paradigms of grammatical categories are hardly more mutually compatible than they used to be prior to language contact.

An example of a different nature was discussed in Section 7.3.2 concerning Singaporean Colloquial English (Singlish): we noted that this variety of an SAE language has turned into a 'typical exemplar of an East Asian language' (Gil 2003: 470) as a result of contact with Sino-Tibetan, Austronesian, and other languages spoken in Singapore. Grammatical replication in this case had the effect that the coexistence of inherited, largely optional English morphology and of newly created functional categories on the model of East Asian languages has given rise to a mixed situation of highly complex marking, and to a type of language that contains some cross-linguistically unusual structures. Thus, rather than leading to structural isomorphism or 'convergence', the result is that Singlish now stands out typologically both against Standard English and against its Asian model languages.

Fourth, the evidence that we were able to access suggests that aiming to achieve 'convergence' is not necessarily the primary motivation characterizing the behaviour of bilinguals in contact situations. We have seen cases in the preceding chapters where speakers of minority languages who are strongly exposed to contact with a dominant language exhibit a particularly defensive behaviour *vis-à-vis* that dominant language. In Chapter 6 we saw, for example, that modern Basque speakers try to rid their language of the 'Romance subordination type', even though that type has been part of the language for at least two centuries (Haase 1992: 151–3). And it is perhaps no coincidence that it is exactly those two Slavic languages that were most strongly exposed to language contact with German, namely Sorbian and Slovenian, that turn out to be particularly conservative in some respects, being the only Slavic languages to have preserved the Proto-Slavic dual category—and this in spite of the fact that there is no comparable structure in German (Breu 1994: 43, 63).

The phenomena discussed here tend to be described in the literature on language contact as being due to calquing and, in fact, calquing has been shown to be a powerful strategy in lexical replication, for example when the English term *skyscraper* was translated as *Wolkenkratzer* in German, *gratte-ciel* in French, *rascacielos* in Spanish, or *nebo skrjób* in Russian. But the situation is different in the case of grammatical replication, as we hope to have demonstrated in the preceding chapters: speakers of Slavic languages in contact with Germanic or Romance languages did not adopt the article system or the possessive perfect of their model languages as fully-fledged functional categories; rather, they created these categories anew, going through various stages of grammaticalization, and in many cases, the replicated category has not (or not yet) developed beyond the initial stages of grammaticalization. What this suggests is that, while the motivation underlying lexical and grammatical replication may be the same, the actual mechanism employed to achieve the latter is more complex than that used for the former.

Another major problem that we were constantly confronted with concerns the question of whether, or to what extent, the patterns of structural equivalence described in this book may not be the result of genetic inheritance or genetically induced parallel development (or drift; Sapir 1921; LaPolla 1994) rather than of areal relationship. After all, Europe is predominantly an Indo-European territory; almost nineteen out of twenty Europeans speak Indo-European languages as their mother tongue and, as has been maintained by some, the history of European languages is to a large extent one of the Indo-Europeanization of Europe. In a number of cases there is no conclusive answer to this question. For example, the development from interrogative to subordination marker can be traced back to Latin (Chapter 6); hence the interrogative–subordination polysemy to be found in the modern Romance languages is likely to be, at least to some extent, the result of genetic inheritance. And much the same applies to the rise of possessive perfects (Chapter 4).

But there are other cases where genetic relationship can essentially be ruled out. As we saw in Chapter 3, all modern Romance languages have fully grammaticalized articles—a fact which might suggest that they inherited this property from their common ancestor language. However, there are a number of observations that cast doubt on this hypothesis: for example, there is the fact that most Romance languages use preposed definite articles whereas Rumanian has a postposed article. Rumanian belongs to the Balkan sprachbund, and postposed articles are a salient property of this sprachbund. Accordingly, there appear to have been factors other than genetic relationship at work that can be held responsible for the fact that Rumanian diverges from other Romance languages in the placement of the definite article.[1]

The objective of this book was a complex one, since we were confronted with a number of variables that may influence grammatical change. Perhaps the main problem that we were confronted with concerned grammaticalization, which is a universal process. The development from demonstrative attribute to definite article, from numeral 'one' to indefinite article, or from comitative to instrumental case marker can be observed in a number of languages across the world. Can we therefore really claim that such developments in Europe were contact-induced? It is hoped that the evidence we have provided is sufficient to establish that language contact must have contributed in propelling or accelerating these processes in European languages. For example, that the Slavic languages Upper and Lower Sorbian have undergone such developments whilst the fellow Slavic language Russian has not, can be, and has been, accounted for plausibly with reference to the fact that the two Sorbian languages share a 1000 years' history of intense contact with German, while there is no such a history in the case of Russian.

[1] That it is possible on the basis of text analyses to distinguish to some extent between genetically, areally, and typologically induced similarities has been demonstrated by Stolz, Stroh and Urdze (2003) on the basis of data on the comitative–instrumental polysemy in European languages that we discussed in Chapter 5.

References

Abbi, Anvita (1992). *Reduplication in South Asian languages: An areal, typological, and historical study.* New Delhi: Allied Publishers.

Abraham, Werner (ed.) (2004). Focus on Germanic Typology. (Studia Typologica, Beihefte zu Sprachtypologie und Universalienforschung [STUF], 6) Berlin: Akademie-Verlag.

Abraham, Werner & C. Jac Conradie (2001). *Präteritumschwund und Diskursgrammatik.* Amsterdam, Philadelphia: Benjamins.

Adamović, Milan (1985). *Konjugationsgeschichte der türkischen Sprache.* Leiden: E.J. Brill.

Aikhenvald, Alexandra Y. (1996). 'Areal diffusion in northwest Amazonia: the case of Tariana'. *Anthropological Linguistics* 38: 73–116.

—— (2002). *Language contact in Amazonia.* New York: Oxford University Press.

—— (2003). 'Language contact and language change in Amazonia'. In Blake & Burridge 2003: 1–20.

Aikhenvald, Alexandra Y. & Robert M. W. Dixon (1998). 'Evidentials and areal typology: a case study from Amazonia'. *Language Sciences* 20(3): 241–57.

—— (eds) (1999). *The Amazonian languages.* Cambridge: Cambridge University Press.

—— (eds) (2001). *Areal diffusion and genetic inheritance: Problems in comparative linguistics.* Oxford: Oxford University Press.

—— (eds) (2003). *Studies in evidentiality.* (Typological Studies in Language, 54) Amsterdam, Philadelphia: Benjamins.

Askedal, John Ole (1982). 'Zur semantischen Analyse deutscher Auxiliarkonstruktionen unter dem Aspekt der Unterscheidung von summativer und nicht-summativer Bedeutung'. *Deutsch als Fremdsprache* 19: 159–67.

Alanne, Eero (1972). 'Zur Rolle der syntaktischen Interferenz der verwandten und unverwandten Sprachen'. *Neuphilologische Mitteilungen* 73: 568–74.

Alsagoff, Lubna and Ho Chee Lick (1998). 'The relative clause in colloquial Singapore English'. *World Englishes* 17(2): 127–38.

Andersen, Henning (ed.) (1995). *Historical linguistics 1993: Selected Papers from the 11th International Conference on Historical Linguistics, Los Angeles, 16–20 August 1993.* (Amsterdam Studies in the Theory and History of Linguistic Science, 124) Amsterdam, Philadelphia: Benjamins.

—— (ed.) (2001). *Actualization.* Papers from a workshop held at the 14th International Conference on Historical Linguistics, Vancouver, BC, 14th August 1999. Amsterdam/Philadelphia: John Benjamins.

Anderson, John M. (1997). 'Remarks on the structure and development of the *have* perfect'. *Folia Linguistica Historica* 18(1–2): 3–23.

Appel, R. & Pieter Muysken (1987). *Language contact and bilingualism.* London: Edward Arnold.

Arends, Jacques (1986). 'Genesis and development of the equative copula in Sranan'. In Muysken & Smith 1986: 103–27.

Asenova, Petja (1999). 'Bulgarian'. In Hinrichs & Büttner 1999: 211–37.

Bahner Werner (1986). 'Balkanlinguistik in wissenschaftshistorischer Sicht'. *Zeitschrift für Phonetik, Sprachwissenschaft und Kommunikationsforschung* 39(6): 629–40.

Bailey, C.-J. N. and K. Maroldt (1977). 'The French lineage of English'. In Meisel 1977: 21–53.

Baker, Philip (ed.) (1995). *From contact to creole and beyond.* London: University of Westminster Press.

Baker, Philip & Anand Syea (eds) (1996). *Changing meanings, changing functions: Papers relating to grammaticalization in contact languages.* (Westminster Creolistics Series, 2) London: University of Westminster Press.

Bakker, Peter & Maarten Mous (eds) (1994). *Mixed languages: 15 case studies in language intertwining.* Amsterdam: Institute for Functional Research into Language and Language Use (IFOTT).

Banfi, Emanuele (1990). 'The infinitive in south-east European languages'. In Bechert *et al.* 1990: 165–83.

Bascom, William R. & Melville J. Herskovits (eds) (1959). *Continuity and change in African cultures.* Chicago: University of Chicago Press.

Bashir, Elena, Madhav Deshpande, & Peter Edwin Hook (eds) (1985). *Select papers from SALA-7: South Asian Languages Analysis, Round Table Conference, Ann Arbor, Michigan, May 1985*, Bloomington, Indiana: Indiana University Linguistics Club.

Bechert, Johannes (1990). 'The structure of the noun in European languages'. In Bechert *et al.* 1990: 115–40.

Bechert, Johannes, Giuliano Bernini, & Claude Buridant (eds) (1990). *Toward a typology of European languages.* (Empirical Approaches to Language Typology, 8) Berlin: Mouton de Gruyter.

Beck, David (2000). 'Grammatical convergence and the genesis of diversity in the Northwest Coast *Sprachbund*'. *Anthropological Linguistics* 42(2) 147–213.

Becker, Henrick (1948). *Der Sprachbund.* Leipzig: Humboldt Bücherei Gerhard Mindt.

Bender, Marvin L., J. D. Bowen, R. L. Cooper, & Charles A. Ferguson (eds) (1976). *Language in Ethiopia.* London: Oxford University Press.

Benveniste, Emile (1952). 'The passive construction of the transitive perfect'. *Bulletin de la Société Linguistique* 48: 52–62.

Berger, T. (n.d.). *Das System der tschechischen Demonstrativpronomina: Textgrammatische und stilspezifische Gebrauchsbedingungen.* Unpublished Habilitationsschrift, Munich.

Bergs, Alexander & Dieter Stein (2001). 'The role of markedness in the actuation and actualization of linguistic change'. In Andersen 2001: 79–93.

Bernini, Guliano (ed.) (to appear). *Pragmatic organization of discourse in the languages of Europe.* Berlin: Mouton de Gruyter.

BERNINI, GIULIANO & PAOLO RAMAT (1992). *La frase negativa nelle lingue d'Europa.* Bologna: Il Mulino.

—— (1996). *Negative sentences in the languages of Europe: A typological approach.* (Empirical Approaches to Language Typology, 16) Berlin: Mouton de Gruyter.

BETZ, WERNER (1944). Die Lehnbildungen und der abendländische Sprachausgleich. *Beiträge zur Geschichte der deutschen Sprache und Literatur* 67: 275–302.

BICKERTON, DEREK (1981). *Roots of language.* Ann Arbor: Karoma.

BIRKEN-SILVERMAN, GABRIELE & GERDA RÖSSLER (eds) (1992). *Beiträge zur sprachlichen, literarischen und kulturellen Vielfalt in den Philologien: Festschrift Ruprecht Rohr.* Stuttgart: Steiner,

BISANG, WALTER (1996*a*). 'Areal typology and grammaticalization: Processes of grammaticalization based on nouns and verbs in East and Mainland South East Asian languages'. *Studies in Language* 20(3): 519–97.

—— (1996*b*). 'Sprachliche Areale in Asien am Beispiel der Satzverknüpfung'. In Boretzky 1996: 24–50.

—— (1998). 'Grammaticalization and language contact, constructions and positions'. In Giacalone Ramat & Hopper 1998: 13–58.

—— (ed.) (2001*a*). *Aspects of typology and universals.* (Studia typologica, 1) Berlin: Akademie-Verlag.

—— (2001*b*). 'Areality, grammaticalization and language typology: on the explanatory power of functional criteria and the status of Universal Grammar'. In Bisang 2001*a*: 175–223.

BISANG, WALTER, NIKOLAUS HIMMELMANN & BJÖRN WIEMER (eds) (2004): *What makes grammaticalization? A look from its fringes and its components.* (Trends in Linguistics, Studies and Monographs, 158) Berlin, New York: Mouton de Gruyter.

BLAKE, BARRY J. & KATE BURRIDGE (eds) (2003). *Historial linguistics 2001: Selected papers from the 15th International Conference on Historical Linguistics, Melbourne, 13–17 August 2001.* (Amsterdam Studies in the Theory and History of Linguistic Science, 237.) Amsterdam, Philadelphia: Benjamins.

BLATT, FRANZ (1957). 'Latin influence on European syntax'. *Travaux du Cercle Linguistique de Copenhague* 11: 33–69.

BLENCH, R. and M. SPRIGGS (eds) (1997). *Archaeology and language.* Volume 1: *Theoretical and methodological orientations.* London: Routlege.

BLISS, A. J. (1972). 'Languages in contact: Some problems of Hiberno-English'. *Proceedings of the Royal Irish Academy* 72, Section C: 63–82.

BOEDER, WINFRIED, CHRISTOPH SCHROEDER, KARL HEINZ WAGNER, & WOLFGANG WILDGEN (eds) (1998). *Sprache in Raum und Zeit: In memoriam Johannes Bechert.* Volume 2: *Beiträge zur empirischen Sprachwissenschaft.* Tübingen: Gunter Narr.

BOESCHOTEN, HENDRIK E. & LARS JOHANSON (eds) (in print). *Turkic language contacts.* Amsterdam, Philadelphia: Benjamins.

BOLONYAI, AGNES (2000). ' "Elective affinities": Language contact in the Abstract Lexicon and its structural consequences'. *International Journal of Bilingualism* 4(1): 81–106.

BOLTON, K. & H. KWOK (eds) (1992). *Sociolinguistics today: international perspectives.* London: Routledge.

BORETZKY, NORBERT (1975). *Der türkische Einfluss auf das Albanische.* Part 1: *Phonologie und Morphologie der albanischen Turzismen.* (Albanische Forschungen, 11) Wiesbaden: Otto Harrassowitz.

BORETZKY, NORBERT (1983). *Kreolsprachen, Substrate und Sprachwandel.* Wiesbaden: Otto Harrassowitz.

—— (1986). Regelentlehnung und Substrateinfluss in Kreolsprachen. In Boretzky *et al.* 1986: 9–39.

—— (1989). 'Zum Interferenzverhalten des Romani'. *Zeitschrift für Phonetik, Sprachwissenschaft und Kommunikationsforschung* 42(3): 357–74.

—— (ed.) (1996). *Areale, Kontakte, Dialekte, Sprachen und ihre Dynamik in mehrsprachigen Situationen.* (Bochum-Essener Beiträge zur Sprachwandelforschung, 24) Bochum: Brockmeyer.

—— (2000). 'The definite article in Romani dialects'. In Elšik & Matras 2000: 31–63.

BORETZKY, NORBERT & BIRGIT IGLA (1994). 'Romani mixed dialects'. In Bakker & Mous 1994: 35–68.

—— (1999). 'Balkanische (südosteuropäische) Einflüsse im Romani'. In Hinrichs & Büttner 1999: 709–31.

BORETZKY, NORBERT, WERNER ENNINGER, & THOMAS STOLZ (eds) (1986). *Beiträge zum 2. Essener Kolloquium über 'Kreolsprachen und Sprachkontakte'.* (Essener Beiträge zur Sprachwandelforschung, 2) Bochum: N. Brockmeyer.

—— (eds) (1989). *Beiträge zum 5. Essener Kolloquium über 'Grammatikalisierung: Natürlichkeit und Systemökonomie'.* Volume 1. (Essener Beiträge zur Sprachwandelforschung, 7) Bochum: Brockmeyer.

BORG, ALBERT & MANWEL MIFSUD (2002). 'Maltese object marking in a Mediterranean context'. In Ramat & Stolz 2002: 33–46.

BRENDEMOEN, BERNDT, ELIZABETH LANZA, & ELSE RYEN (eds) (1999). *Language encounters across time and space: studies in language contact.* Oslo: Novus Forlag.

BREU, WALTER (ed.) (1990*a*). *Slavistische Linguistik 1989.* Munich: Otto Sagner.

—— (1990*b*). 'Sprache und Sprachverhalten in den slavischen Dörfern des Molise (Süditalien)'. In Breu 1990*a*: 35–65.

—— (1992). 'Das italokroatische Verbsystem zwischen slavischem Erbe und kontaktbedingter Entwicklung'. In Reuther 1992: 93–122.

—— (1994). Der Faktor Sprachkontakt in einer dynamischen Typologie des Slavischen. In Mehlig 1994: 41–64.

—— (1996). Überlegungen zu einer Klassifizierung des grammatischen Wandels im Sprachkontakt (am Beispiel slavischer Kontaktfälle). *Sprachtypologie und Universalienforschung* 49(1): 21–38.

BRIGHT, WILLIAM (ed.) (1992*a*). *International encyclopedia of linguistics.* Volume 1. New York, Oxford: Oxford University Press [See under Areal linguistics, Balkan languages].

—— (ed.) (1992*b*). *International encyclopedia of linguistics.* Volume 2). New York, Oxford: Oxford University Press [See chapter 2].

BRUYN, ADRIENNE (1995). *Grammaticalization in creoles: The development of determiners and relative clauses in Sranan.* Amsterdam: IFOTT.

—— (1996). 'On identifying instances of grammaticalization in Creole languages'. In Baker & Syea 1996: 29–46.

—— (1997). *The history of locative verbs in Sranan.* Paper presented at the 1997 annual meeting of the Society for Pidgin and Creole Linguistics. London.

BUNTE, PAMELA A. & MARTHA B. KENDALL (1981). 'When is an error not an error? Notes on language contact and the question of interference'. *Anthropological Linguistics* 23(1): 1–7.

BURRIDGE, KATE (1992). 'Creating grammar: Examples from Pennsylvania German, Ontario'. In Burridge & Enninger 1992: 199–241.

—— (1995). 'Evidence of grammaticalization in Pennsylvania German'. In Andersen 1995: 59–75.

BURRIDGE, KATE & WERNER ENNINGER (eds) (1992). *Diachronic studies on the languages of the Anabaptists.* (Bochum-Essener Beiträge zur Sprachwandelforschung, 17) Bochum: N. Brockmeyer.

BYBEE, JOAN L. (2003). 'Mechanisms of change in grammaticization: the role of frequency'. In Joseph & Janda 2003: 602–23.

BYBEE, JOAN L. & ÖSTEN DAHL (1989). 'The creation of tense and aspect systems in the languages of the world'. *Studies in Language* 13, 1: 51–103.

BYBEE, JOAN L. & SUZANNE FLEISCHMAN (eds) (1995). *Modality in grammar and discourse.* Amsterdam, Philadelphia: Benjamins.

BYBEE, JOAN L. & PAUL HOPPER (2001). *Frequency and the emergence of linguistic structure.* (Typological Studies in Language, 45) Amsterdam, Philadelphia: John Benjamins.

BYBEE, JOAN L., WILLIAM PAGLIUCA & REVERE D. PERKINS (1991). 'Back to the future'. In Traugott & Heine 1991*b*: 17–58.

BYBEE, JOAN L., REVERE D. PERKINS & WILLIAM PAGLIUCA (1994). *The evolution of grammar: Tense, Aspect and Modality in the Languages of the World.* Chicago: University of Chicago Press.

CAMPBELL, LYLE (1985). *The Pipil language of El Salvador.* (Mouton Grammar Library, 1) Berlin, New York, Amsterdam: Mouton.

—— (1987). 'Syntactic change in Pipil'. *International Journal of American Linguistics* 53(3): 253–80.

CAMPBELL, LYLE & RICHARD JANDA (2001). 'Introduction: conceptions of grammaticalization and their problems'. *Language Sciences* 23, 2–3: 93–112.

CAMPBELL, LYLE & MARIANNE MITHUN (eds) (1979). *The language of Native America: Historical and comparative assessment.* Austin: University of Texas Press.

CAMPBELL, LYLE, TERRENCE KAUFMAN, & THOMAS C. SMITH-STARK (1986). 'Meso-America as a linguistic area'. *Language* 62(3): 530–70.

Cao, Jun (2002). *Temporal structures in English and Chinese.* MA dissertation, University of Düsseldorf.

Cárdenas, Hernán Urrutia (1995). 'Morphosyntactic features in the Spanish of the Basque country'. In Silva-Corvalán 1995: 243–59.

Cennamo, Michela (2005). *The rise and development of analytic perfects in Italo-Romance.* Paper presented at the Conference on Linguistic Theory and Grammatical Change, Rosendal (Norway), 31 May to 4 June 2005.

Chambers, J. K. & P. Trudgill (1986). *Dialectology.* 2nd edn. Cambridge: Cambridge University Press.

Chappell, Hilary (2001). 'Language contact and areal diffusion in Sinitic languages'. In Aikhenvald & Dixon 2001: 328–57.

Clyne, Michael (1972). *Perspectives on language contact based on a study of German in Australia.* New York: W. S. Heinman.

Comrie, Bernard (1981). *The languages of the Soviet Uniion.* Cambridge: Cambridge University Press.

Corne, Chris (1995). 'A contact-induced and vernacularized language: how Melanesian is Tayo?' In Baker 1995: 121–148.

—— (1999). *From French to Creole: The development of new vernaculars in the French colonial world.* London: University of Westminster Press.

Cornillie, Bert (2004*a*). 'The shift from lexical to subjective readings in Spanish *prometer* "to promise" and *amenazar* "to threaten": a corpus-based account'. *Pragmatics* 14(1): 1–30.

—— (2004*b*). *Evidentiality and epistemic modality in Spanish (semi-) auxiliaries: a functional-pragmatic and cognitive-linguistic account.* Ph.D. dissertation, University of Leuven.

—— (2005*a*). 'Agentivity and subjectivity in Spanish *prometer* and *amenazar*: a study of constructional and diatopical variation'. *Revista Internacional de Lingüística Iberoamericana* 1(5): 171–96.

—— (2005*b*). *Subjectification as a cognitive semantic operation: on Spanish* amenazar *'to threaten' and* prometer *'to promise'.* Paper presented at the conference From Gram to Mind: Grammar as Cognition, Bordeaux, 19–21 May 2005.

Costello, John R. (1985). 'Pennsylvania German and English: languages in contact'. In Kloss 1985: 111–20.

—— (1992). 'The periphrastic *duh* construction in Anabaptist and nonsectarian Pennsylvania German: synchronic and diachronic perspectives'. In Burridge & Enninger 1992: 242–63.

Cotter, Colleen (1994). 'Focus in Irish and English: contrast and contact'. *Berkeley Linguistics Society* 20: 134–44.

Craig, Colette G. (1991). 'Ways to go in Rama: a case study in polygrammaticalization'. In Traugott & Heine 1991*b*: 455–92.

Cristofaro, Sonia (2000). 'Linguistic areas, typology and historical linguistics: an overview with particular respect to Mediterranean languages'. In Cristofaro & Putzu 2000: 65–81.

CRISTOFARO, SONIA & IGNAZIO PUTZU (eds) (2000). *Languages in the Mediterranean area: typology and convergence.* Milan: Franco Angeli.

CRITCHLEY, DAVID H. (1983). 'Application of a case framework to grammaticalization in German'. *Studia Linguistica* 37(2): 135–45.

CROFT, WILLIAM (1990). *Typology and universals.* Cambridge: Cambridge University Press.

CSATÓ, ÉVA ÁGNES (1996). 'Some typological properties of North-Western Karaim in areal perspectives'. In Boretzky 1996: 68–83.

—— (2001). 'Syntactic code-copying in Karaim'. In Dahl & Koptjevskaja-Tamm 2001*a*: 271–83.

—— (2002). 'Karaim: a high-copying language'. In Jones & Esch 2002: 315–27.

CSATÓ, ÉVA ÀGNES, BO ISAKSSON, and CARINA JAHANI (eds) (2003). *Linguistic convergence and areal diffusion: case studies from Iranian, Semitic and Turkic.* London, New York: Routledge Curzon.

CUMMINGS, III, GEORGE M. (1998). 'Definiteness in Czech'. *Studies in Language* 22(3): 567–96.

CURNOW, TIMOTHY JOWAN (2001). 'What language features can be "borrowed"?' In Aikhenvald & Dixon 2001: 412–36.

DAHL, ÖSTEN (1990). 'Standard Average European as an exotic language'. In Bechert *et al.* 1990: 3–8.

—— (1996). 'Das Tempussystem des Deutschen im typologischen Vergleich'. In Lang & Zifonun 1996: 359–68.

—— (ed.) (2000*a*). *Tense and aspect in the languages of Europe.* (Empirical Approaches to Language Typology, Eurotyp, 20–6) Berlin, New York: Mouton de Gruyter.

—— (2000*b*). 'The grammar of future time reference in European languages'. In Dahl 2000*a*: 309–28.

—— (2000*c*). 'Verbs of becoming as future copulas'. In Dahl 2000*a*: 351–61.

—— (2001). 'Principles of areal typology'. In Haspelmath *et al.* 2001: 1456–70.

—— (2004). 'Definite articles in Scandinavian: Competing grammaticalization processes in standard and non-standard varieties'. In Kortmann 2004: 147–80.

DAHL, ÖSTEN & MARIA KOPTJEVSKAJA-TAMM (eds) (2001*a*). *Circum-Baltic languages: Typology and contact.* Volume 1: *Past and present.* (Studies in Language and Companion Series, 54) Amsterdam, Philadelphia: Benjamins.

—— (2001*b*). *Circum-Baltic languages: Typology and contact.* Volume 2: *Grammar and typology.* (Studies in Language and Companion Series, 55) Amsterdam, Philadelphia: Benjamins.

DANCHEV, ANDREI (1984). 'Translation and syntactic change'. In Fišiak 1984: 47–60.

—— (1988). 'Language contact and language change'. *Folia Linguistica* 22: 37–53.

—— (1989). Language change typology and adjectival comparison in contact situations. *Folia Linguistica Historica* 9(2): 161–74.

DANCHEV, ANDREI & MERJA KYTÖ (1994). 'The construction *be going to + infinitive* in Early Modern English'. In Kastovsky 1994: 59–77.

DANYLENKO, ANDRII (2000). 'The genitive of agent and the instrumental of means in Old Ukranian: an old idea worth revising?' *General Linguistics* 37(1): 41–70.

—— (2001*a*). Russian *čto za*, Ukrainian *ščo za*, Polish *co za* 'was für ein': A case of contact-induced or parallel change? *Diachronica* 18(2): 241–65.

—— (2001b). 'The verb "have" in East Slavic'. In *The Proceedings of the 13th UCLA Indo-European Conference.* Los Angeles.

DANYLENKO, ANDRII & SERHII VAKULENKO (1995). *Ukranian.* Munich and Newcastle: Lincom Europa.

DELANCEY, SCOTT & RUSSEL TOMLIN (eds) (1988). *Papers from the 3rd Pacific Linguistics Conference.* Eugene: University of Oregon.

DEMIRAJ, SHABAN (1985). 'About the origin of the possessive perfect in Albanian and in some other languages'. In Ölberg, Schmidt, & Bothien 1985: 81–5.

DEMSKE, ULRIKE (2001). *Merkmale und Relationen: diachrone Studien zur Nominalphrase des Deutschen.* (Studia Linguistica Germanica, 56) Berlin, New York: Walter de Gruyter.

DENISON, N. (1968). 'Sauris: a trilingual community in diatypic perspective'. *Man*, n.s., 3: 578–92.

—— (1988). 'Language contact and language norm'. *Folia Linguistica* 22: 11–35.

DÉCSY, GYULA (1973). *Die linguistische Struktur Europas: Vergangenheit, Gegenwart, Zukunft.* Wiesbaden: Harrassowitz.

DETGES, ULRICH (2000). 'Time and truth: the grammaticalization of resultatives and perfects within a theory of subjectification'. *Studies in Language* 24(2): 345–77.

DIESSEL, HOLGER (1999). *Demonstratives: Form, function, and grammaticalization.* (Typological Studies in Language, 42) Amsterdam, Philadelphia: Benjamins.

DIHOFF, IVAN R. (ed.) (1983). *Current approaches to African linguistics (vol. 1).* Dordrecht: Foris Publications.

DIL, ANWAR (ed.) (1980). *Language and linguistic area.* Stanford: Stanford University Press.

DIXON, ROBERT M. W. (2002). *Australian languages: their origin and development.* Cambridge: Cambridge University Press.

DOERFER, GERHARD (1967). *Türkische Lehnwörter im Tadschikischen.* (Abhandlungen für die Kunde des Morgenlandes, 37, 3.) Wiesbaden: Steiner.

DORIAN, NANCY C. (ed.) (1989). *Investigating obsolescence.* Cambridge: Cambridge University Press.

—— (1993). 'Internally and externally motivated change in language contact settings: doubts about dichotomy'. In Jones 1993: 131–55.

DREWES, A. J. (1994). 'Borrowing in Maltese'. In Bakker & Mous 1994: 83–111.

DRINKA, BRIDGET (1998). 'The evolution of grammar'. In Schmid, Austin & Stein 1998: 117–33.

—— (2003*a*). 'Areal factors in the development of the European periphrastic perfect'. *Word* 54(1): 1–38.

—— (2003*b*). 'The formation of periphrastic perfects and passives in Europe: an areal approach'. In Blake & Burridge 2003: 105–28.

—— (2004). 'Präteritumschwund: evidence for areal diffusion'. In Abraham 2004: 211–40.

DRYER, MATTHEW S. (1989*a*). 'Article-noun order'. *Chicago Linguistic Society* 25: 83–97.

—— (1989*b*). 'Large linguistic areas and language sampling'. *Studies in Language* 13: 257–92.

—— (1992). 'The Greenbergian word order correlations'. *Language* 68: 81–138.

—— (1998). 'Aspects of word order in the languages of Europe'. In Siewierska 1998: 283–319.

DUBOIS, JOHN W. (1987). 'The discourse basis of ergativity'. *Language* 63: 805–55.

DULIČENKO, ALEKSANDR (1998). 'Das Resianische'. In Rehder 1998: 246–9.

DUPUY-ENGELHARDT, HILTRAUD, SILVIA PALMA, & JEAN EMMANUEL TYVAERT (eds) (2001). *Les phrases dans les textes, les sons et les mots pour les dire, les connecteurs du discours, l'opposition verbo-nominale en acte.* (Recherches en Linguistique et Psychologie cognitive, EA 2071, 16.) Reims: Presses Universitaires de Reims.

DURÁN, RICHARD P. (ed.) (1981). *Latino language and communicative behavior.* Norwood, NJ: Ablex.

DURIE, MARK & MALCOLM D. ROSS, M. (eds) (1996). *The comparative method reviewed: regularity and irregularity in language change.* New York: Oxford University Press.

EBERT, KAREN (2001). 'Südasien als Sprachbund'. In Haspelmath *et al.* 2001: 1529–39.

EICHHOFF, J. (1971). 'German in Wisconsin'. In Gilbert 1971: 43–57.

ELŠIK, VIKTOR & YARON MATRAS (eds) (2000). *Grammatical relations in Romani: The noun phrase.* Amsterdam: Benjamins.

EMENEAU, MURRAY B. (1956). 'India as a linguistic area'. *Language* 32, (1): 3–16.

—— (1980). 'Bilingualism and structural borrowing'. In Dil 1980: 38–65.

ENFIELD, NICK J. (2001). 'On genetic and areal linguistics in mainland south-east Asia: Parallel polyfunctionality of "acquire" '. In Aikhenvald & Dixon 2001: 255–90.

—— (2003). *Linguistic epidemiology: semantics and grammar of language contact in mainland Southeast Asia.* London, New York: Routledge Curzon.

ENNINGER, WERNER (1980). 'Syntactic convergence in a stable triglossia plus trilingualism situation in Kent County, Delaware, U.S.A.' In Nelde 1980: 343–50.

EPSTEIN, R. (1993). 'The definite article: early stages of development'. In van Marle 1993: 111–34.

FARACLAS, NICHOLAS G. (1996). *Nigerian Pidgin.* (Descriptive Grammars Series.) London, New York: Routledge.

FAßKE, HELMUT & SIEGFRIED MICHALK (1981). *Grammatik der obersorbischen Schriftsprache der Gegenwart. Morphologie.* Leipzig: INTERDRUCK.

FEHLING, DETLEV (1980). The origins of European syntax. *Folia Linguistica Historica* 1: 353–87.

FEOKTISTOVA, A.S. (1961). Kistorii sostavnogo skazuemogo s prisvjazočnoj častju vyražennoj pričastiem stradatelnogo zaloga prošedšego vremeni (na materiale Novgorodskich pamjatnikov pis'mennosti XII–XVI vv.). *Issledovanija po lexikologii i grammatike russkogo jazyka.* Moskva: 194–208.

FERGUSON, CHARLES A. (1976). 'The Ethiopian language area'. In Bender *et al.* 1976: 63–76.

FEUILLET, JACK (2001). 'Aire linguistique balkanique'. In Haspelmath *et al.* 2001: 1510–28.

FIEDLER, WILFRIED (1987). 'Zur Typologie der grammatischen Interferenz zwischen den Balkansprachen im Bereich der Konnektive'. *Linguistische Studien* 157: 45–68.

—— (1999). 'Tempus, Modus und Aspekt in den Sprachen Südosteuropas'. In Hinrichs & Büttner 1999: 487–517.

FILIN, F. P. (1972). *Proisxoždenie russkogo, ukrainskogo i belorusskogo jazykov.* Leningrad: Naouka.

FILPPULA, MARKKU (1986). *Some aspects of Hiberno-English in a functional sentence perspective.* (University of Joensuu Publications in the Humanities, 7) Joensuu: University of Joensuu.

—— (1999). *The grammar of Irish English:* Language in *Hibernian Style.* London/New York: Routledge.

FIŠIAK, JAČEK (ed.) (1984). *Historical syntax.* (Trends in Linguistics, 23) Berlin: Mouton de Gruyter.

FLEISCHER, JÜRG (2004). 'A typology of relative clauses in German dialects'. In Kortmann 2004: 211–43.

FLEISCHMAN, SUZANNE (1982*a*). *The future in thought and language: Diachronic evidence from Romance.* (Cambridge Studies in Linguistics, 36) Cambridge: Cambridge University Press.

—— (1982*b*). 'The past and the future: are they *coming* or *going*?' *Berkeley Linguistics Society* 8: 322–34.

—— (1983). 'From pragmatics to grammar. Diachronic reflections on complex pasts and futures in Romance'. *Lingua* 60: 183–214.

FLIER, MICHAEL S. (ed.) (1974). *Slavic Forum: Essays in linguistics and literature.* (Slavistic Printings and Reprintings, 277) The Hague, Paris: Mouton.

FORSSMAN, BERTHOLD (2000). 'Baltisch-finnische Sprachkontakte am Beispiel der Adposition'. In Ofitsch & Zinko 2000: 125–32.

FOULET, LUCIEN (1920). 'La disparition du prétérite'. *Romania* 46: 271–313.

FRAJZYNGIER, ZYGMUNT & TRACI S. CURL (eds.) (2000). *Reflexives: Forms and functions.* (Typological Studies in Language, 40) Amsterdam, Philadelphia: Benjamins.

FRIEDMAN, VICTOR A. (1976). 'Dialectal synchrony and diachronic syntax: The Macedonian perfect'. *Chicago Linguistic Society, Papers from the Parasession on Diachronic Syntax,* 1976: 96–104.

—— (1977). *The grammatical categories of the Macedonian indicative.* Columbus, Ohio: Slavica Publishers, Inc.

—— (1994). 'Variation and grammaticalization in the development of Balkanisms'. *Chicago Linguistic Society* 30(2): 101–15.

—— (1997). 'One grammar, three lexicons: ideological overtones and underpinnings in the Balkan *Sprachbund*'. *Chicago Linguistic Society* 33: 23–44.

—— (2003). *Turkish in Macedonia and beyond: Studies in contact, typology and other phenomena in the Balkans and the Caucasus.* (Turcologica, 52) Wiesbaden: Harrassowitz.

GARVIN, PAUL L. (1949). 'Standard Average European and Czech'. *Studia Linguistica* 3: 65–85.

GARZA CUARÓN, BEATRIZ & PAULETTE LEVY (eds) (1990). *Homenaje a Jorge A. Suárez: Linguística indoamericana e hispánica.* (Estudios de linguística y literatura, 18) Mexico: El Colegio de México.

GEISLER, HANS & DANIEL JACOB (eds) (1998). *Transitivität und Diathese in romanischen Sprachen.* (Linguistische Arbeiten, 392) Tübingen: Max Niemeyer.

GEORGIEV (1957 [1976]). 'Văznikvane na novi složni glagolni formi săs spomagatelen glagol "imam" '. *Izvestija na Instituta za bălgarski ezik.* Volume 5, Sofia.

GERHARDT, DIETRICH (ed.) (1971). *Hugo Schuchardt, Slawo-deutsches und Slawo-italienisches. Mit Schuchardts übrigen Arbeiten zur Slavistik und mit neuen Registern.* (Slavische Propyläen, 66) Munich: Wilhelm Fink.

GIACALONE RAMAT, ANNA & PAUL J. HOPPER (1998) (eds.) *The limits of grammaticalization.* Amsterdam, Philadelphia: Benjamins.

GIL, DAVID (1994). 'Everything also must grab: A unified semantic analysis of Singlish 'also' '. EUROTYP Working Papers VII, 23: 133–45.

—— (2003). 'English goes Asian: Number and (in)definiteness in the Singlish noun phrase'. In Plank 2003: 467–514.

GILBERS, D. G., J. NERBONNE, & J. SCHAEKEN (eds) (2000). *Languages in contact.* (Studies in Slavic and General Linguistics, 28) Amsterdam, Atlanta, GA: Rodopi.

GILBERT, GLENN G. (ed.) (1971). *The German language in America: a symposium.* Austin, London: University of Texas Press.

—— (ed.) (forthcoming). *Pidgin and creole linguistics in the 21st century.* New York: Lang.

GILES, HOWARD, DONALD M. TAYLOR, & RICHARD BOURHIS (1973). 'Towards a theory of interpersonal accommodation through language: some Canadian data'. *Language in Society* 2: 177–92.

GILMAN, CHARLES (1986). 'African areal characteristics: Sprachbund, not substrate?' *Journal of Pidgin and Creole Languages* 1(1): 33–50.

GIVÓN, TALMY (1971). 'Historical syntax and synchronic morphology: an archaeologist's field trip'. *Chicago Linguistic Society* 7: 394–415.

—— (1981). 'On the development of the numeral "one" as an indefinite marker'. *Folia Linguistica Historica* 2(1): 35–53.

GOŁAB, ZBIGNIEW (1959). 'Some Arumanian-Macedonian isogrammatisms and the social background of their development'. *Word* 15: 415–35.

—— (1960). 'The influence of Turkish upon the Macedonian Slavonic dialects'. *Folia Orientalia* (Cracow) 1: 26–45.

GOLDBERG, ADELE E. (1995). *Constructions: A construction grammar approach to argument structure.* Chicago, London: University of Chicago Press.

GRANDI, N. (2002). *Morphologie in contatto: le construzioni valutative nelle lingue del Mediterraneo.* Milano.

GREENBERG, JOSEPH H. (1959). 'Africa as a linguistic area'. In Bascom & Herskovits 1959: 15–27.

—— (1978*a*). 'How does a language acquire gender markers?' In Greenberg, Ferguson, & Moravcsik 1978: 47–82.

—— (1978*b*). 'Generalizations about numeral systems'. In Greenberg, Ferguson, & Moravcsik 1978: 249–95.

—— (1983). 'Some areal characteristics of African languages'. In Dihoff 1983: 3–21.

Greenberg, Joseph H., Charles A. Ferguson & Edith Moravcsik (eds) (1978). *Universals of human language.* Volume 3: *Word structure.* Stanford: Stanford University Press.

Güldemann, Tom (1997). *The Kalahari Basin as an object of areal typology: A first approach.* Köln, Institut für Afrikanistik. (*Khoisan Forum 3*).

Gumperz, John J. & Robert Wilson (1971). 'Convergence and creolization: A case from the Indo-Aryan/Dravidian border in India'. In Hymes 1971: 151–67.

Gundel, Jeanette, Nancy Hedberg, & Ron Zacharski (1993). 'Cognitive status and the form of referring expressions in discourse'. *Language* 69(2): 274–307.

Gupta, Anthea Fraser (1992*a*). 'The pragmatic particles of Singapore Colloquial English'. *Journal of Pragmatics* 18: 31–57.

Gupta, Anthea Fraser (1992*b*). 'Contact features of Singapore Colloquial English'. In Bolton & Kwok 1992: 323–45.

—— (1994). *The step-tongue: Children's English in Singapore.* Clevedon: Multilingual Matters Ltd.

Haarmann, Harald (1976*a*). *Grundzüge der Sprachtypologie: Methodik, Empirie und Systematik der Sprachen Europas.* (Urban-Taschenbücher, 242) Stuttgart, Berlin, Cologne, Mainz: W. Kohlhammer.

—— (1976*b*). *Aspekte der Arealtypologie: die Problematik der europäischen Sprachbünde.* (Tübinger Beiträge zur Linguistik, 72) Tübingen: Gunter Narr.

Haase, Martin (1992). *Sprachkontakt und Sprachwandel im Baskenland: die Einflüsse des Gaskognischen und Französischen auf das Baskische.* Hamburg: Buske.

—— (1997). Gascon et basque: bilinguisme et substrat. *Sprachtypologie und Universalienforschung* 50(3): 189–228.

Haase, Martin & Nicole Nau (eds) (1996). *Sprachkontakt und Grammatikalisierung. Sprachtypologie und Universalienforschung.* (Special issue, 49, 1) Berlin: Akademie-Verlag.

Hagège, Claude (1993). *The language builder: An essay on the human signature in linguistic morphogenesis.* (Amsterdam Studies in the Theory and History of Linguistic Science, 94) Amsterdam, Philadelphia: Benjamins.

—— (1997). 'Language as a faculty, languages as "contingent" manifestations and humans as function builders'. In Simon-Vandenbergen *et al.* 1997: 29–47.

Haig, Geoffrey (2001). 'Linguistic diffusion in present-day East Anatolia: from top to bottom'. In Aikhenvald & Dixon 2001: 195–224.

Haiman, John & Sandra Thompson (eds) (1988). *Clause combining in grammar and discourse.* Amsterdam, Philadelphia: Benjamins.

Hammond, Michael & Michael Noonan (eds) (1988). *Theoretical morphology: Approaches in modern linguistics.* New York: Academic Press.

Hamp, Eric (1977). 'On some questions of areal linguistics'. *Berkeley Linguistics Society* 3: 279–82.

—— (1979). 'A glance from here on'. In Campbell & Mithun 1979: 1001–15.

Harris, Alice (2003). 'Cross-linguistic perspectives on syntactic change'. In Joseph & Janda 2003: 529–51.

Harris, Alice C. & Lyle Campbell (1995). *Historical syntax in cross-linguistic perspective.* Cambridge: Cambridge University Press.

Harris, John (1984). 'Syntactic variation and dialect divergence'. *Journal of Linguistics* 20: 303–27.

—— (1991). 'Conservatism versus substratal transfer in Irish English'. In Trudgill & Chambers 1991: 191–212.

—— (1993). 'The grammar of Irish English'. In Milroy and Milroy (eds) 1993: 139–86.

Harris, Martin (1978). *The evolution of French syntax: a comparative approach.* London, New York: Longman.

—— (1982). 'The "past simple" and the 'present perfect' in Romance'. In Vincent & Harris 1982: 42–70.

Harris, Martin & Paolo Ramat (eds) (1987). *Historical development of auxiliaries.* (Trends in Linguistics, 35) Berlin, New York: Mouton de Gruyter.

Haspelmath, Martin (1989). 'From purposive to infinitive—a universal path of grammaticization'. *Folia Linguistica Historica* 10(1–2): 287–310.

—— (1998). 'How young is Standard Average European?' *Language Sciences* 20(3): 271–87.

—— (1999). 'Why is grammaticalization irreversible?' *Linguistics* 37(6): 1043–68.

—— (2001). 'The European linguistic area: Standard Average European'. In Haspelmath *et al.* 2001: 1492–510.

Haspelmath, Martin & Ekkehard König (eds.) (1995). *Converbs in cross-linguistic perspective.* (Empirical Approaches to Language Typology, 13.) Berlin, New York: Mouton de Gruyter.

Haspelmath, Martin & Oda Buchholz (1998). 'Equative and similative constructions in the languages of Europe'. In van der Auwera 1998*b*: 277–334.

Haspelmath, Martin, Ekkehard König, Wulf Oesterreicher, & Wolfgang Raible (eds) (2001). *Language typology and language universals: An international handbook.* Volume 2. (Handbücher zur Sprach-und Kommunikationswissenschaft, 20.2.) New York: Walter de Gruyter.

Haugen, Einar (1950*a*). 'Problems of bilingualism'. *Lingua* 2: 271–90.

—— (1950*b*). 'The analysis of linguistic borrowing'. *Language* 26: 210–31.

—— (1953). *The Norwegian language in America: A study in bilingual behavior.* Philadelphia: University of Pennsylvania Press.

—— (1989). 'The rise and fall of an immigrant language: Norwegian in America'. In Dorian 1989: 61–73.

—— (1992). 'Borrowing: an overview'. In Bright 1992*a*: 197–200.

Hawkins, John (2004). *Efficiency and complexity in grammars.* Oxford: Oxford University Press.

HEAD, BRIAN F. (1978). Respect degrees in pronominal reference. In Greenberg *et al.* 1978: 151–211.

HEATH, JEFFREY (1978). *Linguistic diffusion in Arnhem Land.* (Australian Aboriginal Studies Research and Regional Studies, 13) Canberra: Australian Institute of Aboriginal Studies.

HEDIN, EVA (1987). *On the use of the perfect and the pluperfect in modern Greek.* (Studia Graeca Stockholmiensia, 6) Stockholm: University, Almqvist & Wiksell International.

HEINE, BERND (1975). 'Language typology and convergence areas in Africa'. *Linguistics* 144: 26–47.

—— (1976). *A typology of African langages based on the order of meaningful elements.* (Kölner Beiträge zur Afrikanistik, 4) Berlin: Dietrich Reimer.

—— (1992). 'Grammaticalization chains'. *Studies in Language* 16(2): 335–68.

—— (1993). *Auxiliaries: Cognitive forces and grammaticalization.* New York, Oxford: Oxford University Press.

—— (1994). 'Areal influence on grammaticalization'. In Pütz 1994: 56–68.

—— (1997*a*). *Possession: Sources, forces, and grammaticalization.* Cambridge: Cambridge University Press.

—— (1997*b*). *Cognitive foundations of grammar.* Oxford, New York: Oxford University Press.

—— (2002). On the role of context in grammaticalization. In Wischer & Diewald 2002: 83–101.

HEINE, BERND (2003*a*). 'Grammaticalization'. In Joseph & Janda 2003: 575–601.

—— (2003*b*). 'On degrammaticalization'. In Blake & Burridge 2003: 163–79.

HEINE, BERND & TANIA KUTEVA (2001). 'Convergence and divergence in the development of African languages'. In Aikhenvald & Dixon 2001: 393–411.

—— (2002). *World lexicon of grammaticalization.* Cambridge: Cambridge University Press.

—— (2003). 'Contact-induced grammaticalization'. *Studies in Language* 27(3): 529–72.

—— (2005). *Language contact and grammatical change.* Cambridge: Cambridge University Press.

HEINE, BERND & HIROYUKI MIYASHITA (2005). 'The structure of a functional category: German *drohen*'. Typescript, University of Cologne.

HEINE, BERND & MECHTHILD REH (1984). *Grammaticalization and reanalysis in African languages.* Hamburg: Buske.

HEINE, BERND & DEREK NURSE (eds) (2000). *African languages: an introduction.* Cambridge: Cambridge University Press.

HEINE, BERND, ULRIKE CLAUDI, & FRIEDERIKE HÜNNEMEYER (1991). *Grammaticalization: a conceptual framework.* Chicago: University of Chicago Press.

HENDRIKS, P. (1976). *The Radožda-Vevčani dialect of Macedonian.* Lisse: Peter de Ridde Press.

HERMANN, EDUARD (1943). 'Herkunft unsrer Fragefürwörter'. *Sitzungsberichte der Bayerischen Akademie der Wissenschaften, Philosophisch-historische Abteilung* 1943, 3. Munich: Verlag der Bayerischen Akademie der Wissenschaften.

Hermann, T. (forthcoming). *Relative clauses in dialects of English.* Ph.D. Thesis.

Hill, Jane H. & Kenneth C. Hill (1980). 'Mixed grammar, purist grammar, and language attitudes in Modern Nahuatl'. *Language in Society* 9: 321–48.

—— (1986). *Speaking Mexicano: Dynamics of syncretic language in Central Mexico.* Tucson: The University of Arizona Press.

Hill, Kenneth C. (ed.) (1979). *The genesis of language.* (The First Michigan Colloquium, 1979.) Ann Arbor: Karoma Publishers.

Himmelmann, Nikolaus P. (2004). 'Lexicalization and grammaticalization: opposite or orthogonal?' In Bisang *et al.* 2004: 19–40.

Hinrichs, Uwe (1999). 'Die sogenannten "Balkanismen" als Problem der Südosteuropa-Linguistik und der allgemeinen Sprachwissenschaft'. In Hinrichs & Büttner 1999: 429–62.

—— (ed.) (2004). *Die europäischen Sprachen auf dem Wege zum analytischen Sprachtyp.* Wiesbaden: Harrassowitz.

Hinrichs, Uwe & Uwe Büttner (eds) (1999). *Handbuch der Südosteuropa-Linguistik.* (Slavistische Studienbücher, Neue Folge) Wiesbaden: Harrassowitz.

Hinze, Friedhelm (1969). Die Wiedergabe des deutschen Substantiv-Verbalabstrakt-Kompositums im Slovinzischen. In Krauss *et al.* 1969: 63–8.

Hock, Hans Heinrich (1986). *Principles of historical linguistics.* (Trends in Linguistics, 34) Berlin: Mouton de Gruyter.

Hodge, Carleton T. (1970). 'The linguistic cycle'. *Language Sciences* 13: 1–7.

Hollenbach, Barbara E. (1990). 'Semantic and syntactic extensions of Copala Trique body-part nouns'. In Garza Cuarón & Levy 1990: 275–96.

—— (1991). 'On some principles of grammaticization'. In Traugott & Heine 1991*a*: 17–35.

Holtus, Günter, Michael Metzeltin, & Christian Schmitt (eds) (1998). *Lexikon der Romanistischen Linguistik.* Volume 7. Tübingen: Max Niemeyer.

Hopper, Paul J. (1991). 'On some principles of grammaticization'. In Traugott & Heine 1991*a*: 17–35.

Hopper, Paul J. & Elizabeth C. Traugott ([1993] 2003). *Grammaticalization.* Cambridge: Cambridge University Press.

Houis, Maurice (1980). 'Propositions pour une typologie des langues négro-africaines'. *Afrique et langage* 13: 5–47.

Huber, Dieter & Erika Worbs (eds) (1997). *Ars transferendi: Sprache, Übersetzung, Interkulturalität: Festschrift für Nikolai Salnikow zum 65. Geburtstag.* Wuppertal: Peter Lang.

Huber, Magnus (1996). 'The grammaticalization of aspect markers in Ghanaian Pidgin English'. In Baker & Syea 1996: 53–70.

—— (1999). *Ghanaian Pidgin English in its West African context: a sociohistorical and structural analysis.* (Varieties of English Around the World, 24) Amsterdam, Philadelphia: Benjamins.

Huffines, Marion Lois (1986). 'The function of aspect in Pennsylvania German and the impact of English'. *Yearbook of German-American Studies* 21: 137–54.

HUFFINES, MARION LOIS (1988). 'Building progressives: evidence from cognate structures'. *Journal of English Linguistics* 21(2): 137–48.

—— (1991). 'Pennsylvania German: convergence and change as strategies of discourse'. In Seliger & Vago 1991: 125–37.

HURCH, BERNHARD (1989). 'Hispanisierung im Baskischen'. In Boretzky *et al.* 1989: 11–35.

HURLEY, JONI KAY (1995). 'The impact of Quichua on verb forms used in Spanish requests in Otavalo, Ecuador'. In Silva-Corvalán 1995: 39–51.

HYMES, DELL (ed.) (1971). *Pidginization and creolization of languages: Proceedings of a conference held at the University of the West Indies, Mona, Jamaica, April 1968.* Cambridge: Cambridge University Press.

IGLA, BIRGIT (1989). 'Kontakt-induzierte Sprachwandelphänomene im Romani von Ajia Varvara (Athen)'. In Boretzky *et al.* 1989: 67–80.

ISAČENKO, ALEXANDER V. (1974). 'On "have" and "be" languages: A typological sketch'. In Flier 1974: 43–77.

JACOB, DANIEL (1994). *Die Auxiliarisierung von* habere *und die Entstehung des romanischen periphrastischen Perfekts, dargestellt an der Entwicklung vom Latein zum Spanischen.* Habilitationsschrift, University of Freiburg.

—— (1998). 'Transitivität, Diathese und Perfekt: zur Entstehnung der romanischen *haben*-Periphrasen'. In Geisler & Jacob 1998: 105–26.

JAHR, ERNST HAKON (ed.) (1992). *Language contact: theoretical and empirical studies.* (Trends in Linguistics, Studies and Monographs, 60) Berlin, New York: Mouton de Gruyter.

JEFFERS, ROBERT & ILSE LEHISTE (1979). *Principles and methods for historical linguistics.* Cambridge, MA: MIT Press.

JENKINS, REBECCA SUE (2002). *Language contact and composite structures in New Ireland, Papua New Guinea.* Ann Arbor: UMI Dissertation Services.

JOHANSON, LARS (1992). 'Strukturelle Faktoren in türkischen Sprachkontakten'. (*Sitzungsberichte der Wissenschaftlichen Gesellschaft an der Johann Wolfgang Goethe-Universität Frankfurt am Main,* volume 29(5): 169–299.) Stuttgart: Franz Steiner.

—— (1996*a*). 'On Bulgarian and Turkish indirectives'. In Boretzky 1996: 84–94.

—— (1996*b*). 'Kopierte Satzjunktoren im Türkischen'. *Sprachtypologie und Universalienforschung* 49(1): 39–49.

—— 'Kopien russischer Konjunktionen in türkischen Sprachen'. In Huber & Worbs 1997: 115–21.

—— (1998). 'Code-copying in Irano-Turkic'. *Language Sciences* 20(3): 325–37.

—— (1999). 'The dynamics of code-copying in language encounters'. In Brendemoen *et al.* 1999: 37–62.

—— (2002*a*). *Structural factors in Turkic language contacts.* London: Curzon.

—— (2002*b*). 'Contact-induced linguistic change in a code-copying framework'. In Jones & Esch 2002: 285–313.

—— (2000*c*). 'Linguistic convergence in the Volga area'. In Gilbers *et al.* 2000: 165–78.

JONES, CHARLES (ed.) (1993). *Historical linguistics: problems and perspectives.* London, New York: Longman.

JONES, MARI C. & EDITH ESCH (eds) (2002). *Language change: the interplay of internal, external and extra-linguistic factors.* (Contributions to the Sociology of Language, 86) Berlin: Mouton de Gruyter.

JOSEPH, BRIAN D. (1983). *Thee synchrony and diachrony of the Balkan infinitive: A study in areal, general, and historical linguistics.* (Cambridge Studies in Linguistics, Supplementary Volume) Cambridge: Cambridge University Press.

—— (1992). 'The Balkan languages'. In Bright 1992*a*: 153–55.

JOSEPH, BRIAN & RICHARD JANDA (1988). 'The how and why of diachronic morphologization and demorphologization'. In Hammond and Noonan 1988: 193–210.

—— (eds) (2003). *The handbook of historical linguistics.* Oxford: Blackwell.

JUVONEN, PÄIVI (2000). *Grammaticalizing the definite article: a study of definite adnominal determiners in a genre of spoken Finnish.* Stockholm: Stockholm Universiy, Department of Linguistics.

KARTTUNEN, FRANCES (1976). Uto-Aztecan and Spanish-type dependent clauses in Nahuatl. (Papers from the Parasession on Diachronic Syntax.) *Chicago Linguistic Society* 1976: 150–8.

KARSKIJ, E. F. (1956). *Belorusy: Jazyk belorusskogo naroda.* Moscow: Academy of Sciences Press.

KASTOVSKY, DIETER (ed.) (1994). *Studies in Early Modern English.* Berlin, New York: Mouton de Gruyter.

KAZAZIS, KOSTAS (1965). *Some Balkan constructions corresponding to Western European infinitives.* Ph.D. dissertation, Indiana University.

—— (1967). 'On a generative grammar of the Balkan languages'. *Foundations of Language* 3: 117–23.

KEENAN, EDWARD & BERNARD COMRIE (1977). 'Noun phrase accessibility and universal grammar'. *Linguistic Inquiry* 8: 77–100.

KEESING, ROGER M. (1988). *Melanesian Pidgin and the Oceanic Substrate.* Stanford: Stanford University Press.

—— (1991). 'Substrates, calquing and grammaticalization in Melanesian Pidgin'. In Traugott & Heine 1991*a*: 315–42.

KEMMER, SUZANNE E. (1993). *The middle voice.* (Typological Studies in Language, 23.) Amsterdam, Philadelphia: Benjamins.

KISSINE, MIKHAIL (2004). 'Les emplois figurés des verbes illocutoires: exprimer la causalité et la nécessité'. *Revue Romane* 39(2): 214–38.

KLEE, CAROL A. & ALICIA M. OCAMPO (1995). 'The expression of past reference in Spanish narratives of Spanish-Quechua bilingual speakers'. In Silva-Corvalán 1995: 52–70.

KLOSS, HEINZ (ed.) (1985). *Deutsch als Muttersprache in den Vereinigten Staaten.* Part 2. (Deutsche Sprache in Europa und Übersee, Berichte und Forschungen, 10) Stuttgart: Franz Steiner.

KONESKI, BLAŽE (1965). *Istorija na makedonskiot jazik.* Skopie: Kočo Racin/Belgrad: Prosveta.

KÖNIG, EKKEHARD & MARTIN HASPELMATH (1999). Der europäische Sprachbund. In Reiter 1999: 111–27.

KÖNIG, EKKEHARD & PETER SIEMUND (2000). 'Intensifiers and reflexives: A typological perspective'. In Frajzyngier & Curl 2000: 41–74.

KOPITAR, JERNEJ (1829). Albanische, walachische und bulgarische Sprache. *Jahrbücher der Literatur* 46: 59–106.

KOPTJEVSKAJA-TAMM, MARIA (2002). 'The Circum-Baltic languages—a coastal contact-superposition zone in the European periphery'. In Ramat & Stolz 2002: 209–22.

—— (2003). 'Genitives and possessive NPs in the languages of Europe'. In Plank 2003.

KOPTJEVSKAJA-TAMM, MARIA & BERNHARD WÄLCHLI (2001b). 'The Circum-Baltic languages: an areal-typological approach'. In Dahl & Koptjevskaja-Tamm 2001*b*: 615–750.

KORTMANN, BERND (1998*a*). 'The evolution of adverbial subordinators in Europe'. In Schmid *et al.* 1998: 213–27.

—— (1998*b*). 'Adverbial subordinators in the languages of Europe'. In van der Auwera 1998*b*: 457–561.

—— (ed.) (2004). *Dialectology meets typology: Dialect grammar from a cross-liguistic perspective.* (Trends in Linguistics, 153) Berlin, New York: Mouton de Gruyter.

KOSCHMIEDER, ERWIN & MAXIMILIAN BRAUN (eds) (1968). *Slavistische Studien zum VI. Internationalen Slavistenkongress in Prag 1968.* Munich: Rudolf Trofenik.

KOSTOV, KIRIL (1973). 'Zur Bedeutung des Zigeunerischen für die Erforschung grammatischer Interferenzerscheinungen'. *Linguistique Balkanique* 16(2): 99–113.

KRAUSS, W., Z. STIEBER, J. BĚLIČ, & V. I. BORKOVSKIJ (eds) (1969). *Slawisch-deutsche Wechselbeziehungen in Sprache, Literatur und Kultur.* (Veröffentlichungen des Instituts für Slawistik, 44) Berlin: Akademie-Verlag.

KUNZMANN-MÜLLER, BÄRBEL (1994), Grammatikhandbuch des Kroatischen und Serbischen. Frankfurt am Main, Berlin, Bern, New York, Paris, Wein: Peter Lang Verlag (= Heidelberger Publikationen zur Slavistik: A. Linguistische Reine. Bd. 7). 293 + V S.

KUTEVA, TANIA (1994). 'Iconicity and auxiliation'. *Journal of Pragmatics* 22: 71–81.

—— (1998). 'Large linguistic areas in grammaticalization: auxiliation in Europe'. *Language Sciences* 20(3): 289–311.

—— (2000). 'Areal grammaticalization: The case of the Bantu-Nilotic borderland'. *Folia Linguistica* 34(3–4): 267–83.

—— (2001). *Auxiliation: An enquiry into the nature of grammaticalization.* Oxford: Oxford University Press.

—— in prep. 'Grammaticalization: universal and specific'. Typescript, University of Düsseldorf.

KUTEVA, TANIA and BERND HEINE (2004). 'On the possessive perfect in North Russian'. *Word, Vol.* 55, No 1: 37–71.

KUZ'MINA, I. (1993) *Sintaksis russkix govorov v lingvogeografičeskom aspekte.* Moscow.

KUZ'MINA, I. & E. NEMČENKO (1971). *Sintaksis pričastnyx form v russkix govorax.* Moscow.

LÄGREID, ANNELIES (1984). The Scandinavians in Russia: on the extra-linguistic factors in the language contact between North Germanic and East Slavic peoples in the early middle ages. In Ureland & Clarkson 1984: 97–110.

LAKOFF, GEORGE & MARK JOHNSON (1980). *Metaphors we live by.* Chicago: University of Chicago Press.

LANG, EWALD & G. ZIFONUN (eds) (1996). *Deutsch—Typologisch.* Berlin: Mouton de Gruyter.

LANGACKER, RONALD W. (1975). 'Relative clauses in Classical Nahuatl'. *International Journal of American Linguistics* 41(1): 46–68.

LAPOLLA, RANDY J. (1994). 'Parallel grammaticalizations in Tibeto-Burman languages: Evidence of Sapir's "drift" '. *Linguistics of the Tibeto-Burman Area* 17(1): 61–80.

—— (2001). 'The role of migration and language contact in the development Sino-Tibetan language family'. In Aikhenvald & Dixon 2001: 225–54.

LARSSON, LARS-GUNNAR (2001). 'Baltic influence on Finnic languages'. In Dahl & Koptjevskaja-Tamm 2001*a*: 237–53.

LAURY, RITVA (1997). *Demonstratives in interaction: The emergence of a definite article in Finnish.* Amsterdam, Philadelphia: Benjamins.

LAZARD, GILBERT (1990). 'Characteristiques actancielles de "l'européen moyen type" '. In Bechert *et al.* 1990: 241–53.

LE GOFFIC, PIERRE (2001). 'Sur les sources et le développement de la subordination dans le langage: l'exemple de l'indo-européen'. In Dupuy-Engelhardt *et al.* 2001: 25–56.

—— (2002). 'Marqueurs d'interrogation/indéfinition/subordination: essai de vue d'ensemble'. *Verbum* 24(4): 315–40.

LEFEBVRE, CLAIRE (1998). *Creole genesis and the acquisition of grammar: The case of Haitian Creole.* Cambridge: Cambridge University Press.

LE GOFFIC, PIERRE & XIU LI WANG (2002). 'Les pronoms interrogatif—indéfinis du chinois: l'example de *shéi* "qui/quelqu'un/ quiconque" '. *Verbum* 24(4): 452–71.

LEHISTE, ILSE (1999). 'Successive translations as source of evidence for linguistic change'. *International Journal of the Sociology of Language* 139: 39–48.

LEHMANN, CHRISTIAN ([1982] 1995). *Thoughts on grammaticalization.* Munich: Lincom Europa.

—— (1984). *Der Relativsatz.* Tübingen: Gunter Narr Verlag.

—— (1988). 'Towards a typology of clause linkage'. In Haiman & Thompson 1988: 181–225.

LESKIEN, A. (1962). *Handbuch der altbulgarischen (altkirchenslavischen) Sprache. Grammatik-Texte-Glossar.* (8, verbesserte und erweiterte Auflage). Heidelberg: Karl Winter-Universitätsverlag.

LEVINSON, STEPHEN C. (1983). *Pragmatics.* Cambridge: Cambridge University Press.

—— (1994). 'Vision, shape, and linguistic description: Tzeltal body-part terminology and object description'. *Linguistics* 32(4/5): 791–855.

LEWY, E. ([1942] 1964). *Der Bau der europäischen Sprachen.* (Proceedings of the Royal Irish Academy, 48) Dublin: Hodges & Figgis. Reprinted 1964: Tübingen: Gunter Niemeyer.

LI, CHARLES N. (ed.) (1976). *Subject and topic.* New York, San Francisco, London: Academic Press.

—— (1983). 'Languages in contact in western China'. *Papers in East Asian Languages* 1: 31–51.

LICHTENBERK, FRANTISEK (1991). 'Semantic change and heterosemy in grammaticalization'. *Language* 67(3): 475–509.

LINDSTEDT, JOUKO (1994). 'On the development of the South Slavonic perfect'. *EUROTYP Working papers,* Series VI, No 5.

LOCKWOOD, W. B. (1968). *Historical German syntax.* Oxford: Clarendon.

LORD, CAROL DIANE (1993). *Historical change in serial verb constructions.* (Typological Studies in Language, 26) Amsterdam, Philadelphia: Benjamins.

LORIMER, D. L. R. (1937). 'Burushaski and its alien neighbors: problems in linguistic contagion'. *Transactions of the Philological Society* 1937: 63–98.

LÖTZSCH, RONALD (1969). 'Zum indirekten Passiv im Deutschen und Slawischen'. In Krauss *et al.* 1969: 102–9.

—— (1996). 'Interferenzbedingte grammatische Konvergenzen und Divergenzen zwischen Sorbisch und Jiddisch'. *Sprachtypologie und Universalienforschung* 49(1): 50–9.

LURAGHI, SILVIA (2001). 'Some remarks on instrument, comitative, and agent in Indo-European'. *Sprachtypologie und Universalienforschung* 54(4): 385–401.

LUTIN, S. A. (1990). 'Sistemno-tipologičeskij analiz rezul'tativnyx konstrukcij russkix govorov severa i severo-zapada'. Ph.D. Thesis, Moscow.

MACAULAY, DONALD (ed.) (1992). *The Celtic languages.* (Cambridge Language Surveys) Cambridge: Cambridge University Press.

MCCLOSKEY, JAMES (1985). 'The modern Irish English double relative and and syntactic binding'. *Eriu* 36: 45–86.

MCCONVELL, PATRICK (2004). 'Some issues in the contact linguistics of possessives'. Typescript.

MACLAURY, ROBERT (1989). 'Zapotec body-part locatives: prototypes and metaphoric extensions'. *International Journal of American Linguistics* 55(2): 119–54.

MACSWAN, JEFF (1999). *A minimalist approach to intrasentential code switching.* New York: Garland.

MCWHORTER, JOHN H. (ed.) (2000). *Language change and language contact in pidgins and creoles.* (Creole Language Library, 21) Amsterdam, Philadelphia: Benjamins.

MARTINET, ANDRÉ (1979). 'Shunting on to ergative or accusative'. In Plank 1979: 39–43.

MASALA, CARLO (ed.) (2002). *Der Mittelmeerraum—Brücke oder Grenze?* (Schriften für Europäische Integrationsforschung, 48) Baden-Baden: Nomos.

MASICA, COLIN P. (1976). *Defining a linguistic area: South Asia.* Chicago, London: University of Chicago Press.

—— (1992). 'Areal linguistics'. In Bright 1992*a*: 108–12.

Maslov, J. S. (1949). 'K voprosu o proischoždenii possessivnogo perfekta'. (*Učenye Zapiski LGU*, 97.) *Serija filologičeskich nauk* 14: 76–104.

Matras, Yaron (1996). 'Prozedurale Fusion: Grammatische Interferenzschichten im Romanes'. *Sprachtypologie und Universalienforschung* 49(1): 60–78.

—— (1998*a*). 'Utterance modifiers and universals of grammatical borrowing'. *Linguistics* 36(1): 281–331.

—— (1998*b*). 'Convergent development, grammaticalization, and the problem of "mutual isomorphism." ' In Boeder *et al.* 1998: 89–103.

Matras, Yaron & Peter Bakker (eds) (2003). *The mixed language debate: theoretical and empirical advances.* (Trends in Linguistics, Studies and Monographs, 145) Berlin, New York: Mouton de Gruyter.

Matras, Yaron, Anthony McMahon, & Nigel Vincent (eds) (forthcoming) *Linguistic areas.* Houndsmill: Palgrave Macmillan.

Meeussen, A. E. (1975). 'Possible linguistic Africanisms'. Fifth Hans Wolff Memorial Lecture. *Language Sciences* 35.

Mehlig, Hans Robert (ed.) (1994). *Slavistische Linguistik 1993.* Munich: Otto Sagner.

Meillet, Antoine (1914). Le problème de la parenté des langues. *Scientia* 15/35.

Meisel, J. M. (ed.) (1977). *Langues en contact.* Tübingen: Narr.

Mélanges de linguistique et de philologie offerts à Jacq. van Ginneken à l'occasion du soixantième anniversaire de sa naissance. (1937) Paris: Librairie C. Klincksieck.

Messner, Dieter (ed.) (1984). *Das Romanische in den Ostalpen.* (Veröffentlichungen der Kommision für Linguistik und Kommunikationsforschung, 15) Vienna: Verlag der Österreichischen Akademie der Wissenschaften.

Mian-Lian, Ho & John T. Platt (1993). *Dynamics of a contact continuum: Singaporean English.* (Oxford Studies in Language Contact) Oxford: Clarendon Press.

Michelena, L. (1978). Miscelánea filológica vasca, I. *Fontes Linguae Vasconum* 10(29): 205–28.

Milroy, J. & L. Milroy (eds) (1993). *Real English: The grammar of English dialects in the British Isles.* London/New York: Longman.

Mirčev, Kiril (1963). *Istoričeska gramatika na bălgarskija ezik.* 2nd edn. Sofia: Naouka i Izkustvo.

—— (1978). *Istoričeska gramatika na bălgarskija ezik.* Sofia: Nauka i Izkustvo.

Mitchell, Bruce (1985). *Old English syntax.* Two volumes. Oxford: Oxford University Press.

Mithun, Marianne (1992). 'The substratum in grammar and discourse'. In Jahr 1992: 103–15.

Mladenov, S. (1935). Prinos kăm izučavane na bălgarskite govori v iztočna i zapadna Trakija. *Trakijski cbornik* (Sofia) 6: 66–105.

Moravcsik, Edith (1978). 'Language contact'. In Greenberg *et al.* 1978: 93–123.

Morfill, W. R. ([1885] 1971). Review of Schuchardt 1884. *The Academy, Edinburgh*, 11. IV, 1885: 261f. Reprinted in Gerhardt 1971: 266–71.

MOSER, MICHAEL (1998). *Die polnische, ukrainische und weißrussische Interferenzschicht im russischen Satzbau des 16. und 17. Jahrhunderts.* Frankfurt am Main: Peter Lang.

MUFWENE, SALIKOKO S. (1986). 'The universalist and substrate hypotheses complement one another'. In Muysken & Smith 1986*a*: 129–62.

—— (1996). 'Creolization and grammaticization: what creolistics could contribute to research on grammaticization'. In Baker & Syea 1996: 5–28.

—— (2000). 'La fonction et les formes réfléchies dans le mauricien et le haitien'. In Véronique 2000: 114–23.

—— (2001). *The ecology of language evolution.* (Cambridge Approaches to Language Contact) Cambridge: Cambridge University Press.

MÜHLHÄUSLER, PETER & ROM HARRÉ (1990). *Pronouns and people: the linguistic construction of social and personal identity.* (Language in Society, 15) Oxford: Blackwell.

MUSTANOJA, T. (1960). *A Middle English syntax.* Part I: *Parts of speech.* (Mémoires de la Société Néophilologique, 23) Helsinki.

MUYSKEN, PIETER & NORVAL SMITH (eds) (1986*a*). *Substrata versus universals in Creole genesis.* (Creole Language Library, 1) Amsterdam, Philadelphia: Benjamins.

—— (1986*b*). 'Introduction: Problems in the identification of substratum features in the creole languages'. In Muysken & Smith 1986*a*: 1–13.

MYERS-SCOTTON, CAROL (1993). *Duelling languages.* Oxford, New York: Oxford University Press.

—— (2002). *Contact linguistics: Bilingual encounters and grammatical outcomes.* Oxford: Oxford University Press.

NADKARNI, MANGESH V. (1975). 'Bilingualism and syntactic change in Konkani'. *Language* 51(3): 672–83.

NAU, NICOLE (1992/3). 'Der ostseefinnische Superlativ im arealen Kontext'. *Finnisch-Ugrische Mitteilungen* 16–17: 13–23.

NAU, NICOLE (1995). *Möglichkeiten und Mechanismen kontaktbewegten Sprachwandels unter besonderer Berücksichtigung des Finnischen.* (Edition Linguistik, 08) Munich, Newcastle: LINCOM Europa.

—— (1996). 'Ein Beitrag zur Arealtypologie der Ostseeanrainersprachen'. In Boretzky 1996: 51–67.

NELDE, PETER HANS (ed.) (1980). *Sprachkontakt und Sprachkonflikt.* (Zeitschrift für Dialektologie, Beihefte, 32) Wiesbaden: Franz Steiner.

NELDE, PETER HANS, P. STURE URELAND, & IAIN CLARKSON (eds) (1986). *Language contact in Europe: Proceedings of the Working Groups 12 and 13 at the XIIIth International Congress of Linguists, August 29–September 4, 1982, Tokyo.* Tübingen: Max Niemeyer.

NEUMANN-HOLZSCHUH, INGRID & EDGAR W. SCHNEIDER (eds) (2000). *Degrees of restructuring in creole languages.* (Creole Language Library, 22) Amsterdam, Philadelphia: Benjamins.

NEWMEYER, FREDERICK J. (1998). *Language form and language function.* Cambridge, MA: MIT Press.

NICHOLS, JOHANNA (1995). 'Europe as a linguistic area'. Typescript, University of California, Berkeley.

NITSCH, KAZIMIERZ (1960). *Wybór polskich tekstów gwarowych* [Selection of Polish Dialect Texts]. Warszawa: Pa'nstwowe Wydawnictwo Naukowe.

NOCENTINI, ALBERTO (1996). 'Tipologica e genesi dell'articolo nelle lingue europee'. *Archivo Glottologico Italiano* 81(1): 3–44.

NURSE, DEREK (1994). 'South meets north: Ilwana = Bantu + Cushitic on Kenya's Tana River'. In Bakker & Mous 1994: 213–22.

—— (2000). *Inheritance, contact, and change in two East African languages.* (Sprachkontakt in Afrika, 4) Cologne: Köppe.

Ò DOCHARTAIGH, CATHAIR (1992). 'The Irish language'. In Macaulay 1992: 11–99.

OFITSCH, MICHAELA & CHRISTIAN ZINKO (eds) (2000). *125 Jahre Indogermanistik in Graz.* Graz: Leykam.

ÖLBERG, HERRMANN M., GERNOT SCHMIDT, & HEINZ BOTHIEN (eds) (1985). *Sprachwissenschaftliche Forschungen: Festschrift für Johann Knobloch.* (Innsbrucker Beiträge zur Kulturwissenschaft, 23) Innsbruck: Amoe.

ORR, ROBERT (1989). 'A Russo-Goidelic syntactic parallel: u nego svoja izba postavlena/ Tá sé déanta agam'. *General Linguistics* 29: 1–21.

—— (1992). 'Slavo-Celtica'. *Canadian Slavonic Papers (Revue canadienne des slavistes)* 34(3): 245–68.

ÖSTMANN, JAN OLA (1981). *You know: A discourse-functional approach.* Amsterdam, Philadelphia: Benjamins.

PAGLIARI, ANTONINO & WALTER BELARDI (1963). *Linee di storia linguistica dell' Europa.* Rome: Edizioni dell'Ateneo.

PANZER, BALDUR (1984). 'Parallel internal development or interference? Post-positive article and possessive perfect in North Germanic and northern Russian'. In Ureland & Clarkson 1984: 111–32.

PAWLEY, ANDREW (1992). 'Formulaic speech'. In Bright 1992*b*: 22–5.

—— (1994). *Beyond the grammar lexicon model: The central role of speech formulas in linguistic competence.* Paper presented at the International Symposium on Phraseology, University of Leeds, 18–20 April.

PETRUCCI, PETER R. (1993). 'The areal distribution of a Slavic language shift feature'. *Berkeley Linguistics Society* 9: 291–9.

PFAFF, MEIKE (2004). *A comparative case study in contact-induced change: Irish English relativization versus Scottish English relativization.* Unpublished MA Thesis, University of Düsseldorf.

PIETSCH, LUKAS (2004*a*). 'Re-inventing the "Perfect" wheel: grammaticalization and the Irish English medial-object perfects'. *Arbeiten zur Mehrsprachigkeit,* University of Hamburg.

—— (2004*b*). 'Nominative subjects in nonfinite clause constructions in Irish English'. *Arbeiten zur Mehrsprachigkeit,* University of Hamburg.

—— (2004*c*). 'Argument omission in Irish English'. *Arbeiten zur Mehrsprachigkeit,* University of Hamburg.

PLAG, INGO (1992). 'From speech act verb to conjunction: the grammaticalization of *taki* in Sranan'. *Journal of Pidgin and Creole Languages* 7(1): 55–73.

—— (1993). *Sentential complementation in Sranan: On the formation of an English-based creole language.* Tübingen: Niemeyer.

—— (Forthcoming) 'On the role of grammaticalization in creolization'. In Gilbert forthcoming.

PLARK, FRANS (ed.) (1979) *Ergativity: Towards a theory of grammatical relations.* London: Academic Press.

—— (2003). *Noun phrase structure in the languages of Europe.* (Empirical Approaches to Language Typology, 20–7) Berlin, New York: Mouton de Gruyter.

PLATT, JOHN T. (1975). 'The Singapore English speech continuum and its basilect "Singlish" as a "creoloid"'. *Anthropological Linguistics* 17(7): 363–74.

POLINSKY, MARIA (1995). 'Cross-linguistic parallels in language loss'. *Southwest Journal of Linguistics* 14(1/2): 87–123.

POPLACK, SHANA (1981). 'Syntactic structure and the social function of codeswitching'. In Durán 1981: 169–84.

POPLACK, SHANA & SALI TAGLIAMONTE (1996). 'Nothing in context: variation, grammaticization and past time marking in Nigerian Pidgin English'. In Baker & Syea 1996: 71–94.

PRESS, IAN (1986). *A grammar of Modern Breton.* (Mouton Grammar Library, 2) Berlin, New York, Amsterdam: Mouton de Gruyter.

PÜTZ, MARTIN (ed.) (1994). *Language contact and language conflict.* Amsterdam, Philadelphia: Benjamins.

PUTZU, IGNAZIO (2002). 'Total/universal quantifiers and definite articles in the Mediterranean languages: a typological, diachronic, and areal point of view'. In Ramat & Stolz 2002: 247–57.

PUTZU, IGNAZIO & PAOLO RAMAT (2001). 'Articles and quantifiers in the Mediterranean languages: a typological-diachronic analysis'. In Bisang 2001*a*: 99–132.

RAMAT, PAOLO (1990). 'Area influence versus typological drift in Western Europe: the case of negation'. In Bechert *et al.* 1990: 25–46.

—— (1998). 'Typological comparison and linguistic areas: some introductory remarks'. *Language Sciences* 20(3): 227–40.

RAMAT, PAOLO & GIULIANO BERNINI (1990). 'Area influence versus typological drift in western Europe: the case of negation'. In Bechert *et al.* 1990: 25–46.

RAMAT, PAOLO & THOMAS STOLZ (eds) (2002). *Mediterranean languages: Papers from the MEDITYP workshop, Tirrenia, June 2000.* (Diversitas Linguarum, 1) Bochum: N. Brockmeyer.

RAYFIELD, JOAN RACHEL (1970). *The language of a bilingual community.* The Hague: Mouton.

RAZ, SHLOMO (1989). 'Areal features as a further criterion in elucidating the term "Ethiopian Semitic"'. *African Languages and Cultures* 2(1): 93–108.

REED, CARROLL E. (1947). 'The question of aspect in Pennsylvania German'. *Germanic Review* 20: 5–12.

REHDER, PETER (ed.) (1998). *Einführung in die Slavischen Sprachen.* Darmstadt: Wissenschaftliche Buchgesellschaft.

REICHENKRON, G. (1958). 'Der lokativische Zähltypus für die Reihe 11 bis 19: "eins auf zehn"'. *Südost-Forschungen* 17(1): 152–74.

REITER, NORBERT (ed.) (1999). *Eurolinguistik: ein Schritt in die Zukunft.* Wiesbaden: Harrassowitz.

REUTHER, TILMANN (ed.) (1992). *Slavistische Linguistik 1991.* Munich: Otto Sagner.

RIEHL, CLAUDIA MARIA (1996). 'Deutsch-romanische Sprachkontakte: Gemeinsamkeiten der Kontaktphänomene am Beispiel des Deutschen'. In Boretzky 1996: 189–206.

—— (2001). *Schreiben, Text und Mehrsprachigkeit: Zur Textproduktion in mehrsprachigen Gesellschaften am Beispiel der deutschsprachigen Minderheiten in Südtirol und Ostbelgien.* (Tertiärsprachen. Drei-und Mehrsprachigkeit, 4) Tübingen: Stauffenberg.

ROMAINE, SUZANNE (1982). *Socio-historical linguistics: its status and methodology.* Cambridge: Cambridge University Press.

—— (1984). 'Towards a typology of relative-clause formation strategies in Germanic'. In Fišiak 1984: 437–70.

—— (1988). *Pidgin and creole languages.* London, New York: Longman.

—— (1989). *Bilingualism.* Oxford: Blackwell.

—— (1995). 'The grammaticalization of irrealis in Tok Pisin'. In Bybee & Fleischman 1995: 1–39.

—— (1999). 'The grammaticalization of the proximative in Tok Pisin'. *Language* 75(2): 322–46.

ROSENBACH, ANETTE (2002). *Genitive variation in English.* Berlin: Mouton de Gruyter.

ROSENTHAL, JANE M. (1972). 'On the relative clauses of Classical Nahuatl'. (The Chicago Which Hunt, Papers from the Relative Clause Festival) *Chicago Linguistic Society* 1972: 246–55.

ROSS, MALCOLM D. (1996). 'Contact-induced change and the comparative method: cases from Papua New Guinea'. In Durie & Ross 1996: 180–217.

—— (1997). 'Social networks and kinds of speech-community event'. In Blench & Spriggs 1997: 209–61.

—— (2001). 'Contact-induced change in Oceanic languages in North-West Melanesia'. In Aikhenvald & Dixon 2001: 134–66.

—— (forthcoming) 'Metatypy'. *The encyclopedia of language and linguistics.* 2nd edn. Oxford: Elsevier.

ROT, SÁNDOR (1991). *Language contact.* (Bamberger Beiträge zur Englischen Sprachwissenschaft, 29) Frankfurt, Berne, New York, Paris: Peter Lang.

RUGE, HANS (1986). *Grammatik des Neugriechischen: Lautlehre, Formenlehre, Syntax.* Cologne: Romiosini.

RUSAKOV, ALEKSANDR YU (2001). 'The North Russian Romani dialect: Interference and code switching'. In Dahl & Koptjevskaja-Tamm 2001*a*: 313–37.

ŠAFRANOV, S. (1852). *O vidax russkix glagolov v sintaksičeskom otnošenii.* Moscow.

SALMONS, JOE (1990). 'Bilingual discourse marking: code-switching, borrowing and convergence in some German-American dialects'. *Linguistics* 28: 453–80.

SANDFELD, KR. (1930). *Linguistique balkanique: problèmes et résultats.* (Collection Linguistique, 31) Paris: Champion.

SANKOFF, GILLIAN (1979). 'The genesis of a language'. In Hill 1979: 23–47.

SANKOFF, GILLIAN & PENELOPE BROWN (1976). 'The origins of syntax in discourse'. *Language* 52: 631–66.

SANKOFF, GILLIAN & SUZANNE LABERGE (1973). 'On the acquisition of native speakers by a language'. *Kivung* 6: 32–47.

SAPIR, EDWARD (1921). *Language: An introduction to the study of speech.* New York: Harcourt Brace Jovanovich.

SARHIMAA, A. (1991). 'Karelian Sprachbund? Theoretical basis of the study of Russian/Baltic-Finnic contacts'. *Finnisch-Ugrische Forschungen* 50: 209–19.

SASSE, HANS-JÜRGEN (1985). 'Sprachkontakt und Sprachwandel: Die Gräzisierung der albanischen Mundarten Griechenlands'. *Papiere zur Linguistik* 32: 37–95.

SASSE, HANS-JÜRGEN (1992). 'Zum Ausdruck von Referentialität und Nichtreferentialität im Arvanitischen'. In Birken-Silverman & Rössler 1992: 179–91.

SAVIĆ, JELENA M. (1995). 'Structural convergence and language change: Evidence from Serbian/English code-switching'. *Language in Society* 24(4): 475–92.

SAXENA, ANJU (1988*a*). 'On syntactic convergence: the case of the verb "say" in Tibeto-Burman'. *Berkeley Linguistics Society* 15: 375–88.

—— (1988*b*). 'On the grammaticalization of the verb "say": a typological and diachronic study'. In Delancey & Tomlin 1988.

SCHAFROTH, ELMAR (1993). *Zur Entstehung und vergleichenden Typologie der Relativpronomina in den romanischen Sprachen. Mit besonderer Berücksichtigung des Substandards.* Tübingen: Max Niemeyer Verlag.

SCHALLER, HELMUT WILHELM (1975). *Die Balkansprachen: Eine Einführung in die Balkanphilologie.* Heidelberg: Carl Winter.

SCHIFFRIN, DEBORAH (1987). *Discourse markers.* Cambridge: Cambridge University Press.

SCHMID, MONIKA S., JENNIFER R. AUSTIN, & DIETER STEIN (eds) (1998). *Historical Linguistics 1997*: Selected papers from the 13th International Conference on Historical Linguistics, Düsseldorf, 10–17 August 1997. (Amsterdam Studies in the Theory and History of Linguistic Science, 164) Amsterdam, Philadelphia: Benjamins.

SCHMITT, ELENA (2000). 'Overt and covert codeswitching in immigrant children from Russia'. *International Journal of Bilingualism* 4: 9–28.

—— (2001). 'Beneath the surface: signs of language attrition in immigrant children from Russia'. Ph.D. dissertation, Columbia, SC: University of South Carolina.

SCHOURUP, LAWRENCE (1985). *Common discourse particles in English conversation.* New York: Garland.

SCHROEDER, CHRISTOPH (to appear). 'Articles and article systems in some areas of Europe'. In Bernini forthcoming.

SCHUCHARDT, HUGO (1884). *Slawo-deutsches und Slawo-italienisches.* Graz: Leuschner und Lubensky.

SCHWARTZ, ARTHUR (1971). 'General aspects of relative clause formation'. *Working Paper on Language Universals*, No 6, Stanford University.

SEBEOK, T. (ed.) (1973). *Current trends in linguistics.* Volume 10. The Hague: Mouton.

SELIGER, HERBERT W. & ROBERT M. VAGO (eds.) (1991). *First language attrition.* Cambridge: Cambridge University Press.

SHANNON, Thomas F. & Johan P. SNAPPER (eds.) (2000). *The Berkeley conference on Dutch linguistics 1997: the Dutch language at the Millennium.* Lanham, MD: University Press of America.

SHERZER, J. (1973). 'Areal linguistics in North America'. In Sebeok 1973: 749–95.

SHEVELOV, GEORGE (1991). *In and around Kiev.* Heidelberg: Carl Winter Universitätsverlag.

SHOPEN, TIMOTHY (ed.) (1985). *Complex constructions.* (Language typology and syntactic description, 2) Cambridge: Cambridge University Press.

SIEMUND, PETER (2004*a*). 'Independent developments in the genesis of Irish English'. Typescript, University of Hamburg.

—— (2004*b*). 'Substrate, superstrate and universals: perfect constructions in Irish English'. Typescript, University of Hamburg.

SIEWIERSKA, ANNA (ed.) (1998). *Constituent order in the languages of Europe.* Berlin: Mouton de Gruyter.

SILVA-CORVALÁN, CARMEN (1994). *Language contact and change: Spanish in Los Angeles.* (Oxford Studies in Language Contact) Oxford: Clarendon Press.

—— (ed.) (1995). *Spanish in four continents: studies in language contact and bilingualism.* (Georgetown Studies in Romance Linguistics) Washington, DC: Georgetown University Press.

SILVERSTEIN, MICHAEL (1974). 'Dialectal developments in Chinookan tense–aspect systems: an areal-historical analysis'. *International Journal of American Linguistics*, Memoir 29.

SIMON, HORST J. (1997). Die Diachronie der deutschen Anredepronomina aus Sicht der Universalienforschung. *Sprachtypologie und Universalienforschung* (STUF, Berlin) 50(3): 267–81.

SIMON-VANDENBERGEN, ANNE-MARIE, KRISTIN DAVIDSE, & DIRK NOEL (eds) (1997). *Reconnecting language. Morphology and syntax in functional perspectives.* Amsterdam & Philadelphia: John Benjamins.

SMITH, NORVAL S. H., IAN E. ROBERTSON, & KAY WILLIAMSON (1987). 'The Ijo element in Berbice Dutch'. *Language in Society* 16: 49–90.

SOLTA, GEORG RENATUS (1980). *Einführung in die Balkanlinguistik mit besonderer Berücksichtigung des Substrats und des Balkanlateinischen.* Darmstadt: Wissenschaftliche Buchgesellschaft.

SOPER, JOHN DAVID (1987). *Loan syntax in Turkic and Iranian: The verb systems of Tajik, Usbek, and Qashqay.* Ann Arbor, MI: UMI Dissertation Services.

—— (1996). *Loan syntax in Turkic and Iranian.* Bloomington: Eurolingua.

SPIER, LESLIE (ed.) (1941). *Language, culture, and personality: Essays in memory of Edward Sapir.* Menasha, WI: Sapir Memorial Publication Fund.

Squartini, Mario & Pier Marco Bertinetto (2000). 'The simple and compound past in Romance'. In Dahl 2000*a*: 403–39.

Stamenov, Christo (1985). 'Za upotrebata na "edin" kato pokazatel za neopredelenost v bălgarskija ezik (v sravnenie s anglijski)'. *Ezik i Literatura* 3: 33–44.

—— (1987). *Pokazateljat za neopredelenost "edin" i predikativnata imenna fraza. Proceedings of the Second International Congress on Bulgarian Studies.* Vol. 3. *Contemporary Bulgarian Language.* Sofia: Sofia University Press.

Stassen, Leon (1985). *Comparison and universal grammar.* Oxford, New York: Blackwell.

—— (2000). 'AND-languages and WITH-languages'. *Typological Linguistics* 4(1): 1–54.

Steinkrüger, Patrick Oliver (1995). 'Grammatikalisierungen von Auxiliaren und Copulae im Katalanischen der Decadència'. *Zeitschrift für Katalanistik* 8: 35–62.

Stilo, Donald (1985). 'Ambipositions as an areal response: the case study of the Iranian zone'. In Bashir *et al.* 1985: 308–34.

—— (2003). 'Iranian as buffer zone between the universal typologies of Turkic and Semitic'. In Csató *et al.* 2003: 35–63.

Stimm, Helmut (1984). 'Eigenheiten der Kausativkonstruktionen im Surselvischen'. In Messner 1984: 329–50.

Stolz, Christel & Thomas Stolz (1996). 'Funktionswortentlehnung in Mesoamerika: Spanisch–amerindischer Sprachkontakt (Hispanoindiana II). *Sprachtypologie und Universalienforschung* 49(1): 86–123.

—— (2001). 'Mesoamerica as a linguistic area'. In Haspelmath *et al.* 2001: 1542–53.

Stolz, Thomas (1991). *Sprachbund im Baltikum? Estnisch und Lettisch im Zentrum einer sprachlichen Konvergenzlandschaft.* (Bochum-Essener Beiträge zur Sprachwandelforschung, 13) Bochum: N. Brockmeyer.

—— (1996*a*). 'Komitativ-Typologie: MIT-und OHNE-Relationen im crosslinguistischen Überblick'. *Papiere zur Linguistik* 51(1): 3–65.

—— (1996*b*). 'Some instruments are really good companions—some are not: on syncretism and the typology of instrumentals and comitatives'. *Theoretical Linguistics* 23(1/2): 113–200.

—— (1998). 'UND, MIT und/oder UND/MIT? Koordination, Instrumental und Komitativ—kymrisch, typologisch und universell'. *STUF* (Sprachtypologie und Universalienforschung, Berlin) 51(2): 107–30.

Stolz, Thomas (2001). 'On Circum-Baltic instrumentals and comitatives'. In Dahl & Koptjevskaja-Tamm 2001*b*: 591–612.

—— (2002*a*). 'No *Sprachbund* beyond this line! On the age-old discussion of how to define a linguistic area'. In Ramat & Stolz 2002: 259–81.

—— (2002*b*). 'Crosscurrents—the Mediterranean region as a potential linguistic area'. In Masala 2002: 52–73.

—— (2002*c*). 'Mediterraneanism vs. universal process: Word iteration in an areal perspective'. Typescript, University of Bremen.

—— (2003). 'Not quite the right mixture: Chamorro and Malti as candidates for the status of mixed language'. In Matras & Bakker 2003: 271–315.

—— (2003–4). 'A new Mediterraneanism: word iteration in an areal perspective, a pilot study'. *Mediterranean Language Review* 15: 1–47.

—— (2004). 'Sardinian in areal perspective: morphonological interaction of definite articles and adjacent words'. Typescript, University of Bremen.

—— (2006) 'Europe (as a linguistic area)'. *The encyclopedia of language and linguistics*. 2nd edn. Oxford: Elsevier.

Stolz, Thomas, Cornelia Stroh, & Aina Urdze (2006). *On comitatives and related categories: a typological study with special focus on the languages of Europe*. Typescript, University of Bremen.

Sullivan, James P. (1980). 'The validity of literary dialect: Evidence from the theatrical portrayal of Hiberno-English forms'. *Language in Society* 9: 195–219.

Suttles, W. (ed.) (1990). *Northwest Coast*. (Handbook of North American Indians, 7) Washington, DC: Smithsonian Institute.

Svane, Gunar Olaf (1958). *Grammatik der slowenischen Schriftsprache*. Copenhagen: Rosenkilde & Bagger.

Švedova, N. Ju (1964). 'O nekotoryx aktivnyx processax v sovremennom russkom sintaksise'. *Voprosy Jazykoznanija* 13(2): 3–18.

Swan, Torik & Olaf Jansen Westvik (eds) (1996). *Modality in Germanic Languages*. Berlin: Mouton de Gruyter.

Šwela, B. (1952). *Grammatik der niedersorbischen Sprache*. Zweite Auflage. Bautzen: Publisher.

Taeldeman, Johan (1978). Französisch-flämische Sprachinterferenz in Flandern. In Ureland 1978*a*: 43–66.

Tagliamonte, Sali A. (2000). 'The story of *kom* in Nigerian Pidgin English'. In McWhorter 2000: 253–82.

Tchekhov, Claude (1978). *Aux fondements de la syntaxe: l'ergatif*. Paris: Presses Universitaires de France.

Tenser, Anton (2004). *Grammatical description of a Lithuanian Romani Dialect*. Ph.D. Thesis, University of Manchester.

Ternes, Elmar (1978). Zur inneren Gliederung der keltischen Sprachen. *Zeitschrift für vergleichende Sprachforschung* 92: 195–217.

—— (1979). 'Die Sonderstellung des Bretonischen innerhalb der keltischen Sprachen'. *Zeitschrift für Celtische Philologie* 37: 214–28.

—— (1988). 'Zur Typologie der Vergangenheitstempora in den Sprachen Europas (synthetische vs. analytische Bildungsweise)'. *Zeitschrift für Dialektologie und Linguistik* 55: 332–41.

—— (1992). 'The Breton language'. In Macaulay 1992: 371–452.

—— (1998). 'Keltisch und Romanisch'. In Holtus *et al.* 1998: 266–91.

—— (1999). 'Ist Bretonisch SVO oder VSO? Typologische Überlegungen zu einer umstrittenen Frage'. In Zimmer *et al.* 1999: 236–53.

THIEROFF, ROLF (2000). 'On the areal distribution of tense–aspect categories in Europe'. In Dahl 2000*a*: 265–305.

—— (2001). 'The German tense–aspect–mood system from a typological perspective'. In Watts *et al.* 2001: 211–30.

THOMAS, ALAN R. (1992). 'The Welsh language'. In Macaulay 1992: 251–345.

THOMAS, GEORGE (1975). 'The calque—an international trend in the lexical development of the literary languages of eighteenth-century Europe'. *Germano-Slavica* 6: 21–41.

THOMASON, SARAH GREY (ed.) (2000). *Contact languages: an introduction.* Washington, DC: University Press.

—— (2001*a*). 'Contact-induced typological change'. In Haspelmath *et al.* 2001: 1640–8.

—— (2001*b*). *Language contact.* Edinburgh: Edinburgh University Press.

—— (2003). 'Contact as a source of language change'. In Joseph & Janda 2003: 686–712.

THOMASON, SARAH GREY & TERRENCE KAUFMANN (1988). *Language contact, creolization, and genetic linguistics.* Berkeley, Los Angeles, London: University of California Press.

THOMPSON, L. C. & M. D. KINKADE (1990). 'Languages'. In Suttles 1990: 30–51.

THOMPSON, SANDRA A. & ROBERT E. LONGACRE (1985). 'Adveribal clauses'. In Shopen 1985: 171–234.

THURSTON, W. R. (1982). *A comparative study in Anêm and Lusi.* Pacific Linguistics B-83. Canberra: The Australian National University.

—— (1987). *Processes of change in the languages of north-western New Britain.* Pacific Linguistics B-99. Canberra: The Australian National University.

TIMBERLAKE, ALAN (1974). *The nominative object in Slavic, Baltic, and West Finnic.* (Slavistische Beiträge, 82.) Munich: Otto Sagner.

—— (1976). 'Subject properties in the North Russian passive'. In Li 1976: 547–71.

TOMMOLA, HANNU (2000). 'On the perfect in North Slavic'. In Dahl 2000*a*: 441–78.

TOWEETT, TAITTA (1979). *Kalenjin linguistics.* Nairobi: Kenya Literature Bureau.

TOSCO, MAURO (2000). 'Is there an "Ethiopian language area"?' *Anthropological Linguistics* 42(3): 329–65.

TRASK, ROBERT L. (1998). 'The typological position of Basque: then and now'. *Language Sciences* 20(3): 313–24.

TRAUGOTT, ELIZABETH CLOSS (1972). *A history of English syntax. A transformational approach to the history of English sentence structure.* London/New York/Sydney: Holt, Rinehart and Winston Inc.

TRAUGOTT, ELIZABETH CLOSS (1993). 'The conflict *promises/threatens* to escalate into war'. *Berkeley Linguistics Society* 19: 348–58.

—— (1997). 'Subjectification and the development of epistemic meaning: the case of *promise* and *threaten*'. In Swan & Jansen Westvik 1996: 185–210.

TRAUGOTT, ELIZABETH C. & BERND HEINE (eds) (1991*a*). *Approaches to grammaticalization.* Volume 1. Amsterdam, Philadelphia: Benjamins.

—— (eds) (1991*b*). *Approaches to grammaticalization.* Volume 2. Amsterdam, Philadelphia: Benjamins.

Trésor de la langue française (informatisé). http://atilf.inalf.fr/tlfv3.htm

TRUBETZKOY, NIKOLAI SERGEJEWITSCH (1923). 'Vavilonskaja basnja i smesenie jazykov'. [The tower of Bable and the confusion of languages.] *Evrazijskij vremennik* [The Eurasian compatriot] 3: 107–24.

TRUBINSKIJ, V. I. (1979). 'O russkom razgovornom posessivnom prfekte'. In Trubinskij, V. I. (ed.), *Severnorusskie govory.* Leningrad.

TRUDGILL, PETER (1983). *On dialect. Social and geographical perspectives.* Oxford: Basil Blackwell.

—— (1986). *Dialects in contact.* Cambridge: Cambridge University Press.

TRUDGILL, PETER & J. K. CHAMBERS (eds.) (1991). *Dialects of English: Studies in grammatical variation.* Rev edn. New York: Longman.

TSITSIPIS, LUKAS D. (1998). *A linguistic anthropology of praxis and language shift: Arvanítika (Albanian) and Greek in contact.* (Oxford Studies in Language Contact) Oxford: Clarendon Press.

TUCKER, ARCHIBALD N. (1994). *A grammar of Kenya Luo (Dholuo), edited by C. A. Creider.* Two volumes. (Nilo-Saharan, 8.1, 8.2.) Cologne: Köppe.

TUFAN, SIRIN (forthcoming). 'A grammar of Macedonian Turkish'. Ph.D thesis, Manchester, University of Manchester.

URELAND, PER STURE (ed.) (1978*a*). *Sprachkontakte im Nordseegebiet: Akten des 1. Symposions über Sprachkontakt in Europa, Mannheim 1977.* (Linguistische Arbeiten, 66) Tübingen: Max Niemeyer.

—— (1978*b*). Die Bedeutung des Sprachkontakts in der Entwicklung der Nordseesprachen. In Ureland 1978*a*: 83–128.

—— (ed.) (1985*a*). *Entstehung von Sprachen und Völkern: glotto-und ethnogenetische Aspekte europäischer Sprachen.* (Akten des 6. Symposions über Sprachkontakte in Europa, Mannheim 1984) Tübingen: Niemeyer.

—— (1985*b*). 'Sprachkontakt und Glottogenese in Europa'. In Ureland 1985*a*: 7–43.

—— (2004). 'Eurolinguistik and Europäistik als Fächer an den Universitäten'. In Hinrichs 2004: 1–15.

URELAND, PER STURE & IAIN CLARKSON (eds) (1984). *Scandinavian language contacts.* Cambridge: Cambridge University Press.

VAN DER AUWERA, JOHAN (1998*a*). 'Revisiting the Balkan and Meso-American linguistic areas'. *Language Sciences* 20(3): 259–70.

—— (ed.) (1998*b*). *Adverbial constructions in the languages of Europe.* (Empirical Approaches to Language Typology, EUROTYP, 20–3) Berlin: Mouton de Gruyter.

—— (1998*c*). 'Conclusion'. In van der Auwera 1998*b*: 813–36.

VAN HAMEL, A. G. (1912). 'On Anglo-Irish syntax'. *Englische Studien* 45: 272–92.

VAN KEMENADE, ANS & NIGEL VINCENT (eds) (1997). *Parameters of morphosyntactic change.* Cambridge: Cambridge University Press.

VAN MARLE, JAAP (ed.) (1993). *Historical linguistics 1991.* Amsterdam, Philadelphia: Benjamins.

Van Ness, Silke (1992). 'The New Order Amish in Ohio: A grammatical change in progress'. In Burridge & Enninger 1992: 182–98.

Van Pottelberge, Jeroen (2005). *Linguistics online* 8, 1/01 (ISSN 1615–3014).

Vasilev, Christo (1968). 'Der romanische Perfekttyp im Slavischen'. In Koschmieder & Braun 1968: 215–30.

Večerka, Radoslav (1993). 'Altkirchenslavische (Altbulgarische) Syntax II'. Die innere Satzstruktur. U.W. Weiher-Freiburg I. Br.

Veenker, Wolfgang (1967). *Die Frage des finnougrischen Substrats in der russischen Sprache.* (Uralic and Altaic Series, 82.) Bloomington, The Hague: Mouton.

Vendryes, J. (1937). 'Sur l'emploi de l'auxiliaire "avoir" pour marquer le passé'. In *Mélanges* 1937: 85–92.

Vennemann, Theo (1994). 'Linguistic reconstruction in the context of European prehistory'. *Transactions of the Philological Society* 92: 213–82.

Verhagen, Arie (2000). '"The girl that promised to become something": an exploration into diachronic subjectification in Dutch'. In Shannon & Snapper 2000: 197–208.

Véronique, Daniel (ed.) (2000). *Syntaxe des langues créoles.* (Langages, 138.) Paris: Larousse.

Veselinović, Elvira (2002). *Suppletion im irischen Verbum.* Ph.D. dissertation, University of Cologne, in preparation.

Vincenot, Claude (1975). *Essai de grammaire slovène.* Ljubljana: Mladinska knjiga.

Vincent, Nigel (1982). The development of the auxiliaries *habere* and *esse* in Romance. In Vincent & Harris 1982: 71–96.

—— (1997). 'The emergence of the D-system in Romance'. In van Kemenade & Vincent 1997: 149–69.

Vincent, Nigel & Martin Harris (eds) (1982). *Studies in the Romance verbs.* London: Croom Helm.

Wagner, Heinrich (1959). *Das Verbum in den Sprachen der britischen Inseln: ein Beitrag zur geographischen Typologie des Verbums.* Tübingen: Niemeyer.

—— (1964). Nordeuropäische Lautgeographie. *Zeitschrift für Celtische Philologie* 29: 225–98.

—— (1970). *The origin of the Celts in the light of linguistic geography.* (Transactions of the Philological Society, 1969) Hertford: Austin.

Watts, Sheila, Jonathan West & Hans-Joachim Solms (eds) (2001). *Zur Verbalmorphologie germanischer Sprachen.* (Linguistische Arbeiten, 446). Tübingen: Max Niemeyer.

Wehr, Barbara (1984). *Diskurs-Strategien im Romanischen: ein Beitrag zur romanischen Syntax.* Tübingen: Narr.

Wehr, Barbara (1998). 'Typologische Parallelen in der französischen und irischen Syntax. In Boeder *et al.* 1998: 335–54.

Weinreich, Uriel ([1953] 1964). *Languages in contact.* London, The Hague, Paris: Mouton.

—— (1958). 'On the compatibility of genetic relationship and convergent development'. *Word* 14: 373–9.

WEISS, DANIEL (2004). 'The rise of an indefinite article: the case of Macedonian *eden*'. In Bisang *et al.* 2004.

WESTERMANN, DIEDRICH (1930). *A study of the Ewe language.* London: Oxford University Press.

WHORF, BENJAMIN LEE (1941). 'The relation of habitual thought and behavior to language'. In Spier 1941: 75–93.

—— (1956). *Language, thought, and reality: Selected writings of Benjamin Lee Whorf.* Edited by John B. Carroll. Cambridge, MA: MIT Press.

WHITNEY, WILLIAM DWIGHT (1881). 'On mixture in language'. *Transactions of the American Philosophical Association* 12: 1–26.

WINTSCHALEK, WALTER (1993). *Die Areallinguistik am Beispiel syntaktischer Übereinstimmungen im Wolga-Kama-Areal.* (Studia Uralica 7) Wiesbaden: Harrassowitz.

WISCHER, ILSE & GABRIELE DIEWALD (eds) (2002). *New reflections on grammaticalization.* (Typological Studies in Language, 49) Amsterdam, Philadelphia: Benjamins.

YASUGI, YOSHIHO (1995). *Native Middle American languages: An areal-typological perspective.* (Senri Ethological Studies, 39.) Osaka: National Museum of Ethnology.

ZALIZNJAK, A. A. (1995). *Drevnenovgorodskij dialekt.* Moscow.

ZIEGELER, DEBRA (2000). *Hypothetical modality: Grammaticalization in an L2 dialect.* (Studies in Language Companion Series, 51) Amsterdam, Philadelphia: Benjamins.

ZIMA, PETR (ed.) (1995). *Time in languages.* Prague: Institute for Advanced Studies at Charles University and the Academy of Sciences of the Czech Republic.

ZIMMER, STEFAN, ROLF KÖDDERITZSCH, & ARNDT WIGGER (eds) (1999). *Akten des Zweiten Deutschen Keltologen-Symposiums.* Tübingen: Niemeyer.

Glossary

ABLATIVE (CASE): a grammatical CASE expressing instrument, cause, location, source, and time

ABSOLUTIVE (CASE): in absolutive-ergative languages the typically unmarked CASE of NOUNS which would be the subject of INTRANSITIVE VERBS or the OBJECT of TRANSITIVE VERBS in NOMINATIVE-ACCUSATIVE languages such as English

ACCESSIBILITY HIERARCHY: a term introduced by Keenan & Comrie (1977) to describe the universal dependencies of the relativizability of NOUN PHRASE positions. The relative accessibility to relativization of these positions in main clauses is expressed in the following Accessibility Hierarchy: *subject* > DIRECT OBJECT > INDIRECT OBJECT > *oblique* > GENITIVE > *object of comparison*, with '>' meaning 'is more accessible than'

ACCOMMODATION, GRAMMATICAL: in non-monolingual communities without a dominant language the CONVERGENCE process in which the languages' grammars become more similar than formerly

ACCOMPANIMENT: the semantic role of an entity that participates in close association with an AGENT, causer, or that is affected in an event, e.g. *I ate lunch with my friend*

ACCUSATIVE (CASE): in NOMINATIVE-accusative languages, the grammatical CASE that marks DIRECT OBJECTS

ACTION SCHEMA: **[X takes Y]**; a source schema according to which the notion of PREDICATIVE POSSESSION is conceptually derived. It involves an AGENT, a PATIENT and some action or activity, typically denoted by verbs like Engl. *take, seize, grab, catch,* etc.

ADJECTIVE: a NOUN MODIFIER, usually specifying the NOUN's meaning. Adjectives are used in predicative (*the sky is blue*) or attributive (*it is a cold day*) manner

ADJUNCT: a type of adverbial that expresses the circumstances of the action denoted by the verb like time (*I saw her yesterday*), manner (*he spoke calmly*), place (*it is near Boston*), frequency (*she would often eat in the car*), reason (*I get the back seat, because I want to sleep*), and degree (*you are very smart*)

ADPOSITION: a function word which in prepositional/postpositional clauses represents the head that indicates a relationship between two entities. Two types of adpositions are to be differentiated: PREPOSITIONS are adpositions preceding the NOUN PHRASE complement, POSTPOSITIONS are those which follow it, cf. Engl. *to the school* vs. japan. *gakkō e*

ADVERB: 1) a verb MODIFIER for such categories as time, manner, place, or direction. 2) a MODIFIER for verbs, ADJECTIVES, adverbs, phrases, clauses, or sentences. In this case, the possible type of modification depends on the class of the constituent being modified. Typical Engl. PLACE ADVERBS are e.g. *here, inside, there,* etc., QUANTIFYING ADVERBS are e.g. *rather, quite, very,* etc.

ADVERBIAL CLAUSE: a clause that functions to modify another clause, whereby it typically exhibits distinct syntactical features or verb morphology, e.g. Engl. *he ate dinner although he was not hungry*

AGENT: the case of the PARTICIPANT instigating or performing the action denoted by the main verb

AGGLUTINATION: type of word formation whereby distinct morphemes, all of which bear a single component of meaning, are arranged in a linear sequence

AGREEMENT: the congruence between elements regarding their morphosyntactic categories as a means to express grammatical relationships within a sentence

AGREEMENT MARKER: a free or bound morpheme that indicates congruence between two or more elements regarding their morphosyntactic categories

ALEMANNIC: a western Upper German DIALECT union, which borders at its western and southern boundaries on French, Italian, and Raeto-Romance and at its northern and eastern boundaries on Rhine-Franconian, Eastern Franconian, and Bavarian

ANALYTIC(ITY): in analytic languages one word is typically represented by a single isolated morpheme whereby all the words are invariable and syntactic relationships are primarily expressed by means of WORD ORDER

ANAPHORIC DEMONSTRATIVE: a demonstrative, i.e. deictic element, deriving its interpretation from the ANTECEDENT

ANAPHORIC FUNCTION: the referential function of a linguistic unit deriving its interpretation from some previously expressed unit or meaning

ANIMACY: nominal subcategory which refers to 'living' beings, i.e. human beings and animals

ANTECEDENT: a word, phrase, or clause referred to endophorically by another expression, typically following it

ANTERIOR: a tense referring to an action or event which took place prior to a certain point of reference

ANTICAUSATIVE: a marker that typically reduces the valence of a verb by one PARTICIPANT, which as the rule is the AGENT

AORIST: *also* **perfective**; a past tense form of the verb expressing distinctive aspectual notions, especially the lack of completion, duration, or repetition

APPOSITIONAL THEORY: a theory saying that the postposed definite ARTICLE could have arisen from the appositional function

ARAWAKAN LANGUAGES: a large language family that links a number of highly dispersed languages ranging from Belize to Paraguay with 50–120 languages assigned to the family

AREAL DIFFUSION: the spread of a linguistic form or a linguistic change across the boundaries of languages or of families

AREAL LINGUISTICS: the study of LINGUISTIC AREAS or of individual linguistic features across language boundaries

AREAL RELATIONSHIP: a factor that accounts for shared properties among languages which cannot be accounted for with reference to genetic relationship but require an account in terms of AREAL DIFFUSION

ARGUMENT: within a verb phrase a NOUN PHRASE that presents part of the proposition, e.g. Engl. *Jim watched the soccer game*

ARTICLE: a type of determiner that identifies a NOUN's definite or indefinite reference, and its new or given status

ASPECT: a grammatical category associated with verbs that express a temporal view of the event or state expressed by the verb. It refers primarily to the way grammar marks the duration or type of temporal activity denoted by the verb

ATTRIBUTIVE POSSESSION: nominal possession taking the form of GENITIVE constructions, e.g. Engl. *her car, John's nose, the money of my friend*

AUGMENTATIVE SUFFIX: *see* SUFFIX, AUGMENTATIVE

AUSTRONESIAN LANGUAGES: a vast language family, with nearly 1000 languages, extending from the western Indian Ocean to the eastern Pacific, e.g. Fijian, Javanese, Malagasy, Samoan, Tagalog, etc.

AUXILIARY: a verb which accompanies the main lexical verb of a verb phrase, and expresses grammatical distinctions not carried by the lexical verb, such as **mood**, ASPECT, VOICE, etc.

AUXILIATION: the process by which AUXILIARY verbs such as Engl. *do, may, must, will,* and *have,* develop from former lexical verbs meaning 'exist', 'possess', 'hold', etc.

BALKAN SPRACHBUND: a LINGUISTIC AREA in the Balkans, comprising ROMANCE and SLAVIC LANGUAGES, as well as Albanian and Greek, which together share a number of structural features that cannot be accounted for in terms of genetic inheritance

BASILECT: in CREOLIZATION, processes that variety of a linguistic continuum which differs most from the superstrate variety (**acrolect**)

BENEFACTIVE: a marker introducing a PARTICIPANT indicating that the action of the main verb is for the benefit or on behalf of someone else

'BE'- PERFECT: PERFECT constructions using 'be'-COPULAS as AUXILIARIES

BORROWING: the transfer of form–meaning units from one language into a second language, as a result of some kind of contact between speakers of the two

BRIDGING STAGE: Stage I in the process of CONTEXT-INDUCED REINTERPRETATION: a given linguistic form acquires, in addition to its core sense, an extra sense when occurring in a specific context (cf. Heine *et al.* 1991)

BUFFER ZONE: a geographical region which separates two other regions in which a single word has conflicting senses and within which the word is either absent or has only a superordinate sense

CALQUING: *also* LOAN TRANSLATION; the transfer of lexical or grammatical meaning from a MODEL LANGUAGE into a REPLICA LANGUAGE whereby the latter replicates a formal expression typically via translation

CASE: a grammatical category determined by the syntactic or semantic function of a NOUN or PRONOUN and used to identify the syntactic relationship between words in a sentence, through such contrasts as 'NOMINATIVE', 'ACCUSATIVE', etc.

CATAPHORIC FUNCTION: the co-referential function of one expression with another following expression. The latter provides the information necessary for the interpretation of the former

CELTIC LANGUAGES: a branch of the INDO-EUROPEAN LANGUAGE family; originally spoken in western mainland Europe. Nowadays, restricted to the British Isles (Irish Gaelic, Scottish Gaelic, Welsh, Cornish†, and Manx†) and to the northwestern outskirts of France (Breton)

CHANGE-OF-STATE VERB: type of verb indicating an INCHOATIVE or ingressive meaning: 'become', 'turn into', e.g. Engl. *break, grow, wither,* etc.

CHARLEMAGNE SPRACHBUND: according to van der Auwera (1998*c*), a minimal area consisting of French, Dutch, and German, with Italian and Polish being close to this central area. Haspelmath (1998) limits its nucleus to northern Italian DIALECTS, while (Standard) Italian and Polish are in the same areal grouping as SLAVIC LANGUAGES

CLAUSE, COORDINATING: a clause within a series of two or more independent clauses, which are typically linked by means of a coordinating conjunction (**coordinator**), a connective, or PARATAXIS, e.g. Engl. *Mary likes cats and John likes dogs*

CLAUSE, MATRIX: a clause into which a subordinate clause is embedded as a constituent, e.g. Engl. *if it rains we'll stay home*

CLAUSE, SUBORDINATE: a **dependent clause** that is embedded as a constituent into a MATRIX CLAUSE in which it functions like a NOUN, ADJECTIVE, or ADVERB, e.g. Engl. *she got sick after having eaten raw fish*

CLEFTING: a focusing device whereby a simple sentence is expressed by means of a complex sentence consisting of a main clause and SUBORDINATE CLAUSE, so as to highlight a particular constituent, e.g. Engl. *it is his accent that I like*

CLITIC: a morpheme with the syntactic characteristics of a word, which is phonologically and structurally dependent on an adjacent word, e.g. the Engl. contracted form *you're*

COGNATE: a word or morpheme which shares a common origin with another word or morpheme without BORROWING being involved

COMITATIVE (CASE): a grammatical CASE expressing ACCOMPANIMENT

COMPARATIVE OF EQUALITY: *also* EQUATIVE (CONSTRUCTION); a comparative construction expressing 'sameness of extent', e.g. Engl. *Jane is as smart as her brother*

COMPARATIVE OF INEQUALITY: a comparative construction expressing 'sameness of manner'; e.g. Engl. *she swims like a fish*

COMPAREE: in comparative constructions the item of comparison, e.g. Engl. *David is smarter than Bob,* or *David is as smart as Bob*

COMPATIBILITY, LINGUISTIC: the relative degree of structural similarity among the languages involved

COMPLEMENT CLAUSE: a clause functioning as a NOUN, e.g. Engl. *for Sally to win would be a surprise*

COMPLEMENTIZER: a marker introducing COMPLEMENT CLAUSES, e.g. Engl *I know that she will win*

COMPLEX SENTENCE: a sentence consisting of at least one **main clause** and one SUBORDINATE CLAUSE

COMPOUNDING: a word formation process, whereby two (or more) existing words are combined for the purpose of creating a new word, e.g. Engl. *boyfriend, breakup,* etc.

CONCEPTUAL TRANSFER: a universal strategy operating in GRAMMATICALIZATION processes whereby an item of concrete meaning comes to be used to express a more abstract notion

CONCLUSIVE PERFECT: *see* PERFECT, CONCLUSIVE

CONDITIONAL (CONJUNCTION): marker of conditional protasis expressing hypotheses or conditions, e.g. Engl. *if, unless*

CONTACT-INDUCED GRAMMATICALIZATION: a process of grammatical language change which is triggered by language contact and which involves mechanisms typically operating in processes of GRAMMATICALIZATION, such as EXTENSION, CONTEXT-INDUCED REINTERPRETATION, DESEMANTICIZATION, DECATEGORIALIZATION, or EROSION

CONTEXT GENERALIZATION: *see* EXTENSION

CONTEXT-INDUCED REINTERPRETATION: *see* EXTENSION

CONVENTIONALIZATION STAGE: Stage III in the process of CONTEXT-INDUCED REINTERPRETATION: a formerly additional sense of a given linguistic form, acquired in Stage I and contextually extended in Stage II, is conventionalized, i.e. the linguistic form has become 'polysemous' (cf. Heine *et al.* 1991)

CONVERB: a NON-FINITE VERB form whose central function is to mark adverbial subordination, i.e. a verbal ADVERB, e.g. Portug. *despenhou-se um avião military, morrendo o piloto* vs. Engl. *a military plane crashed, and the pilot was killed* (Haspelmath & König 1995)

CONVERGENCE: a phenomenon observable in situations of language contact—especially in the context of LINGUISTIC AREAS—whereby two or more languages come to be more similar as a result of individual contact-induced changes

COPULA: 'be'; predicate marker used in propositions of the type 'X is (a) Y', i.e. linking a subject to a NOUN PHRASE, ADJECTIVE, or other constituent which expresses the predicate

CORRELATIVE: constructions which use a pair of connecting words e.g. Engl. *either ... or, both ... and*, etc.

CREOLE (LANGUAGES): *see* CREOLIZATION

CREOLIZATION: the formation of a contact language, in situations of extreme language contact that do not involve any kind of bilingualism, either through the nativization of a prior PIDGIN, or through the abrupt or gradual development without a prior pidgin stage, whereby the CREOLE comes to serve as a first language being used in an all domains of communication. Such CREOLE LANGUAGES typically derive their lexicon from the dominant language whereas the grammar typically represents a cross-linguistic mixture

DATIVE (CASE): a grammatical CASE marking INDIRECT OBJECTS and NOUNS having the role of the recipient, the beneficiary of an action, or the POSSESSOR of an item

DE-ALLATIVE FUTURE: a grammaticalized FUTURE form that has a goal-directed motion schema 'direction toward' (**allative**) as its source concept

DECATEGORIALIZATION: a mechanism operating in processes of GRAMMATICALIZATION: the loss in morphosyntactic properties characteristic of lexical or other less grammaticalized forms

DEGREE MARKER: in comparative constructions the lexical or inflectional marker that signals degree ('more'), e.g. Engl. *more beautiful*, *faster-er*

DEIXIS: linguistic reference to the personal, temporal, or locational characteristics of the situation within which an utterance takes place by means of an expression whose interpretation is relative to the usually extra-linguistic context of the utterance, such as who is speaking, the time or place of speaking, the gestures of the speaker, or the current location in the discourse

DEIXIS, DISTAL: 'far away'; a marker in **place deixis** that indicates spatial distance, i.e. a location far from the speaker or other deictic centre

DERIVATION: a morphological process of word formation whereby the syntactic category of a lexeme may be changed, e.g. verb-to-ADJECTIVE as in Engl. *drink* → *drink-able*, or its meaning becomes modified, e.g. Engl. *healthy* → *un-healthy*.

DESEMANTICIZATION: *also* SEMANTIC BLEACHING; a mechanism operating in processes of GRAMMATICALIZATION: the loss in meaning content

DE-VOLITIVE FUTURE: a grammaticalized FUTURE form that has volitional schema [X wants Y] as its source concept

DIACHRONY: linguistic time dimension. A diachronic approach to a language is one which examines language change over some period of time

DIALECT: any regionally distinctive variety of a given language with characteristic pronunciation (**accent**) as well as characteristic lexical and/or grammatical features

DOUBLE ARTICULATION: *also* **duality of patterning;** the structural organization of human language according to two levels: a higher level consisting of meaningful units (**bound** and **free morphemes**), and a lower level consisting of meaningless phonemes that only in combination come to form morphemes

DOUBLE DETERMINATION: both a preposed and a postposed definite ARTICLE in the ADJECTIVE-NOUN PHRASE

DOUBLE MARKING: the co-existence of morphosyntactic segments expressing the same grammatical function, typically as the result of a process of contact-induced language change whereby a construction of the MODEL LANGUAGE does not come to replace a structure in the recipient language (REPLACEMENT), but is added to it. This may be a transitional phenomenon or a permanent feature

DRAVIDIAN LANGUAGES: a major language family of South Asia, including languages like Brahui (spoken in Pakistan), Kannada, Telugu (spoken in southern India) and Tamil (spoken in southern India and Sri Lanka)

DRIFT: the general trend or tendency of a language to keep changing in a certain direction over many generations

DYNAMIC TYPOLOGY: the cross-linguistic classification of grammatical categories according to salient structural properties, which at the same time reflects the evolution of these categories

DYNAMIC VERB: type of verb denoting activity and process, and which may occur in the PROGRESSIVE and IMPERATIVE verb forms, e.g. Engl. *walk*

EAST TUSCANOAN LANGUAGES: a language family consisting of fifteen languages spoken in Colombia and Brazil

EMPHATIC PARTICLE: particle expressing emphasis or contrast

ENDOPHORIC DEMONSTRATIVE: a deictic determiner referring to another expression which provides the information necessary to interpret the other, e.g. Engl. *a well-dressed man was speaking; he had a foreign accent*, or *if you need one, there's a towel in the top drawer*

EQUATIVE (CONSTRUCTION): *also* COMPARATIVE OF EQUALITY; expressing comparison of equality, e.g. Engl. *Nancy is as tall as her mother*

EQUIVALENCE (RELATION): *see* EQUIVALENCE, FORMULA OF

EQUIVALENCE, FORMULA OF: a term introduced by Keesing (1991) to describe some mechanism for equating 'similar' concepts and categories across languages which speakers tend to develop in situations of intense language contact. In this volume referred to as EQUIVALENCE RELATIONS or, in short, as EQUIVALENCE (or **isomorphism**), whereby it is referred to corresponding structures of different languages (or DIALECTS) that are conceived and/or described as being the same

EROSION: *also* PHONETIC REDUCTION; mechanism operating in processes of GRAMMATICALIZATION: the loss in phonetic substance

EUROPÄISCHER SPRACHAUSGLEICH: a term introduced by Betz (1944) denoting a continuous levelling process whereby neighbouring languages constantly adjust to one another—with the effect that over a period of more than 1,000 years the languages concerned accumulate larger amounts of structures of other languages spoken in the same area

EUROPEAN CORE AREA: a linguistic areal nucleus of Europe, though it is largely unclear which languages exactly belong to it. There is, however, agreement to the effect that if there are European languages that occupy a central position on account of their linguistic properties then they are located mostly or exclusively in the western half of the continent (*see* Section 1.2.2)

EUROPEANISM: *see* STANDARD AVERAGE EUROPEAN

EUROVERSAL: *also* **europeme;** 1) linguistic properties to be found in most or all European languages, i.e. properties that may as well be found in other languages. 2) linguistic properties that set European languages off from languages in other parts of the world, i.e. that are specific to Europe (*see* Section 1.2.3)

EVIDENTIAL: marker used by the speaker to indicate the source of the information on which a given assertion is based. The term is generally used to describe devices indicating perceptual evidence and devices indicating evidence that is obtained from someone else

EVIDENTIALITY: a type of EPISTEMIC MODALITY that connotes the speaker's estimation of the evidence for his or her proposition

EXOPHORIC DEMONSTRATIVE: a deictic determiner which directly refers to an extra-linguistic REFERENT whereby that referent does not need another expression for its interpretation

EXPERIENCER: the case of a PARTICIPANT which is affected by the action denoted by the main verb, e.g. Engl. *Sally likes ice cream* or *Robert surprised me*

EXTENSION: *also* CONTEXT GENERALIZATION, CONTEXT-INDUCED REINTERPRETATION; mechanism operating in processes of GRAMMATICALIZATION: the rise of novel grammatical meanings when linguistic expressions are extended to new contexts

FINITE VERB: a form of the verb that may be inflected according to the inflectional categories of a particular language, and which can occur by itself in a main clause

FUNCTIONALIZATION: a process in GRAMMATICALIZATION whereby a grammatical form becomes even more grammaticalized (cf. Matras 1998*b*)

FUTURE: a TENSE form which refers to a time subsequent to the moment of utterance

FUTURE PERFECT: an absolute-relative tense that refers to a time before a contextually determined temporal reference point that must be located in the future relative to the moment of utterance, e.g. Engl. *she will have returned by noon*

GAP STRATEGY: a relativization strategy without overt reference to the head noun in the modifying clause, e.g. Engl. *the car_I bought yesterday*

GENITIVE (CASE): a grammatical CASE denoting a relationship of possession whereby the REFERENT of the marked NOUN is the POSSESSOR of the referent of another noun. English has both a synthetic and ANALYTIC expression for possession (**periphrastic genitive**), cf. Engl. *my father's* car vs. *the car of my father*

GOAL SCHEMA: **[Y exists to/for X]**; a source schema according to which possessive constructions have conceptually derived. It consists of a verb of existence or of location and a DATIVE or BENEFACTIVE POSSESSOR

GRAMMATICAL TRANSFER: *see* INTERFERENCE

GRAMMATICAL USE PATTERN: a recurrent piece of discourse, which may consist of a clause, a phrase or a single form which is associated with the same grammatical meaning

GRAMMATICALIZATION: a process leading from lexical to grammatical and from grammatical to more grammatical forms. The linguistic item being affected undergoes loss in pragmatic significance, semantic complexity, syntactic freedom, morphological structure and phonetic substance

GRAMMATICALIZATION, ORDINARY (CONTACT-INDUCED): a process of CONTACT-INDUCED GRAMMATICALIZATION, whereby speakers of a replica language (R) on the model of a CATEGORY (MX), which exists in the MODEL LANGUAGE (M), create an equivalent category (Rx) in their language R and to this end draw on universal strategies of GRAMMATICALIZATION

GRAMMATICALIZATION, REPLICA: a process of CONTACT-INDUCED GRAMMATICALIZATION, whereby rather than a grammatical concept, a whole grammaticalization process is transferred from the MODEL LANGUAGE (M) to the replica language (R), i.e. whereby M provides a model for both a category as well as the way that category is replicated

'HAVE'-PERFECT: *see* POSSESSIVE PERFECT

HETEROSEMY: a lexical item having different but (etymologically) related meanings which are associated with distinct grammatical contexts, e.g. Engl. *mother*, *drive*, *stone*, and *talk*, each of which have related NOUN and verb meanings

HISTORICAL LINGUISTICS: a branch of linguistics, investigating the processes of language change, identifying all types of historical and prehistoric connections between languages, and establishing genetic relationships between languages

HOT-NEWS PERFECT: a verbal ASPECT category, which expresses an event that is located at a point that is separated from but temporally close to the moment of speaking, for example *John has just arrived*

HYPOTAXIS: *also* **interdependency**; in grammar, the syntactic subordination of one clause or construction to another

IBERIAN LANGUAGES: *also* **Ibero-Romance languages**: the southwestern ROMANCE LANGUAGE group, consisting of one East-Iberian Language (Catalan), the Oc languages (e.g. Gascon) and the West-Iberian languages (e.g. Portuguese, Spanish, etc.)

IMPERATIVE: a grammatical **mood** carrying a directive connotation like commands or permission. An IMPERATIVE verb is typically non-inflected for most grammatical categories for verbs, especially TENSE and person

IMPERFECT: a TENSE category, which denotes a past tense with imperfective ASPECT. It corresponds to the English past-continuous tense, for example, *Tom was going to the mall*

INCHOATIVE: a verbal ASPECT category, which refers to an action soon to take place, for example, *John is about to leave.* In those languages, which use AUXILIARY verbs to express an INCHOATIVE ASPECT, the term **near future** is more commonly used

INCIPIENT CATEGORY: 'beginning', 'commencing' category; a MINOR USE PATTERN developing into a MAJOR USE PATTERN associated with a particular grammatical meaning

INDIC LANGUAGES: *also* INDO-ARYAN LANGUAGES; a major subgroup of the Indo-Iranian branch of the INDO-EUROPEAN LANGUAGES, such as Bengali, Gujarati, Punjabi, Urdu, Hindi, Romani and Sanskrit

INDO-ARYAN LANGUAGES: *see* INDIC LANGUAGES

INDO-EUROPEAN LANGUAGES: a vast language family occupying most of Europe, much of western and southern Asia, formerly also occupying much of Anatolia and central Asia, now also predominating in the Americas, Australia, New Zealand and elsewhere. Its principal branches include Celtic, Germanic, Italic, Albanian, Greek, Balto-Slavic, Armenian, Indo-Iranian, Anatolian†, and Tocharian†

INFERENTIAL: a grammatical **mood** carrying a deducive connotation like inference, conjecture, assumption, etc.

INFINITIVE: the base form of a verb, unmarked for inflectional categories such as ASPECT, **modality**, NUMBER, person, TENSE

INFLECTION: the modification or marking of a lexeme that reflects grammatical information, such as ASPECT, **modality**, NUMBER, TENSE, etc. In contrast to DERIVATION, inflection does not result in a change of word class, and usually produces a predictable, non-idiosyncratic change of meaning, e.g. Engl. *he walk-ed, she sing-s*

INNOVATION: any kind of language change

INSTRUMENTAL (CASE): a CASE that indicates that the REFERENT denoted by the NOUN is the means of the action's achievement expressed by the clause

INTEGRATIVE MODEL OF GRAMMATICALIZATION: a model of how GRAMMATICALIZATION works overall. It is based on the assumption that universal conceptual-semantic mechanisms underlying grammatical change play a crucial role and that language contact is not a factor working against grammaticalization but is rather in conspiracy *with* grammaticalization

INTENSIFIER: *also* **emphatic** REFLEXIVES; a linguistic means to heighten or lower the intensity of meaning of a linguistic element. In English, intensifiers are considered ADVERBS, such as *very* or *hardly*

INTERFERENCE: the non-deliberate transfer of linguistic features from a first language into a second language due to language contact

INTERNAL LANGUAGE CHANGE: any linguistic change in a certain language which is not the result of the influence of another language

INTERPERSONAL FUNCTION: interaction between speakers and hearers

INTERROGATIVE: a clause type expressing a question, or an interrogative word introducing an interrogative clause (**interrogative pronoun** e.g. Engl. *who,* **interrogative adjective** e.g. Engl. *which,* or **interrogative adverb**, e.g. Engl. *why*)

INTRANSITIVE VERB: a verb which does not allow a DIRECT OBJECT; e.g. Engl. *I ran to the station*

IRANIAN LANGUAGES: a major subgroup of the Indo-Iranian branch of the INDO-EUROPEAN LANGUAGES, comprising almost 50 languages, e.g. Alanic, Kurdish, Talishi, Persian, etc.

ISOGLOSS: a line drawn on a DIALECT map marking the boundary between two competing linguistic forms used in neighbouring areas

ISOMORPHY: a language's situation in which a single linguistic form always has the same meaning or function, and a single meaning or function is always expressed by the same form

ISOPLETH: a line drawn on a dialectal map marking the boundary of the frequencies of occurrence of some linguistic form above and below a specified reference value

JUXTAPOSITION: uninflected listing of single linguistic items. Close appositional constructions such as *Queen Mum, Mister Minit,* etc. are called **determinative** JUXTAPOSITION

LANGUAGE DEATH: the disappearance of a language as a mother tongue

LANGUE: the abstract system of signs and rules, i.e. 'language' (in contrast to PAROLE, i.e. 'speech'). Introduced in F. de Saussure's *Cours de linguistique générale* (1916), LANGUE is marked as a static, monolinguistic system of social validity based on the invariance and functionality of its elements

LEXICAL REPLICATION: the replication of lexical structures commonly referred to as LOANSHIFT

LEXICAL TONE: the pitch level carried by the syllable of a lexeme, which distinguishes meaning

LINGUA FRANCA: any learned second language which serves as a means of communication between groups that do not speak each other's language, so as for international commerce or other cultural exchanges, such as diplomacy. Originally, the term lingua franca denoted an Italian-based PIDGIN, which evolved in the Mediterranean area some time during the Crusades (eleventh to fifteenth centuries)

LINGUISTIC AREA: *see* SPRACHBUND

LOAN TRANSLATION: *see* CALQUING

LOANSHIFT: *see* LEXICAL REPLICATION

LOCATION SCHEMA: **[Y is located at X]**; a source schema according to which possessive constructions are conceptually derived. This schema involves a subject POSSESSEE, locative complement POSSESSOR and a locative COPULA predicate or verb

MAJOR USE PATTERN: a use pattern which is regularly associated with a specific grammatical function, and which, in comparison to MINOR USE PATTERNS, is employed more frequently and exhibits a wider range of different contexts

MESO-AMERICA: a LINGUISTIC AREA covering languages spoken in central Mexico and parts of Central America, which together share a number of structural features that cannot be accounted for in terms of genetic inheritance

METATYPY: the wholesale RESTRUCTURING of a language's semantic and syntactic structures as a result of language contact, leading to a new TYPOLOGICAL PROFILE in the REPLICA LANGUAGE on the one hand, and to a large degree of direct inter-translatability between the model and the replica language on the other (cf. e.g. Ross 1996)

MINOR USE PATTERN: an infrequently employed use pattern which is restricted to specific contexts

MODAL VERB: a verb expressing **modality** (*see* MODALITY, DEONTIC and MODALITY, EPISTEMIC), such as Engl. *order, assume, allow*, etc.

MODALITY, DEONTIC: a modal category connoting the speaker's degree of requirement of desire for, or commitment to the realization of the proposition expressed by an utterance, e.g. Engl. *you may go at four o'clock*

MODALITY, EPISTEMIC: a modal category denoting the speaker's degree of certainty or evidence for the proposition expressed by an utterance, e.g. Engl. *there's no answer; she must have already left*

MODEL CATEGORY: the concept or structure Mx of a MODEL LANGUAGE (M) which serves as a model for the contact-induced development of Rx in the recipient language (R)

MODEL LANGUAGE: a language (M) providing the model for contact-induced change in a recipient language (R)

MODIFIER: a constituent carrying information that refers to the head of the construction, e.g. Engl. *the very hot soup*

MORIBUND LANGUAGE: a language in danger of imminent extinction, usually a language no longer being learned by children

MORPHOLOGY: the study of the construction of words out of morphemes as well as the study of the parts of speech and their criteria for classification

MORPHOSYNTAX: a grammatical category for whose definition criteria of MORPHOLOGY and **syntax** both apply, e.g. NUMBER contrasts, affecting syntax (e.g. subject–verb AGREEMENT) and requiring morphological definition (e.g. PLURAL-*s*)

NEGATION: a morphosyntactic operation in which the meaning of a lexical item or construction is denied or inverted

NEUTER: a grammatical gender including those NOUNS having REFERENTS which do not have distinctions of sex, e.g. ger. *das Festmahl* ('the banquet'), and often including some which do have a natural sex distinction, e.g. Ger. *das Mädchen* ('the girl')

NIGER-CONGO LANGUAGES: a vast language family of 1,000–1,500 languages occupying most of sub-Saharan Africa, major branches being Mande, Kordofanian, West Atlantic, Ijoid, Kru, Gur, Adamawa-Ubangi, Kwa, and the vast Benue-Congo

NOMINALIZER: a grammatical means for the formation of a new NOUN from another word or stem, e.g. the formation of the NOUN *singer* from the verb *to sing* + *-er*

NOMINATIVE (CASE): in NOMINATIVE-ACCUSATIVE languages, the CASE identifying clause subjects

NON-EQUIVALENCE: *see* EQUIVALENCE

NON-FINITE VERB: verb form (comprising infinitival and participial forms), which lacks categorical distinctions, and which occurs by itself in subordinate clauses only

NOUN PHRASE: a phrasal category composed of a determiner and a NOUN with a noun as its head

NOUN, COLLECTIVE: a NOUN agreeing grammatically with the verb either as a SINGULAR or a PLURAL noun, and taking either a singular or a plural PRONOUN

NOUN: a syntactic category including lexical items which refer to a group of entities that may be considered either as individuals or as one larger entity

NUMBER: a grammatical category of NOUNS, PRONOUNS, and verb AGREEMENT expressing count distinctions, such as SINGULAR, i.e. 'one', or PLURAL, i.e. 'more than one', which usually correspond to the actual number of the REFERENTS of the marked item

NUMERAL: typically an ADJECTIVE or PRONOUN expressing a number or a relation to NUMBER, such as quantity, sequence, frequency or fraction

OBJECT, DIRECT VS. INDIRECT: the major subdivision of the notion of OBJECT, the relationship between the two being illustrated by e.g. *the man gave the boy a book* with *a book* being the DIRECT OBJECT, i.e. the more central in clause structure, and *the boy* being the INDIRECT OBJECT, i.e. the element requiring a DIRECT OBJECT to relate to

OBJECT: a major grammatical constituent of sentence or clause structure, associated with the 'receiver' or 'goal' of an action denoted by the main verb, e.g. Engl. *the cat bit the dog*

OBLIQUE QUESTION: indirect question

ONTOLOGICAL CATEGORY: a lexical category of possible concrete objects, substances, persons, etc. expressed by an abstraction, such as an activity, emotion, or idea

OPTATIVE: a grammatical **mood** carrying a volitive connotation like desire, hope, or wish. Optative expressions in English use MODAL VERBS or the SUBJUNCTIVE, cf. *may they get home safely, Heaven help us!*

PARAMETER MARKER: in EQUATIVE CONSTRUCTIONS a functional element which marks an element (typically an adjectival form) as the parameter of comparison, e.g. Engl. *Jim is as smart as Marcia*

PARATAXIS: a grammatical term referring to constructions of equal status which are linked solely through JUXTAPOSITION and punctuation or intonation, e.g. Engl. *she bought tea, bread, and butter*

PAROLE: the concrete realization of LANGUE, i.e. 'speech'. Resting on these LANGUE-systems, introduced in F. de Saussure's *Cours de linguistique générale* (1916), PAROLE-events are individual speech events marked by variability and redundancy

PARTICIPANT: an interlocutor with regard to his/her involvement in a speech event with a major subdivision into CORE and PERIPHERAL PARTICIPANT, the former being the participant that is central to the event or state, e.g. an addressee, a speaker, etc., and the latter being the participant not being central to the event or state, e.g. an audience, a bystander, etc.

PARTICIPANT, CORE: *see* PARTICIPANT

PARTICIPANT, PERIPHERAL: *see* PARTICIPANT

PARTICIPLE: a grammatical term denoting an ADJECTIVE derived from a verb, as in Engl. *a laughing face.* Therefore, distinct from the notion of **gerund**, where the word derived from the verb is used as a NOUN, e.g. Engl. *smoking is forbidden*

PARTITIVE: a grammatical category referring to a part or quantity, e.g. Engl. *some*, occurring with almost any quantifiable lexical item, or *blade* (*of grass*), restricted to a single lexical item, or to a very small set

PASSIVE: a grammatical category referring to a sentence, clause, or verb form in which the grammatical subject is the semantic OBJECT of the action denoted by the verb, e.g. Engl. *the letter was written by the girl*

PAST PASSIVE PARTICIPLE (PPP): a PARTICIPLE formed by adding the SUFFIX *-ed.* Clauses with past passive participle always replace subordinate clauses in the PASSIVE VOICE, for example, *when invited, Tom felt happy*

PATIENT: PARTICIPANT that suffers or is affected by the action denoted by the main verb

PERFECT: a syntactic category which typically marks a contrast of a temporal or durative kind, thus sometimes assigned to TENSE (e.g. 'perfect', '**future perfect**', 'PLUPERFECT') and sometimes to ASPECT (e.g. 'perfective', 'non-perfective')

PERFECT, CONCLUSIVE: a PERFECT construction formed with a 'have' AUXILIARY plus PASSIVE PARTICIPLE plus OBJECT construction, e.g. Engl. *Jenny has a postcard sent*

PHONETIC REDUCTION: *see* EROSION

PHRASAL CONSTRUCTION: a combination of two or more words that form a single semantic and syntactic unit, e.g. Engl. *on television, on the request of*

PIDGIN (LANGUAGES): *see* PIDGINIZATION

PIDGINIZATION: the formation of a language as the result of intense language contact whereby the speaker groups involved lack a common means of communication, but need to communicate for limited purposes such as trade. A PIDGIN LANGUAGE resulting from such contact scenario typically has only highly restricted lexical and structural resources and is nobody's native language

PLACE ADVERB: *see* ADVERB

PLUPERFECT: *also* **past perfect**, e.g. Engl. *I had eaten*

PLURAL: *see* NUMBER

POLAR QUESTION (**yes–no question**): type of question that permits *yes* or *no* as an acceptable answer

POLYGENESIS: the hypothesis that all languages have emerged spontaneously in several communities. In PIDGIN studies, the theory that the development of a pidgin in one place is independent of the development of a pidgin in another

POLYSEMY: a term referring to a form that has multiple etymologically related meanings, e.g. Engl. *fly* for either 'propel oneself through air' or (coll.) 'go very fast'

POSSESSEE: in a POSSESSION SCHEMA the head which is modified by another entity (POSSESSOR), e.g. Engl. *the money of my friend*

POSSESSION SCHEMA: a grammatical construction (possessive construction) involving two interrelated entities, the POSSESSOR and POSSESSEE (each typically being expressed by means of a NOUN PHRASE), the relationship between which is denoted by a possessive marker

POSSESSIVE PERFECT: *also* 'HAVE'-PERFECT; a PERFECT construction formed with a 'have' AUXILIARY plus PASSIVE PARTICIPLE

POSSESSOR: in a POSSESSION SCHEMA the entity that modifies the head (POSSESSEE), e.g. Engl. *the money of my friend*

POSSESSOR, EXTERNAL: a POSSESSOR that is not part of the same phrase as the entity conceived of as inalienable

POSTPOSITION: *see* ADPOSITION

PREDICATIVE POSSESSION: possessive constructions with a clausal syntax involving event-like contents, e.g. Engl. *I have a dog, the dog belongs to me*

PREFIX: an **affix**, i.e. a bound morpheme which precedes the stem of a word to which it is attached, as opposed to a SUFFIX, which succeeds the stem

PREPOSITION: *see* ADPOSITION

PRESENT ACTIVE PARTICIPLE: a PARTICIPLE formed by adding the SUFFIX *-ing* to a verb. Clauses with present active participle always replace subordinate clauses in the active voice, for example, *having cleaned her bike, Sally left*

PRETERIT: the simple past tense of a language which is typically unmarked with respect to ASPECT and **modality**, e.g. Engl. *she went to the grocery store*

PRO-DROP: from 'PRONOUN-dropping'; a **pro-drop language** is a language in which the subject of a clause can be omitted when pragmatically inferable. Typical pro-drop languages are Japanese and ROMANCE LANGUAGES such as Italian and Spanish; cf. Span. *ø han comido* vs. Engl. *they have eaten*

PROGRESSIVE (ASPECT): a verbal ASPECT category indicating a continuous activity

PRONOUN, DEMONSTRATIVE: type of pronoun denoting the REFERENT's spatial, temporal, or discourse location, e.g. *these, those, this, that,* etc.

PRONOUN, PERSONAL: type of pronoun expressing a distinction of person DEIXIS, e.g. *he, she, it, they, my, mine,* etc.

PROXIMATIVE: an aspectual gram expressing a temporal phase located close before the initial boundary of the situation denoted by the main verb, thus imminence: *being on the point of V-ing*

QUANTIFYING ADVERB: *see* ADVERB

RAISING: type of rule with a major distinction between **object-** and **subject-raising**: while object-raising brackets the constituents of a main clause + COMPLEMENT CLAUSE with the effect that the complement clause's subject is 'raised' to become the OBJECT of the main clause (e.g. Engl. *he wants it* + *Mary is honest* becoming *he wants Mary* + *to be honest*), subject-RAISING 'raises' the complement clause's subject to become the subject of the main clause (e.g. Engl. *it seems that the girl is sad* to *the girl seems sad*)

REANALYSIS: a mechanism operating in processes of GRAMMATICALIZATION, whereby the syntactic, morphological, and semantic features are remodelled, especially owing to changes in constituency (**rebracketing**), caused by a hearer's assignment of a different structure to a certain output (cf. Hopper & Traugott 2003: 39–70)

RECOGNITIONAL DEMONSTRATIVE: a demonstrative, i.e. deictic element, indicating that the REFERENT can be identified by the addressee, based on specific shared knowledge, whereby the preceding discourse or the surrounding situation does not provide a referent

REDUPLICATION: in MORPHOLOGY the repetition of the root or stem, or certain segments of it, as a means of INFLECTION or DERIVATION. Thereby reduplicated elements may be PREFIXES, SUFFIXES, or infixes; cf. Lat. 1. person sg. perf. *cucurri*, 'I went' of the INFINITIVE *currere*, 'to go'

REFERENT: the real world object or notion referred to by a linguistic expression

REFLEXIVE (PRONOUN): pronoun denoting **coreference** with the subject, e.g. Engl. *I saw myself in the mirror*

REIFIER: a NOMINALIZER, e.g. Engl. *the red one* (cf. Gil 2003)

RELATIONAL NOUN: class of body part terms, like Engl. *head*, *back*, etc., which are utilized to function as PREPOSITIONS, i.e. to express the location of objects in relation to others

RELATIVE CLAUSE: a subordinate clause which modifies a NOUN PHRASE (e.g. Engl. *the man that I saw yesterday*). A major distinction is made between **restrictive** and **non-restrictive relative clauses**: while restrictive relative clauses confine the REFERENT of the head noun, non-restrictive relative clauses only serve to add further information about it

RELATIVE PRONOUN: marker introducing RELATIVE CLAUSES, e.g. Engl. *who*, *which*, *that*

RELATIVIZER: a **subordinating conjunction** that serves as a linkage between a RELATIVE CLAUSE and its head noun. Relativizers, in contrast to RELATIVE PRONOUNS, do not have a nominal function within the relative clause

RENEWAL: the REPLACEMENT of one form of grammatical expression, typically inflectional affixes, which have come to lose their meaning, by a new, lexical or grammatical form

REPLACEMENT: in a given language the replacement of an existing structure by a new one

REPLICA LANGUAGE: a language (R) which creates a new grammatical structure on the model of some structure of another language called the MODEL LANGUAGE (M)

RESTRUCTURING: processes of grammatical replication that cannot be accounted for with reference to GRAMMATICALIZATION

RESULTATIVE: aspectual notion expressing 'having reached a new state'

RESULTATIVE (ASPECT): a verbal ASPECT category coming under non-durative or perfective and indicating activities which do not lead to a close

RESUMPTIVE RELATIVE PRONOUN: a PERSONAL PRONOUN which serves to reinforce the grammatical function of the relativized NOUN PHRASE within the RELATIVE CLAUSE by explicitly indicating the co-referential relationship between the relativized noun phrase and the ANTECEDENT, e.g. Engl. *this is the boy that, whenever it hails, he hides*

ROMANCE LANGUAGES: the languages that have Latin as their common ancestor, e.g. French, Italian, Portuguese, Romansh, and Spanish

SEMANTIC BLEACHING: *see* DESEMANTICIZATION

SIMILATIVE (CASE): a grammatical CASE denoting equal manner or quality, e.g. Engl. *she sings like an angel*

SINGLISH: English-based CREOLE spoken in Singapore

SINGULAR: *see* NUMBER

SINO-TIBETAN LANGUAGES: a language family comprising approx. 250 languages of East-Asia with a further major subdivision into **Chinese** and **Tibeto-Burman**

SLAVIC LANGUAGES: languages belonging to one of the two sub-branches of the Balto-Slavic branch of the INDO-EUROPEAN LANGUAGE family with further subdivisions into **East Slavic** (Belarusian, Russian, etc.), **South Slavic** (Bulgarian, Macedonian, etc.), and **West Slavic** (Czech, Polish, etc.)

SPRACHBUND: *also* LINGUISTIC AREA; a geographical region that consists of several languages that, due to their geographical proximity rather than to common descent, share a number of structural features

STANDARD AVERAGE EUROPEAN (SAE): LINGUISTIC AREA in Europe, comprising the ROMANCE, Germanic, Balto-Slavic, Balkan, and westernmost Finno-Ugrian languages, that together share certain structural features (EUROPEANISMS, **Europemes**), which cannot be accounted for in terms of genetic inheritance

STANDARD MARKER: in EQUATIVE and SIMILATIVE constructions a functional element which marks a REFERENT as the standard of comparison, e.g. Engl. *Jim is as smart as Marcia*

STATIVE VERB: denotes a state of affairs rather than an activity or process, e.g. Engl. *to possess*

SUBJUNCTIVE: a grammatical **mood** marked on the verb, carrying an irrealis connotation like uncertainty, possibility, necessity, desire, etc.

SUBORDINATOR (**subordinating conjunction**): a marker that serves as a linkage between a dependent clause (SUBORDINATE CLAUSE) and an independent clause (**main clause**), e.g. Engl. *after, although, because*

SUBSTRATUM (**substrate**): in a language contact situation, a language which is less prestigious than another language (**superstrate**), but which exerts a considerable influence on the latter, mainly as a consequence of substrate speakers acquiring the superstrate language

SUFFIX: an **affix**, i.e. a bound morpheme which succeeds the stem of a word to which it is attached, as opposed to a PREFIX which precedes the stem

SUFFIX, AUGMENTATIVE: a SUFFIX which bears, in opposition to the diminutive, the general meaning of 'large'. Therefore, it is usually used to express a sense of higher intensity and thereby often implies discomfort or ugliness

SUPERESSIVE (CASE): a grammatical CASE denoting the positioning 'on top' of the REFERENT of the marked NOUN. Whereas this notion in most languages is expressed by means of ADPOSITIONS, especially members of the Finno-Ugric language family, in particular, employ this case marking strategy

SUPERLATIVE: an adjectival or adverbial form expressing the comparison between more than two items, as opposed to the **comparative** form involving only two items of comparison, and the **positive** form, which does not involve any comparison, e.g. Engl. *good* (positive), *better* (comparative), *best* (superlative)

SUPERSTRATUM **(superstrate)**: in a language contact situation a language which is more prestigious than another language (**substrate**) and which has a measurable impact on the latter in terms of contact-induced change

SUPPLETIVE: an etymologically unrelated form within a paradigm, e.g. the Engl. past tense form *went* in relation to the present tense or participial forms *go, gone*

SWITCH STAGE: Stage II in the process of CONTEXT-INDUCED REINTERPRETATION: a given linguistic form can, after having acquired an additional sense in **Stage I**, be used in new contexts, which are compatible with the additional sense but rule out the original sense (cf. Heine *et al.* 1991)

SYNCRETISM: *see* CASE SYNCRETISM

SYNTHETIC MARKER: an **affix**, i.e. a bound morpheme, signalling a morphosyntactic operation, e.g. DERIVATION or INFLECTION

TENSE: a grammatical category, which deictically refers to the time of the action denoted by the verb in relation to some other temporal reference point. In inflecting languages, tense is typically expressed by means of verbal INFLECTION, whereas in isolating languages it is commonly expressed by means of time adverbials

TOPIC CONTINUITY: the taking up of a theme, which has already been introduced in the preceding discourse, for the purpose of further elaboration, which is commonly achieved through the employment of definite ARTICLES, or other topic-marking devices

TRANSITIVE VERB: a verb which allows a DIRECT OBJECT; e.g. Engl. *I saw the man*

TRANSNUMERAL: neutral with respect to NUMBER

TURKIC LANGUAGES: a group of closely related agglutinating languages spoken mainly in Asia and Eastern Europe with the highest number of speakers in Turkey (representatives are e.g. Turkish, Azerbaijani, Kyrgyz, etc.)

TYPOLOGICAL PROFILE: the structural characteristics of a given language

UNIDIRECTIONALITY PRINCIPLE: a rule according to which GRAMMATICALIZATION processes typically proceed in one, but not in the opposite direction, viz. from less grammaticalized forms involving more concrete concepts to more grammaticalized forms involving less concrete, thus more abstract notions

UTO-AZTECAN LANGUAGES: a language family comprising native American languages which are spoken in Mexico and the western United States with a major subdivision into Northern Uto-Aztecan languages (Hopi, Northern Paiute, etc.) and Southern Uto-Aztecan languages (Nahuatl, Pipil, etc.)

VERB OF COGNITION: a verb denoting a mental process (e.g. Engl. *think*, *know*, *remember*, etc.)

VERB SERIALIZING: the sequencing of several verbs or verb phrases within a single clause without overt marking indicating coordination or subordination

VERB-MEDIAL ORDER: SVO WORD ORDER

VOICE: grammatical category denoting the semantic functions of the REFERENTS of a clause. It indicates whether the subject is an **actor**, PATIENT, or **recipient**

WORD ITERATION: reduplication or repetition of a word as a grammatical means, e.g. marking of plurality as in Jap. *hito* ('person') vs. *hitobito* ('people'), or as a lexical means, e.g. word formation, cp. Jap. *toki* ('time') and *tokidoki* ('sometimes')

WORD ORDER: the sequential arrangement of words in larger linguistic units. Some languages rely on word order as a means of expressing grammatical relationships

WORD QUESTION **(wh-question)**: a question containing an INTERROGATIVE pro-form, e.g. Engl. *who, which, where, when*

Index-Authors

Index-Languages

Index-Subjects